Holt McDougal Geometry

Practice and Problem Solving Workbook

HOLT McDOUGAL

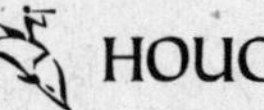
HOUGHTON MIFFLIN HARCOURT

Printed in the U.S.A.

ISBN 978-0-547-71000-6

1 2 3 4 5 6 7 8 9 10 1689 20 19 18 17 16 15 14 13 12 11

4500303394 A B C D E F G

Contents

Practice

Problem Solving

Name ______________________ Date ______________ Class ______________

LESSON 1-1

Practice

Understanding Points, Lines, and Planes

Use the figure for Exercises 1–7.

1. Name a plane. ______________________

2. Name a segment. ______________________

3. Name a line. ______________________

4. Name three collinear points.

____

5. Name three noncollinear points.

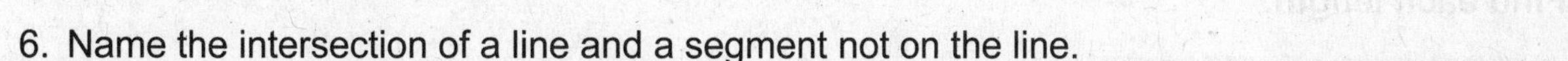

6. Name the intersection of a line and a segment not on the line. ______________

7. Name a pair of opposite rays. ______________________

Use the figure for Exercises 8–11.

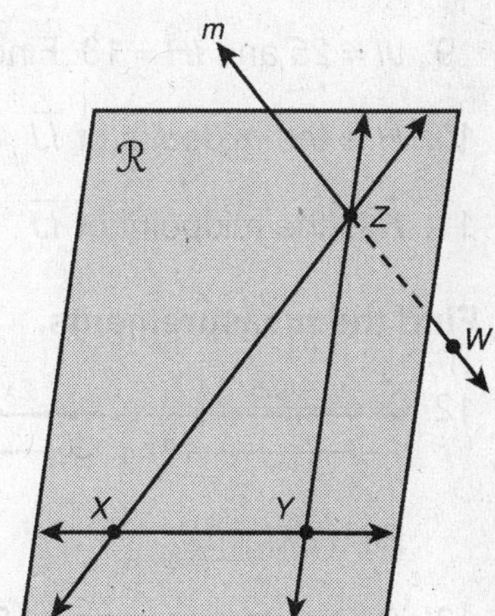

8. Name the points that determine plane ℛ.

____

9. Name the point at which line *m* intersects plane ℛ. ______________________

10. Name two lines in plane ℛ that intersect line *m*.

____

11. Name a line in plane ℛ that does not intersect line *m*. ______________________

Draw your answers in the space provided.

Michelle Kwan won a bronze medal in figure skating at the 2002 Salt Lake City Winter Olympic Games.

12. Michelle skates straight ahead from point *L* and stops at point *M*. Draw her path.

13. Michelle skates straight ahead from point *L* and continues through point *M*. Name a figure that represents her path. Draw her path.

14. Michelle and her friend Alexei start back to back at point *L* and skate in opposite directions. Michelle skates through point *M*, and Alexei skates through point *K*. Draw their paths.

Name ______________________ Date ______________ Class ______________

LESSON 1-2

Practice

Measuring and Constructing Segments

Draw your answer in the space provided.

1. Use a compass and straightedge to construct $\overline{XY}$ congruent to $\overline{UV}$.

Find the coordinate of each point.

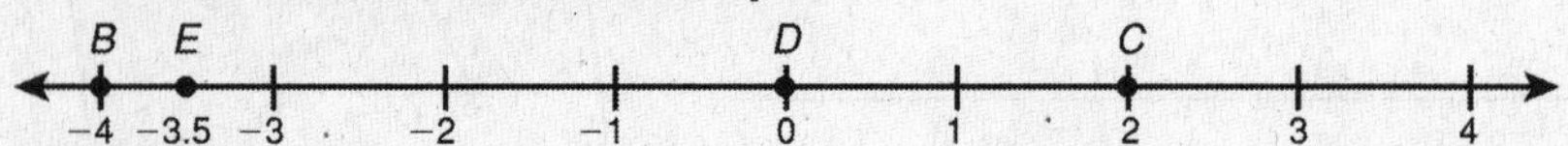

2. D _____ 3. C _____ 4. E _____

Find each length.

5. BE _____ 6. DB _____ 7. EC _____

For Exercises 8–11, *H* is between *I* and *J*.

8. $HI = 3.9$ and $HJ = 6.2$. Find IJ. _____

9. $JI = 25$ and $IH = 13$. Find HJ. _____

10. H is the midpoint of $\overline{IJ}$, and $IH = 0.75$. Find HJ. _____

11. H is the midpoint of $\overline{IJ}$, and $IJ = 9.4$. Find IH. _____

Find the measurements.

12. K $x + 0.5$ L $3x - 2$ M

$3x + 1.5$

Find LM. _____

13. A pole-vaulter uses a 15-foot-long pole. She grips the pole so that the segment below her left hand is twice the length of the segment above her left hand. Her right hand grips the pole 1.5 feet above her left hand. How far up the pole is her right hand? _____

Name ______________________ Date ______________ Class ______________

LESSON 1-3

Practice

Measuring and Constructing Angles

Draw your answer on the figure.

1. Use a compass and straightedge to construct angle bisector $\overrightarrow{DG}$.

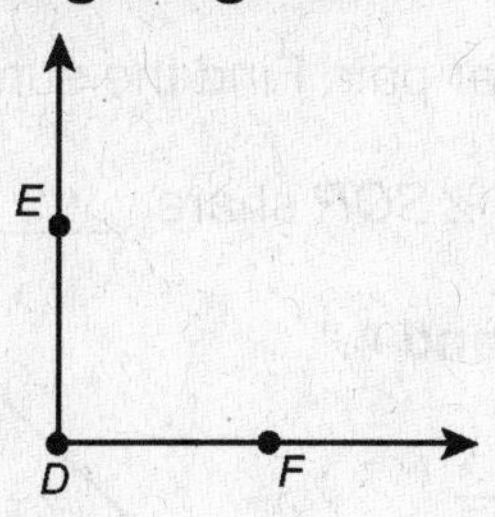

2. Name eight different angles in the figure.

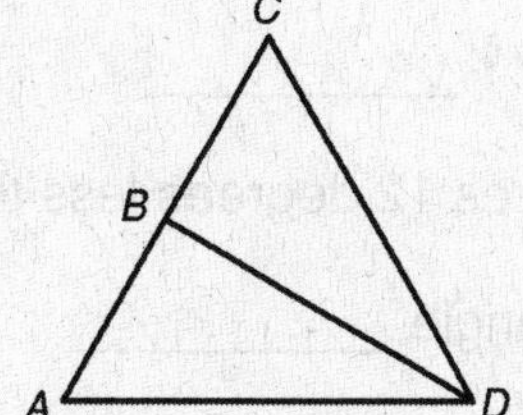

____

____

Find the measure of each angle and classify each as acute, right, obtuse, or straight.

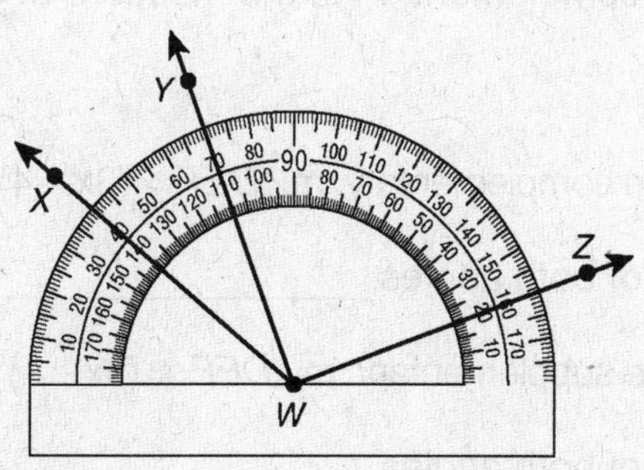

3. $\angle YWZ$ ______________

4. $\angle XWZ$ ______________

5. $\angle YWX$ ______________

***T* is in the interior of $\angle PQR$. Find each of the following.**

6. $m\angle PQT$ if $m\angle PQR = 25°$ and $m\angle RQT = 11°$. ________

7. $m\angle PQR$ if $m\angle PQR = (10x - 7)°$, $m\angle RQT = 5x°$, and $m\angle PQT = (4x + 6)°$. ________

8. $m\angle PQR$ if $\overrightarrow{QT}$ bisects $\angle PQR$, $m\angle RQT = (10x - 13)°$, and $m\angle PQT = (6x + 1)°$. ________

9. Longitude is a measurement of position around the equator of Earth. Longitude is measured in degrees, minutes, and seconds. Eachs degree contains 60 minutes, and each minute contains 60 seconds. Minutes are indicated by the symbol ′ and seconds are indicated by the symbol ″. Williamsburg, VA, is located at 76°42′25″. Roanoke, VA, is located at 79°57′30″. Find the difference of their longitudes in degrees, minutes, and seconds. ______________

10. To convert minutes and seconds into decimal parts of a degree, divide the number of minutes by 60 and the number of seconds by 3,600. Then add the numbers together. Write the location of Roanoke, VA, as a decimal to the nearest thousandths of a degree. ______________

Name ______________________ Date ______________ Class ______________

LESSON 1-4

Practice

Pairs of Angles

1. $\angle PQR$ and $\angle SQR$ form a linear pair. Find the sum of their measures. ________

2. Name the ray that $\angle PQR$ and $\angle SQR$ share. ________

Use the figures for Exercises 3 and 4.

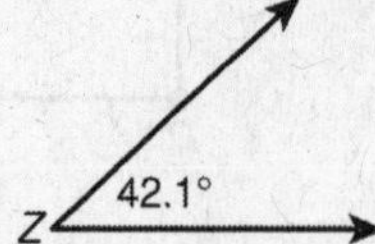

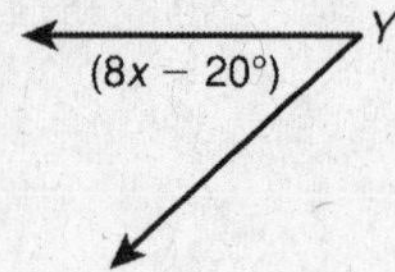

3. supplement of $\angle Z$ ________

4. complement of $\angle Y$ ________

5. An angle measures 12 degrees less than three times its supplement. Find the measure of the angle. ________

6. An angle is its own complement. Find the measure of a supplement to this angle. ________

7. $\angle DEF$ and $\angle FEG$ are complementary. $m\angle DEF = (3x - 4)°$, and $m\angle FEG = (5x + 6)°$.

   Find the measures of both angles. ________________

8. $\angle DEF$ and $\angle FEG$ are supplementary. $m\angle DEF = (9x + 1)°$, and $m\angle FEG = (8x + 9)°$.

   Find the measures of both angles. ________________

Use the figure for Exercises 9 and 10.

In 2004, several nickels were minted to commemorate the Louisiana Purchase and Lewis and Clark's expedition into the American West. One nickel shows a pipe and a hatchet crossed to symbolize peace between the American government and Native American tribes.

9. Name a pair of vertical angles.

   ____

   ____

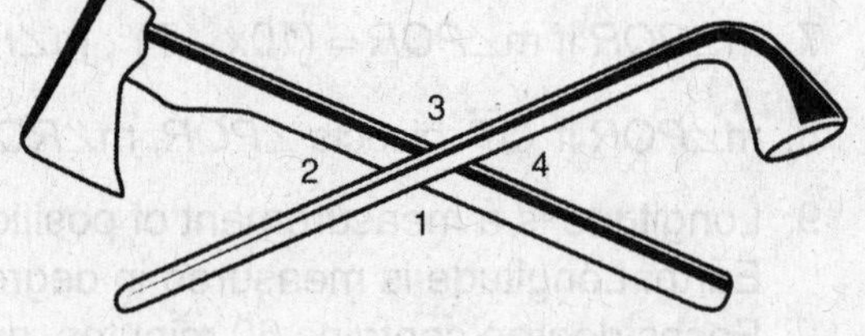

10. Name a linear pair of angles.

    ____

11. $\angle ABC$ and $\angle CBD$ form a linear pair and have equal measures. Tell if $\angle ABC$ is acute, right, or obtuse. ________________

12. $\angle KLM$ and $\angle MLN$ are complementary. $\overline{LM}$ bisects $\angle KLN$. Find the measures of $\angle KLM$ and $\angle MLN$. ________________

Name ______________________ Date ______________ Class ______________

LESSON 1-5

Practice

Using Formulas in Geometry

Use the figures for Exercises 1–3.

1. Find the perimeter of triangle *A*. ____________

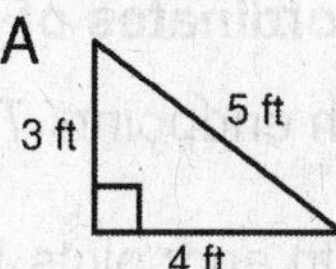

2. Find the area of triangle *A*. ____________

3. Triangle *A* is identical to triangle *B*.
   Find the height *h* of triangle *B*. ____________

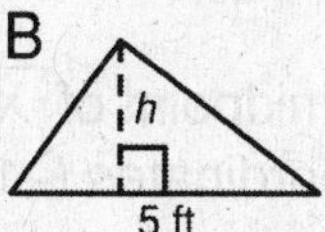

Find the perimeter and area of each shape.

4. square with a side 2.4 m in length

5. rectangle with length $(x + 3)$ and width 7

____________________ ____________________

6. Although a circle does not have sides, it does have a perimeter.
   What is the term for the perimeter of a circle? ____________

Find the circumference and area of each circle.

7. 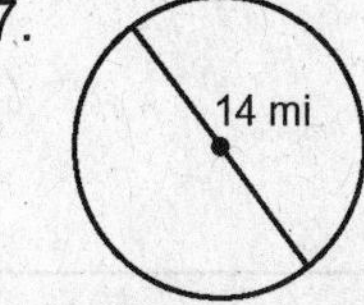

Use $\frac{22}{7}$ for π.

8. 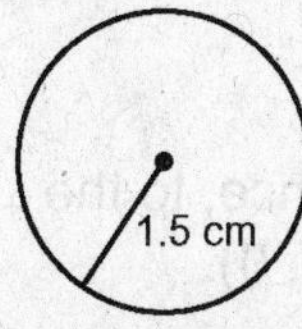

Use 3.14 for π.

9. 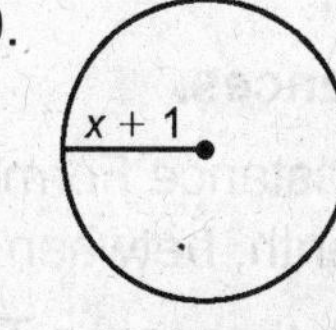

Leave π as π.

____________ ____________ ____________

10. The area of a square is $\frac{1}{4}$ in^2. Find the perimeter. ____________

11. The area of a triangle is 152 m^2, and the height is 16 m. Find the base. ____________

12. The circumference of a circle is 25π mm. Find the radius. ____________

Use the figure for Exercises 13 and 14.

Lucas has a 39-foot-long rope. He uses all the rope to outline this T-shape in his backyard. All the angles in the figure are right angles.

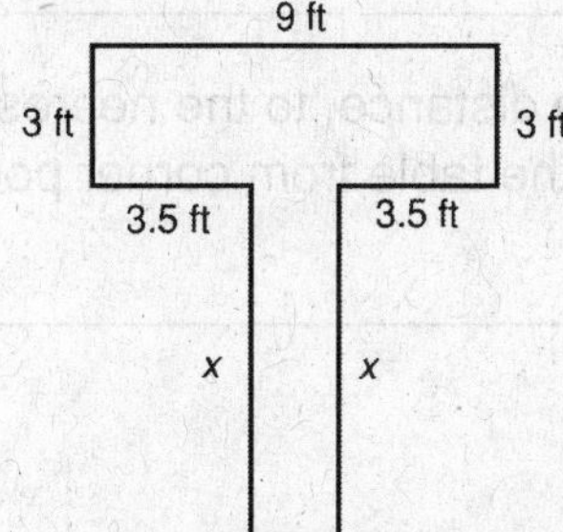

13. Find *x*. ____________

14. Find the area enclosed by the rope. ____________

Name ______________________ Date ______________ Class ______________

LESSON 1-6

Practice

Midpoint and Distance in the Coordinate Plane

Find the coordinates of the midpoint of each segment.

1. $\overline{TU}$ with endpoints $T(5, -1)$ and $U(1, -5)$ ______________

2. $\overline{VW}$ with endpoints $V(-2, -6)$ and $W(x + 2, y + 3)$ ______________

3. Y is the midpoint of $\overline{XZ}$. X has coordinates (2, 4), and Y has coordinates (–1, 1). Find the coordinates of Z. ______________

Use the figure for Exercises 4–7.

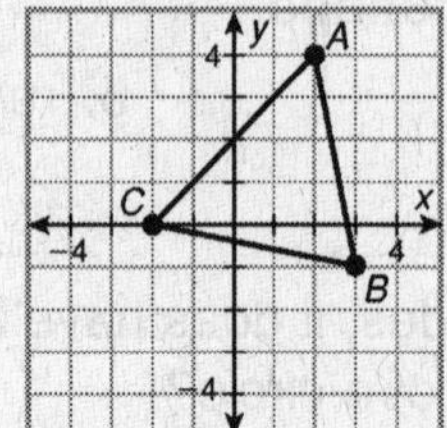

4. Find AB. ______________

5. Find BC. ______________

6. Find CA. ______________

7. Name a pair of congruent segments. ______________

Find the distances.

8. Use the Distance Formula to find the distance, to the nearest tenth, between $K(-7, -4)$ and $L(-2, 0)$. ______________

9. Use the Pythagorean Theorem to find the distance, to the nearest tenth, between $F(9, 5)$ and $G(-2, 2)$. ______________

Use the figure for Exercises 10 and 11.

Snooker is a kind of pool or billiards played on a 6-foot-by-12-foot table. The side pockets are halfway down the rails (long sides).

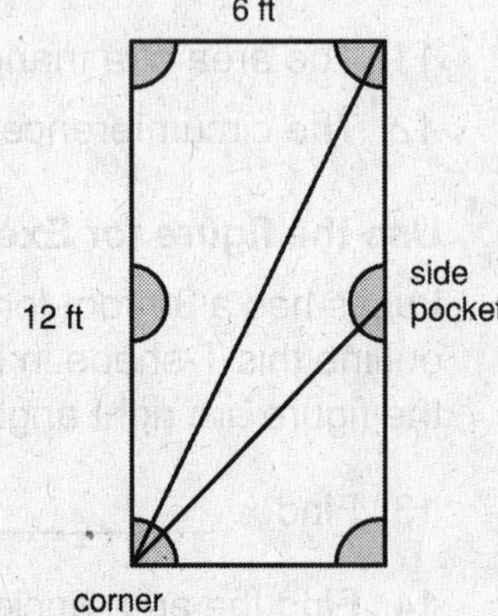

10. Find the distance, to the nearest tenth of a foot, diagonally across the table from corner pocket to corner pocket.

____

11. Find the distance, to the nearest tenth of an inch, diagonally across the table from corner pocket to side pocket.

____

Name ______________________ Date ______________ Class ______________

LESSON 1-7

Practice

Transformations in the Coordinate Plane

Use the figure for Exercises 1–3.

The figure in the plane at right shows the preimage in the transformation *ABCD* → *A′B′C′D′*. Match the number of the image (below) with the name of the correct transformation.

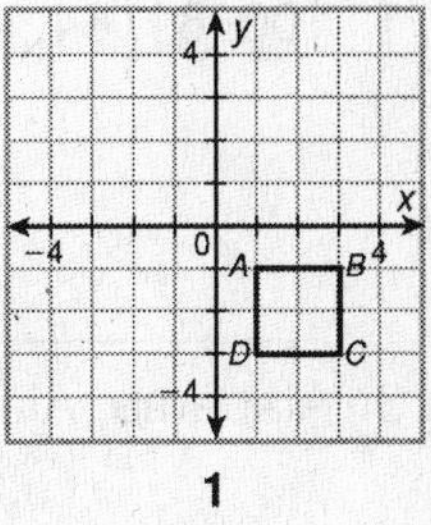

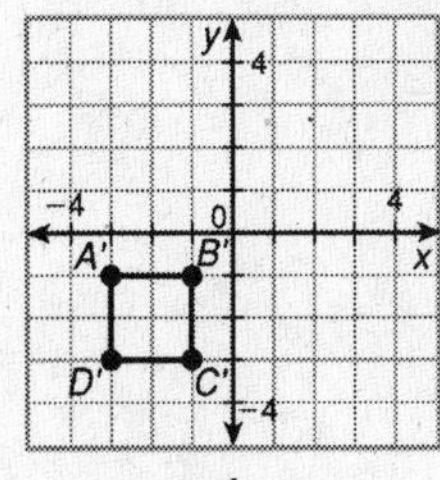

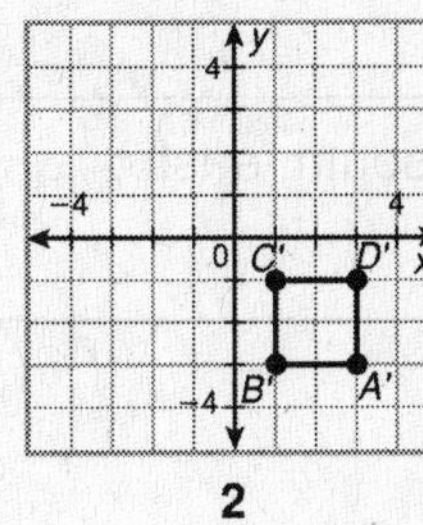

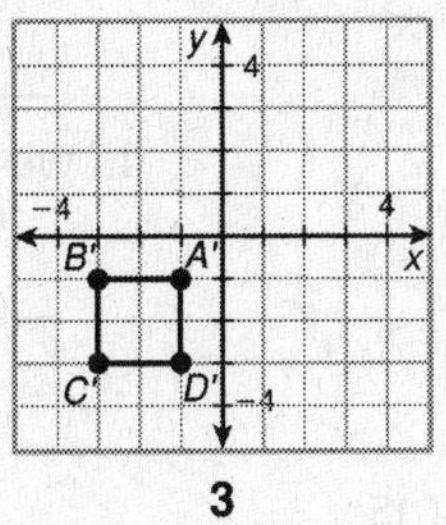

1. rotation ________ 2. translation ________ 3. reflection ________

4. A figure has vertices at *D*(–2, 1), *E*(–3, 3), and *F*(0, 3). After a transformation, the image of the figure has vertices at *D′*(–1, –2), *E′*(–3, –3), and *F′*(–3, 0). Draw the preimage and the image. Then identify the transformation.

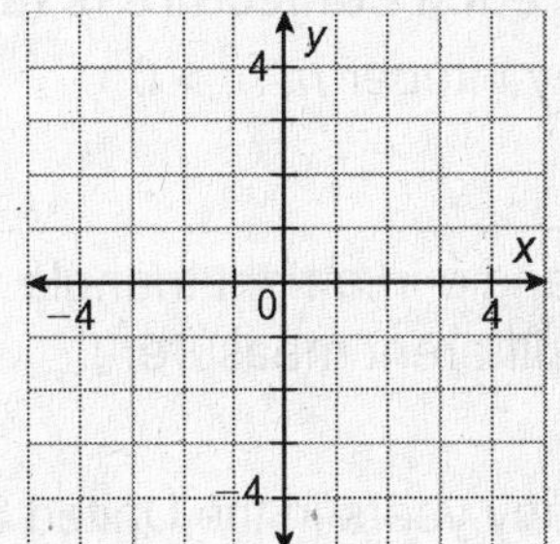

____

5. A figure has vertices at *G*(0, 0), *H*(–1, –2), *I*(–1.5, 0), and *J*(–2.5, 2). Find the coordinates for the image of *GHIJ* after the translation (*x*, *y*) → (*x* – 2.5, *y* + 4).

____

Use the figure for Exercise 6.

6. A parking garage attendant will make the most money when the maximum number of cars fits in the parking garage. To fit one more car in, the attendant moves a car from position 1 to position 2. Write a rule for this translation.

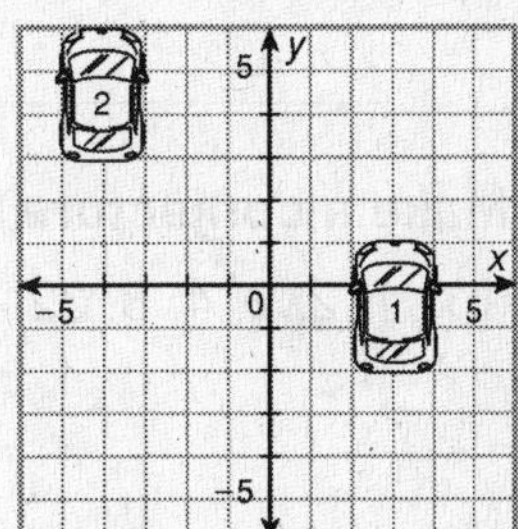

____

7. A figure has vertices at *X*(–1, 1), *Y*(–2, 3), and *Z*(0, 4). Draw the image of *XYZ* after the translation (*x*, *y*) → (*x* – 2, *y*) and a 180° rotation around *X*.

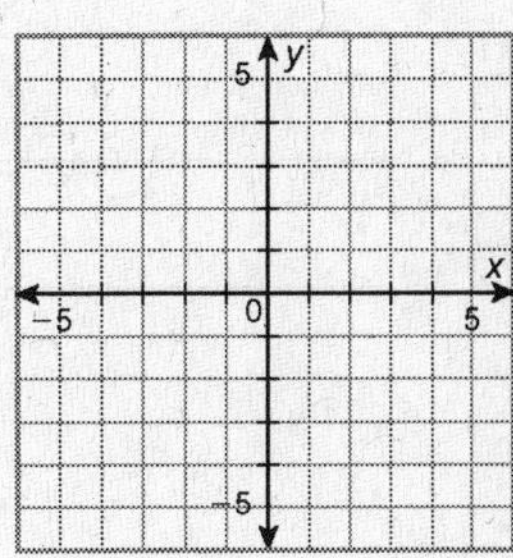

Name ________________________ Date ______________ Class ______________

LESSON 2-1

Practice

Using Inductive Reasoning to Make Conjectures

Find the next item in each pattern.

1. 100, 81, 64, 49, . . .

____

2. . . .

____

3. Alabama, Alaska, Arizona, . . .

____

4. west, south, east, . . .

____

Complete each conjecture.

5. The square of any negative number is ________________.

6. The number of segments determined by *n* points is ________________.

Show that each conjecture is false by finding a counterexample.

7. For any integer n, $n^3 > 0$.

____

8. Each angle in a right triangle has a different measure.

____

9. For many years in the United States, each bank printed its own currency. The variety of different bills led to widespread counterfeiting. By the time of the Civil War, a significant fraction of the currency in circulation was counterfeit. If one Civil War soldier had 48 bills, 16 of which were counterfeit, and another soldier had 39 bills, 13 of which were counterfeit, make a conjecture about what fraction of bills were counterfeit at the time of the Civil War.

____

Make a conjecture about each pattern. Write the next two items.

10. 1, 2, 2, 4, 8, 32, . . .

____

____

____

11. 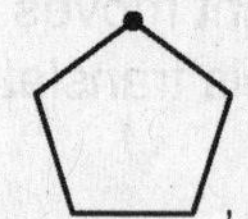, 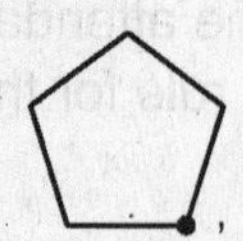, 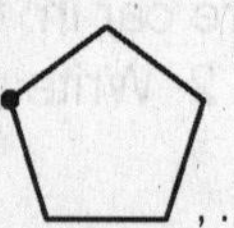, . . .

____

____

Name ______________________ Date ______________ Class ______________

LESSON 2-2

Practice

Conditional Statements

Identify the hypothesis and conclusion of each conditional.

1. If you can see the stars, then it is night.
   Hypothesis: ______________
   Conclusion: ______________

2. A pencil writes well if it is sharp.
   Hypothesis: ______________
   Conclusion: ______________

Write a conditional statement from each of the following.

3. Three noncollinear points determine a plane.

____

4. Fruit
   Kumquats

____

Determine if each conditional is true. If false, give a counterexample.

5. If two points are noncollinear, then a right triangle contains one obtuse angle.

____

6. If a liquid is water, then it is composed of hydrogen and oxygen.

____

7. If a living thing is green, then it is a plant.

____

8. "If G is at 4, then GH is 3." Write the converse, inverse, and contrapositive of this statement. Find the truth value of each.

   H
   −5 0 5

   Converse: ____
   Inverse: ____
   Contrapositive: ____

This chart shows a small part of the *Mammalia* class of animals, the mammals. Write a conditional to describe the relationship between each given pair.

Mammals
Rodents
Primates
Lemurs
Apes

9. primates and mammals ____
10. lemurs and rodents ____
11. rodents and apes ____
12. apes and mammals ____

Name ______________________ Date ____________ Class ____________

LESSON 2-3

Practice

Using Deductive Reasoning to Verify Conjectures

Tell whether each conclusion is a result of inductive or deductive reasoning.

1. The United States Census Bureau collects data on the earnings of American citizens. Using data for the three years from 2001 to 2003, the bureau concluded that the national average median income for a four-person family was $43,527.

____

2. A speeding ticket costs $40 plus $5 per mi/h over the speed limit. Lynne mentions to Frank that she was given a ticket for $75. Frank concludes that Lynne was driving 7 mi/h over the speed limit.

____

Determine if each conjecture is valid by the Law of Detachment.

3. Given: If $m\angle ABC = m\angle CBD$, then $\overrightarrow{BC}$ bisects $\angle ABD$. $\overrightarrow{BC}$ bisects $\angle ABD$.
Conjecture: $m\angle ABC = m\angle CBD$. ____________

4. Given: You will catch a catfish if you use stink bait. Stuart caught a catfish.
Conjecture: Stuart used stink bait. ____________

5. Given: An obtuse triangle has two acute angles. Triangle *ABC* is obtuse.
Conjecture: Triangle *ABC* has two acute angles. ____________

Determine if each conjecture is valid by the Law of Syllogism.

6. Given: If the gossip said it, then it must be true. If it is true, then somebody is in big trouble.
Conjecture: Somebody is in big trouble because the gossip said it. ____________

7. Given: No human is immortal. Fido the dog is not human.
Conjecture: Fido the dog is immortal. ____________

8. Given: The radio is distracting when I am studying. If it is 7:30 P.M. on a weeknight, I am studying.
Conjecture: If it is 7:30 P.M. on a weeknight, the radio is distracting. ____________

Draw a conclusion from the given information.

9. Given: If two segments intersect, then they are not parallel. If two segments are not parallel, then they could be perpendicular. $\overline{EF}$ and $\overline{MN}$ intersect.

____

10. Given: When you are relaxed, your blood pressure is relatively low. If you are sailing, you are relaxed. Becky is sailing.

____

Name ______________________ Date ______________ Class ______________

LESSON 2-4

Practice

Biconditional Statements and Definitions

Write the conditional statement and converse within each biconditional.

1. The tea kettle is whistling if and only if the water is boiling.

   Conditional: ____________________

   Converse: ____________________

2. A biconditional is true if and only if the conditional and converse are both true.

   Conditional: ____________________

   Converse: ____________________

For each conditional, write the converse and a biconditional statement.

3. Conditional: If n is an odd number, then $n - 1$ is divisible by 2.

   Converse: ____________________

   Biconditional: ____________________

4. Conditional: An angle is obtuse when it measures between 90° and 180°.

   Converse: ____________________

   Biconditional: ____________________

Determine whether a true biconditional can be written from each conditional statement. If not, give a counterexample.

5. If the lamp is unplugged, then the bulb does not shine.

   ____

6. The date can be the 29th if and only if it is not February.

   ____

Write each definition as a biconditional.

7. A cube is a three-dimensional solid with six square faces.

   ____

   ____

8. Tanya claims that the definition of *doofus* is "her younger brother."

   ____

   ____

Name ______________________ Date ____________ Class ____________

LESSON 2-5

Practice

Algebraic Proof

Solve each equation. Show all your steps and write a justification for each step.

1. $\frac{1}{5}(a + 10) = -3$

2. $t + 6.5 = 3t - 1.3$

3. The formula for the perimeter P of a rectangle with length ℓ and width w is $P = 2(\ell + w)$. Find the length of the rectangle shown here if the perimeter is $9\frac{1}{2}$ feet. Solve the equation for ℓ and justify each step.

$1\frac{1}{4}$ ft

ℓ

Write a justification for each step.

4. $7x - 3$

H $2x + 6$ I $3x - 3$ J

$HJ = HI + IJ$ ______________

$7x - 3 = (2x + 6) + (3x - 3)$ ______________

$7x - 3 = 5x + 3$ ______________

$7x = 5x + 6$ ______________

$2x = 6$ ______________

$x = 3$ ______________

Identify the property that justifies each statement.

5. $m = n$, so $n = m$.

____

6. $\angle ABC \cong \angle ABC$

____

7. $\overline{KL} \cong \overline{LK}$

____

8. $p = q$ and $q = -1$, so $p = -1$.

____

Name ______________________ Date ______________ Class ______________

LESSON 2-6

Practice

Geometric Proof

Write a justification for each step.

Given: $AB = EF$, B is the midpoint of $\overline{AC}$, and E is the midpoint of $\overline{DF}$.

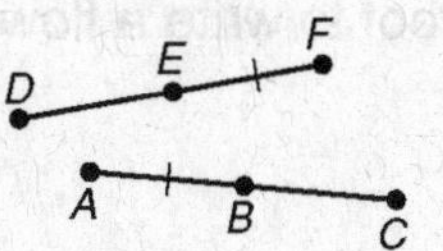

1. B is the midpoint of $\overline{AC}$, and E is the midpoint of $\overline{DF}$. ______________
2. $\overline{AB} \cong \overline{BC}$, and $\overline{DE} \cong \overline{EF}$. ______________
3. $AB = BC$, and $DE = EF$. ______________
4. $AB + BC = AC$, and $DE + EF = DF$. ______________
5. $2AB = AC$, and $2EF = DF$. ______________
6. $AB = EF$ ______________
7. $2AB = 2EF$ ______________
8. $AC = DF$ ______________
9. $\overline{AC} \cong \overline{DF}$ ______________

Fill in the blanks to complete the two-column proof.

10. **Given:** $\angle HKJ$ is a straight angle. $\overrightarrow{KI}$ bisects $\angle HKJ$.
    Prove: $\angle IKJ$ is a right angle.

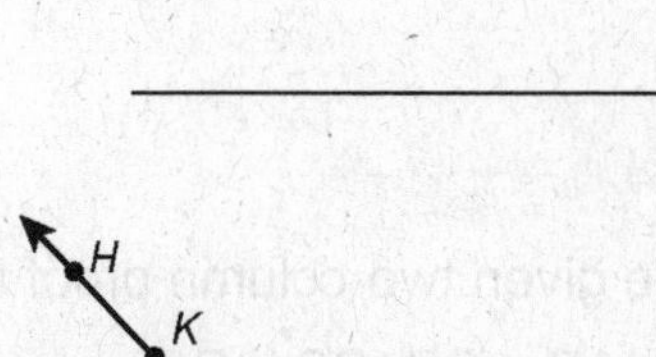

Proof:

Statements	Reasons
1. a. ______________	1. Given
2. $m\angle HKJ = 180°$	2. b. ______________
3. c. ______________	3. Given
4. $\angle IKJ \cong \angle IKH$	4. Def. of $\angle$ bisector
5. $m\angle IKJ = m\angle IKH$	5. Def. of $\cong$ $\angle$s
6. d. ______________	6. $\angle$ Add. Post.
7. $2m\angle IKJ = 180°$	7. e. Subst. (Steps ______)
8. $m\angle IKJ = 90°$	8. Div. Prop. of =
9. $\angle IKJ$ is a right angle.	9. f. ______________

Name ______________________ Date ______________ Class ______________

LESSON 2-7

Practice

Flowchart and Paragraph Proofs

1. Use the given two-column proof to write a flowchart proof.

Given: $\angle 4 \cong \angle 3$

Prove: $m\angle 1 = m\angle 2$

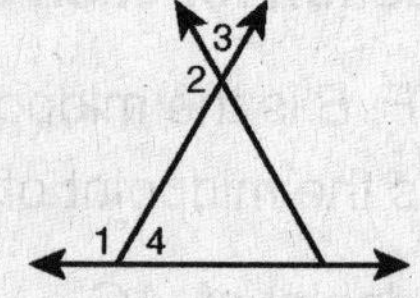

Statements	Reasons
1. $\angle 1$ and $\angle 4$ are supplementary, $\angle 2$ and $\angle 3$ are supplementary.	1. Linear Pair Thm.
2. $\angle 4 \cong \angle 3$	2. Given
3. $\angle 1 \cong \angle 2$	3. $\cong$ Supps. Thm.
4. $m\angle 1 = m\angle 2$	4. Def. of $\cong$ ∡s

2. Use the given two-column proof to write a paragraph proof.

Given: $AB = CD$, $BC = DE$

Prove: C is the midpoint of $\overline{AE}$.

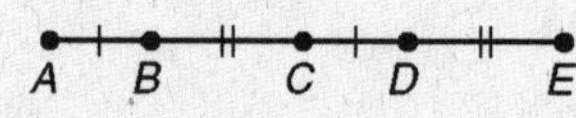

Statements	Reasons
1. $AB = CD$, $BC = DE$	1. Given
2. $AB + BC = CD + DE$	2. Add. Prop. of =
3. $AB + BC = AC$, $CD + DE = CE$	3. Seg. Add. Post.
4. $AC = CE$	4. Subst.
5. $\overline{AC} \cong \overline{CE}$	5. Def. of $\cong$ segs.
6. C is the midpoint of $\overline{AE}$.	6. Def. of mdpt.

____

____

____

____

____

Name ________________ Date ________________ Class ________________

LESSON 3-1

Practice

Lines and Angles

For Exercises 1–4, identify each of the following in the figure.

1. a pair of parallel segments ________________
2. a pair of skew segments ________________
3. a pair of perpendicular segments ________________
4. a pair of parallel planes ________________

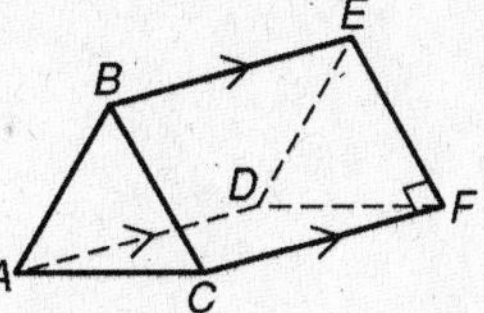

In Exercises 5–10, give one example of each from the figure.

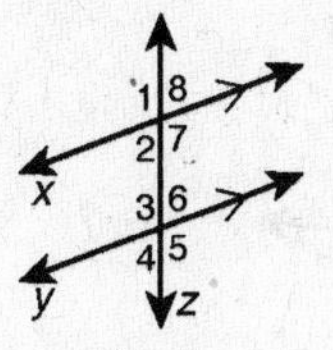

5. a transversal ________________
6. parallel lines ________________
7. corresponding angles ________________
8. alternate interior angles ________________
9. alternate exterior angles ________________
10. same-side interior angles ________________

Use the figure for Exercises 11–14. The figure shows a utility pole with an electrical line and a telephone line. The angled wire is a tension wire. For each angle pair given, identify the transversal and classify the angle pair. (*Hint:* Think of the utility pole as a line for these problems.)

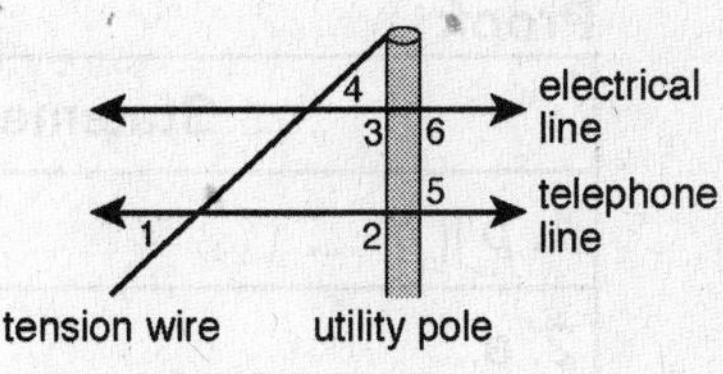

11. ∠5 and ∠6 ________________

12. ∠1 and ∠4 ________________

13. ∠1 and ∠2 ________________

14. ∠5 and ∠3 ________________

Name ______________________ Date ______________ Class ______________

LESSON 3-2

Practice

Angles Formed by Parallel Lines and Transversals

Find each angle measure.

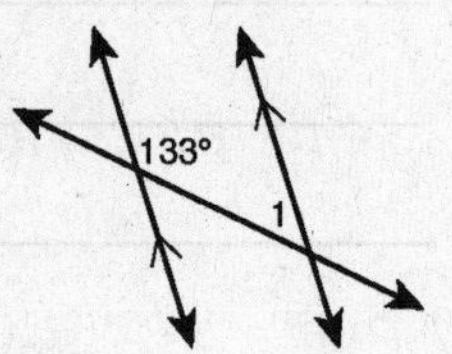

1. $m\angle 1$ ______________

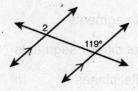

2. $m\angle 2$ ______________

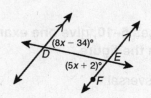

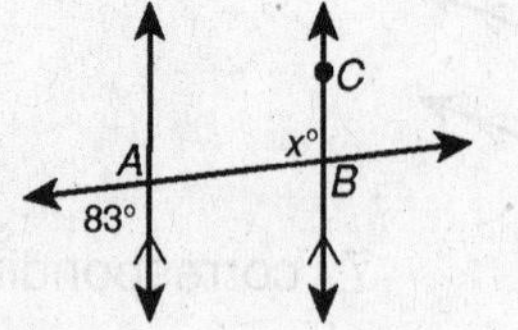

3. $m\angle ABC$ ______________

4. $m\angle DEF$ ______________

Complete the two-column proof to show that same-side exterior angles are supplementary.

5. **Given:** $p \parallel q$

   Prove: $m\angle 1 + m\angle 3 = 180°$

   Proof:

Statements	Reasons
1. $p \parallel q$	1. Given
2. a. ______________	2. Lin. Pair Thm.
3. $\angle 1 \cong \angle 2$	3. b. ______________
4. c. ______________	4. Def. of ≅ ∠s
5. d. ______________	5. e. ______________

6. Ocean waves move in parallel lines toward the shore. The figure shows Sandy Beaches windsurfing across several waves. For this exercise, think of Sandy's wake as a line. $m\angle 1 = (2x + 2y)°$ and $m\angle 2 = (2x + y)°$. Find x and y.

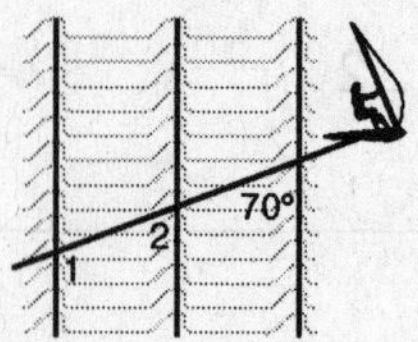

   x = ______________

   y = ______________

Name ______________________ Date ______________ Class ______________

LESSON 3-3

Practice

Proving Lines Parallel

Use the figure for Exercises 1–8. Tell whether lines *m* and *n* must be parallel from the given information. If they are, state your reasoning. (*Hint:* The angle measures may change for each exercise, and the figure is for reference only.)

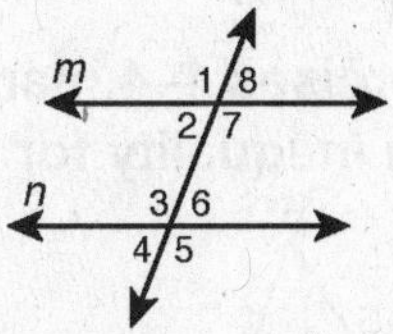

1. $\angle 7 \cong \angle 3$

____

2. $m\angle 3 = (15x + 22)°$, $m\angle 1 = (19x - 10)°$, $x = 8$

____

3. $\angle 7 \cong \angle 6$

____

____

4. $m\angle 2 = (5x + 3)°$, $m\angle 3 = (8x - 5)°$, $x = 14$

____

____

5. $m\angle 8 = (6x - 1)°$, $m\angle 4 = (5x + 3)°$, $x = 9$

____

6. $\angle 5 \cong \angle 7$

____

7. $\angle 1 \cong \angle 5$

____

8. $m\angle 6 = (x + 10)°$, $m\angle 2 = (x + 15)°$

____

9. Look at some of the printed letters in a textbook. The small horizontal and vertical segments attached to the ends of the letters are called *serifs*. Most of the letters in a textbook are in a serif typeface. The letters on this page do not have serifs, so these letters are in a sans-serif typeface. (*Sans* means "without" in French.) The figure shows a capital letter *A* with serifs. Use the given information to write a paragraph proof that the serif, segment $\overline{HI}$, is parallel to segment $\overline{JK}$.

   Given: $\angle 1$ and $\angle 3$ are supplementary.

   Prove: $\overline{HI} \parallel \overline{JK}$

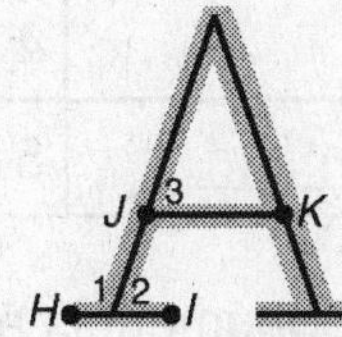

Name ____________________ Date ____________ Class ____________

LESSON 3-4

Practice

Perpendicular Lines

For Exercises 1–4, name the shortest segment from the point to the line and write an inequality for *x*. (*Hint:* One answer is a double inequality.)

1. 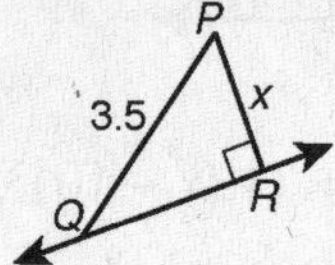

2. 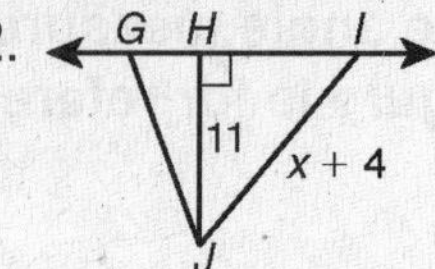

________________________ ________________________

3. 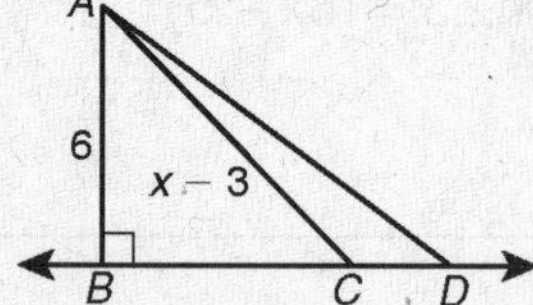

4. 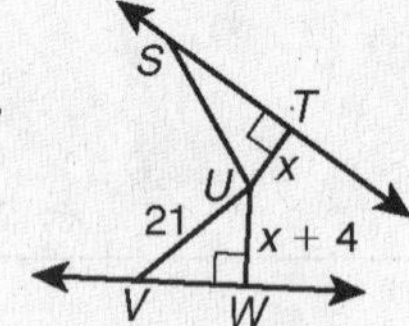

________________________ ________________________

Complete the two-column proof.

5. **Given:** $m \perp n$

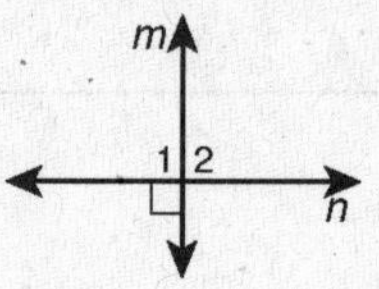

Prove: ∠1 and ∠2 are a linear pair of congruent angles.

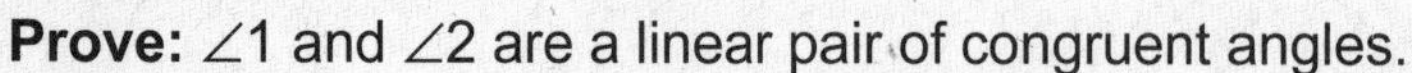

Proof:

Statements	Reasons
1. a. ________________	1. Given
2. b. ________________	2. Def. of ⊥
3. ∠1 ≅ ∠2	3. c. ________________
4. m∠1 + m∠2 = 180°	4. Add. Prop. of =
5. d. ________________	5. Def. of linear pair

6. The Four Corners National Monument is at the intersection of the borders of Arizona, Colorado, New Mexico, and Utah. It is called the four corners because the intersecting borders are perpendicular. If you were to lie down on the intersection, you could be in four states at the same time—the only place in the United States where this is possible. The figure shows the Colorado-Utah border extending north in a straight line until it intersects the Wyoming border at a right angle. Explain why the Colorado-Wyoming border must be parallel to the Colorado–New Mexico border.

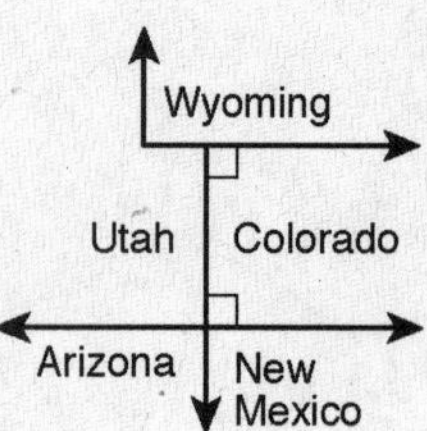

____

____

____

Name ______________________ Date ______________ Class ______________

LESSON 3-5

Practice

Slopes of Lines

Use the slope formula to determine the slope of each line.

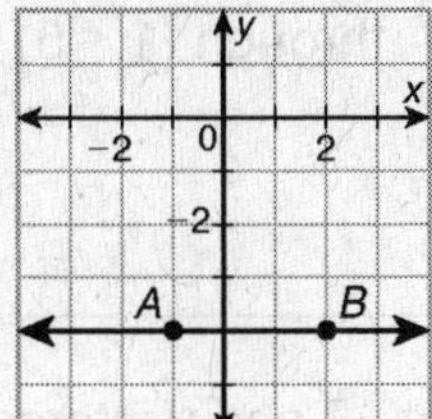

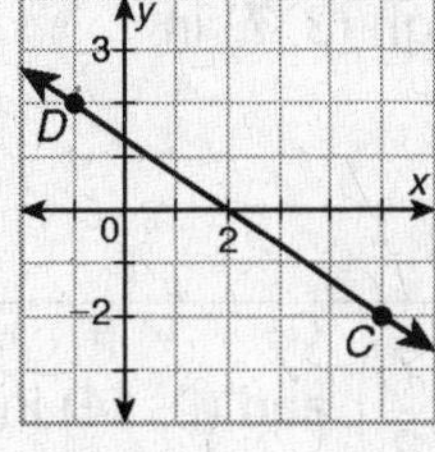

1. $\overleftrightarrow{AB}$ ______________________

2. $\overleftrightarrow{CD}$ ______________________

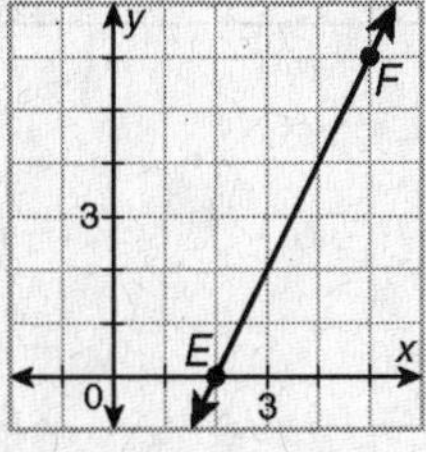

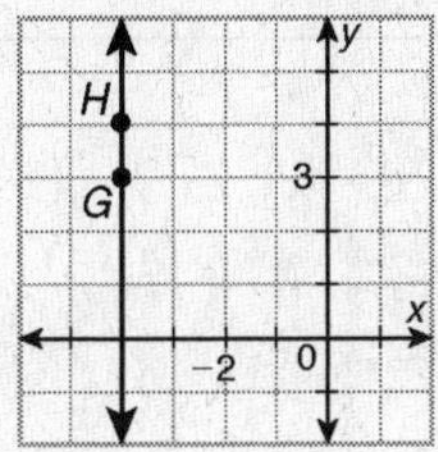

3. $\overleftrightarrow{EF}$ ______________________

4. $\overleftrightarrow{GH}$ ______________________

Graph each pair of lines. Use slopes to determine whether the lines are parallel, perpendicular, or neither.

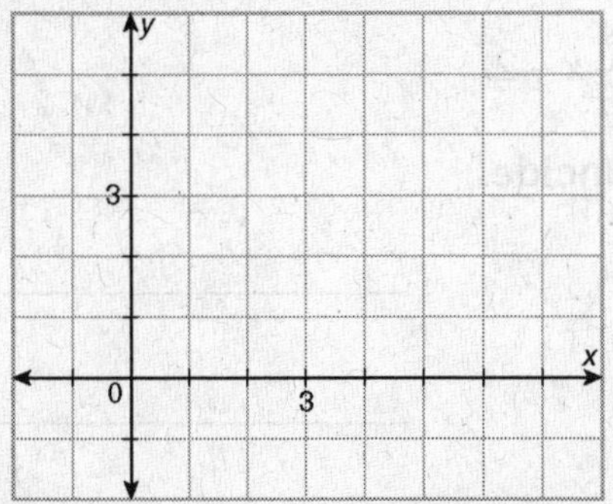

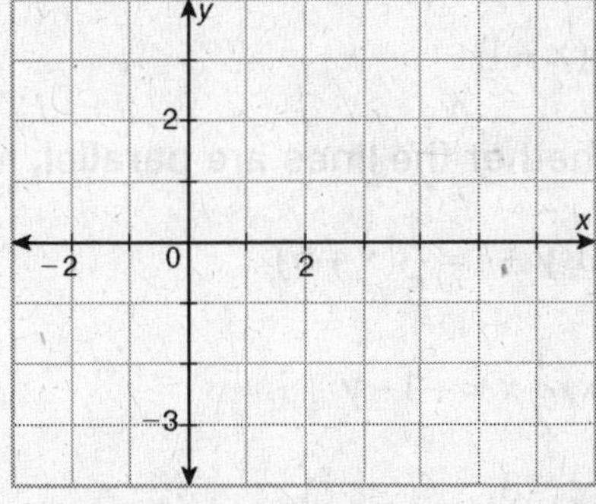

5. $\overleftrightarrow{IJ}$ and $\overleftrightarrow{KL}$ for $I(1, 0)$, $J(5, 3)$, $K(6, -1)$, and $L(0, 2)$ ______________________

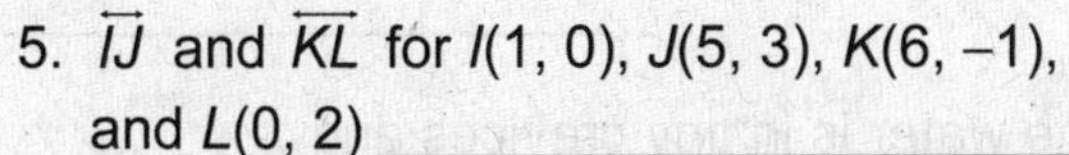

6. $\overleftrightarrow{PQ}$ and $\overleftrightarrow{RS}$ for $P(5, 1)$, $Q(-1, -1)$, $R(2, 1)$, and $S(3, -2)$ ______________________

7. At a ski resort, the different ski runs down the mountain are color-coded according to difficulty. Green is easy, blue is medium, and black is hard. Assume that the ski runs below are rated only according to their slope (steeper is harder) and that there is one green, one blue, and one black run. Assign a color to each ski run.

Emerald $\left(m = \frac{4}{7}\right)$ Diamond $\left(m = \frac{5}{4}\right)$ Ruby $\left(m = \frac{5}{8}\right)$

______________________ ______________________ ______________________

Name ______________________ Date ______________ Class ______________

LESSON 3-6

Practice

Lines in the Coordinate Plane

Write the equation of each line in the given form.

1. the horizontal line through (3, 7) in point-slope form

   ____

2. the line with slope $-\frac{8}{5}$ through (1, –5) in point-slope form

   ____

3. the line through $\left(-\frac{1}{2}, -\frac{7}{2}\right)$ and (2, 14) in slope-intercept form

   ____

4. the line with *x*-intercept –2 and *y*-intercept –1 in slope-intercept form

   ____

Graph each line.

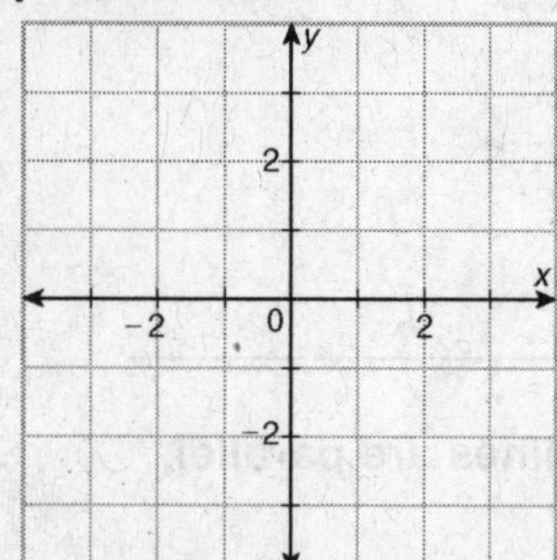

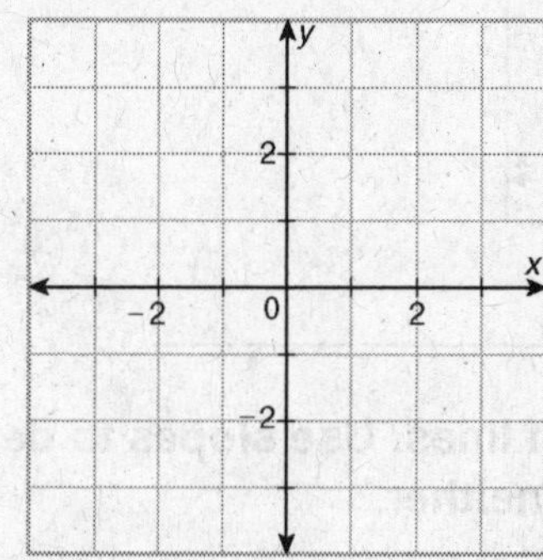

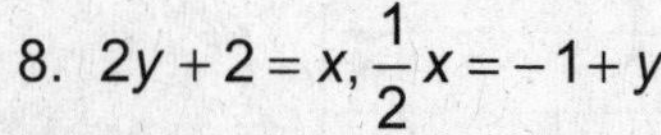

5. $y + 3 = \frac{3}{4}(x + 1)$

6. $y = -\frac{4}{3}x + 2$

Determine whether the lines are parallel, intersect, or coincide.

7. $x - 5y = 0,\ y + 1 = \frac{1}{5}(x + 5)$ ______________

8. $2y + 2 = x,\ \frac{1}{2}x = -1 + y$ ______________

9. $y = 4(x - 3),\ \frac{3}{4} + 4y = -\frac{1}{4}x$ ______________

An *aquifer* is an underground storehouse of water. The water is in tiny crevices and pockets in the rock or sand, but because aquifers underlay large areas of land, the amount of water in an aquifer can be vast. Wells and springs draw water from aquifers.

10. Two relatively small aquifers are the Rush Springs (RS) aquifer and the Arbuckle-Simpson (AS) aquifer, both in Oklahoma. Suppose that starting on a certain day in 1985, 52 million gallons of water per day were taken from the RS aquifer, and 8 million gallons of water per day were taken from the AS aquifer. If the RS aquifer began with 4500 million gallons of water and the AS aquifer began with 3000 million gallons of water and no rain fell, write a slope-intercept equation for each aquifer and find how many days passed until both aquifers held the same amount of water. (Round to the nearest day.)

    ____

Name ______________________ Date ______________ Class ______________

LESSON 4-1

Practice

Congruence and Transformations

Apply the transformation *M* to the polygon with the given vertices. Identify and describe the transformation.

1. $M: (x, y) \rightarrow (x - 2, y + 3)$

   $A(-1, -3)$, $B(2, -1)$, $C(2, -4)$

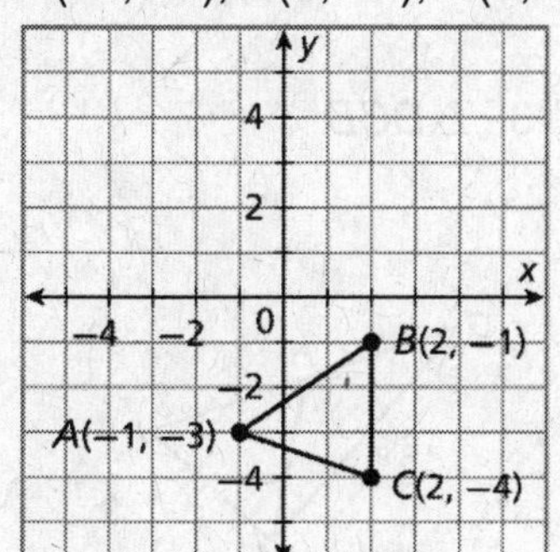

____

2. $M: (x, y) \rightarrow (-x, y)$

   $P(-1, 2)$, $Q(-2, -3)$, $R(1, -2)$

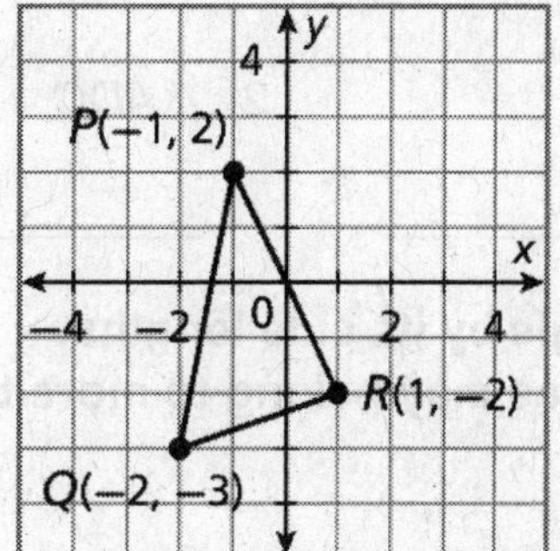

____

3. $M: (x, y) \rightarrow (y, -x)$

   $G(-4, 3)$, $H(-2, 3)$, $J(-2, -1)$, $K(-4, -1)$

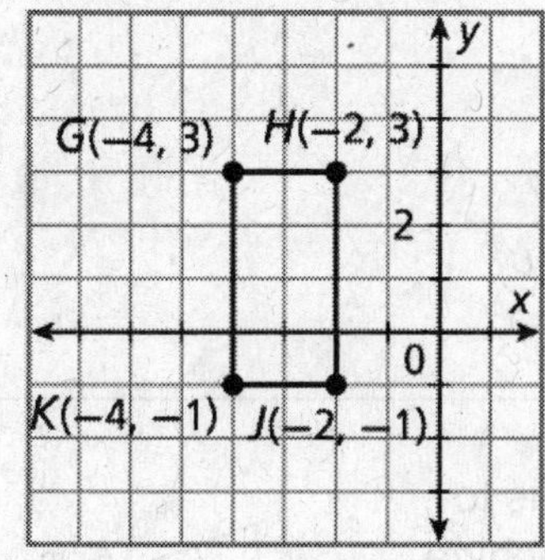

____

4. $M: (x, y) \rightarrow (2x, 2y)$

   $E(-2, 2)$, $F(1, 1)$, $G(2, 2)$

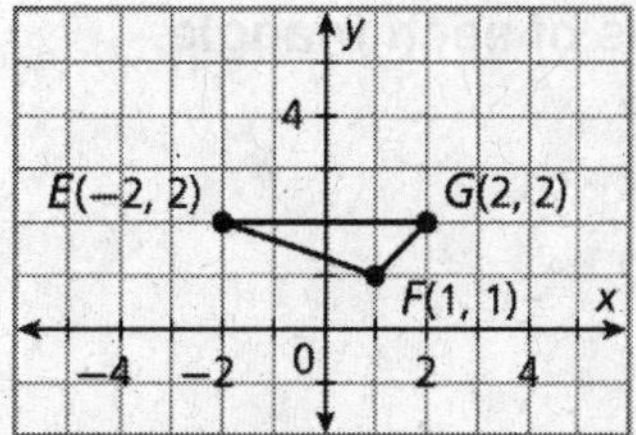

____

Determine whether the polygons with the given vertices are congruent.

5. $A(-4, 4)$, $B(-2, 4)$, $C(-2, 2)$, $D(-3, 1)$, $E(-4, 2)$; $P(2, 6)$, $Q(4, 6)$, $R(4, 4)$, $S(3, 3)$, $T(2, 4)$

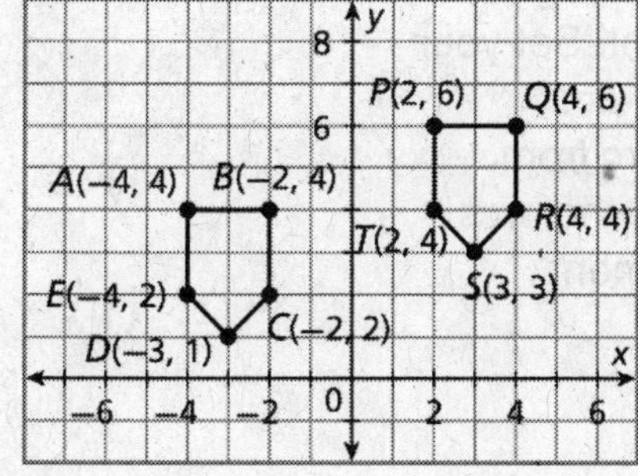

____

6. $P(4, 4)$, $Q(-4, 2)$, $R(-2, 6)$; $J(2, 2)$, $K(-2, 1)$, $L(-1, 3)$

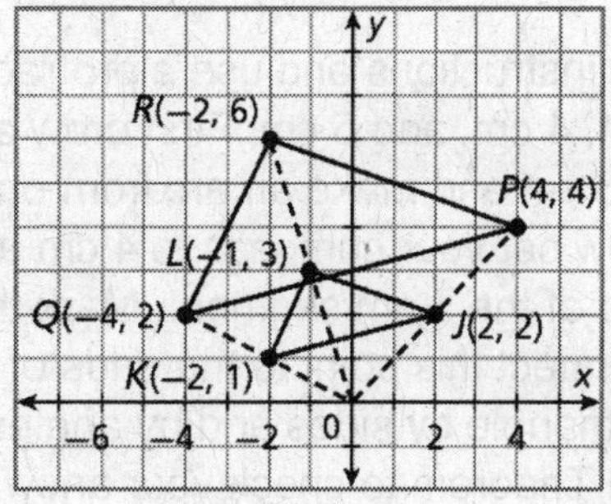

____

Name ______________________ Date ______________ Class ______________

LESSON 4-2

Practice

Classifying Triangles

Classify each triangle by its angle measures. (*Note:* Some triangles may belong to more than one class.)

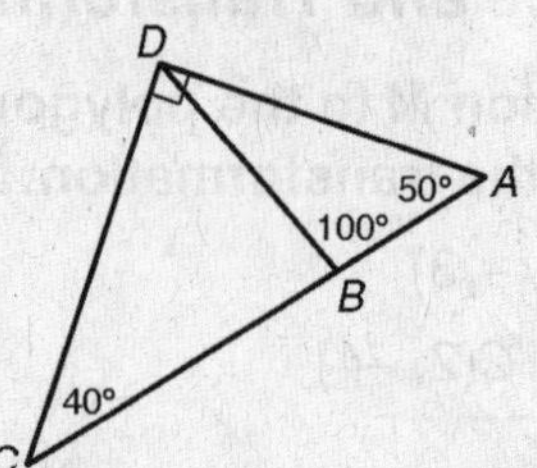

1. $\triangle ABD$ ______________
2. $\triangle ADC$ ______________
3. $\triangle BCD$ ______________

Classify each triangle by its side lengths. (*Note:* Some triangles may belong to more than one class.)

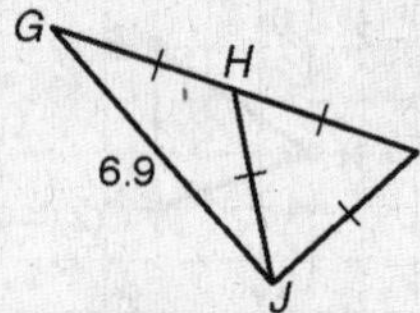

4. $\triangle GIJ$ ______________
5. $\triangle HIJ$ ______________
6. $\triangle GHJ$ ______________

Find the side lengths of each triangle.

7.

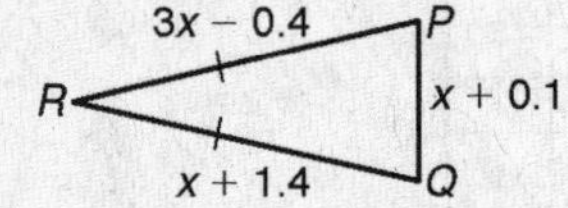

____

8.

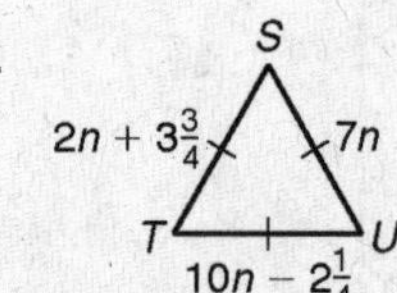

____

9. Min works in the kitchen of a catering company. Today her job is to cut whole pita bread into small triangles. Min uses a cutting machine, so every pita triangle comes out the same. The figure shows an example. Min has been told to cut 3 pita triangles for every guest. There will be 250 guests. If the pita bread she uses comes in squares with 20-centimeter sides and she doesn't waste any bread, how many squares of whole pita bread will Min have to cut up?

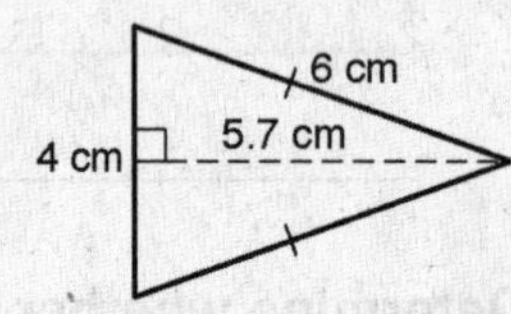

____

10. Follow these instructions and use a protractor to draw a triangle with sides of 3 cm, 4 cm, and 5 cm. First draw a 5-cm segment. Set your compass to 3 cm and make an arc from one end of the 5-cm segment. Now set your compass to 4 cm and make an arc from the other end of the 5-cm segment. Mark the point where the arcs intersect. Connect this point to the ends of the 5-cm segment. Classify the triangle by sides and by angles. Use the Pythagorean Theorem to check your answer.

____

Name ______________________ Date ______________ Class ______________

LESSON 4-3

Practice

Angle Relationships in Triangles

1. An area in central North Carolina is known as the Research Triangle because of the relatively large number of high-tech companies and research universities located there. Duke University, the University of North Carolina at Chapel Hill, and North Carolina State University are all within this area. The Research Triangle is roughly bounded by the cities of Chapel Hill, Durham, and Raleigh. From Chapel Hill, the angle between Durham and Raleigh measures 54.8°. From Raleigh, the angle between Chapel Hill and Durham measures 24.1°. Find the angle between Chapel Hill and Raleigh from Durham. ______________

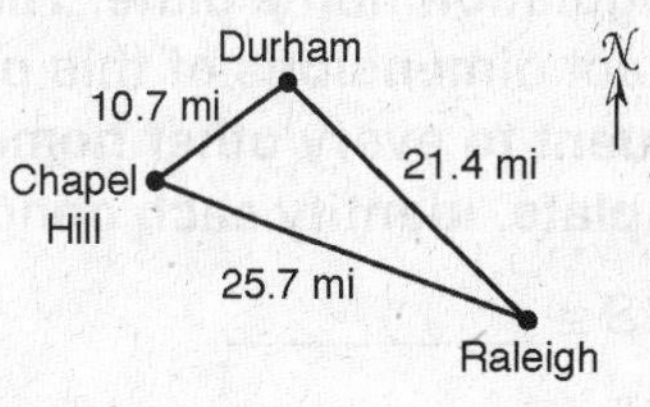

2. The acute angles of right triangle *ABC* are congruent. Find their measures. ______________

The measure of one of the acute angles in a right triangle is given. Find the measure of the other acute angle.

3. 44.9° ______________ 4. $(90 - z)°$ ______________ 5. 0.3° ______________

Find each angle measure.

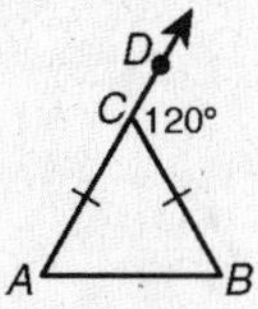

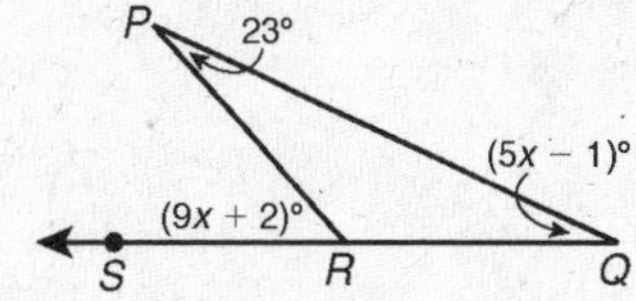

6. $m\angle B$ ______________ 7. $m\angle PRS$ ______________

8. In $\triangle LMN$, the measure of an exterior angle at *N* measures 99°. $m\angle L = \frac{1}{3}x°$ and $m\angle M = \frac{2}{3}x°$. Find $m\angle L$, $m\angle M$, and $m\angle LNM$. ______________

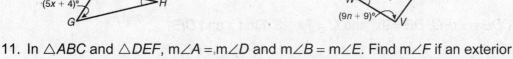

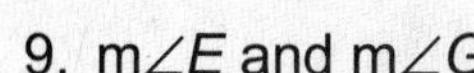

9. $m\angle E$ and $m\angle G$ ______________ 10. $m\angle T$ and $m\angle V$ ______________

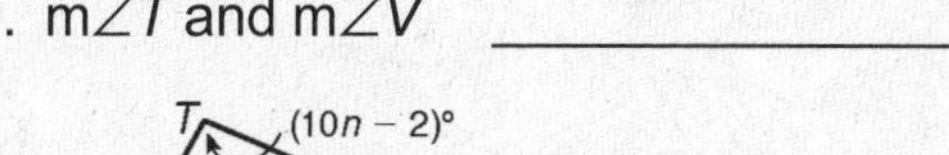

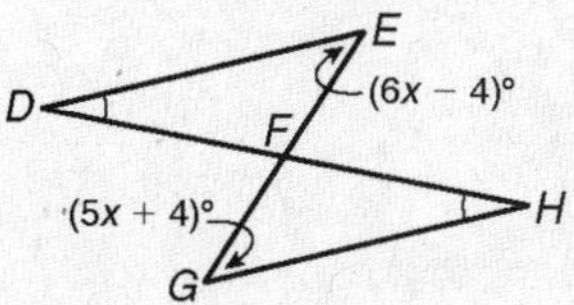

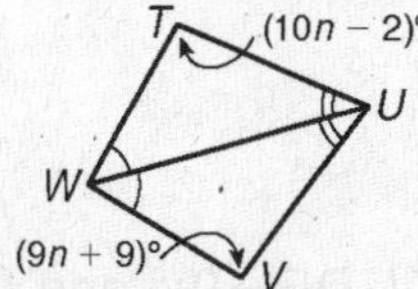

11. In $\triangle ABC$ and $\triangle DEF$, $m\angle A = m\angle D$ and $m\angle B = m\angle E$. Find $m\angle F$ if an exterior angle at *A* measures 107°, $m\angle B = (5x + 2)°$, and $m\angle C = (5x + 5)°$. ______________

12. The angle measures of a triangle are in the ratio 3 : 4 : 3. Find the angle measures of the triangle. ______________

Name ______________________ Date ______________ Class ______________

LESSON 4-4

Practice

Congruent Triangles

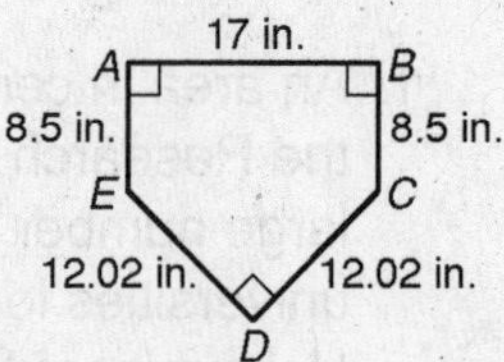

In baseball, home plate is a pentagon. Pentagon *ABCDE* is a diagram of a regulation home plate. The baseball rules are very specific about the exact dimensions of this pentagon so that every home plate is congruent to every other home plate. If pentagon *PQRST* is another home plate, identify each congruent corresponding part.

1. $\angle S \cong$ __________
2. $\angle B \cong$ __________
3. $\overline{EA} \cong$ __________
4. $\angle E \cong$ __________
5. $\overline{PQ} \cong$ __________
6. $\overline{TS} \cong$ __________

Given: $\triangle DEF \cong \triangle LMN$. Find each value.

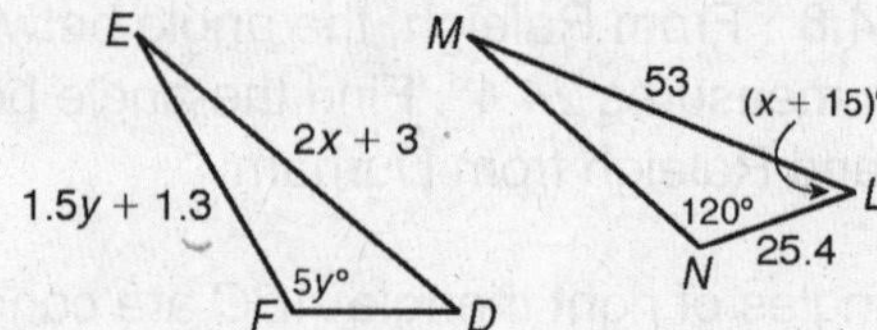

7. m$\angle L =$ __________
8. $EF =$ __________
9. Write a two-column proof.

Given: $\angle U \cong \angle UWV \cong \angle ZXY \cong \angle Z$, $\overline{UV} \cong \overline{WV}$, $\overline{XY} \cong \overline{ZY}$, $\overline{UX} \cong \angle \overline{WZ}$

Prove: $\Delta UVW \cong \Delta XYZ$

Proof:

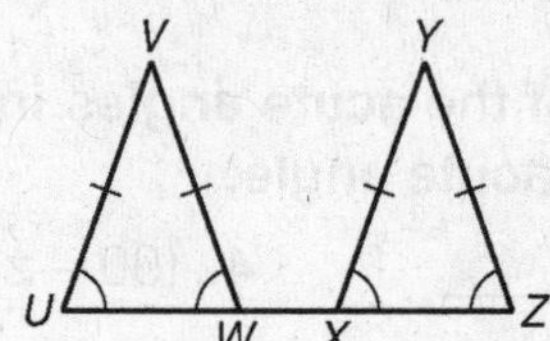

10. **Given:** $\triangle CDE \cong \triangle HIJ$, $DE = 9x$, and $IJ = 7x + 3$. Find x and DE.

____

11. **Given:** $\triangle CDE \cong \triangle HIJ$, m$\angle D = (5y + 1)°$, and m$\angle I = (6y - 25)°$. Find y and m$\angle D$.

____

Name ________________________ Date ______________ Class ______________

LESSON 4-5

Practice

Triangle Congruence: SSS and SAS

Write which of the SSS or SAS postulates, if either, can be used to prove the triangles congruent. If no triangles can be proved congruent, write *neither*.

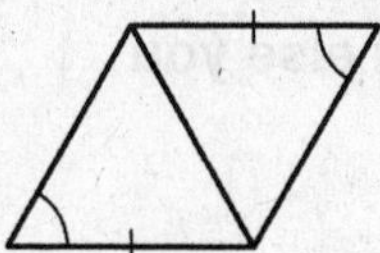

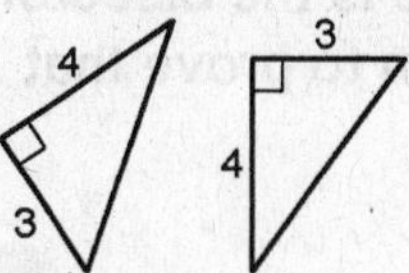

1. ________________________

2. ________________________

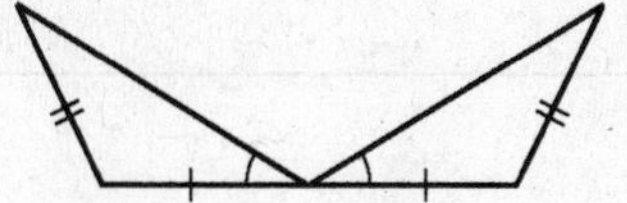

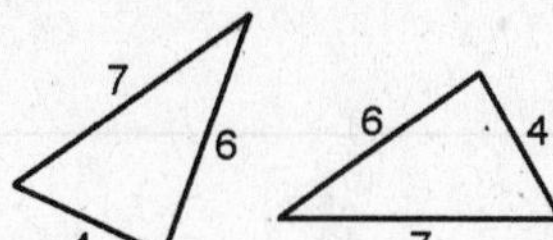

3. ________________________

4. ________________________

Find the value of *x* so that the triangles are congruent.

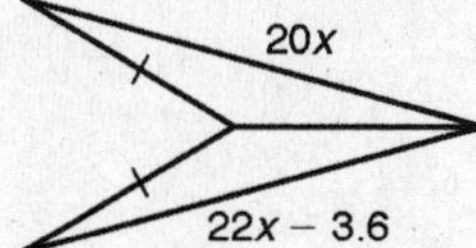

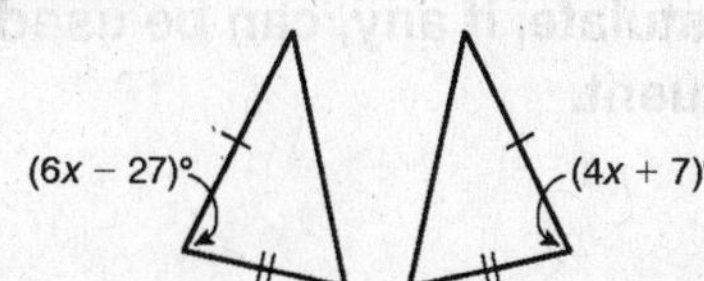

5. $x =$ ________________________

6. $x =$ ________________________

The Hatfield and McCoy families are feuding over some land. Neither family will be satisfied unless the two triangular fields are exactly the same size. You know that *C* is the midpoint of each of the intersecting segments. Write a two-column proof that will settle the dispute.

7. **Given:** C is the midpoint of $\overline{AD}$ and $\overline{BE}$.

   Prove: $\triangle ABC \cong \triangle DEC$

   Proof:

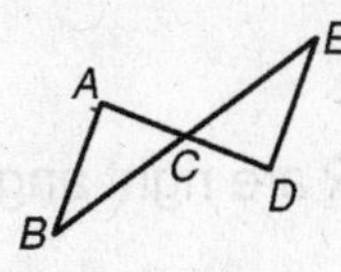

Name ______________________ Date ______________ Class ______________

LESSON 4-6

Practice

Triangle Congruence: ASA, AAS, and HL

Students in Mrs. Marquez's class are watching a film on the uses of geometry in architecture. The film projector casts the image on a flat screen as shown in the figure. The dotted line is the bisector of $\angle ABC$. Tell whether you can use each congruence theorem to prove that $\triangle ABD \cong \triangle CBD$. If not, tell what else you need to know.

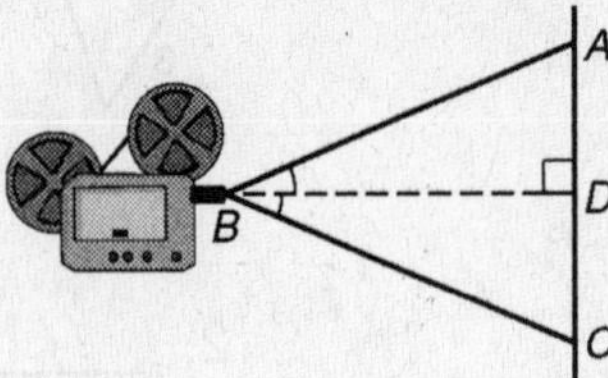

1. Hypotenuse-Leg

____

2. Angle-Side-Angle

____

3. Angle-Angle-Side

____

Write which postulate, if any, can be used to prove the pair of triangles congruent.

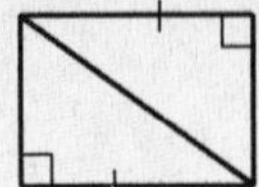

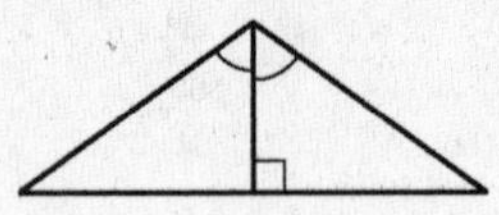

4. ______________________ 5. ______________________

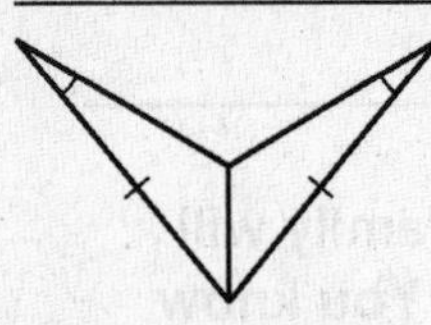

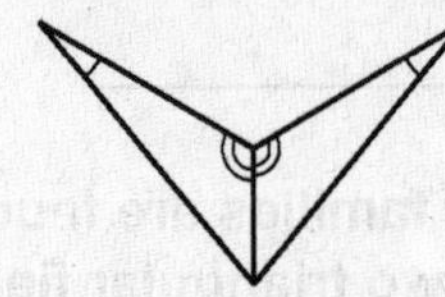

6. ______________________ 7. ______________________

Write a paragraph proof.

8. **Given:** $\angle PQU \cong \angle TSU$,
$\angle QUR$ and $\angle SUR$ are right angles.

Prove: $\triangle RUQ \cong \triangle RUS$

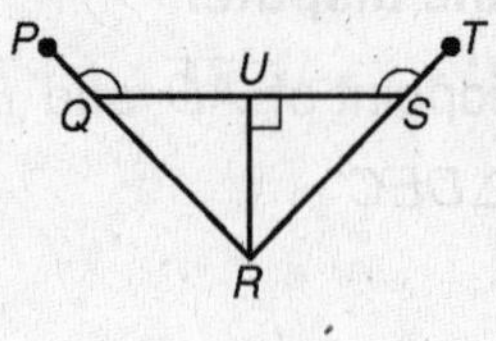

Name ______________________________ Date ______________ Class ______________

LESSON 4-7

Practice

Triangle Congruence: CPCTC

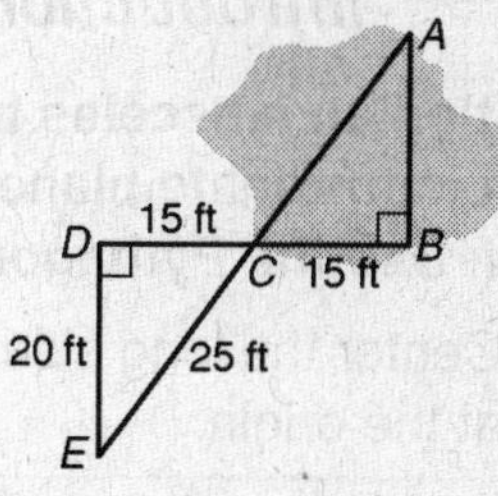

1. Heike Dreschler set the Woman's World Junior Record for the long jump in 1983. She jumped about 23.4 feet. The diagram shows two triangles and a pond. Explain whether Heike could have jumped the pond along path *BA* or along path *CA*.

____

____

____

____

____

Write a flowchart proof.

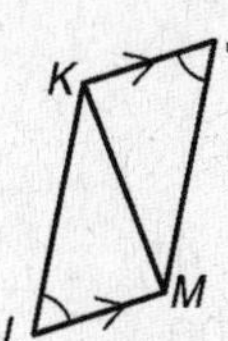

2. **Given:** $\angle L \cong \angle J$, $\overline{KJ} \parallel \overline{LM}$

   Prove: $\angle LKM \cong \angle JMK$

Write a two-column proof.

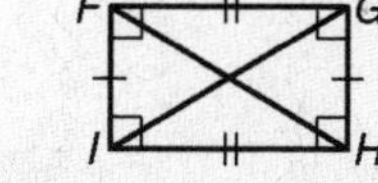

3. **Given:** *FGHI* is a rectangle.

   Prove: The diagonals of a rectangle have equal lengths.

Name ______________________ Date ______________ Class ______________

LESSON 4-8

Practice

Introduction to Coordinate Proof

Position an isosceles triangle with sides of 8 units, 5 units, and 5 units in the coordinate plane. Label the coordinates of each vertex. (*Hint:* Use the Pythagorean Theorem.)

1. Center the long side on the *x*-axis at the origin.

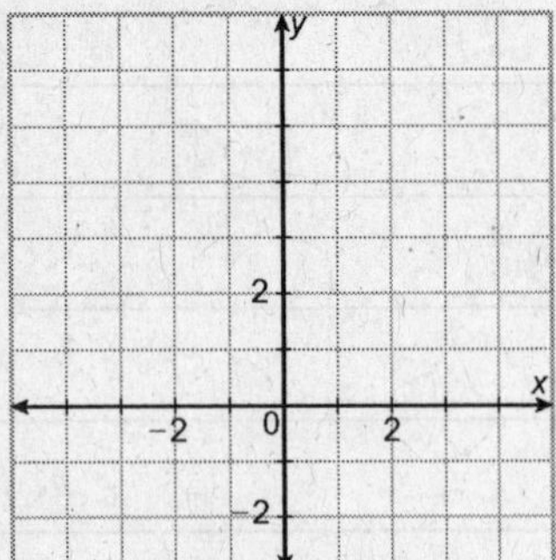

2. Place the long side on the *y*-axis centered at the origin.

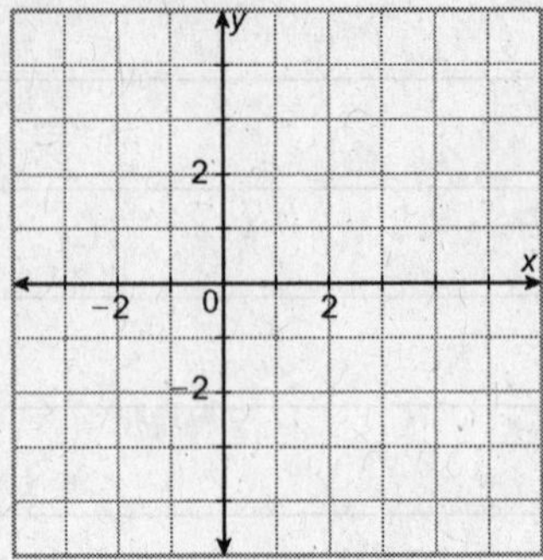

Write a coordinate proof.

3. **Given:** Rectangle *ABCD* has vertices *A*(0, 4), *B*(6, 4), *C*(6, 0), and *D*(0, 0). *E* is the midpoint of $\overline{DC}$. *F* is the midpoint of $\overline{DA}$.

   Prove: The area of rectangle *DEGF* is one-fourth the area of rectangle *ABCD*.

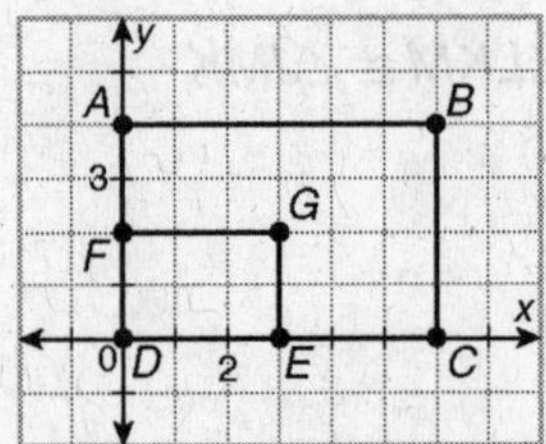

Name ______________________ Date ______________ Class ______________

LESSON 4-9

Practice

Isosceles and Equilateral Triangles

An altitude of a triangle is a perpendicular segment from a vertex to the line containing the opposite side. Write a paragraph proof that the altitude to the base of an isosceles triangle bisects the base.

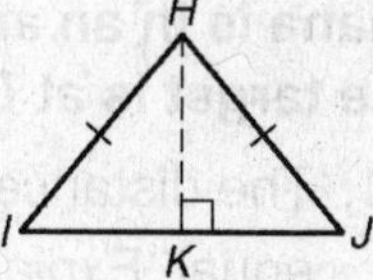

1. **Given:** $\overline{HI} \cong \overline{HJ}$, $\overline{HK} \perp \overline{IJ}$

   Prove: $\overline{HK}$ bisects $\overline{IJ}$.

2. An *obelisk* is a tall, thin, four-sided monument that tapers to a pyramidal top. The most well-known obelisk to Americans is the Washington Monument on the National Mall in Washington, D.C. Each face of the pyramidal top of the Washington Monument is an isosceles triangle. The height of each triangle is 55.5 feet, and the base of each triangle measures 34.4 feet. Find the length, to the nearest tenth of a foot, of one of the two equal legs of the triangle. ________

Find each value.

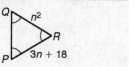

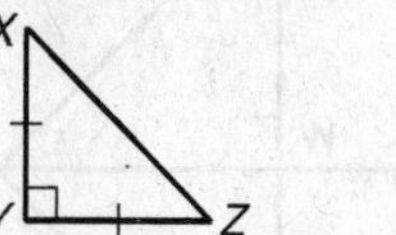

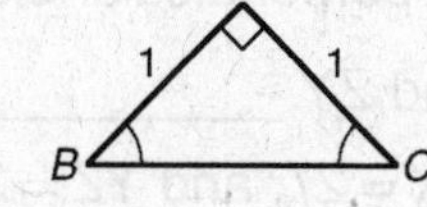

3. m∠X = ____________

4. BC = ____________

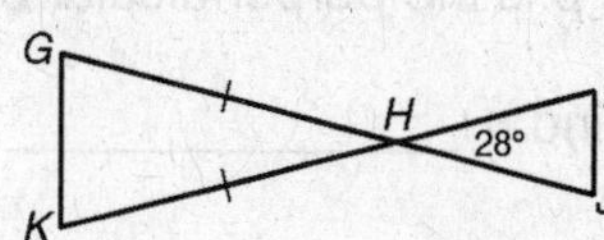

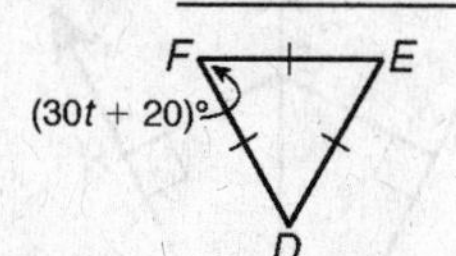

5. PQ = ____________

6. m∠K = ____________

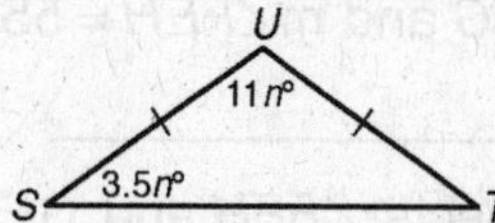

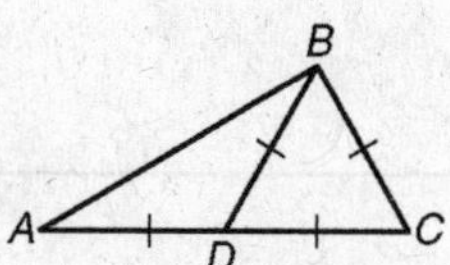

7. t = ____________

8. n = ____________

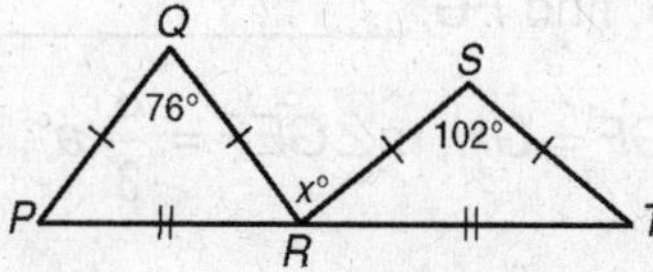

9. m∠A = ____________

10. x = ____________

Name ______________________ Date ______________ Class ______________

LESSON 5-1

Practice

Perpendicular and Angle Bisectors

Diana is in an archery competition. She stands at *A*, and the target is at *D*. Her competitors stand at *B* and *C*.

1. The distance from each of her competitors to her target is equal. Explain whether the flight path of Diana's arrow, $\overline{AD}$, must be a perpendicular bisector of $\overline{BC}$.

____

____

____

____

Use the figure for Exercises 2–5.

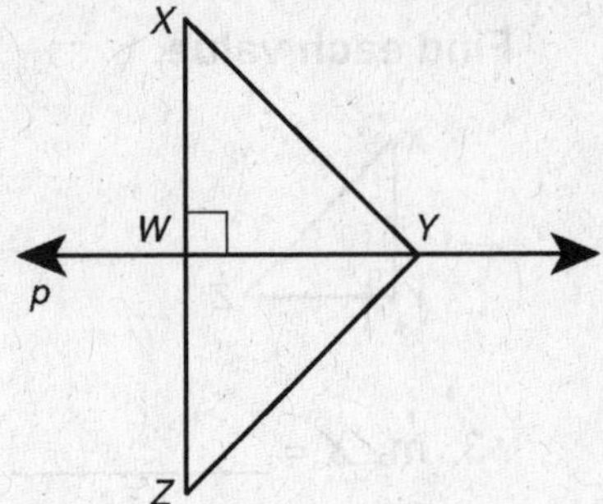

2. Given that line *p* is the perpendicular bisector of $\overline{XZ}$ and $XY = 15.5$, find ZY. ______________
3. Given that $XZ = 38$, $YX = 27$, and $YZ = 27$, find ZW. ______________

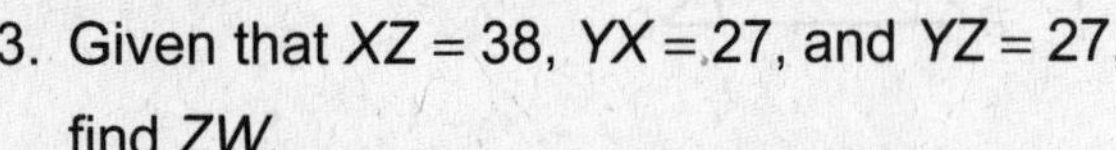

4. Given that line *p* is the perpendicular bisector of $\overline{XZ}$; $XY = 4n$, and $YZ = 14$, find *n*. ______________
5. Given that $XY = ZY$, $WX = 6x - 1$, and $XZ = 10x + 16$, find ZW. ______________

Use the figure for Exercises 6–9.

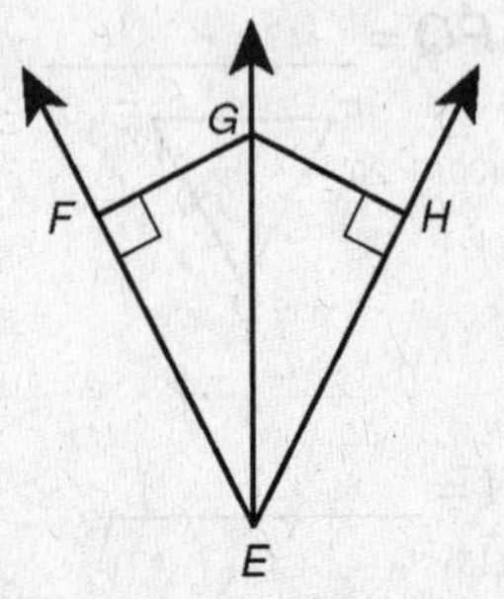

6. Given that $FG = HG$ and $m\angle FEH = 55°$, find $m\angle GEH$. ______________
7. Given that $\overline{EG}$ bisects $\angle FEH$ and $GF = \sqrt{2}$, find GH.

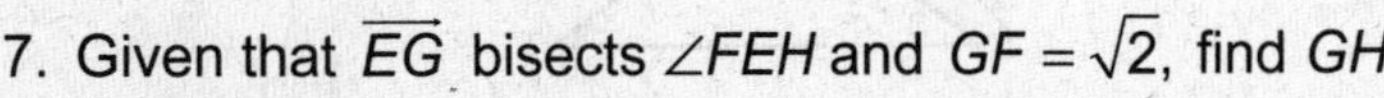

____

8. Given that $\angle FEG \cong \angle GEH$, $FG = 10z - 30$, and $HG = 7z + 6$, find FG. ______________

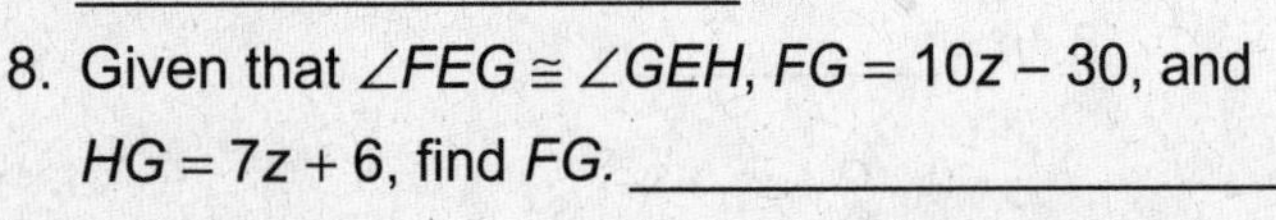

9. Given that $GF = GH$, $m\angle GEF = \frac{8}{3}a°$, and $m\angle GEH = 24°$, find *a*. ______________

Write an equation in point-slope form for the perpendicular bisector of the segment with the given endpoints.

10. $L(4, 0)$, $M(-2, 3)$ ______________
11. $T(0, -3)$, $U(0, 1)$ ______________
12. $A(-1, 6)$, $B(-3, -4)$ ______________

Name ______________________ Date ______________ Class ______________

LESSON 5-2

Practice

Bisectors of Triangles

Use the figure for Exercises 1 and 2. $\overline{SV}, \overline{TV}$, and $\overline{UV}$ are perpendicular bisectors of the sides of $\triangle PQR$. Find each length.

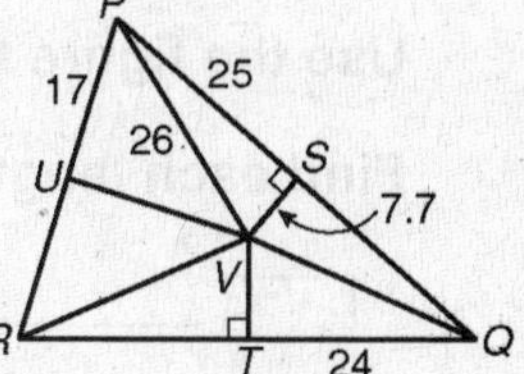

1. *RV* ______________

2. *TR* ______________

Find the circumcenter of the triangle with the given vertices.

3. *A*(0, 0), *B*(0, 5), *C*(5, 0)

4. *D*(0, 7), *E*(–3, 1), *F*(3, 1)

(________, ________) (________, ________)

Use the figure for Exercises 7 and 8. $\overline{GJ}$ and $\overline{IJ}$ are angle bisectors of $\triangle GHI$. Find each measure.

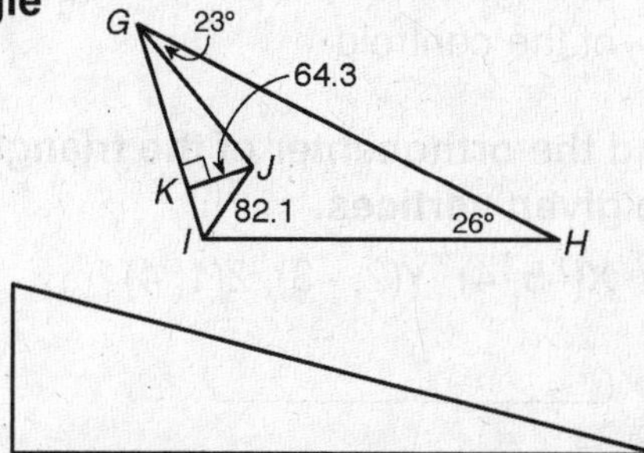

5. the distance from *J* to $\overline{GH}$ ______________

6. m∠*JGK* ______________

Raleigh designs the interiors of cars. He is given two tasks to complete on a new production model.

7. A triangular surface as shown in the figure is molded into the driver's side door as an armrest. Raleigh thinks he can fit a cup holder into the triangle, but he'll have to put the largest possible circle into the triangle. Explain how Raleigh can do this. Sketch his design on the figure.

____

____

____

____

____

8. The car's logo is the triangle shown in the figure. Raleigh has to use this logo as the center of the steering wheel. Explain how Raleigh can do this. Sketch his design on the figure.

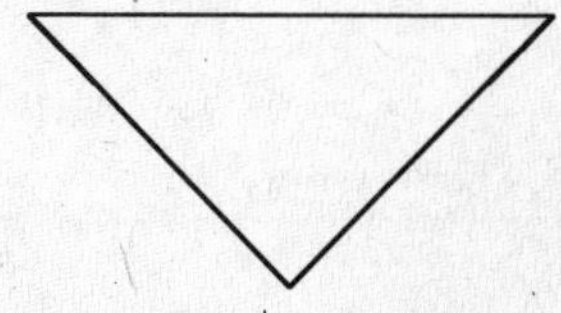

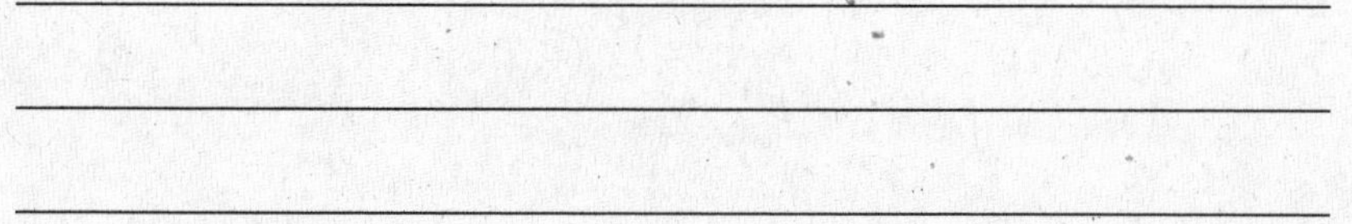

____

____

____

____

____

Name ______________________ Date ______________ Class ______________

LESSON 5-3

Practice

Medians and Altitudes of Triangles

Use the figure for Exercises 1–4. $GB = 12\frac{2}{3}$ and $CD = 10$.

Find each length.

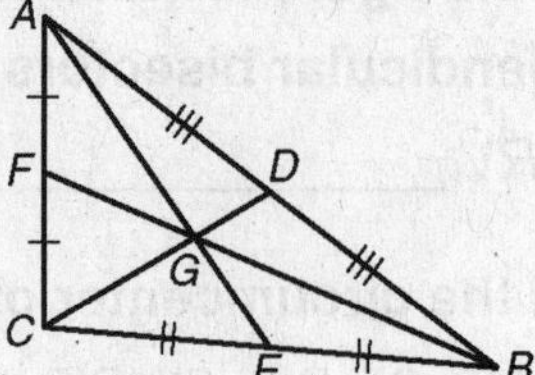

1. *FG* ______________
2. *BF* ______________
3. *GD* ______________
4. *CG* ______________
5. A triangular compass needle will turn most easily if it is attached to the compass face through its centroid. Find the coordinates of the centroid. (______, ______)

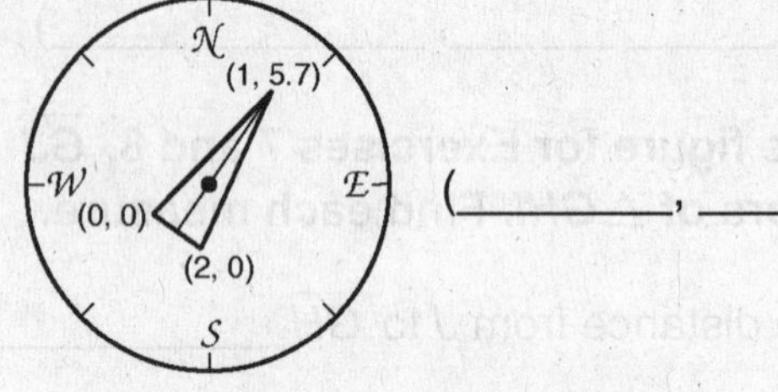

Find the orthocenter of the triangle with the given vertices.

6. *X*(–5, 4), *Y*(2, –3), *Z*(1, 4)

   (______, ______)

7. *A*(0, –1), *B*(2, –3), *C*(4, –1)

   (______, ______)

Use the figure for Exercises 8 and 9. $\overline{HL}$, $\overline{IM}$, and $\overline{JK}$ are medians of $\triangle HIJ$.

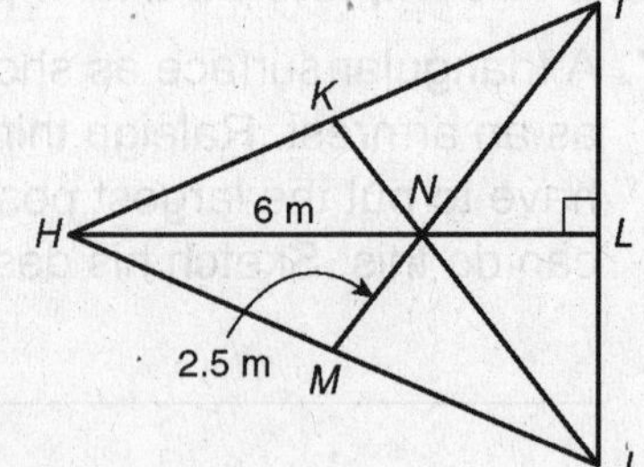

8. Find the area of the triangle. ______________
9. If the perimeter of the triangle is 49 meters, then find the length of $\overline{MH}$. (*Hint:* What kind of a triangle is it?)

   ____

10. Two medians of a triangle were cut apart at the centroid to make the four segments shown below. Use what you know about the Centroid Theorem to reconstruct the original triangle from the four segments shown. Measure the side lengths of your triangle to check that you constructed medians. (*Note:* There are many possible answers.)

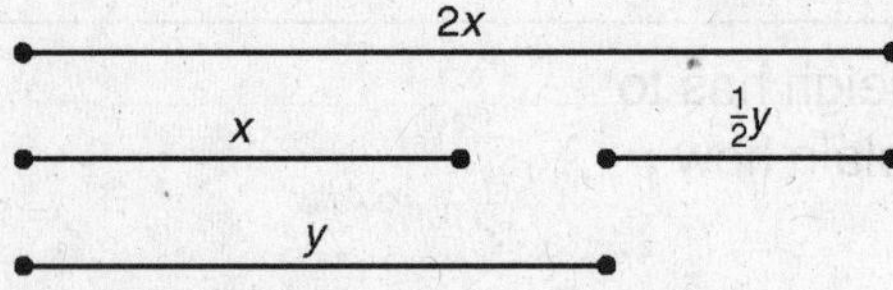

Name ______________________ Date ______________ Class ______________

LESSON 5-4

Practice

The Triangle Midsegment Theorem

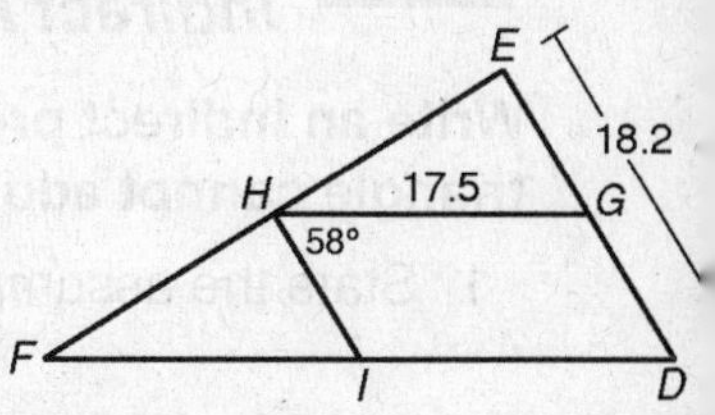

Use the figure for Exercises 1–6. Find each measure.

1. HI ______________ 2. DF ______________
3. GE ______________ 4. $m\angle HIF$ ______________
5. $m\angle HGD$ ______________ 6. $m\angle D$ ______________

The Bermuda Triangle is a region in the Atlantic Ocean off the southeast coast of the United States. The triangle is bounded by Miami, Florida; San Juan, Puerto Rico; and Bermuda. In the figure, the dotted lines are midsegments.

	Dist. (mi)
Miami to San Juan	1038
Miami to Bermuda	1042
Bermuda to San Juan	965

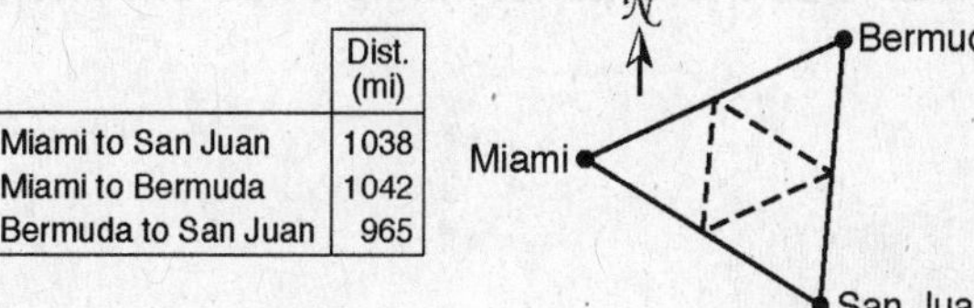

7. Use the distances in the chart to find the perimeter of the Bermuda Triangle. ______________
8. Find the perimeter of the midsegment triangle within the Bermuda Triangle. ______________
9. How does the perimeter of the midsegment triangle compare to the perimeter of the Bermuda Triangle?

____

Write a two-column proof that the perimeter of a midsegment triangle is half the perimeter of the triangle.

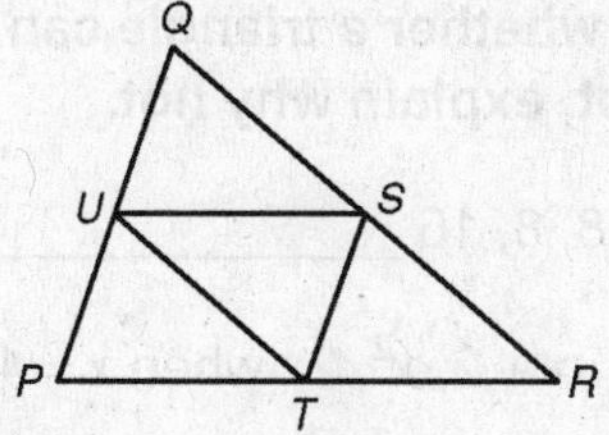

10. **Given:** $\overline{US}$, $\overline{ST}$, and $\overline{TU}$ are midsegments of $\triangle PQR$.

    Prove: The perimeter of $\triangle STU = \frac{1}{2}(PQ + QR + RP)$.

Name ______________________ Date ______________ Class ______________

LESSON 5-5

Practice

Indirect Proof and Inequalities in One Triangle

Write an indirect proof that the angle measures of a triangle cannot add to more than 180°.

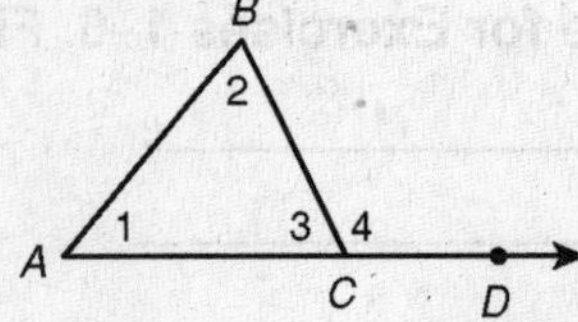

1. State the assumption that starts the indirect proof.

____

2. Use the Exterior Angle Theorem and the Linear Pair Theorem to write the indirect proof.

3. Write the angles of $\triangle DEF$ in order from smallest to largest.

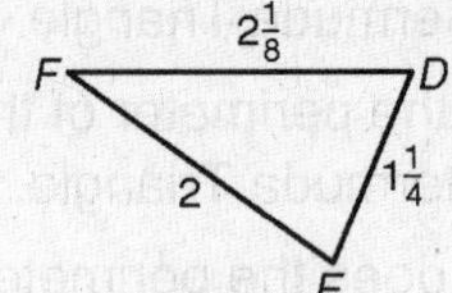

____

4. Write the sides of $\triangle GHI$ in order from shortest to longest.

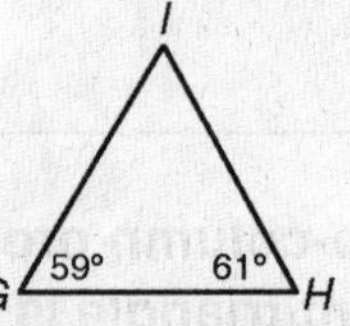

____

Tell whether a triangle can have sides with the given lengths. If not, explain why not.

5. 8, 8, 16 ______________
6. 0.5, 0.7, 0.3 ______________
7. $10\frac{1}{2}$, 4, 14 ______________
8. $3x + 2$, x^2, $2x$ when $x = 4$ ______________
9. $3x + 2$, x^2, $2x$ when $x = 6$ ______________

The lengths of two sides of a triangle are given. Find the range of possible lengths for the third side.

10. 8.2 m, 3.5 m ______________
11. 298 ft, 177 ft ______________
12. $3\frac{1}{2}$ mi, 4 mi ______________

13. The annual Cheese Rolling happens in May at Gloucestershire, England. As the name suggests, large, 7–9 pound wheels of cheese are rolled down a steep hill, and people chase after them. The first person to the bottom wins cheese. Renaldo wants to go to the Cheese Rolling. He plans to leave from Atlanta and fly into London (4281 miles). On the return, he will fly back from London to New York City (3470 miles) to visit his aunt. Then Renaldo heads back to Atlanta. Atlanta, New York City, and London do not lie on the same line. Find the range of the total distance Renaldo could travel on his trip.

____

Name ______________________ Date ______________ Class ______________

LESSON 5-6

Practice

Inequalities in Two Triangles

Compare the given measures.

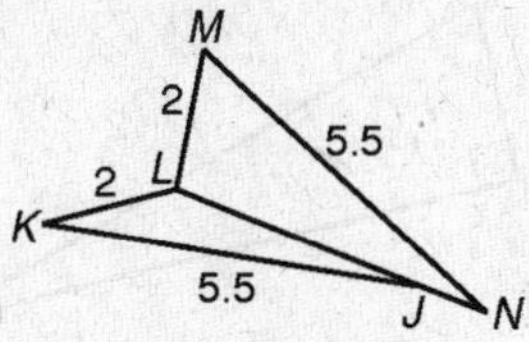

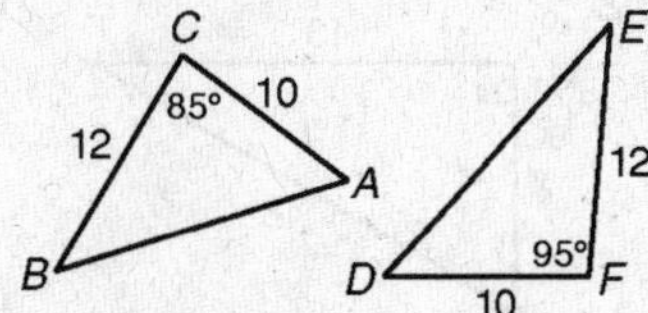

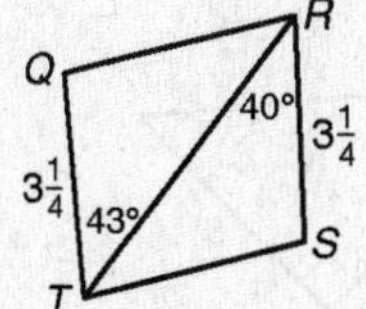

1. m∠*K* and m∠*M*

2. *AB* and *DE*

3. *QR* and *ST*

_______________ _______________ _______________

Find the range of values for *x*.

4.

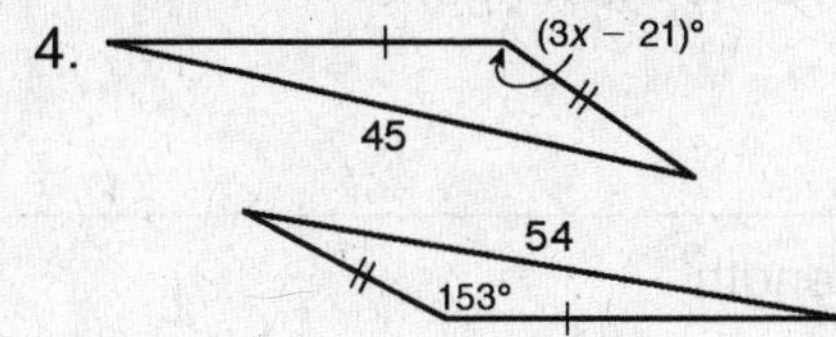

____

6. 12, 11, (3*x* − 5)°, (*x* + 12)°

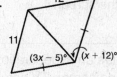

____

5.

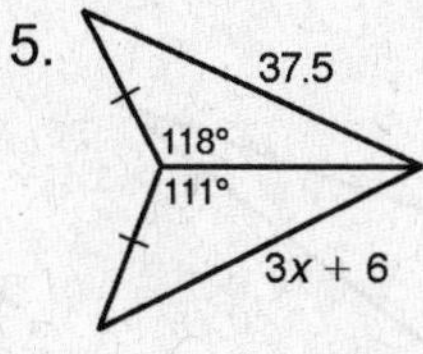

____

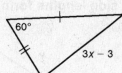

7. 60°, 3*x* − 3

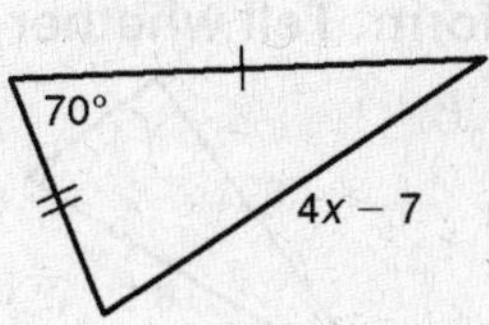

____

8. You have used a compass to copy and bisect segments and angles and to draw arcs and circles. A compass has a drawing leg, a pivot leg, and a hinge at the angle between the legs. Explain why and how the measure of the angle at the hinge changes if you draw two circles with different diameters.

____

____

____

____

____

____

Name ______________________ Date ______________ Class ______________

LESSON 5-7

Practice

The Pythagorean Theorem

Find the value of *x*. Give your answer in simplest radical form.

1.

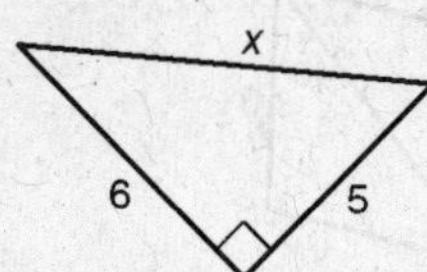

2.

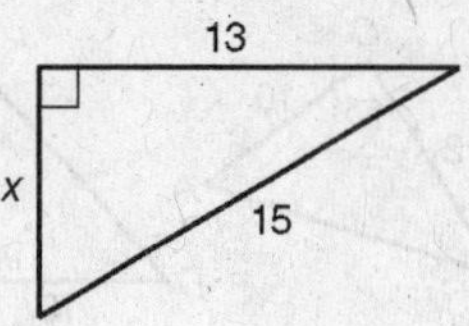

3.

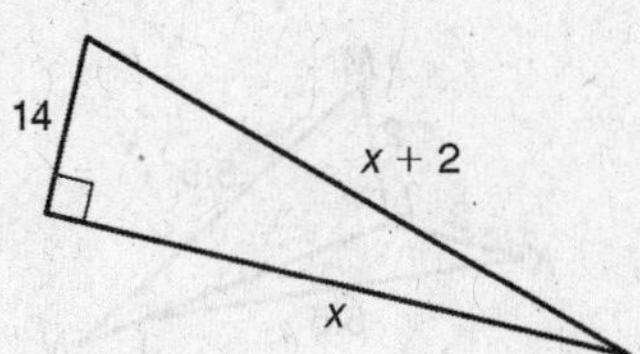

_________________ _________________ _________________

4. The aspect ratio of a TV screen is the ratio of the width to the height of the image. A regular TV has an aspect ratio of 4 : 3. Find the height and width of a 42-inch TV screen to the nearest tenth of an inch. (The measure given is the length of the diagonal across the screen.)

____

5. A "wide-screen" TV has an aspect ratio of 16 : 9. Find the length of a diagonal on a wide-screen TV screen that has the same height as the screen in Exercise 4. _________________

Find the missing side lengths. Give your answer in simplest radical form. Tell whether the side lengths form a Pythagorean Triple.

6.

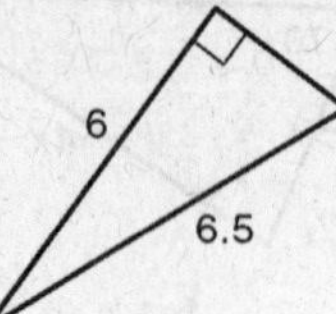

7.

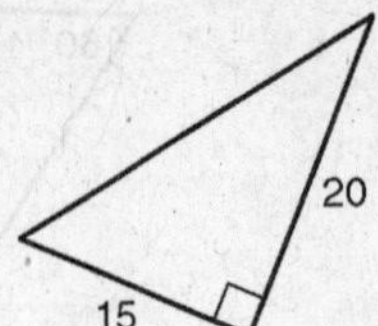

8.

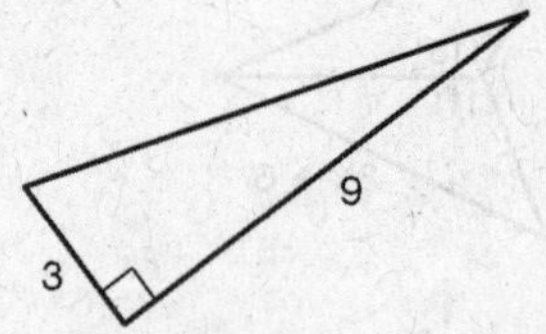

_________________ _________________ _________________

Tell whether the measures can be the side lengths of a triangle. If so, classify the triangle as acute, obtuse, or right.

9. 15, 18, 20

10. 7, 8, 11

11. 6, 7, $3\sqrt{13}$

_________________ _________________ _________________

12. Kitty has a triangle with sides that measure 16, 8, and 13. She does some calculations and finds that $256 + 64 > 169$. Kitty concludes that the triangle is obtuse. Evaluate Kitty's conclusion and Kitty's reasoning.

____

____

____

____

Name ______________________ Date ______________ Class ______________

LESSON 5-8

Practice

Applying Special Right Triangles

Find the value of *x* in each figure. Give your answer in simplest radical form.

1. 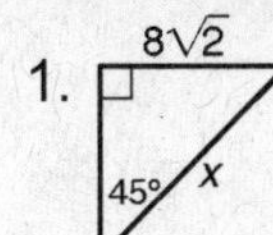

2. 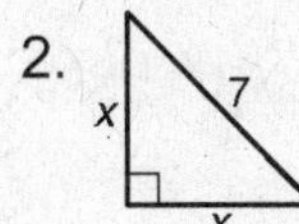

3. 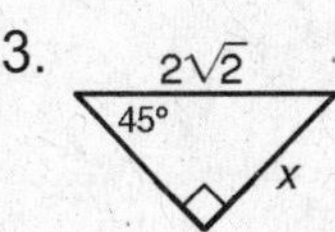

________________________ ________________________ ________________________

Find the values of *x* and *y*. Give your answers in simplest radical form.

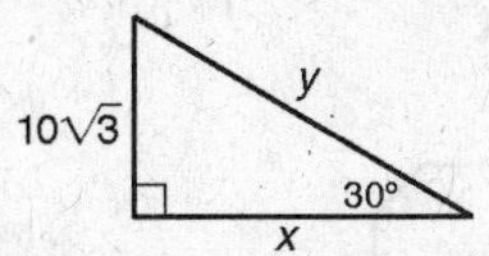

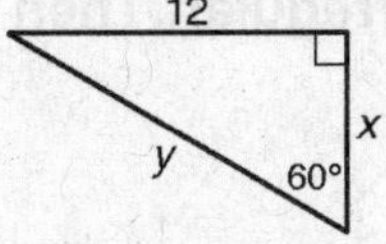

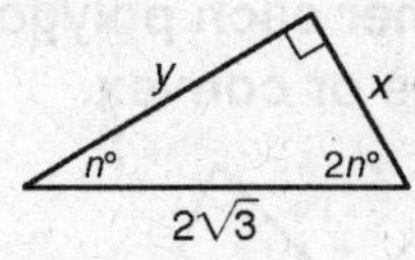

4. $x =$ ________ $y =$ ________ 5. $x =$ ________ $y =$ ________ 6. $x =$ ________ $y =$ ________

Lucia is an archaeologist trekking through the jungle of the Yucatan Peninsula. She stumbles upon a stone structure covered with creeper vines and ferns. She immediately begins taking measurements of her discovery. (*Hint:* Drawing some figures may help.)

7. Around the perimeter of the building, Lucia finds small alcoves at regular intervals carved into the stone. The alcoves are triangular in shape with a horizontal base and two sloped equal-length sides that meet at a right angle. Each of the sloped sides measures $14\frac{1}{4}$ inches. Lucia has also found several stone tablets inscribed with characters. The stone tablets measure $22\frac{1}{8}$ inches long. Lucia hypothesizes that the alcoves once held the stone tablets. Tell whether Lucia's hypothesis may be correct. Explain your answer.

____

____

8. Lucia also finds several statues around the building. The statues measure $9\frac{7}{16}$ inches tall. She wonders whether the statues might have been placed in the alcoves. Tell whether this is possible. Explain your answer.

____

____

____

____

____

Name ______________________ Date ______________ Class ______________

LESSON 6-1

Practice

Properties and Attributes of Polygons

Tell whether each figure is a polygon. If it is a polygon, name it by the number of its sides.

1. 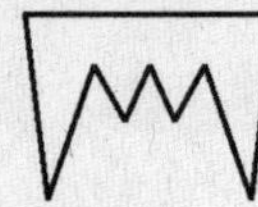

2. 

3. 

4. For a polygon to be regular, it must be both equiangular and equilateral. Name the only type of polygon that must be regular if it is equiangular. ____________

Tell whether each polygon is regular or irregular. Then tell whether it is concave or convex.

5. 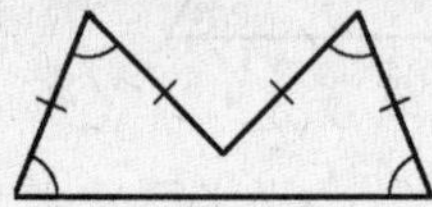

6. 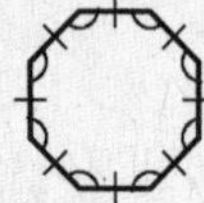

7. 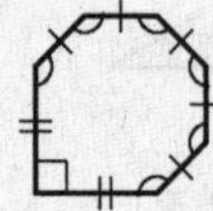

8. Find the sum of the interior angle measures of a 14-gon. ____________

9. Find the measure of each interior angle of hexagon *ABCDEF*.

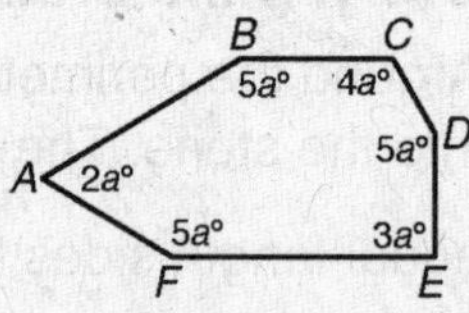

10. Find the value of *n* in pentagon *PQRST*.

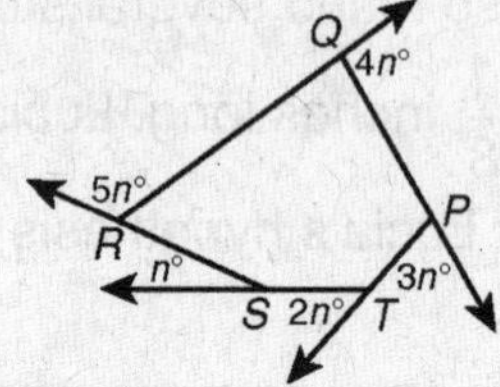

Before electric or steam power, a common way to power machinery was with a waterwheel. The simplest form of waterwheel is a series of paddles on a frame partially submerged in a stream. The current in the stream pushes the paddles forward and turns the frame. The power of the turning frame can then be used to drive machinery to saw wood or grind grain. The waterwheel shown has a frame in the shape of a regular octagon.

11. Find the measure of one interior angle of the waterwheel. ____________

12. Find the measure of one exterior angle of the waterwheel. ____________

Name ______________________ Date ______________ Class ______________

LESSON 6-2

Practice

Properties of Parallelograms

A gurney is a wheeled cot or stretcher used in hospitals. Many gurneys are made so that the base will fold up for easy storage in an ambulance. When partially folded, the base forms a parallelogram. In ▱ *STUV*, *VU* = 91 centimeters, *UW* = 108.8 centimeters, and m∠*TSV* = 57°. Find each measure.

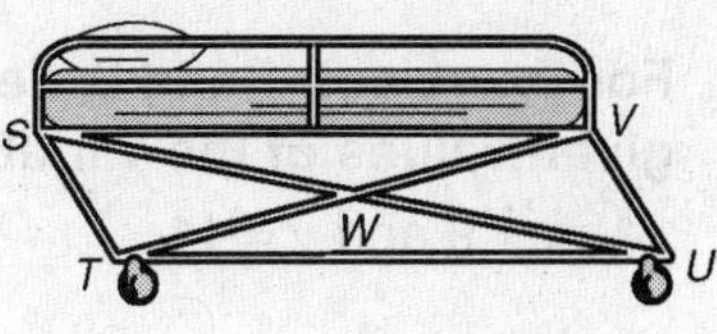

1. *SW* ______________
2. *TS* ______________
3. *US* ______________
4. m∠*SVU* ______________
5. m∠*STU* ______________
6. m∠*TUV* ______________

***JKLM* is a parallelogram. Find each measure.**

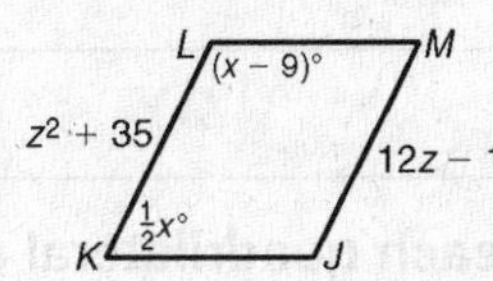

7. m∠*L* ______________
8. m∠*K* ______________
9. *MJ* ______________

***VWXY* is a parallelogram. Find each measure.**

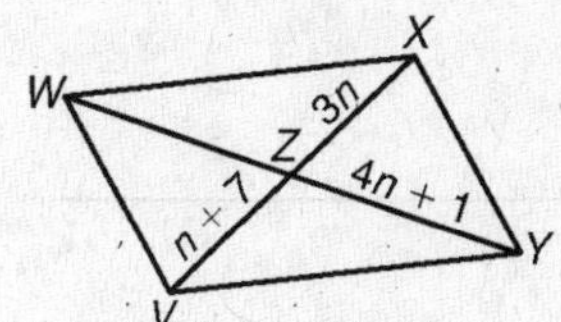

10. *VX* ______________
11. *XZ* ______________
12. *ZW* ______________
13. *WY* ______________

14. Three vertices of ▱ *ABCD* are *B*(−3, 3), *C*(2, 7), and *D*(5, 1). Find the coordinates of vertex *A*. ______________

Write a two-column proof.

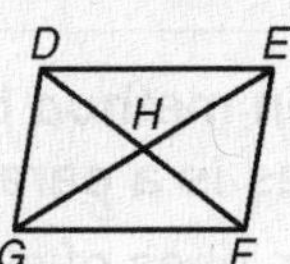

15. **Given:** *DEFG* is a parallelogram.

    Prove: m∠*DHG* = m∠*EDH* + m∠*FGH*

Name ______________________ Date ______________ Class ______________

LESSON 6-3

Practice

Conditions for Parallelograms

For Exercises 1 and 2, determine whether the figure is a parallelogram for the given values of the variables. Explain your answers.

1. $x = 9$ and $y = 11$

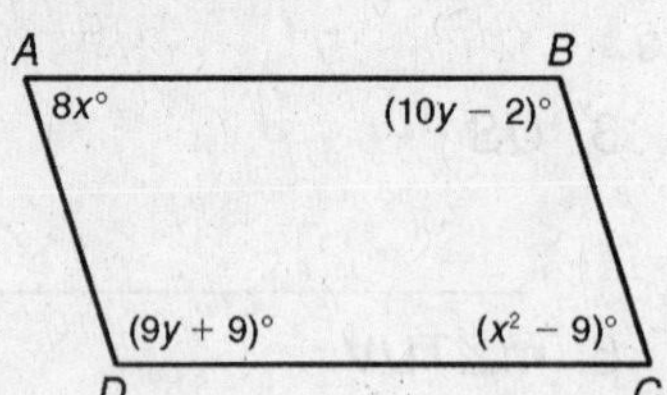

2. $a = 4.3$ and $b = 13$

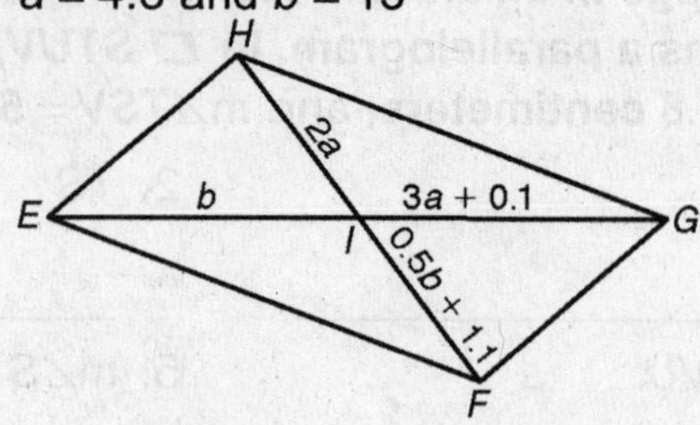

______________________________________ ______________________________________

______________________________________ ______________________________________

______________________________________ ______________________________________

Determine whether each quadrilateral must be a parallelogram. Justify your answers.

3.

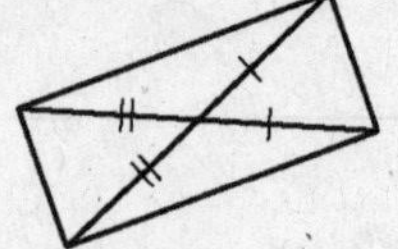

4.

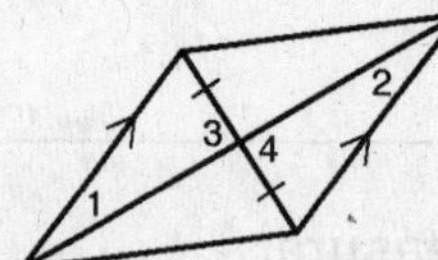

5.

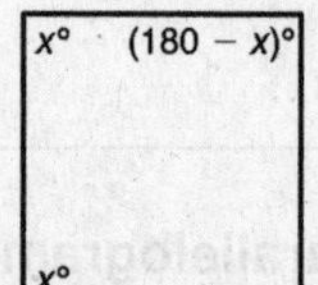

______________________ ______________________ ______________________

______________________ ______________________ ______________________

______________________ ______________________ ______________________

______________________ ______________________ ______________________

______________________ ______________________ ______________________

Use the given method to determine whether the quadrilateral with the given vertices is a parallelogram.

6. Find the slopes of all four sides: $J(-4, -1)$, $K(-7, -4)$, $L(2, -10)$, $M(5, -7)$

____

____

7. Find the lengths of all four sides: $P(2, 2)$, $Q(1, -3)$, $R(-4, 2)$, $S(-3, 7)$

____

8. Find the slopes and lengths of one pair of opposite sides:

$T\left(\frac{3}{2}, -2\right), U\left(\frac{3}{2}, 4\right), V\left(-\frac{1}{2}, 0\right), W\left(-\frac{1}{2}, -6\right)$

____

Name ______________________ Date ______________ Class ______________

LESSON 6-4

Practice

Properties of Special Parallelograms

Tell whether each figure must be a rectangle, rhombus, or square based on the information given. Use the most specific name possible.

1. 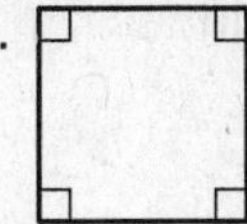

2. 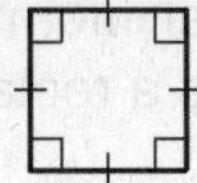

3.

______________________ ______________________ ______________________

A modern artist's sculpture has rectangular faces. The face shown here is 9 feet long and 4 feet wide. Find each measure in simplest radical form. (*Hint:* Use the Pythagorean Theorem.)

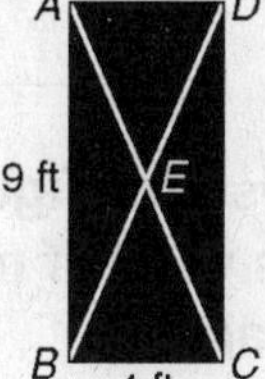

4. $DC =$ ______________________

5. $AD =$ ______________________

6. $DB =$ ______________________

7. $AE =$ ______________________

***VWXY* is a rhombus. Find each measure.**

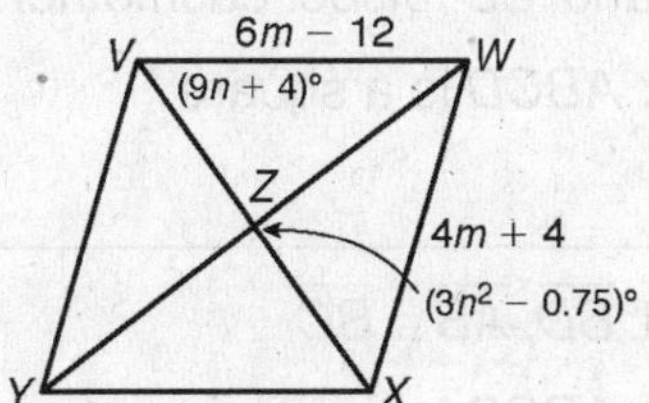

8. $XY =$ ______________________

9. $m\angle YVW =$ ______________________

10. $m\angle VYX =$ ______________________

11. $m\angle XYZ =$ ______________________

12. The vertices of square *JKLM* are $J(-2, 4)$, $K(-3, -1)$, $L(2, -2)$, and $M(3, 3)$. Find each of the following to show that the diagonals of square *JKLM* are congruent perpendicular bisectors of each other.

$JL =$ __________ $KM =$ __________

slope of $\overline{JL} =$ __________ slope of $\overline{KM} =$ __________

midpoint of $\overline{JL} =$ (__________, __________) midpoint of $\overline{KM} =$ (__________, __________)

Write a paragraph proof.

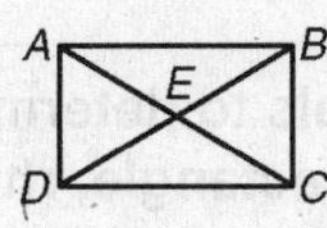

13. **Given:** *ABCD* is a rectangle.
Prove: $\angle EDC \cong \angle ECD$

Name ______________________ Date ______________ Class ______________

LESSON 6-5

Practice

Conditions for Special Parallelograms

1. On the National Mall in Washington, D.C., a reflecting pool lies between the Lincoln Memorial and the World War II Memorial. The pool has two 2300-foot-long sides and two 150-foot-long sides. Tell what additional information you need to know in order to determine whether the reflecting pool is a rectangle. (*Hint:* Remember that you have to show it is a parallelogram first.)

____

____

____

____

Use the figure for Exercises 2–5. Determine whether each conclusion is valid. If not, tell what additional information is needed to make it valid.

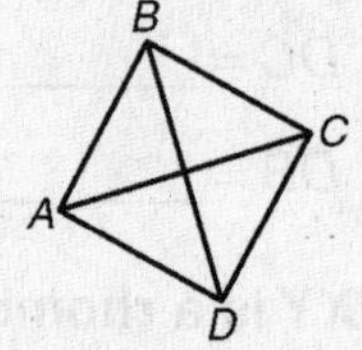

2. **Given:** $\overline{AC}$ and $\overline{BD}$ bisect each other. $\overline{AC} \cong \overline{BD}$

   Conclusion: *ABCD* is a square.

   ____

3. **Given:** $\overline{AC} \perp \overline{BD}$, $\overline{AB} \cong \overline{BC}$

   Conclusion: *ABCD* is a rhombus.

   ____

4. **Given:** $\overline{AB} \cong \overline{DC}$, $\overline{AD} \cong \overline{BC}$, $m\angle ADB = m\angle ABD = 45°$

   Conclusion: *ABCD* is a square.

   ____

5. **Given:** $\overline{AB} \parallel \overline{DC}$, $\overline{AD} \cong \overline{BC}$, $\overline{AC} \cong \overline{BD}$

   Conclusion: *ABCD* is a rectangle.

   ____

Find the lengths and slopes of the diagonals to determine whether a parallelogram with the given vertices is a rectangle, rhombus, or square. Give all names that apply.

6. $E(-2, -4)$, $F(0, -1)$, $G(-3, 1)$, $H(-5, -2)$ ______________________

   $EG =$ ________ $FH =$ ________

   slope of $\overline{EG}$ = ________ slope of $\overline{FH}$ = ________

7. $P(-1, 3)$, $Q(-2, 5)$, $R(0, 4)$, $S(1, 2)$ ______________________

   $PR =$ ________ $QS =$ ________

   slope of $\overline{PR}$ = ________ slope of $\overline{QS}$ = ________

Name ______________________ Date ______________ Class ______________

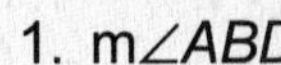

Practice

Properties of Kites and Trapezoids

In kite *ABCD*, m∠*BAC* = 35° and m∠*BCD* = 44°. For Exercises 1–3, find each measure.

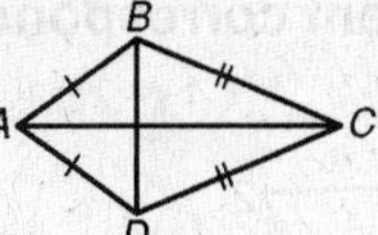

1. m∠*ABD* ______________

2. m∠*DCA* ______________

3. m∠*ABC* ______________

4. Find the area of Δ*EFG*. ______________

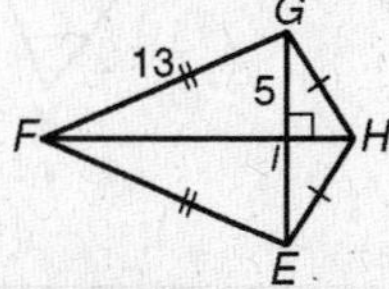

5. Find m∠*Z*.

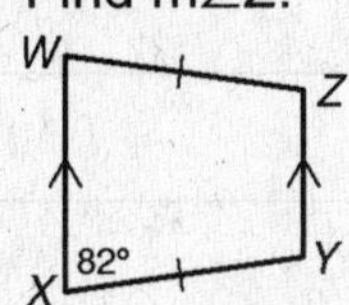

____

6. *KM* = 7.5, and *NM* = 2.6. Find *LN*.

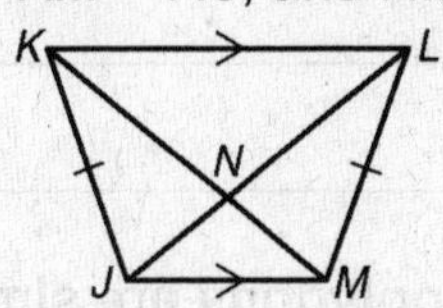

____

7. Find the value of *n* so that *PQRS* is isosceles.

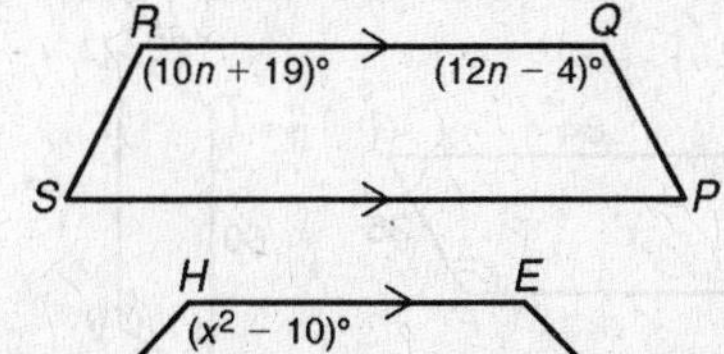

____

8. Find the value of *x* so that *EFGH* is isosceles.

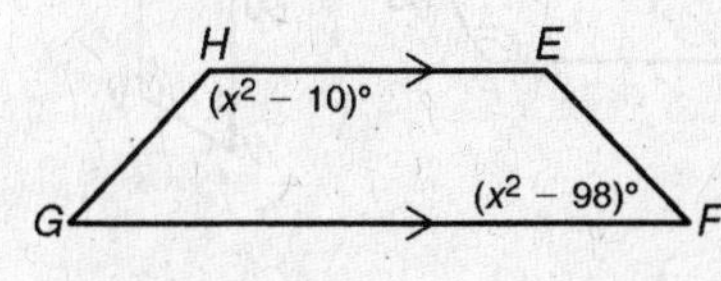

____

9. *BD* = 7*a* – 0.5, and *AC* = 5*a* + 2.3. Find the value of *a* so that *ABCD* is isosceles.

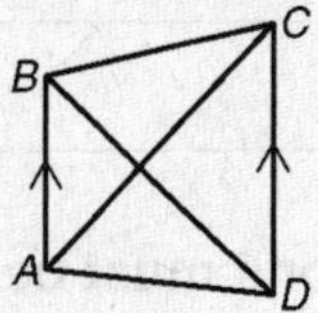

____

10. $QS = 8z^2$, and $RT = 6z^2 + 38$. Find the value of *z* so that *QRST* is isosceles.

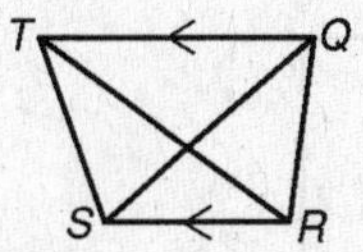

____

Use the figure for Exercises 11 and 12. The figure shows a *ziggurat.* A ziggurat is a stepped, flat-topped pyramid that was used as a temple by ancient peoples of Mesopotamia. The dashed lines show that a ziggurat has sides roughly in the shape of a trapezoid.

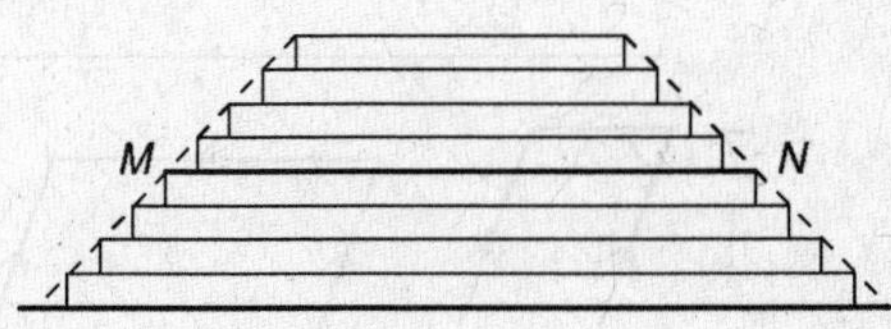

11. Each "step" in the ziggurat has equal height. Give the vocabulary term for $\overline{MN}$.

____

12. The bottom of the ziggurat is 27.3 meters long, and the top of the ziggurat is 11.6 meters long. Find *MN*.

____

Name ______________________ Date ____________ Class ____________

LESSON 7-1

Practice

Ratio in Similar Polygons

Identify the pairs of congruent corresponding angles and the corresponding sides.

1. 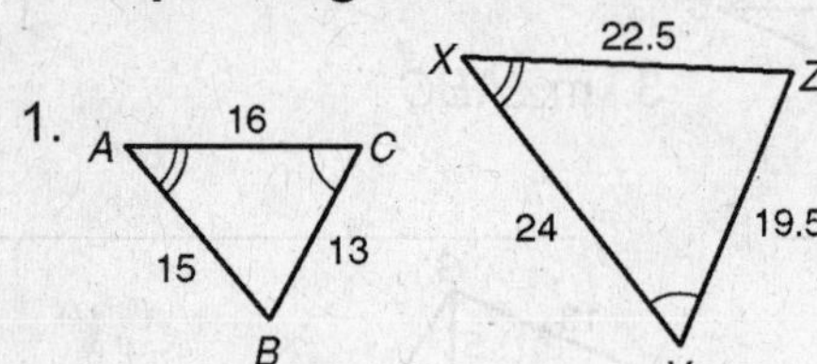

2. 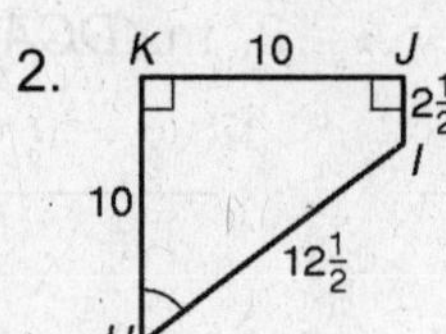

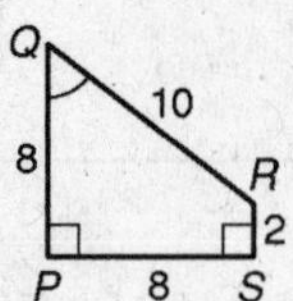

Determine whether the polygons are similar. If so, write the similarity ratio and a similarity statement. If not, explain why not.

3. parallelograms *EFGH* and *TUVW*

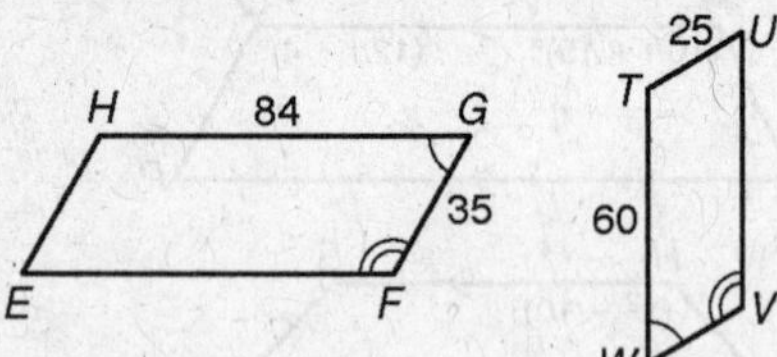

4. $\triangle CDE$ and $\triangle LMN$

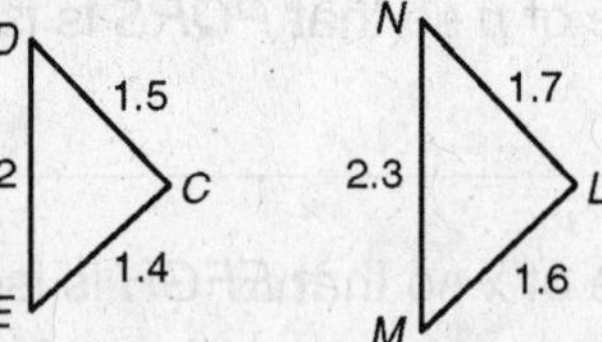

Tell whether the polygons must be similar based on the information given in the figures.

5. 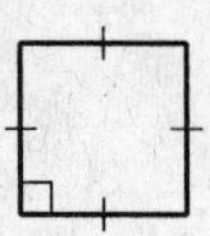 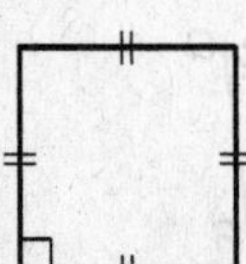

6. 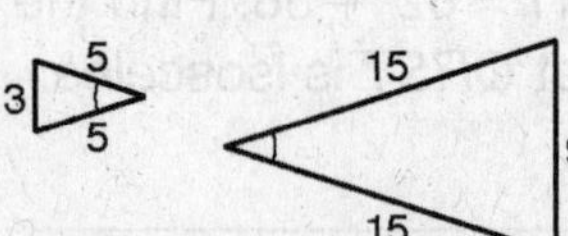

7. 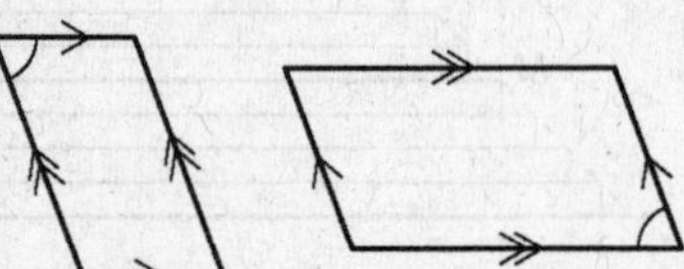

8. 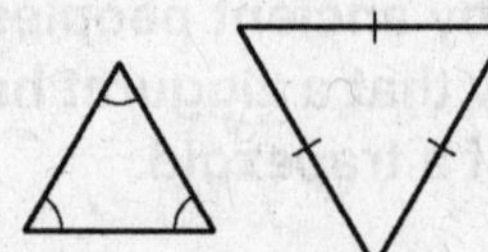

Name ______________________ Date ____________ Class ____________

LESSON 7-2

Practice

Similarity and Transformations

Apply the dilation *D* to the polygon with the given vertices. Describe the dilation.

1. $D: (x, y) \rightarrow (2x, 2y)$
   $A(1, 2)$, $B(3, 3)$, $C(4, 1)$

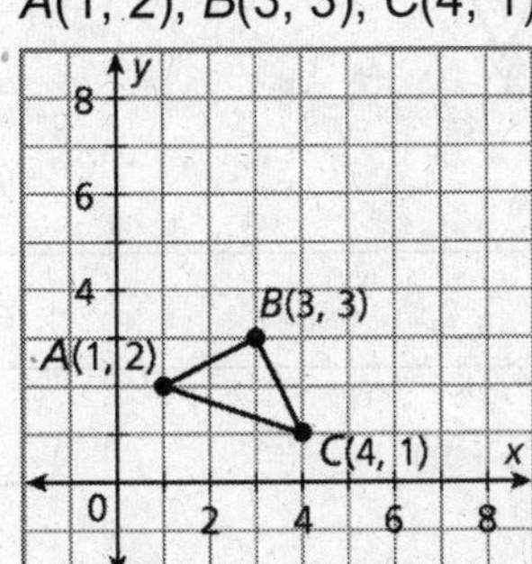

____

2. $D: (x, y) \rightarrow (\frac{1}{2}x, \frac{1}{2}y)$
   $P(-6, 8)$, $Q(0, 6)$, $R(-4, 2)$

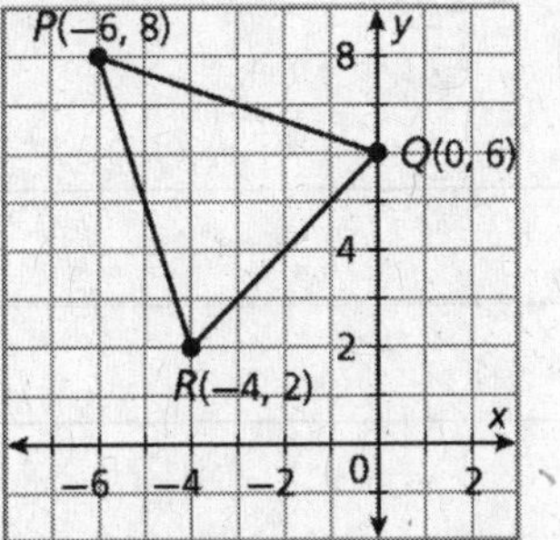

____

3. $D: (x, y) \rightarrow (1.5x, 1.5y)$
   $G(-4, 1)$, $H(-2, 1)$, $J(-2, 6)$, $K(-4, 6)$

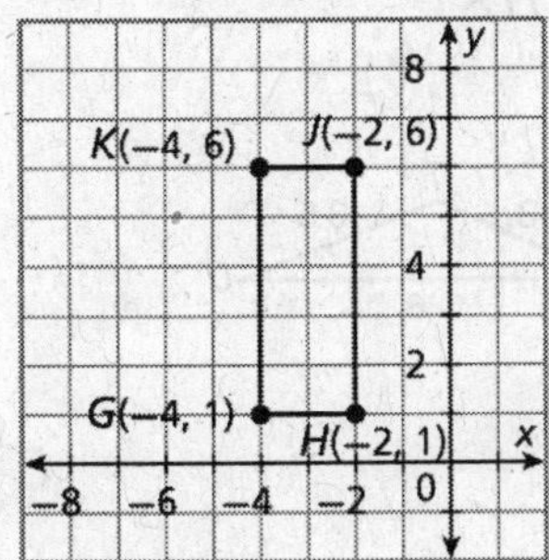

____

4. $D: (x, y) \rightarrow (0.75x, 0.75y)$
   $E(-4, 6)$, $F(-2, 2)$, $G(4, -2)$, $H(4, 4)$

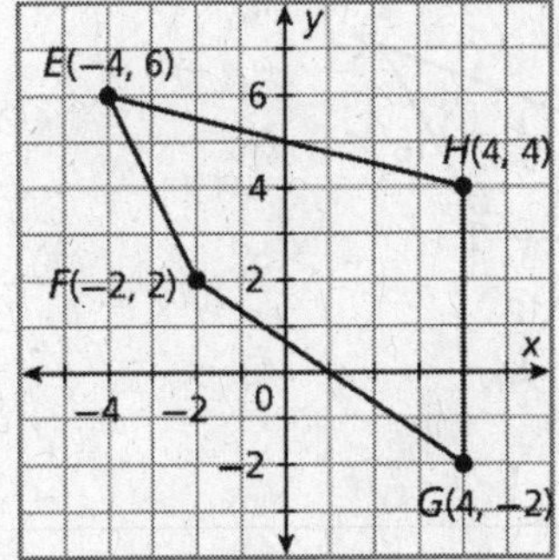

____

Determine whether the polygons with the given vertices are similar.

5. $A(-4, 4)$, $B(0, 4)$, $C(0, 0)$, $D(-2, -2)$, $E(-4, 0)$; $P(-3, 3)$, $Q(-1, 3)$, $R(-1, 1)$, $S(-2, 0)$, $T(-3, 1)$

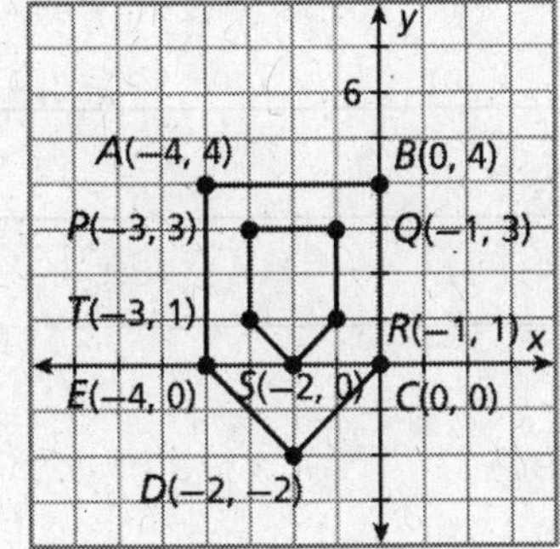

____

6. $J(-4, 6)$, $K(4, 6)$, $L(4, 4)$; $P(-2, 3)$, $Q(2, 3)$, $R(2, 2)$; $S(-4, 1)$, $T(0, 1)$, $O(0, 0)$

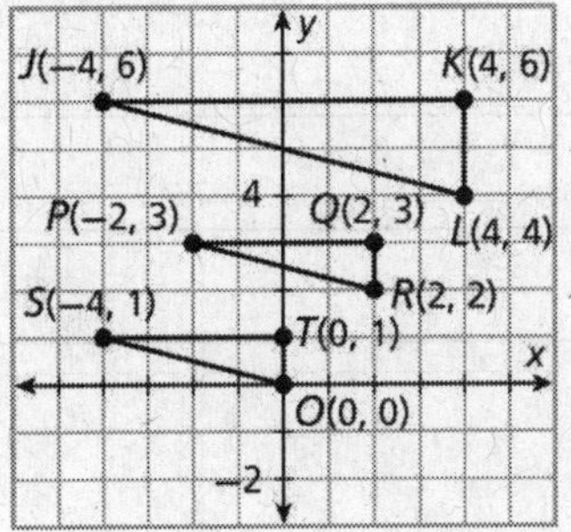

____

Name ______________________ Date ______________ Class ______________

LESSON 7-3

Practice

Triangle Similarity: AA, SSS, SAS

For Exercises 1 and 2, explain why the triangles are similar and write a similarity statement.

1. 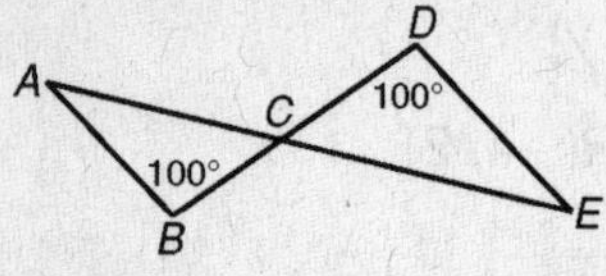

____

2. 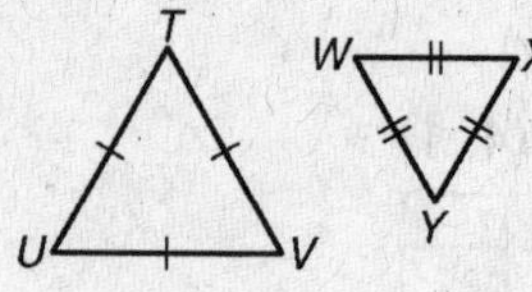

____

For Exercises 3 and 4, verify that the triangles are similar. Explain why.

3. $\triangle JLK$ and $\triangle JMN$

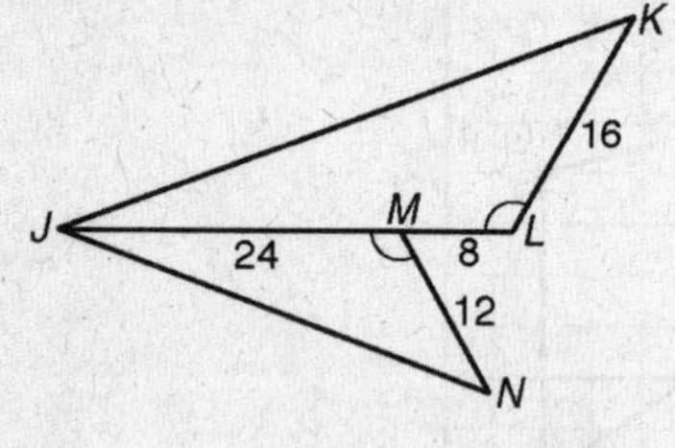

____

4. $\triangle PQR$ and $\triangle UTS$

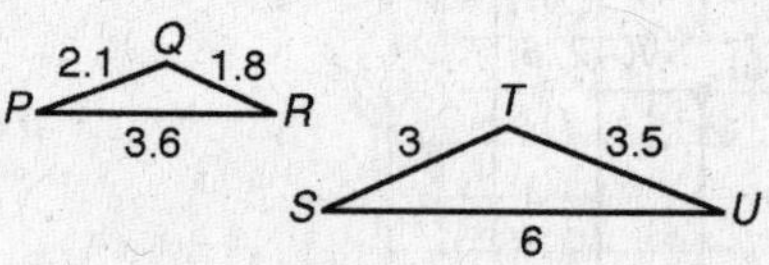

____

For Exercise 5, explain why the triangles are similar and find the stated length.

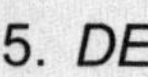

5. *DE*

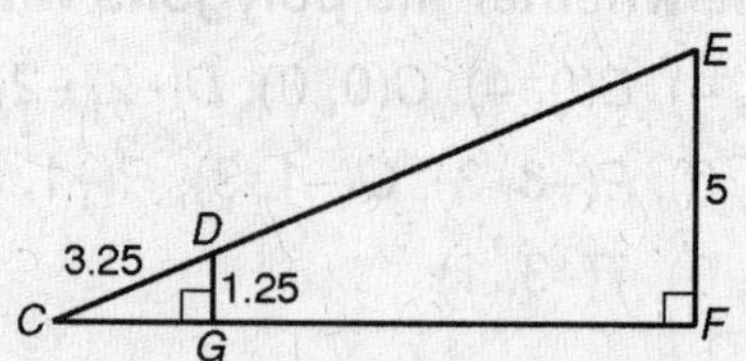

____

Name ______________________ Date ______________ Class ______________

LESSON 7-4

Practice

Applying Properties of Similar Triangles

Find each length.

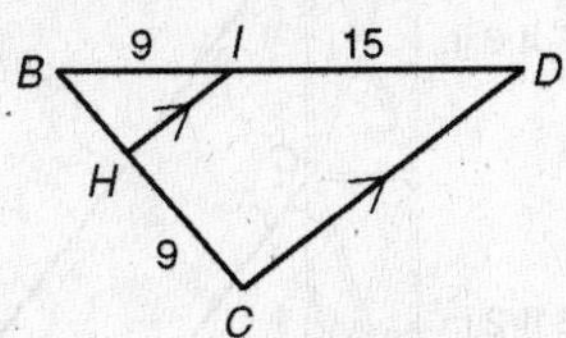

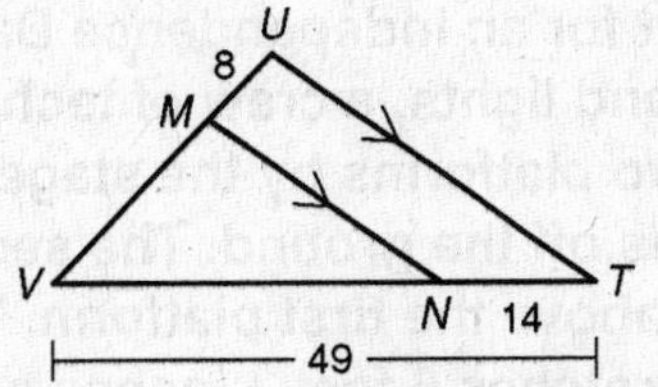

1. BH ______________

2. MV ______________

Verify that the given segments are parallel.

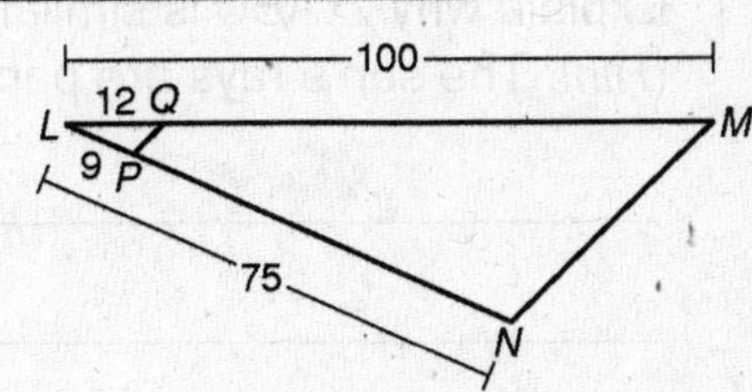

3. $\overline{PQ}$ and $\overline{NM}$

____

____

____

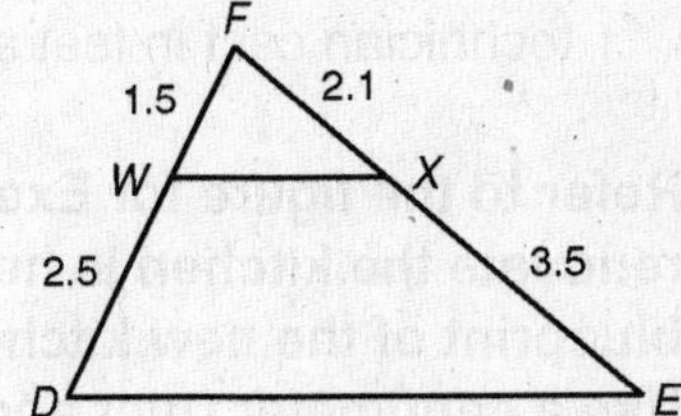

4. $\overline{WX}$ and $\overline{DE}$

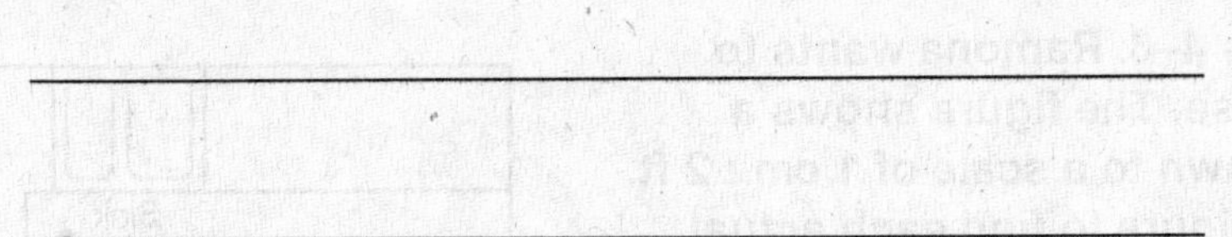

____

____

____

Find each length.

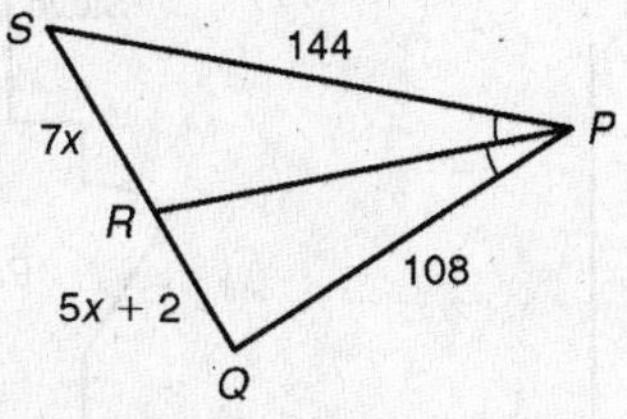

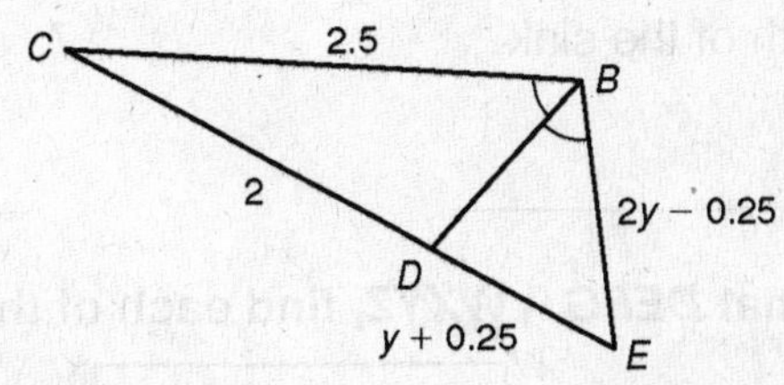

5. SR and RQ ______________

6. BE and DE ______________

7. In $\triangle ABC$, $\overline{BD}$ bisects $\angle ABC$ and $\overline{AD} \cong \overline{CD}$. Tell what kind of $\triangle ABC$ must be. ______________

Name ______________________ Date ______________ Class ______________

LESSON 7-5

Practice

Using Proportional Relationships

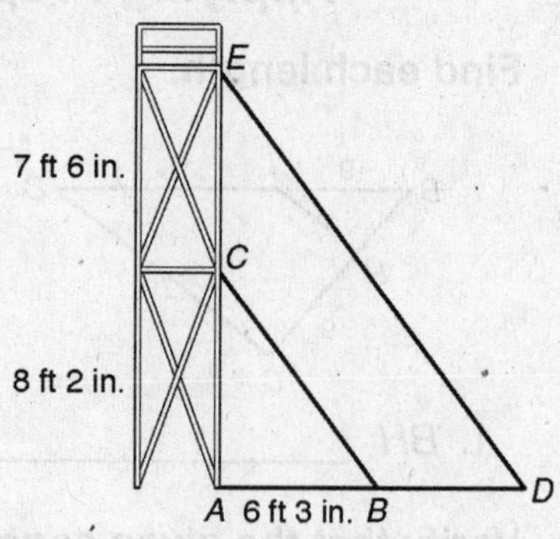

Refer to the figure for Exercises 1–3. A city is planning an outdoor concert for an Independence Day celebration. To hold speakers and lights, a crew of technicians sets up a scaffold with two platforms by the stage. The first platform is 8 feet 2 inches off the ground. The second platform is 7 feet 6 inches above the first platform. The shadow of the first platform stretches 6 feet 3 inches across the ground.

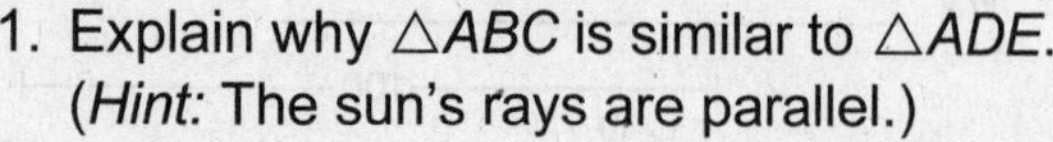

1. Explain why $\triangle ABC$ is similar to $\triangle ADE$. (*Hint:* The sun's rays are parallel.)

____

____

____

2. Find the length of the shadow of the second platform in feet and inches to the nearest inch. ______________

3. A 5-foot-8-inch-tall technician is standing on top of the second platform. Find the length of the shadow the scaffold and the technician cast in feet and inches to the nearest inch. ______________

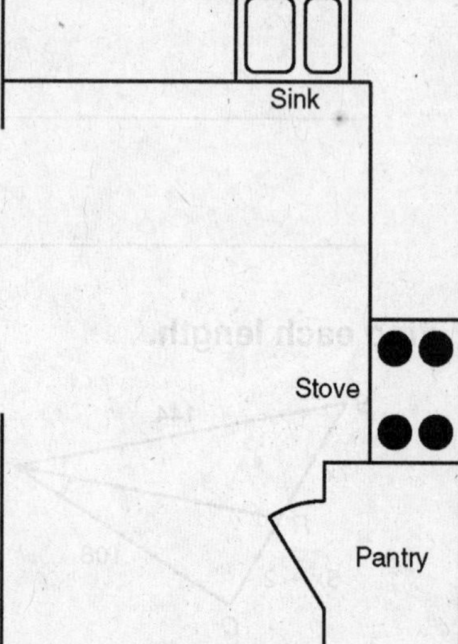

Refer to the figure for Exercises 4–6. Ramona wants to renovate the kitchen in her house. The figure shows a blueprint of the new kitchen drawn to a scale of 1 cm : 2 ft. Use a centimeter ruler and the figure to find each actual measure in feet.

4. width of the kitchen ______________

5. length of the kitchen ______________

6. width of the sink ______________

7. area of the pantry ______________

Given that *DEFG* ~ *WXYZ*, find each of the following.

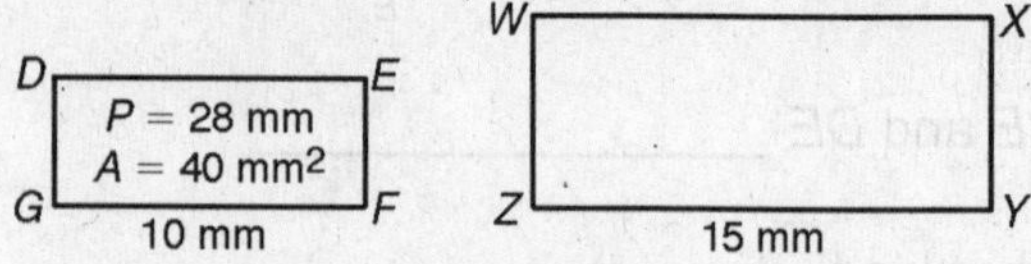

8. perimeter of *WXYZ* ______________

9. area of *WXYZ* ______________

Name ______________________ Date ______________ Class ______________

LESSON 7-6

Practice

Dilations and Similarity in the Coordinate Plane

A jeweler designs a setting that can hold a gem in the shape of a parallelogram. The figure shows the outline of the gem. The client, however, wants a gem and setting that is slightly larger.

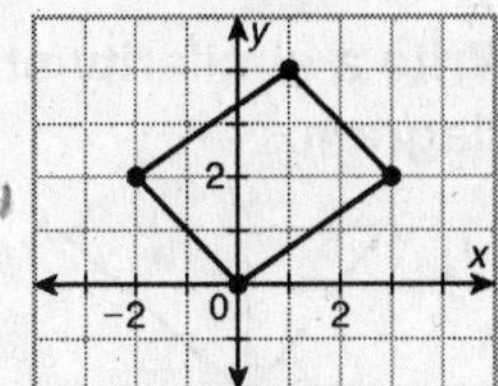

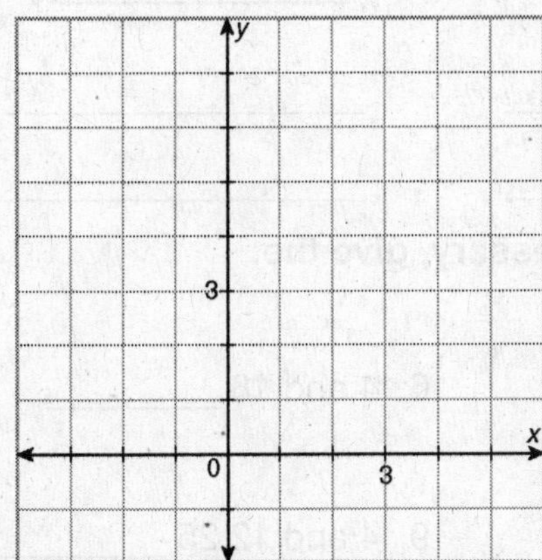

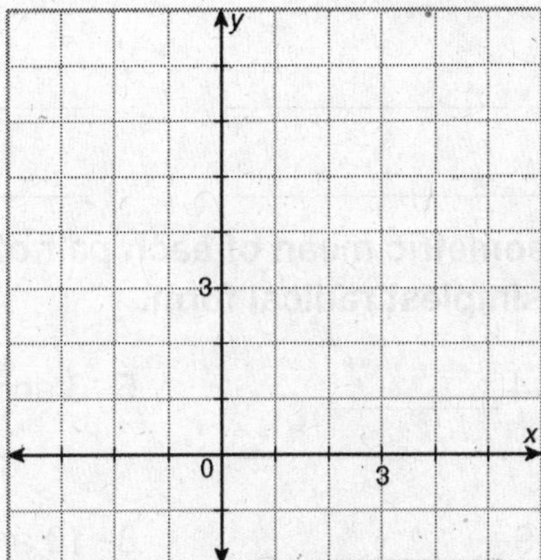

1. Draw the gem after a dilation with a scale factor of $\frac{3}{2}$.

2. The client is so pleased with her ring that she decides to have matching but smaller earrings made using the same pattern. Draw the gem after a dilation from the original pattern with a scale factor of $\frac{1}{2}$.

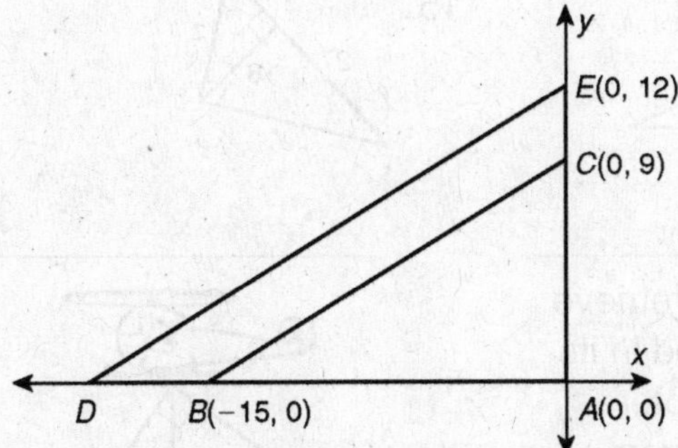

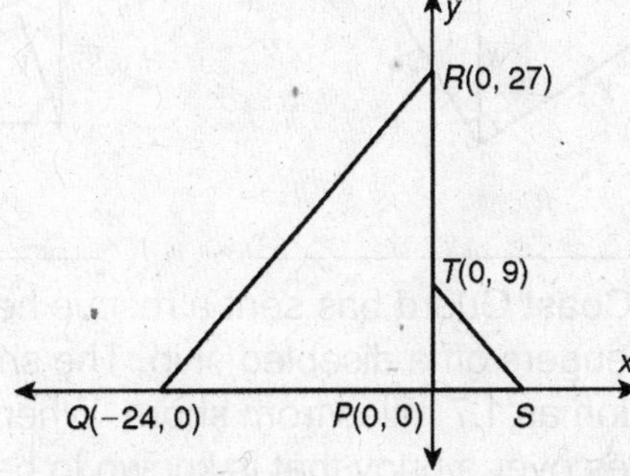

3. Given that $\triangle ABC \sim \triangle ADE$, find the scale factor and the coordinates of D.

____

4. Given that $\triangle PQR \sim \triangle PST$, find the scale factor and the coordinates of S.

____

Name ______________________ Date ______________ Class ______________

LESSON 8-1

Practice

Similarity in Right Triangles

Write a similarity statement comparing the three triangles in each diagram.

1. 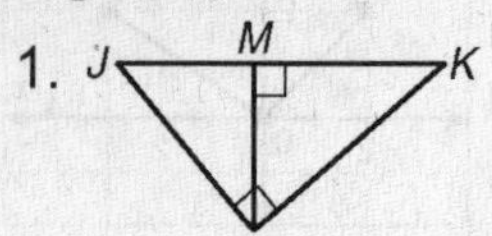

2. D E G F

3. 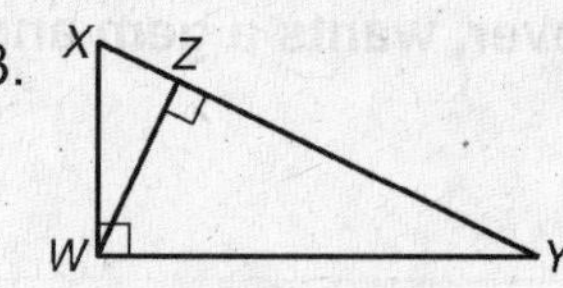

Find the geometric mean of each pair of numbers. If necessary, give the answer in simplest radical form.

4. $\frac{1}{4}$ and 4 ________

5. 3 and 75 ________

6. 4 and 18 ________

7. $\frac{1}{2}$ and 9 ________

8. 10 and 14 ________

9. 4 and 12.25 ________

Find *x*, *y*, and *z*.

10. 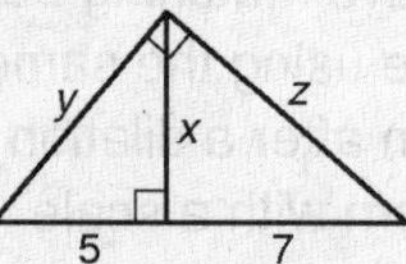

11. 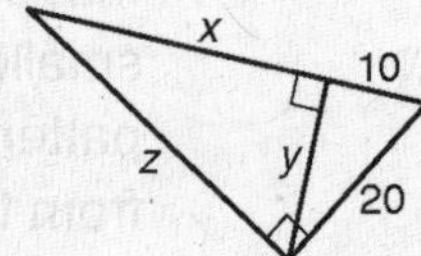

12. 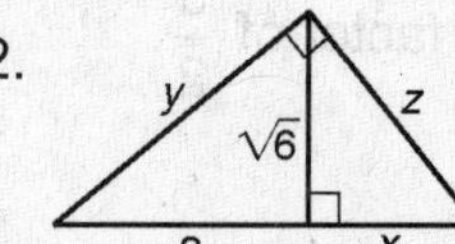

13. 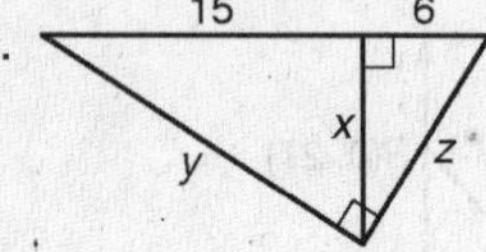

14. 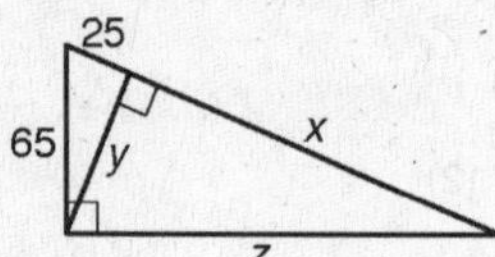

15. 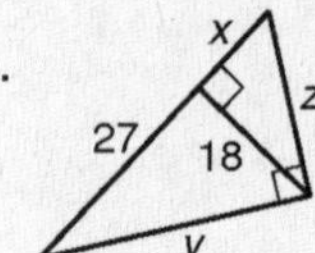

16. The Coast Guard has sent a rescue helicopter to retrieve passengers off a disabled ship. The ship has called in its position as 1.7 miles from shore. When the helicopter passes over a buoy that is known to be 1.3 miles from shore, the angle formed by the shore, the helicopter, and the disabled ship is 90°. Determine what the altimeter would read to the nearest foot when the helicopter is directly above the buoy.

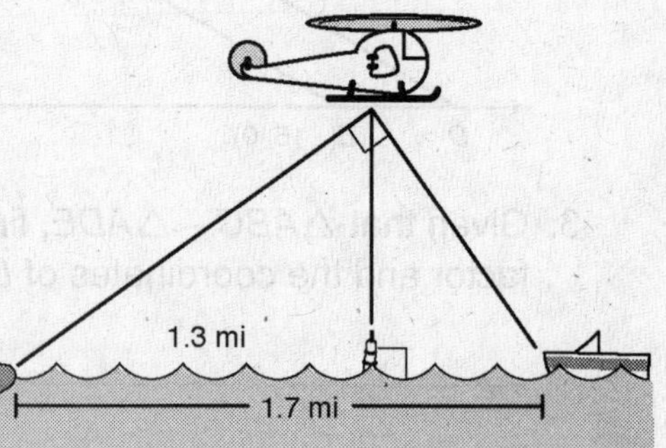

____

Use the diagram to complete each equation.

17. $\frac{e}{b} = \frac{\square}{e}$

18. $\frac{d}{b+c} = \frac{\square}{a}$

19. $\frac{d}{\square} = \frac{a}{e}$

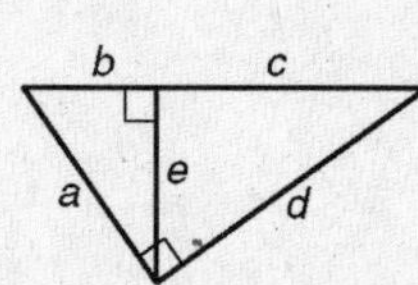

Name ______________________ Date ______________ Class ______________

LESSON 8-2

Practice

Trigonometric Ratios

Use the figure for Exercises 1–6. Write each trigonometric ratio as a simplified fraction and as a decimal rounded to the nearest hundredth.

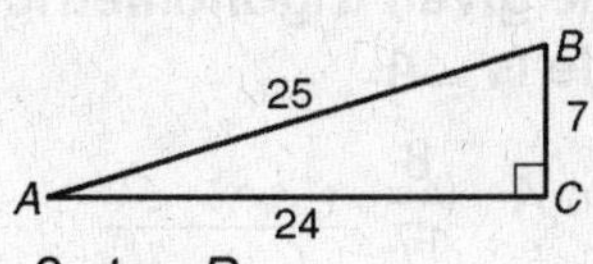

1. sin *A* ______________
2. cos *B* ______________
3. tan *B* ______________
4. sin *B* ______________
5. cos *A* ______________
6. tan *A* ______________

Use special right triangles to write each trigonometric ratio as a simplified fraction.

7. sin 30° ________
8. cos 30° ________
9. tan 45° ________
10. tan 30° ________
11. cos 45° ________
12. tan 60° ________

Use a calculator to find each trigonometric ratio. Round to the nearest hundredth.

13. sin 64° ________
14. cos 58° ________
15. tan 15° ________

Find each length. Round to the nearest hundredth.

16.

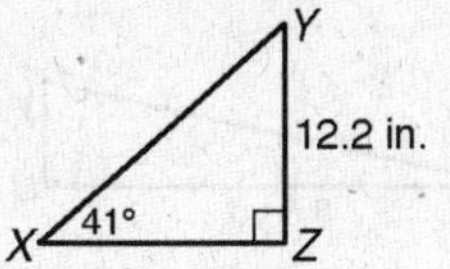

XZ ______________

17.

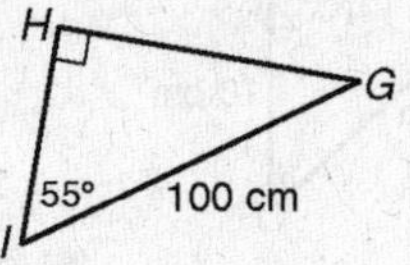

HI ______________

18.

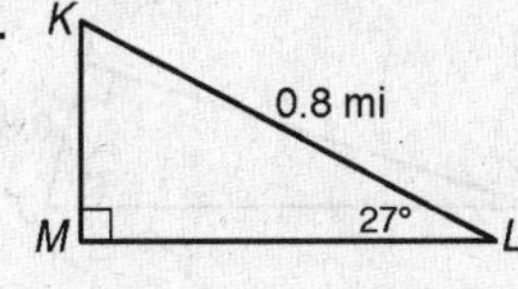

KM ______________

19.

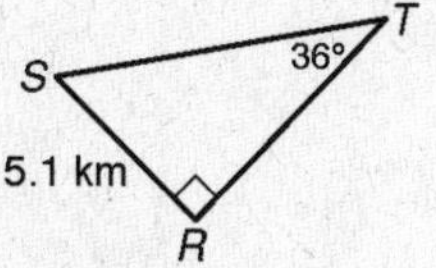

ST ______________

20.

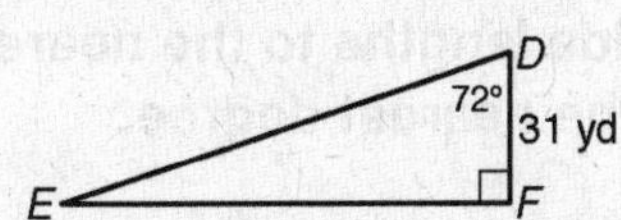

EF ______________

21.

C E

2 ft

51°

D

DE ______________

Name ______________________ Date ______________ Class ______________

LESSON 8-3

Practice

Solving Right Triangles

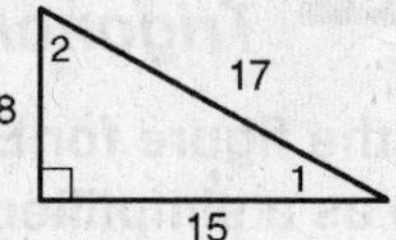

Use the given trigonometric ratio to determine which angle of the triangle is $\angle A$.

1. $\sin A = \dfrac{8}{17}$ ________
2. $\cos A = \dfrac{15}{17}$ ________
3. $\tan A = \dfrac{15}{8}$ ________
4. $\sin A = \dfrac{15}{17}$ ________
5. $\cos A = \dfrac{8}{17}$ ________
6. $\tan A = \dfrac{8}{15}$ ________

Use a calculator to find each angle measure to the nearest degree.

7. $\sin^{-1}(0.82)$ ________
8. $\cos^{-1}\left(\dfrac{11}{12}\right)$ ________
9. $\tan^{-1}(5.03)$ ________
10. $\sin^{-1}\left(\dfrac{3}{8}\right)$ ________
11. $\cos^{-1}(0.23)$ ________
12. $\tan^{-1}\left(\dfrac{1}{9}\right)$ ________

Find the unknown measures. Round lengths to the nearest hundredth and angle measures to the nearest degree.

13.

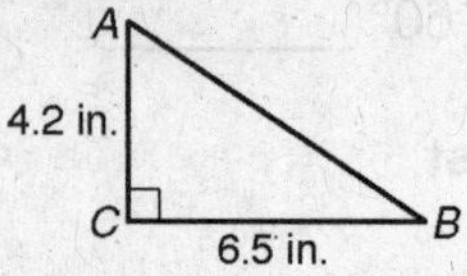

____
____

14.

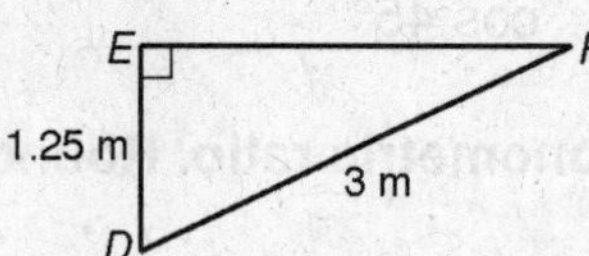

____
____

15.

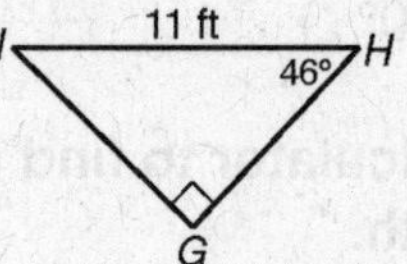

____
____

16.

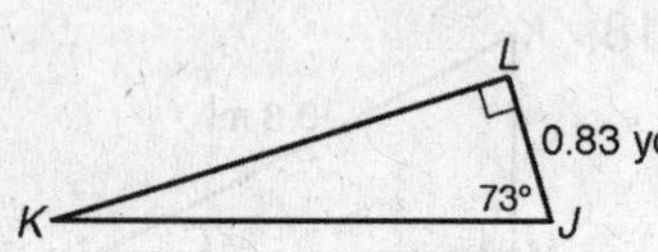

____
____

17.

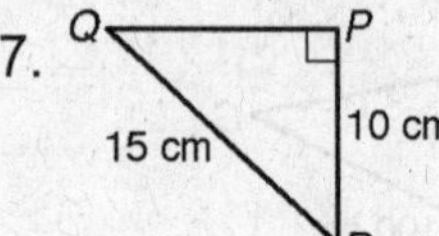

____
____

18.

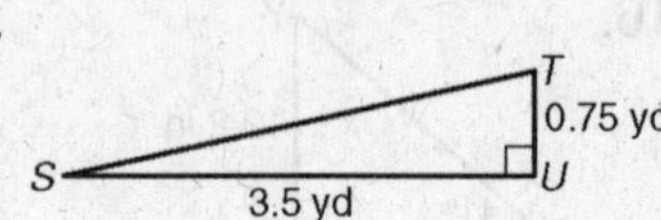

____
____

For each triangle, find all three side lengths to the nearest hundredth and all three angle measures to the nearest degree.

19. $B(-2, -4)$, $C(3, 3)$, $D(-2, 3)$

____

20. $L(-1, -6)$, $M(1, -6)$, $N(-1, 1)$

____

21. $X(-4, 5)$, $Y(-3, 5)$, $Z(-3, 4)$

____

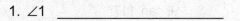

Name ______________________ Date ______________ Class ______________

LESSON 8-4

Practice

Angles of Elevation and Depression

Marco breeds and trains homing pigeons on the roof of his building. Classify each angle as an angle of elevation or an angle of depression.

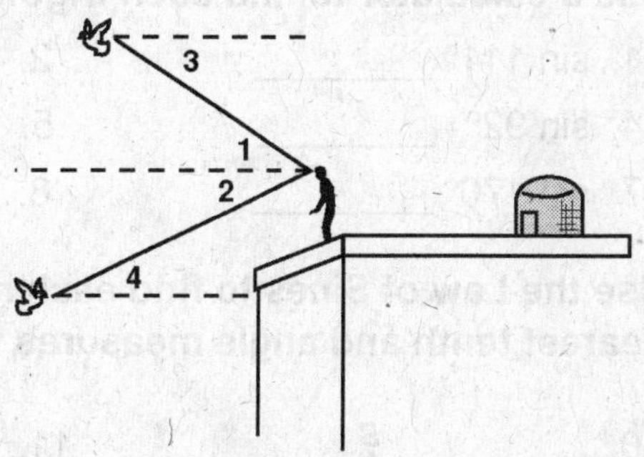

1. ∠1 ______________________

2. ∠2 ______________________

3. ∠3 ______________________

4. ∠4 ______________________

To attract customers to his car dealership, Frank tethers a large red balloon to the ground. In Exercises 5–7, give answers in feet and inches to the nearest inch. (*Note:* Assume the cord that attaches to the balloon makes a straight segment.)

5. The sun is directly overhead. The shadow of the balloon falls 14 feet 6 inches from the tether. Frank sights an angle of elevation of 67°. Find the height of the balloon. ______________________

6. Find the length of the cord that tethers the balloon. ______________________

7. The wind picks up and the angle of elevation changes to 59°. Find the height of the balloon. ______________________

Lindsey shouts down to Pete from her third-story window.

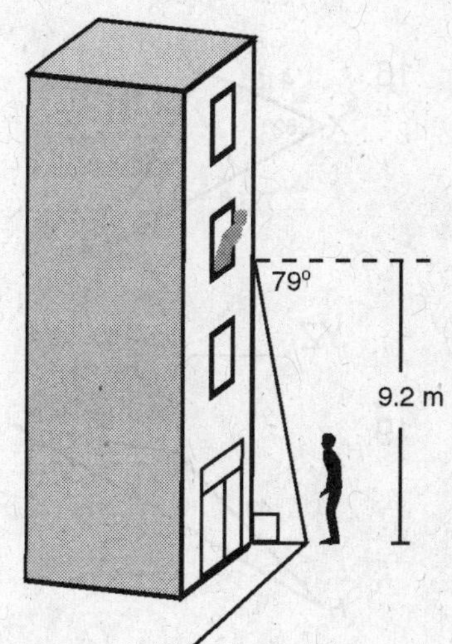

8. Lindsey is 9.2 meters up, and the angle of depression from Lindsey to Pete is 79°. Find the distance from Pete to the base of the building to the nearest tenth of a meter.

____

9. To see Lindsey better, Pete walks out into the street so he is 4.3 meters from the base of the building. Find the angle of depression from Lindsey to Pete to the nearest degree.

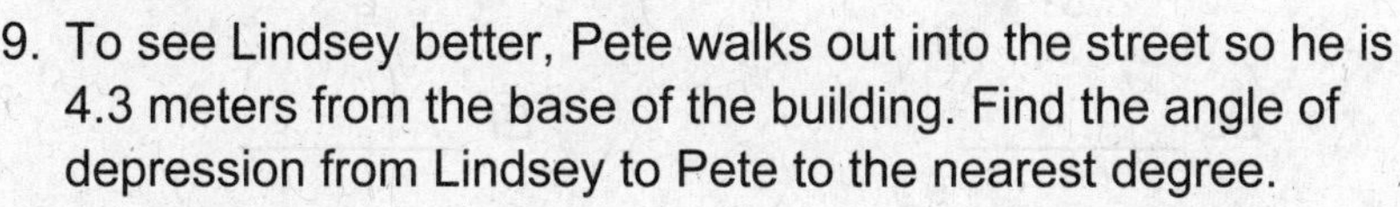

____

10. Mr. Shea lives in Lindsey's building. While Pete is still out in the street, Mr. Shea leans out his window to tell Lindsey and Pete to stop all the shouting. The angle of elevation from Pete to Mr. Shea is 72°. Tell whether Mr. Shea lives above or below Lindsey.

____

Name ______________________ Date ______________ Class ______________

LESSON 8-5

Practice

Law of Sines and Law of Cosines

Use a calculator to find each trigonometric ratio. Round to the nearest hundredth.

1. sin 111° ________ 2. cos 150° ________ 3. tan 163° ________
4. sin 92° ________ 5. cos 129° ________ 6. tan 99° ________
7. sin 170° ________ 8. cos 96° ________ 9. tan 117° ________

Use the Law of Sines to find each measure. Round lengths to the nearest tenth and angle measures to the nearest degree.

10. 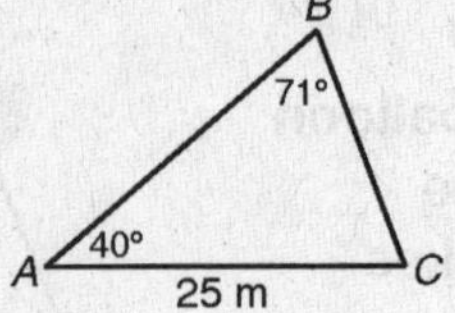

BC ________

11. 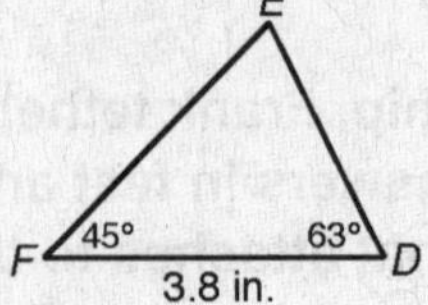

DE ________

12. 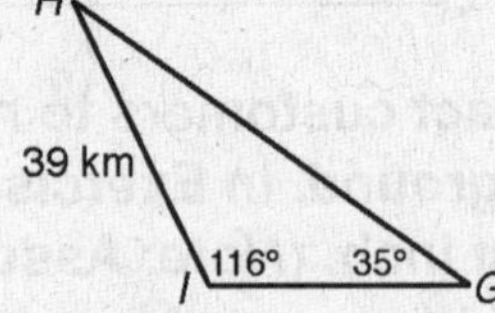

GH ________

13. 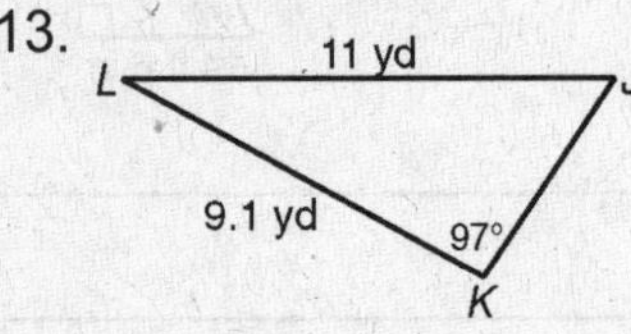

m∠J ________

14. 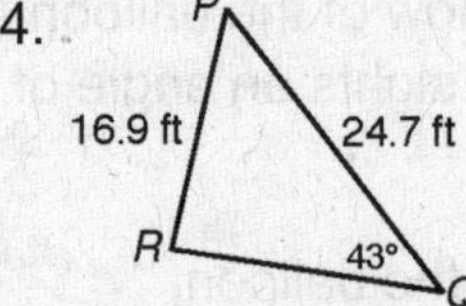

m∠R ________

15. 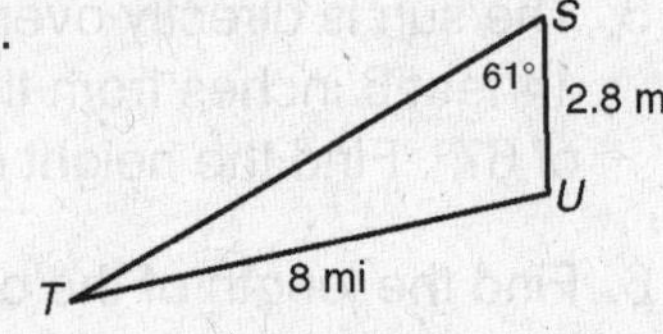

m∠T ________

Use the Law of Cosines to find each measure. Round lengths to the nearest tenth and angle measures to the nearest degree.

16. 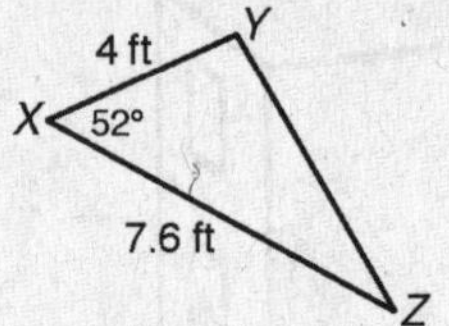

YZ ________

17. 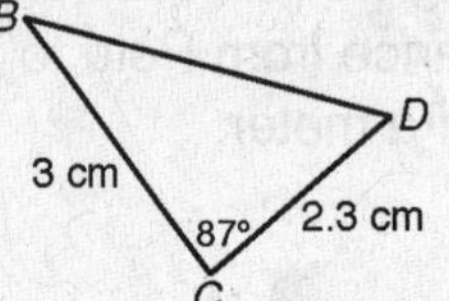

BD ________

18. 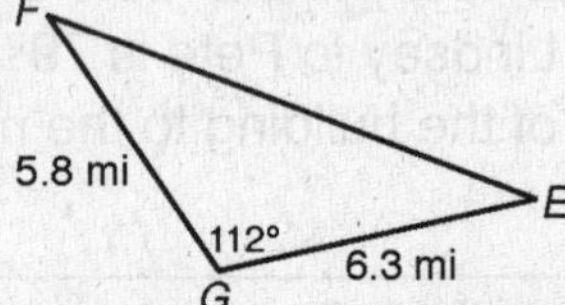

EF ________

19. 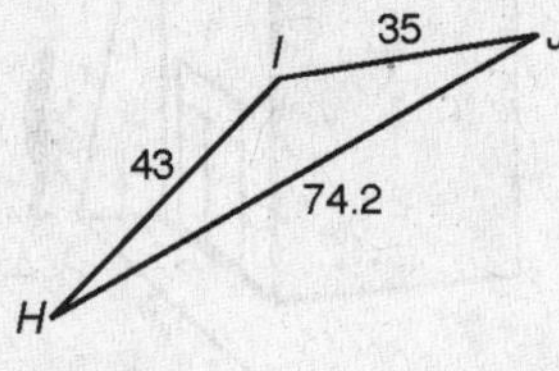

m∠I ________

20. 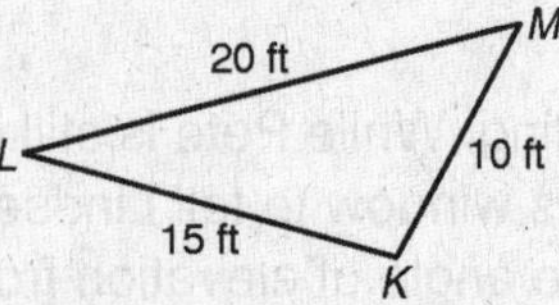

m∠M ________

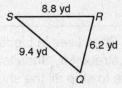

21. S 8.8 yd R
9.4 yd
6.2 yd
Q

m∠S ________

Name ______________________________ Date ________________ Class ________________

LESSON 8-6

Practice

Vectors

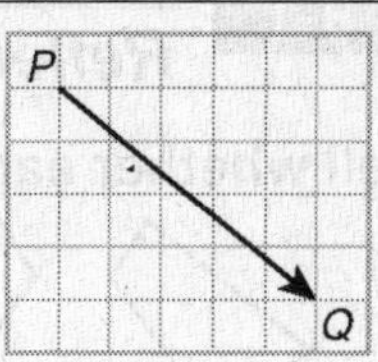

Write each vector in component form.

1. $\overrightarrow{PQ}$ ________________

2. $\overrightarrow{EF}$ with $E(-1, 2)$ and $F(-10, -3)$ ________________

3. the vector with initial point $V(7, 3)$ and terminal point $W(0, -1)$ ________________

Draw each vector on a coordinate plane. Find its magnitude to the nearest tenth.

4.  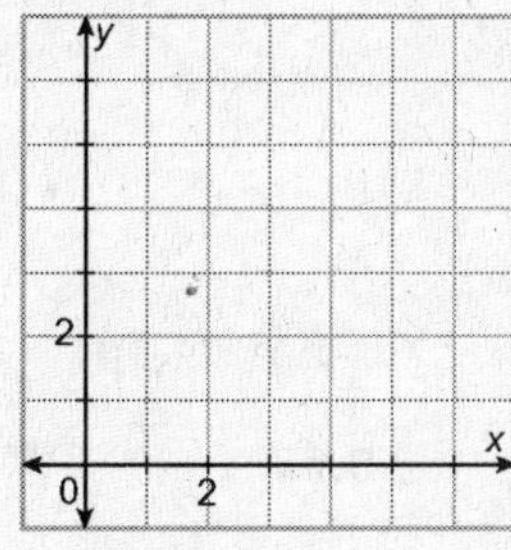

⟨5, 2⟩ ________

5.  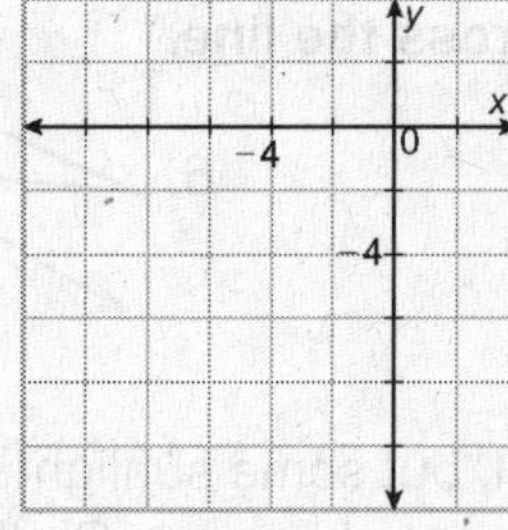

⟨−4, −7⟩ ________

6.  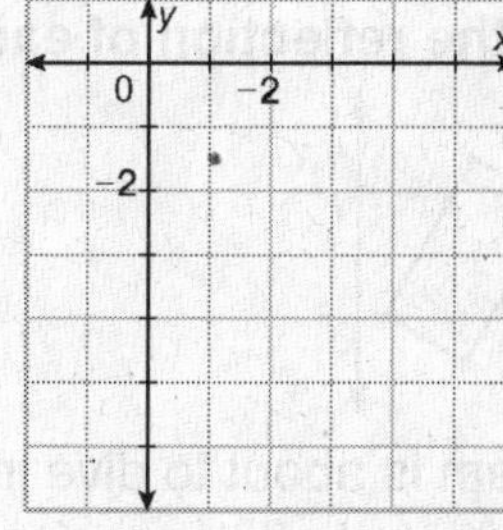

⟨3, −6⟩ ________

Draw each vector on a coordinate plane. Find the direction of the vector to the nearest degree.

7. 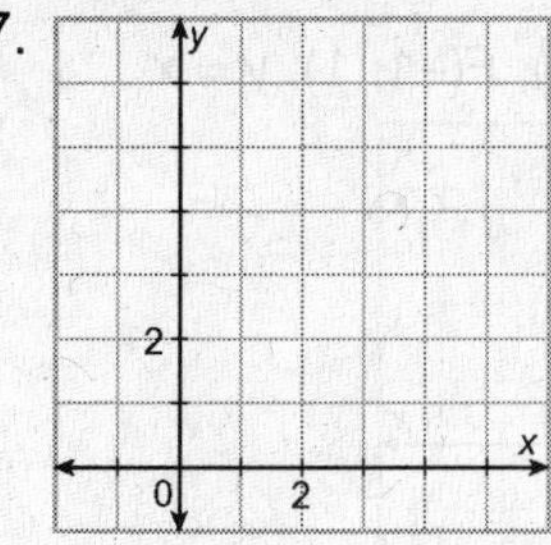

⟨4, 6⟩ ________

8. 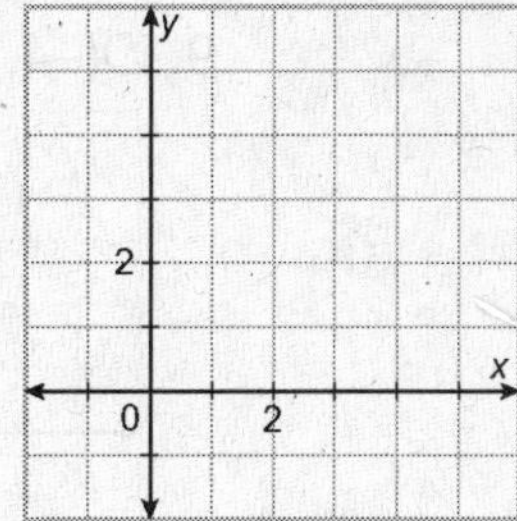

⟨3, 2⟩ ________

9. 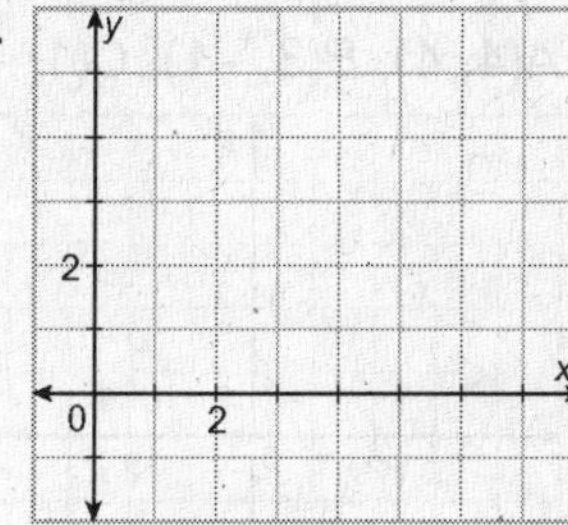

⟨7, 2⟩ ________

Identify each of the following in the figure.

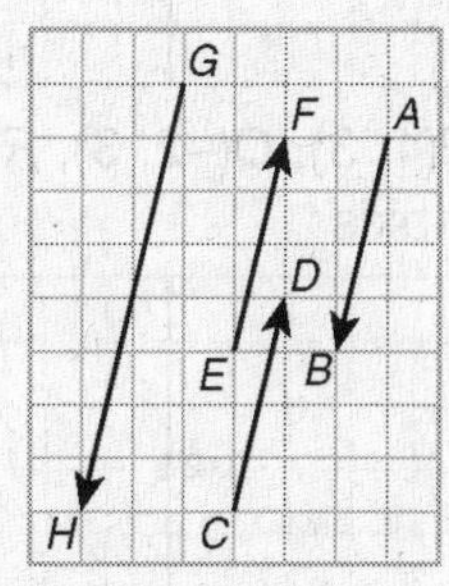

10. equal vectors ________________________________

11. parallel vectors ________________________________

In Exercise 12, round directions to the nearest degree and speeds to the nearest tenth.

12. Becky is researching her family history. She has found an old map that shows the site of her great grandparents' farmhouse outside of town. To get to the site, Becky walks for 3.1 km at a bearing of N 75° E. Then she walks 2.2 km due north. Find the distance and direction Becky could have walked to get straight to the site.

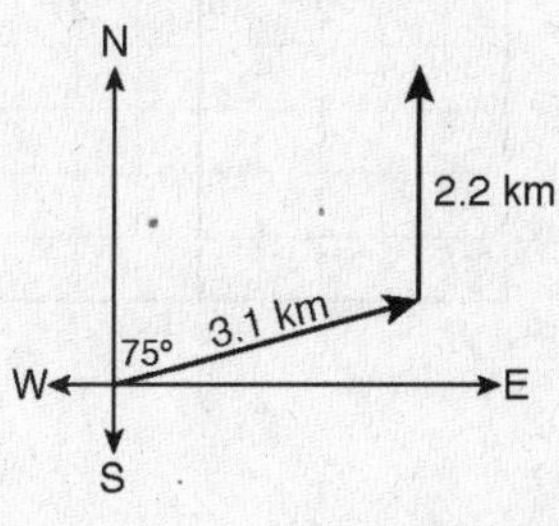

____

Name ________________________ Date ______________ Class ______________

LESSON 9-1

Practice

Reflections

Tell whether each transformation appears to be a reflection.

1. 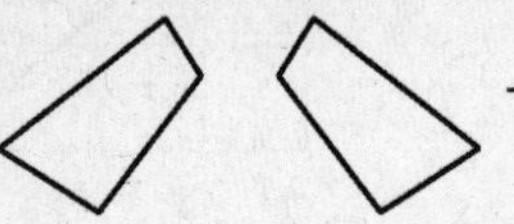 ________

2.  ________

3.  ________

4.  ________

Draw the reflection of each figure across the line.

5. 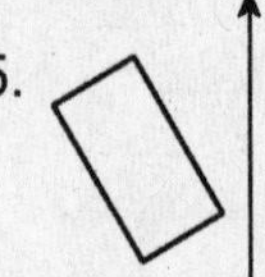

6. 

7. Sam is about to dive into a still pool, but some sunlight is reflected off the surface of the water into his eyes. On the figure, plot the exact point on the water's surface where the sunlight is reflected at Sam.

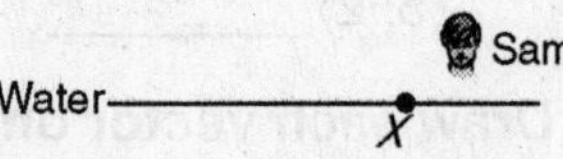

Reflect the figure with the given vertices across the given line.

8. $A(4, 4)$, $B(3, -1)$, $C(1, -2)$; y-axis

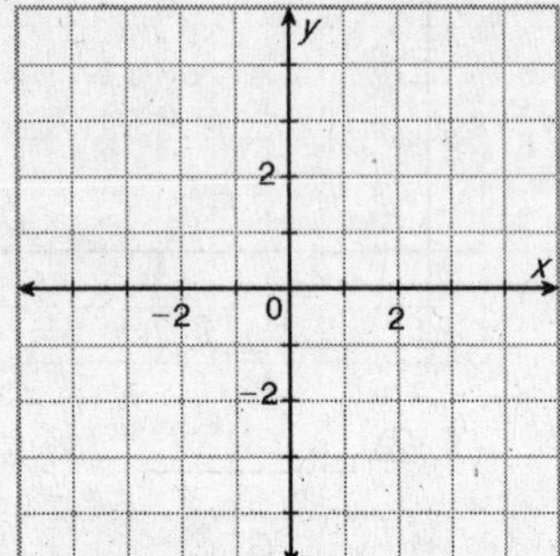

9. $D(-4, -1)$, $E(-2, 3)$, $F(-1, 1)$; $y = x$

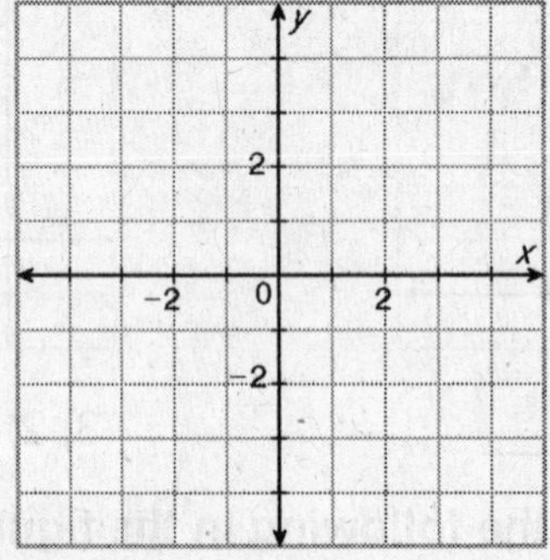

10. $P(1, 3)$, $Q(-2, 3)$, $R(-2, 1)$, $S(1, 0)$; x-axis

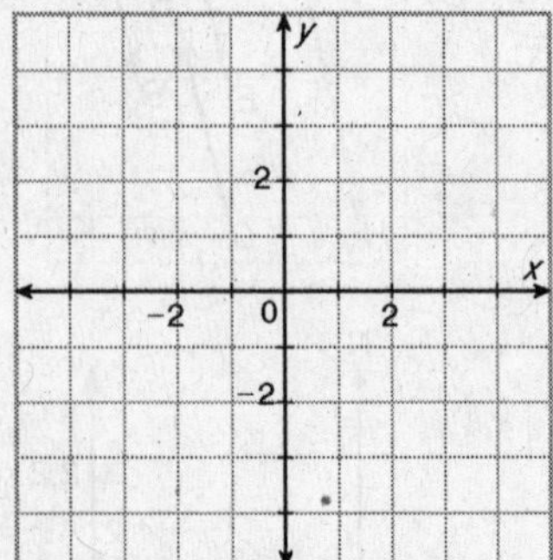

11. $J(3, -4)$, $K(1, -1)$, $L(-1, -1)$, $M(-2, -4)$; $y = x$

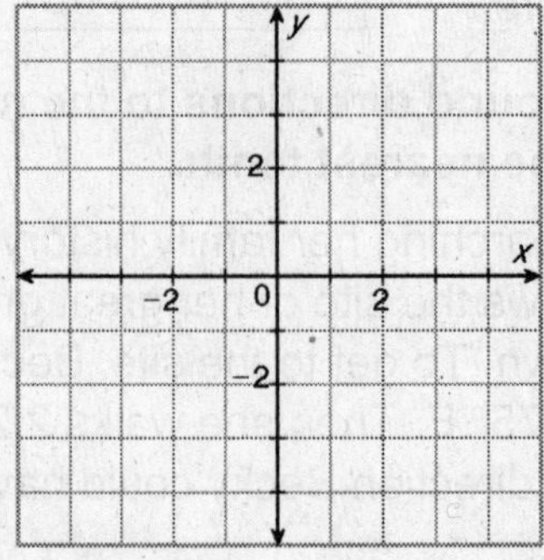

Name ________________________ Date ________________ Class ________________

LESSON 9-2

Practice

Translations

Tell whether each transformation appears to be a translation.

1. ________________

2. ________________

3. ________________

4. ________________

Draw the translation of each figure along the given vector.

5.

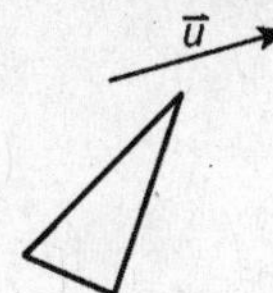

6.

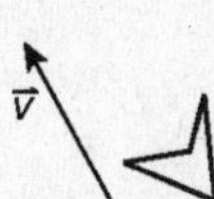

Translate the figure with the given vertices along the given vector.

7. $A(-1, 3)$, $B(1, 1)$, $C(4, 4)$; $\langle 0, -5 \rangle$

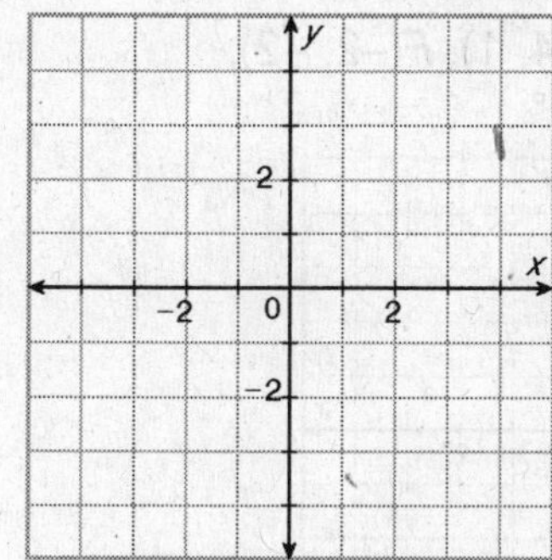

8. $P(-1, 2)$, $Q(0, 3)$, $R(1, 2)$, $S(0, 1)$; $\langle 1, 0 \rangle$

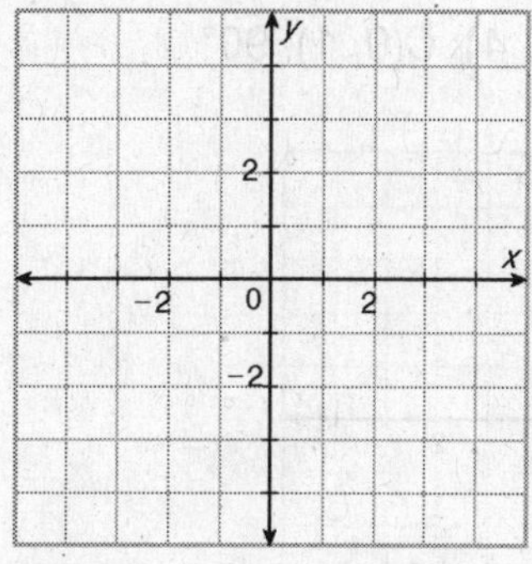

9. $L(3, 2)$, $M(1, -3)$, $N(-2, -2)$; $\langle -2, 3 \rangle$

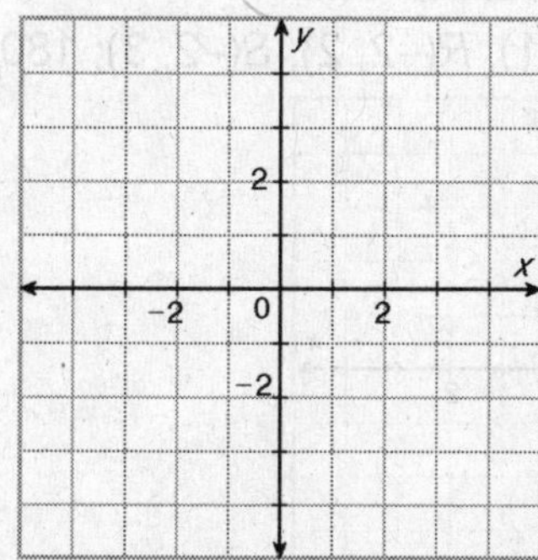

10. $D(2, -2)$, $E(2, -4)$, $F(1, -4)$, $G(-2, -2)$; $\langle 2, 5 \rangle$

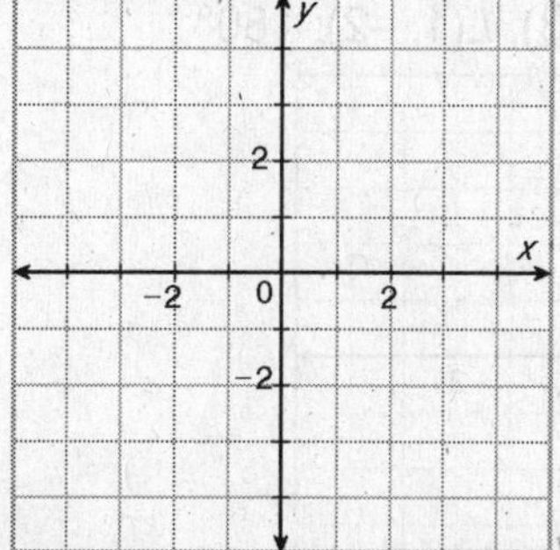

11. A builder is trying to level out some ground with a front-end loader. He picks up some excess dirt at (9, 16) and then maneuvers through the job site along the vectors $\langle -6, 0 \rangle$, $\langle 2, 5 \rangle$, and $\langle 8, 10 \rangle$ to get to the spot to unload the dirt. Find the coordinates of the unloading point. Find a single vector from the loading point to the unloading point.

____

Name ______________________________ Date ______________ Class ______________

LESSON 9-3

Practice

Rotations

Tell whether each transformation appears to be a rotation.

1.  ________

2. ________

3. ________

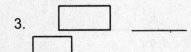

4. ________

Draw the rotation of each figure about point *P* by m∠*A*.

5. 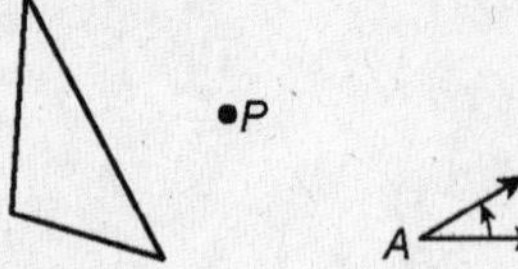

6. 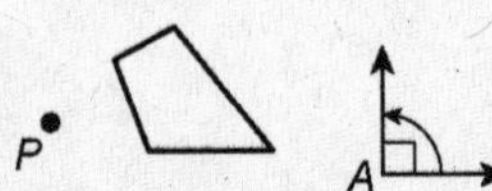

Rotate the figure with the given vertices about the origin using the given angle of rotation.

7. *A*(–2, 3), *B*(3, 4), *C*(0, 1); 90°

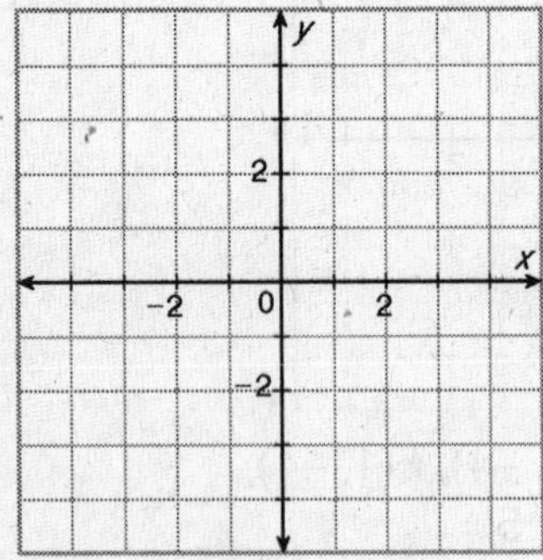

8. *D*(–3, 2), *E*(–4, 1), *F*(–2, –2), *G*(–1, –1); 90°

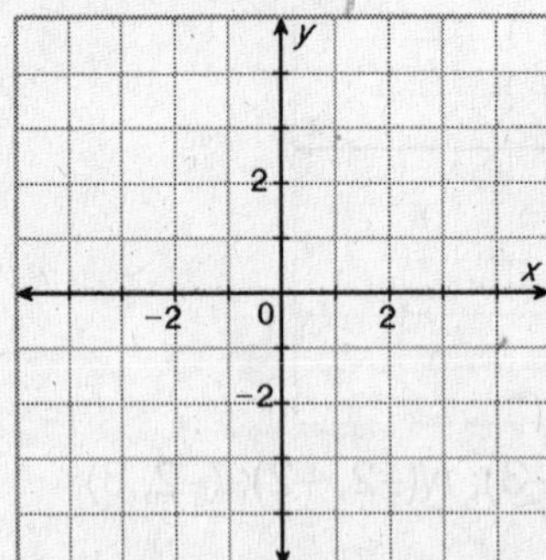

9. *J*(2, 3), *K*(3, 3), *L*(1, –2); 180°

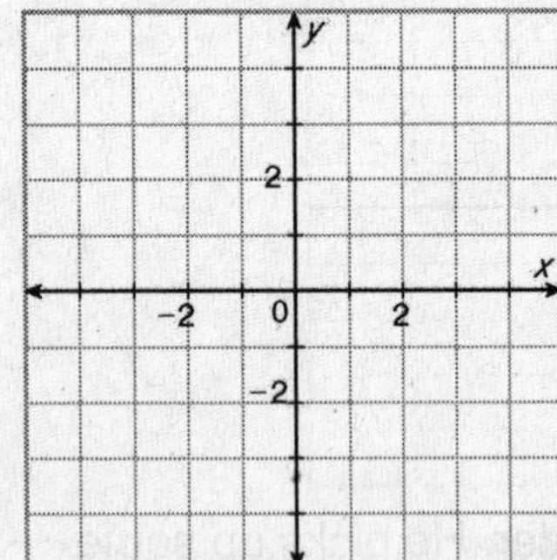

10. *P*(0, 4), *Q*(0, 1), *R*(–2, 2), *S*(–2, 3); 180°

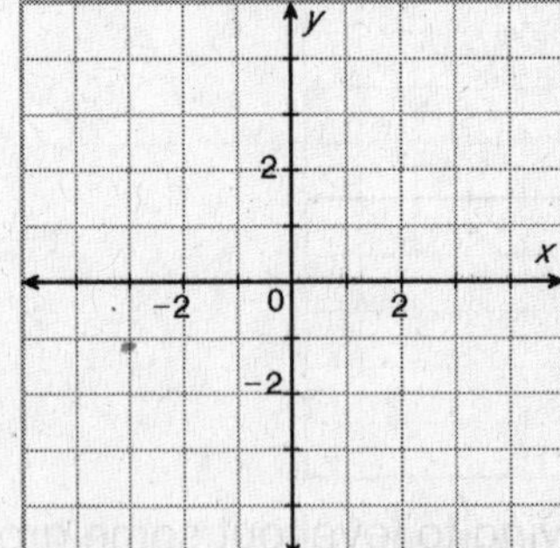

11. The steering wheel on Becky's car has a 15-inch diameter, and its center is at (0, 0). Point *X* at the top of the wheel has coordinates (0, 7.5). To turn left off her street, Becky must rotate the steering wheel by 300°. Find the coordinates of *X* when the steering wheel is rotated. Round to the nearest tenth. (*Hint:* How many degrees short of a full rotation is 300°?) ________________

Name ______________________ Date ______________ Class ______________

LESSON 9-4

Practice

Compositions of Transformations

Draw the result of each composition of isometries.

1. Rotate △*XYZ* 90° about point *P* and then translate it along $\vec{v}$.

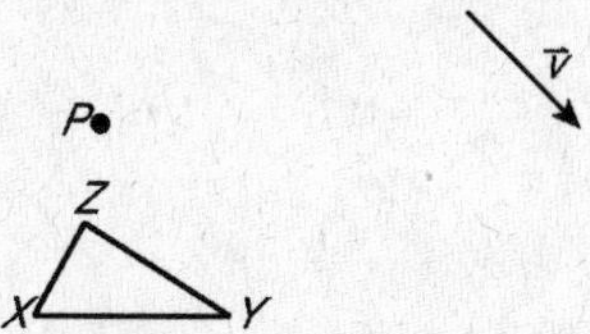

2. Reflect △*LMN* across line *q* and then translate it along $\vec{u}$.

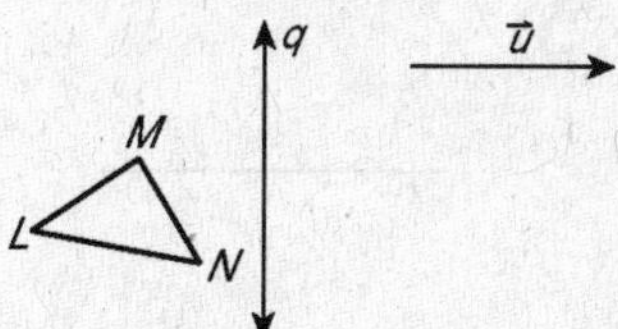

3. *ABCD* has vertices *A*(–3, 1), *B*(–1, 1), *C*(–1, –1), and *D*(–3, –1). Rotate *ABCD* 180° about the origin and then translate it along the vector ⟨1, –3⟩.

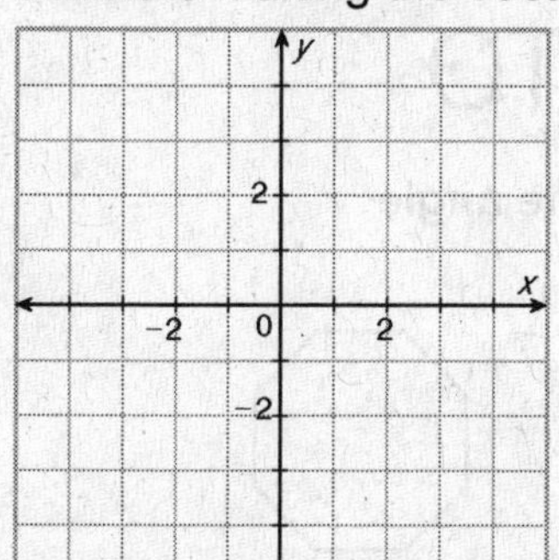

4. △*PQR* has vertices *P*(1, –1), *Q*(4, –1), and *R*(3, 1). Reflect △*PQR* across the *x*-axis and then reflect it across *y* = *x*.

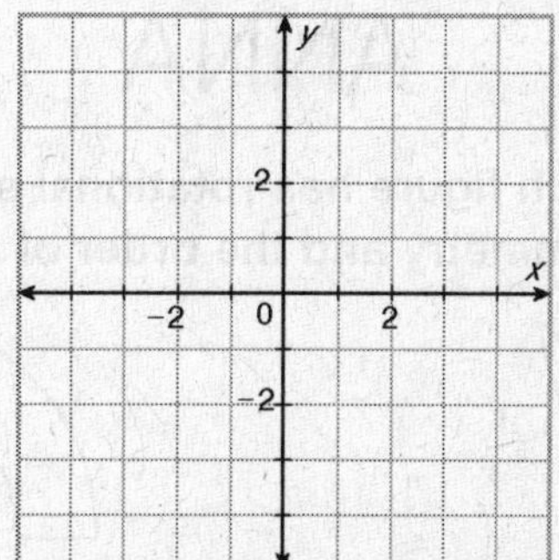

5. Ray draws equilateral △*EFG*. He draws two lines that make a 60° angle through the triangle's center. Ray wants to reflect △*EFG* across ℓ_1 and then across ℓ_2. Describe what will be the same and what will be different about the image of △*E″F″G″* compared to △*EFG*.

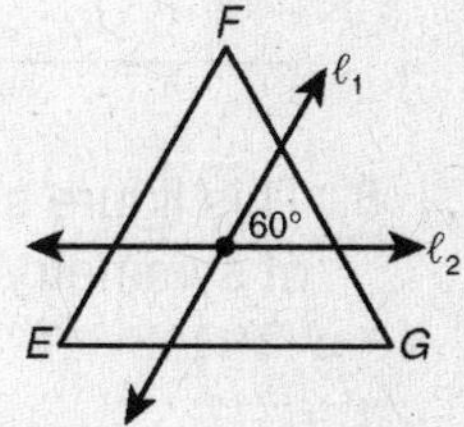

____

____

____

Draw two lines of reflection that produce an equivalent transformation for each figure.

6. translation: *STUV* → *S′T′U′V′*

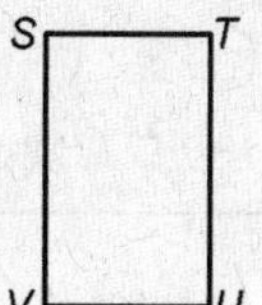

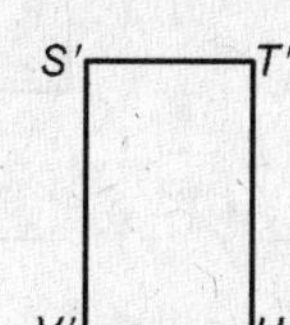

7. rotation with center *P*: *STUV* → *S′T′U′V′*

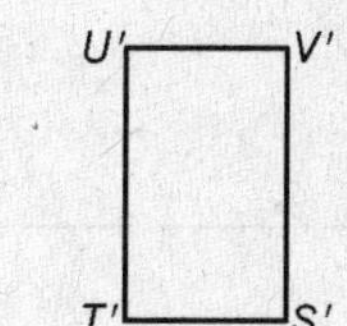

Name ________________________ Date ______________ Class ______________

LESSON 9-5

Practice

Symmetry

Tell whether each figure has line symmetry. If so, draw all lines of symmetry.

1. 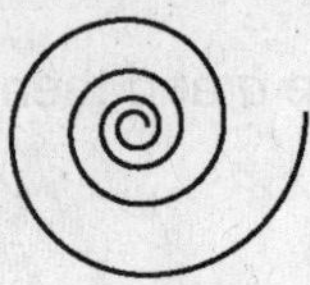 ________________

2. 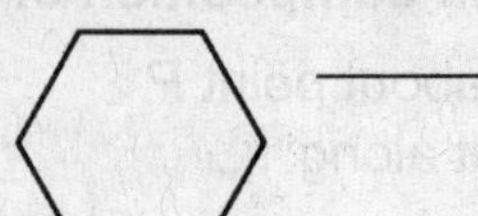 ________________

3.  ________________

4. Anna, Bob, and Otto write their names in capital letters. Draw all lines of symmetry for each whole name if possible.

ANNA BOB 

Tell whether each figure has rotational symmetry. If so, give the angle of rotational symmetry and the order of the symmetry.

5. 

6. 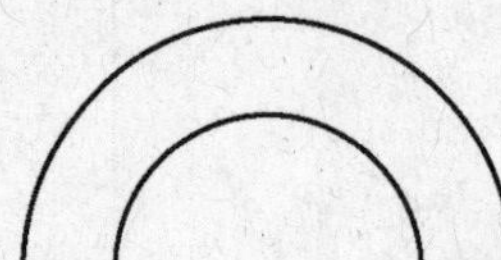

7. 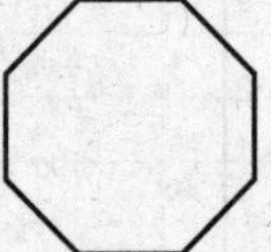

________________ ________________ ________________

8. This figure shows the Roman symbol for Earth. Draw all lines of symmetry. Give the angle and order of any rotational symmetry.

____

Tell whether each figure has plane symmetry, symmetry about an axis, both, or neither.

9. 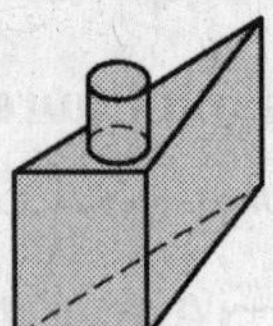

10. 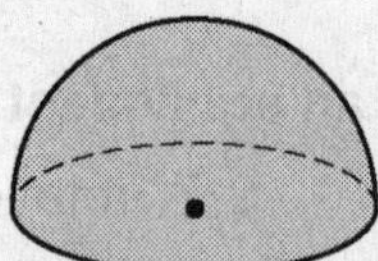

11. 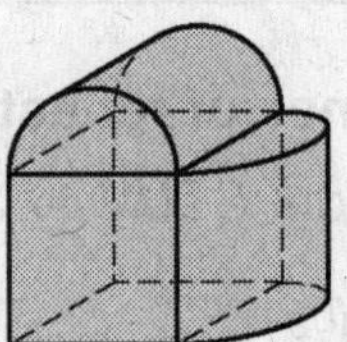

________________ ________________ ________________

Name ______________________ Date ______________ Class ______________

LESSON 9-6

Practice

Tessellations

Tell whether each pattern has translation symmetry, glide reflection symmetry, or both.

1. 

2. 

3. 

________________________ ________________________ ________________________

Use the given figure to create a tessellation.

4. 

5. 

Classify each tessellation as regular, semiregular, or neither.

6. 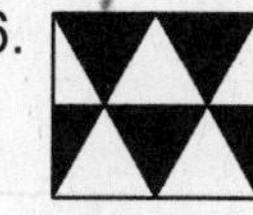

7. 

8. 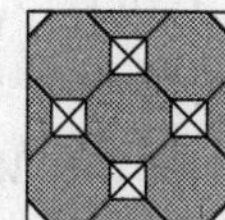

________________________ ________________________ ________________________

Determine whether the given regular polygon(s) can be used to form a tessellation. If so, draw the tessellation.

9. 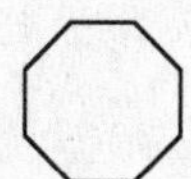

10. 

11. 

________________________ ________________________ ________________________

Name ______________________ Date ______________ Class ______________

LESSON 9-7

Practice

Dilations

Tell whether each transformation appears to be a dilation.

1. ____________

2. ____________

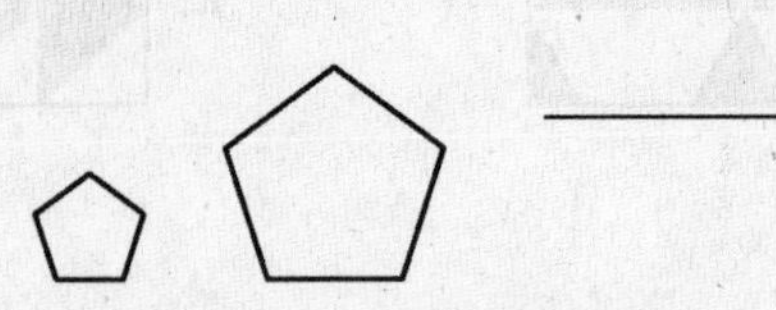

3. ____________

4. ____________

Draw the dilation of each figure under the given scale factor with center of dilation *P*.

5. scale factor: $\frac{1}{2}$

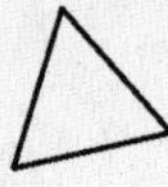

P•

6. scale factor: -2

P•

7. A sign painter creates a rectangular sign for Mom's Diner on his computer desktop. The desktop version is 12 inches by 4 inches. The actual sign will be 15 feet by 5 feet. If the capital *M* in "Mom's" will be 4 feet tall, find the height of the *M* on his desktop version. ____________

Draw the image of the figure with the given vertices under a dilation with the given scale factor centered at the origin.

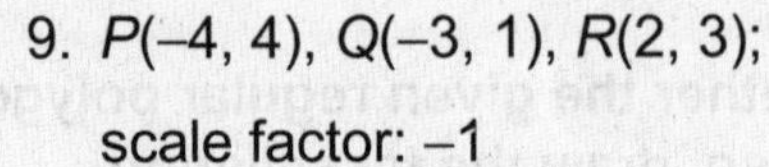

8. $A(2, -2)$, $B(2, 3)$, $C(-3, 3)$, $D(-3, -2)$;
scale factor: $\frac{1}{2}$

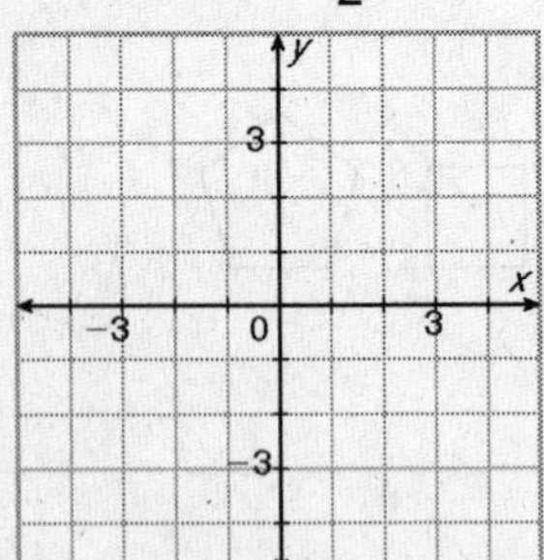

9. $P(-4, 4)$, $Q(-3, 1)$, $R(2, 3)$;
scale factor: -1

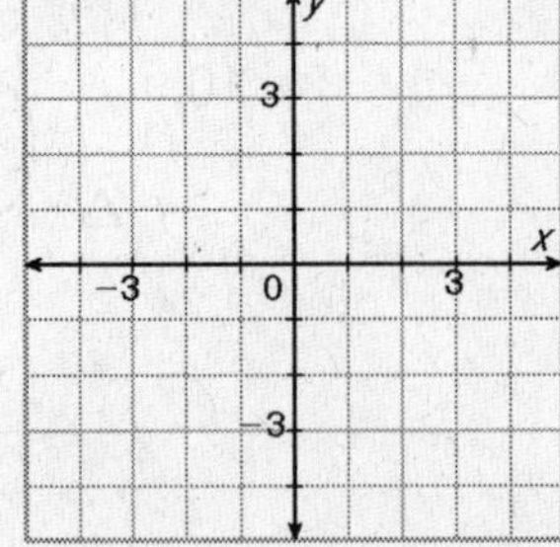

10. $J(0, 2)$, $K(-2, 1)$, $L(0, -2)$, $M(2, -1)$;
scale factor: 2

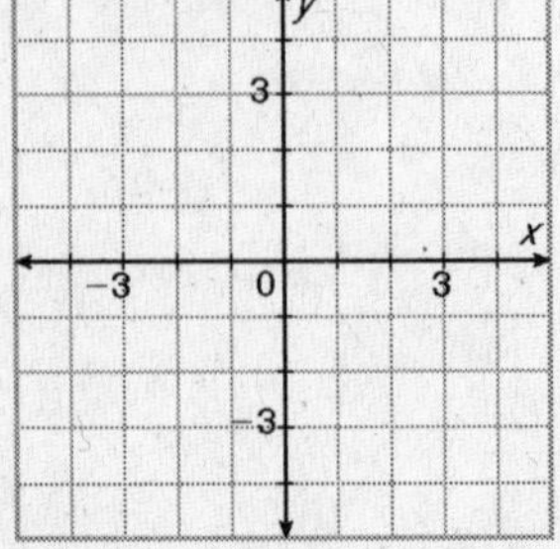

11. $D(0, 0)$, $E(-1, 0)$, $F(-1, -1)$;
scale factor: -2

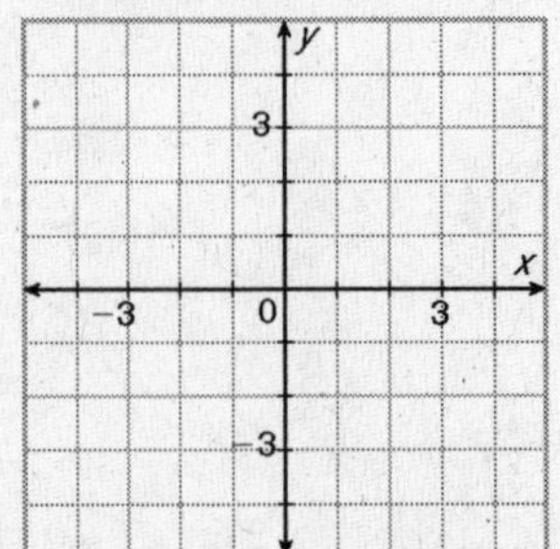

Name ______________________ Date ______________ Class ______________

LESSON 10-1

Practice

Developing Formulas for Triangles and Quadrilaterals

Find each measurement.

1.  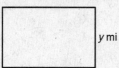

the perimeter of the rectangle in which $A = 2xy$ mi^2

____

2. $(a - b)$ ft

the area of the square

____

3. the height of a parallelogram in which $A = 96$ cm^2 and $b = 8x$ cm ________________________

4. 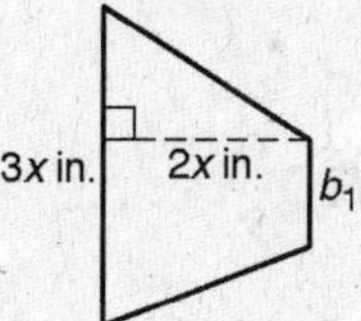

b_1 of the trapezoid in which $A = 4x^2$ in^2

____

5. 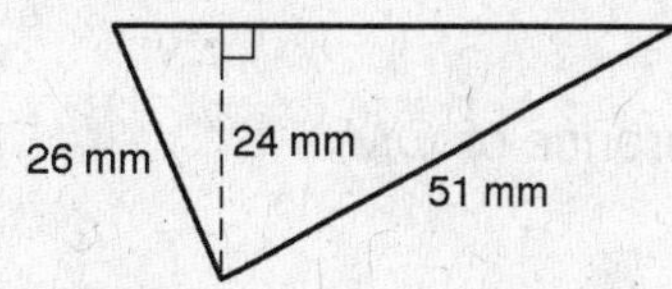

the area of the triangle

____

6. the area of a trapezoid in which $b_1 = 3a$ km, $b_2 = 6a$ km, and $h = (10 + 4c)$ km

____

7. 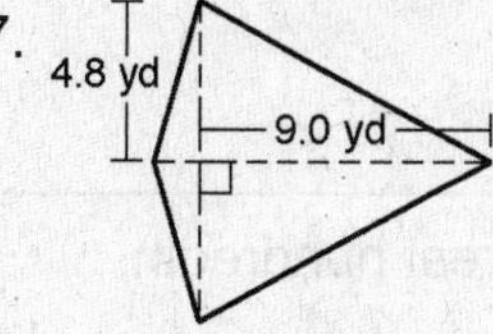

the perimeter of the kite in which $A = 49.92$ yd^2

____

8. 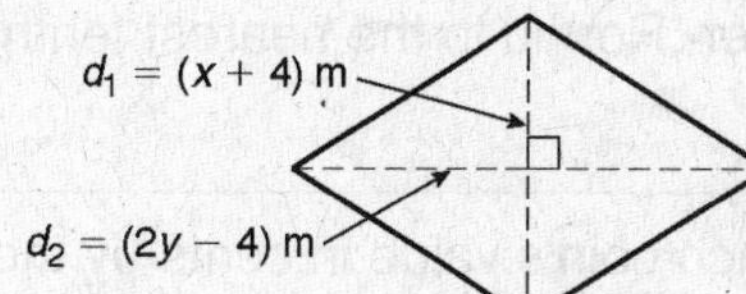

the area of the rhombus

____

9. d_2 of the kite in which $d_1 = (a - 4)$ ft and $A = (2a^2 - 8a)$ ft^2

____

Name ______________________ Date ______________ Class ______________

LESSON 10-2

Practice

Developing Formulas for Circles and Regular Polygons

Find each measurement. Give your answers in terms of π.

1.

the area of $\odot V$

____

2. 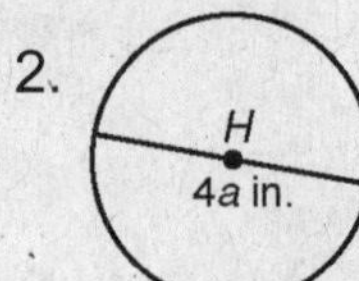

the area of $\odot H$

____

3. 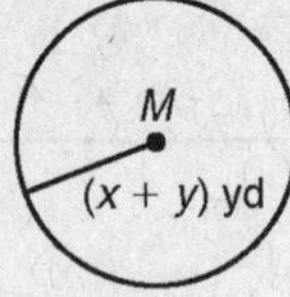

the circumference of $\odot M$

____

4. 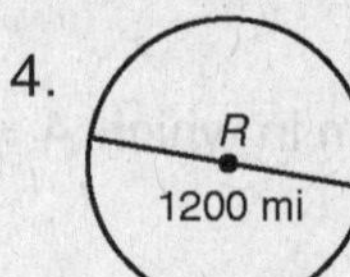

the circumference of $\odot R$

____

5. the radius of $\odot D$ in which $C = 2\pi^2$ cm ______________

6. the diameter of $\odot K$ in which $A = (x^2 + 2x + 1)\pi$ km^2 ______________

Stella wants to cover a tabletop with nickels, dimes, or quarters. She decides to find which coin would cost the least to use.

7. Stella measures the diameters of a nickel, a dime, and a quarter. They are 21.2 mm, 17.8 mm, and 24.5 mm. Find the areas of the nickel, the dime, and the quarter. Round to the nearest tenth.

____

8. Divide each coin's value in cents by the coin's area. Round to the nearest hundredth.

____

9. Tell which coin has the least value per unit of area. ______________

10. Tell about how many nickels would cover a square tabletop that measures 1 square meter. Then find the cost of the coins.

____

Find the area of each regular polygon. Round to the nearest tenth.

11. 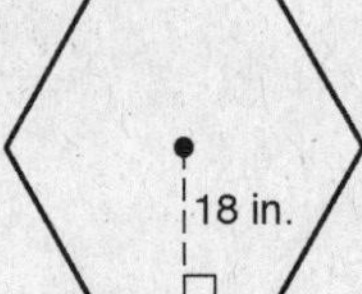

____

12. 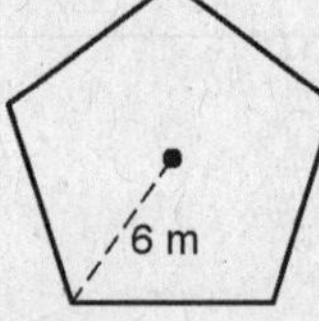

____

Name ______________________ Date ______________ Class ______________

LESSON 10-3

Practice

Composite Figures

Find the shaded area. Round to the nearest tenth if necessary.

1.

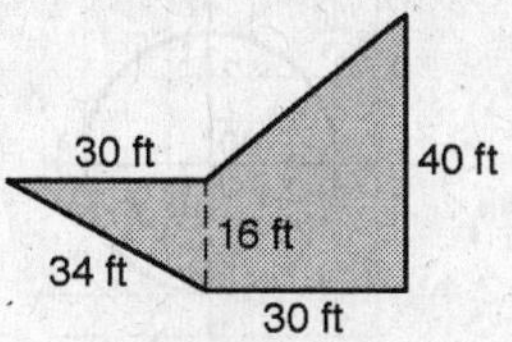

____

2.

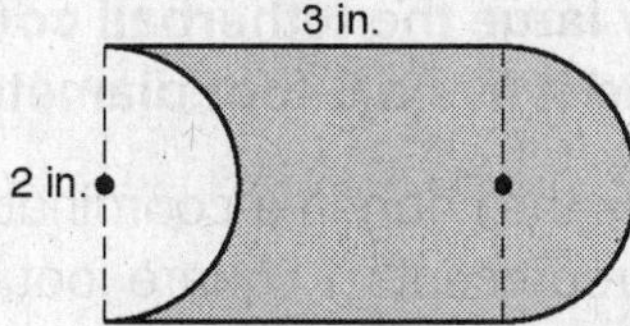

____

3.

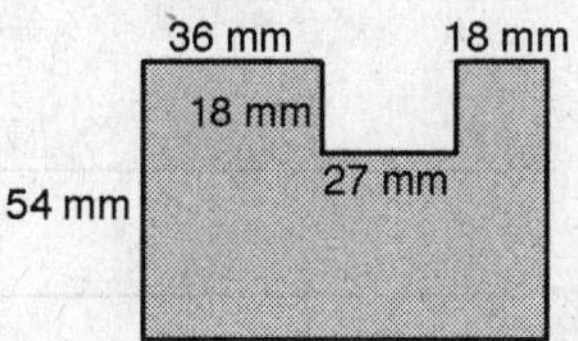

____

4.

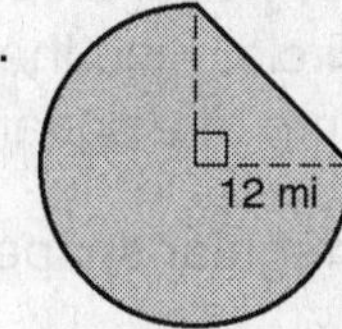

____

5.

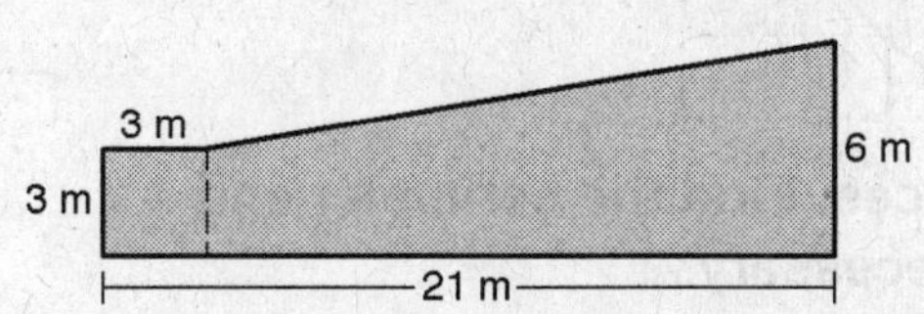

____

6.

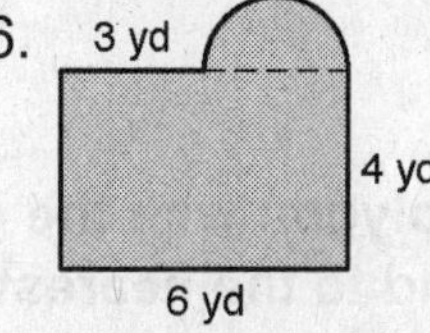

____

7.

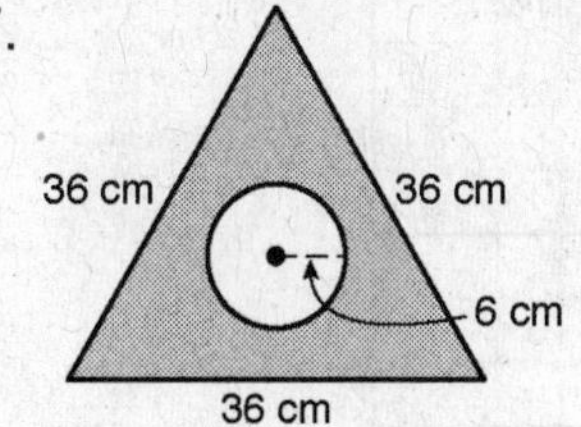

____

8.

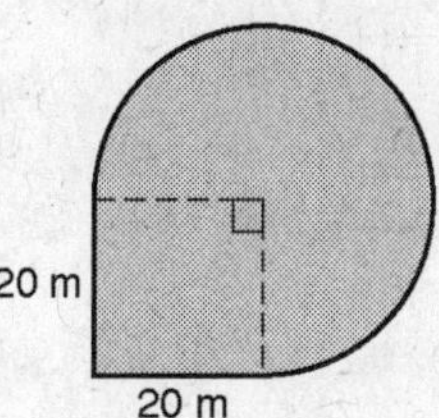

____

9. Osman broke the unusually shaped picture window in his parents' living room. The figure shows the dimensions of the window. Replacement glass costs $8 per square foot, and there will be a $35 installation fee. Find the cost to replace the window to the nearest cent.

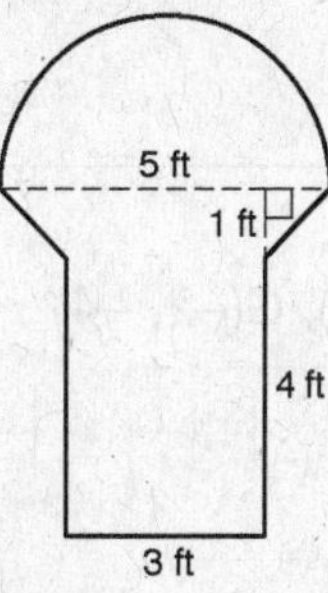

____

Estimate the area of each shaded irregular shape. The grid has squares with side lengths of 1 cm.

10.

____

11.

____

Name ________________________ Date ______________ Class ______________

LESSON 10-4

Practice

Perimeter and Area in the Coordinate Plane

Lena and her older sister Margie love to play tetherball. They want to find how large the tetherball court is. They measure the court and find it has a 6-foot diameter.

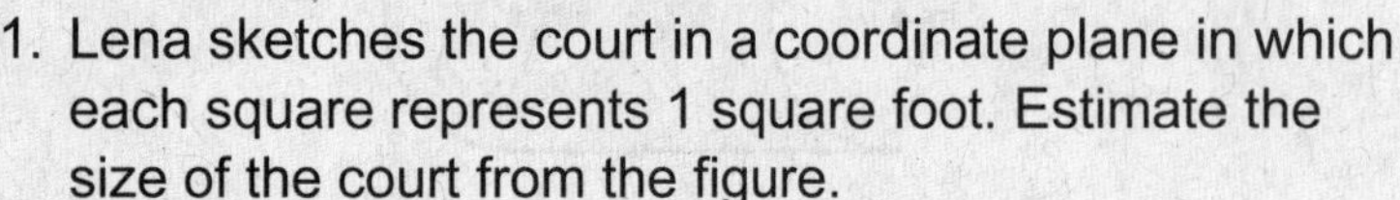

1. Lena sketches the court in a coordinate plane in which each square represents 1 square foot. Estimate the size of the court from the figure.

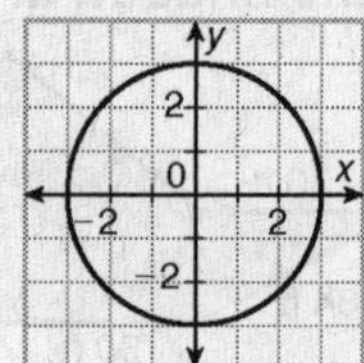

____

2. Margie has taken a geometry course, so she knows the formula for the area of a circle. Find the actual area of the court to the nearest tenth of a square foot.

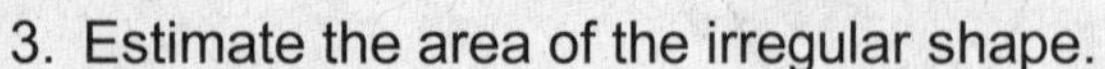

____

3. Estimate the area of the irregular shape.

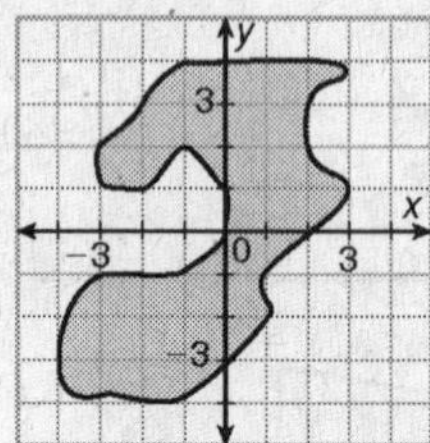

____

Draw and classify each polygon with the given vertices. Find the perimeter and area of the polygon. Round to the nearest tenth if necessary.

4. $A(-2, 3)$, $B(3, 1)$, $C(-2, -1)$, $D(-3, 1)$

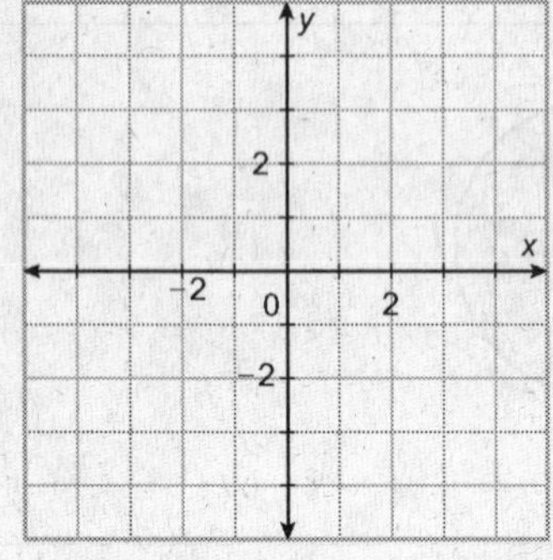

____

5. $P(-3, -4)$, $Q(3, -3)$, $R(3, -2)$, $S(-3, 2)$

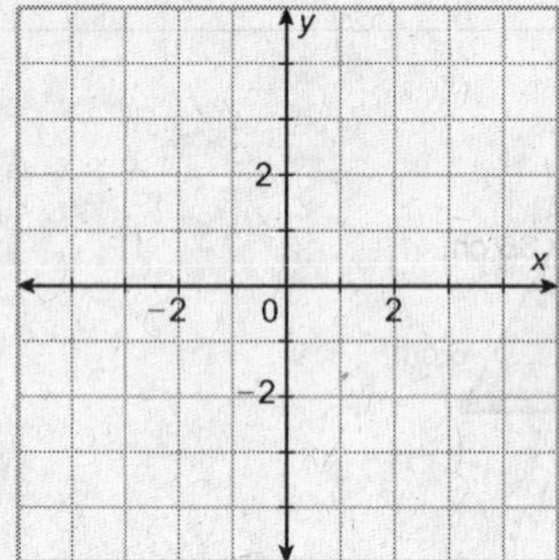

____

6. $E(-4, 1)$, $F(-2, 3)$, $G(-2, -4)$

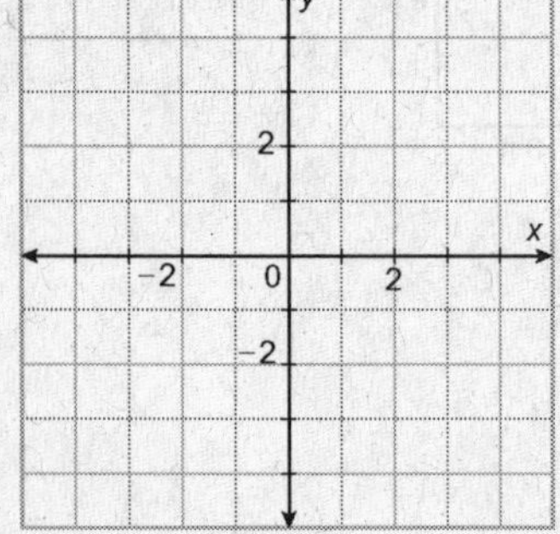

____

7. $T(1, -2)$, $U(4, 1)$, $V(2, 3)$, $W(-1, 0)$

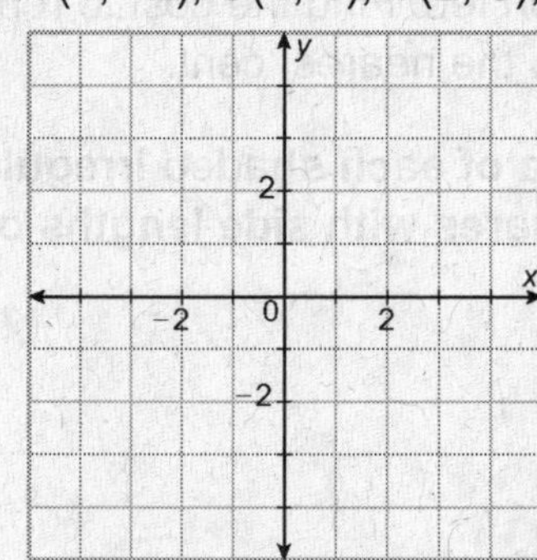

____

Name ________________________ Date ______________ Class ______________

LESSON 10-5

Practice

Effects of Changing Dimensions Proportionally

Describe the effect of each change on the area of the given figure.

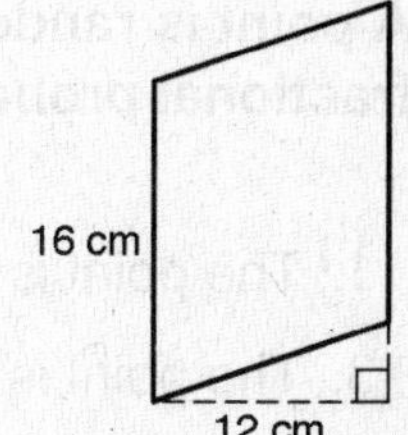
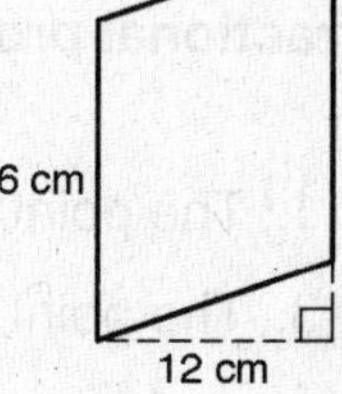

1. The base of the parallelogram is multiplied by $\frac{3}{4}$.

____

2. The length of a rectangle with length 12 yd and width 11 yd is divided by 6.

____

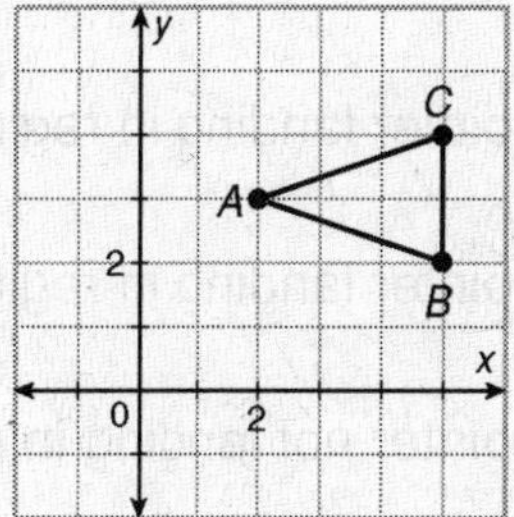

3. The base of a triangle with vertices $A(2, 3)$, $B(5, 2)$, and $C(5, 4)$ is doubled.

____

4. The height of a trapezoid with base lengths 4 mm and 7 mm and height 9 mm is multiplied by $\frac{1}{3}$.

____

In Exercises 5–8, describe the effect of each change on the perimeter or circumference and the area of the given figure.

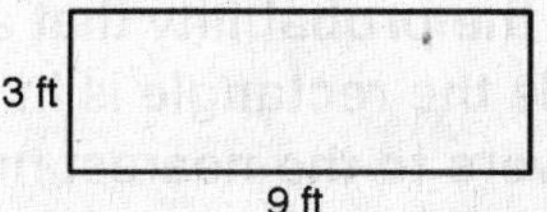

5. The length and width of the rectangle are multiplied by $\frac{4}{3}$.

____

6. The base and height of a triangle with base 1.5 m and height 6 m are both tripled.

____

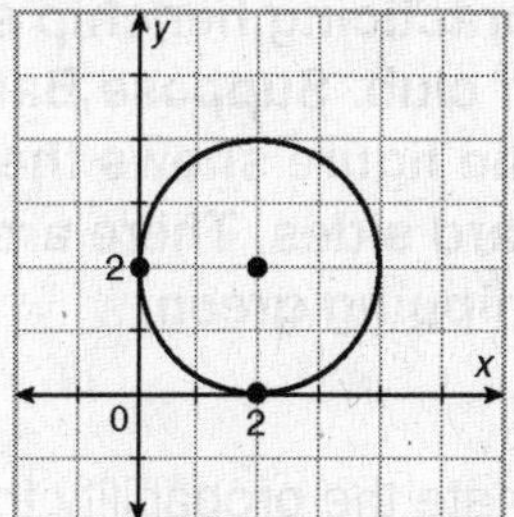

7. The radius of a circle with center (2, 2) that passes through (0, 2) is divided by 2.

____

____

8. The bases and the height of a trapezoid with base lengths 4 in. and 8 in. and height 8 in. are all multiplied by $\frac{1}{8}$.

____

9. A rhombus has an area of 9 cm^2. The area is multiplied by 5. Describe the effects on the diagonals of the rhombus.

____

10. A circle has a circumference of 14π ft. The area is halved. Describe the effects on the circumference of the circle.

____

Name ______________________ Date ______________ Class ______________

LESSON 10-6

Practice

Geometric Probability

A point is randomly chosen on $\overline{AD}$. Find the fractional probability of each event.

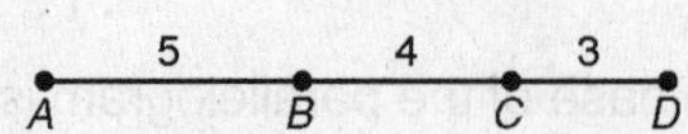

1. The point is on $\overline{AB}$. ____________
2. The point is on $\overline{BD}$. ____________
3. The point is on $\overline{AD}$. ____________
4. The point is not on $\overline{BC}$. ____________

Use the spinner to find the fractional probability of each event.

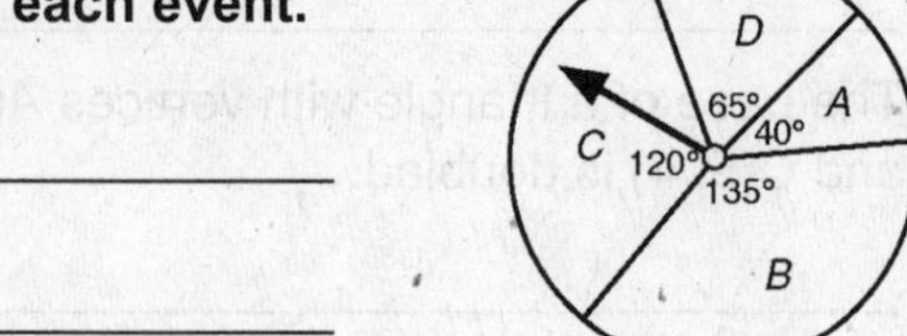

5. the pointer landing in region *C* ____________
6. the pointer landing in region *A* ____________
7. the pointer not landing in region *D* ____________
8. the pointer landing in regions *A* or *B* ____________

Find the probability that a point chosen randomly inside the rectangle is in each given shape. Round answers to the nearest hundredth.

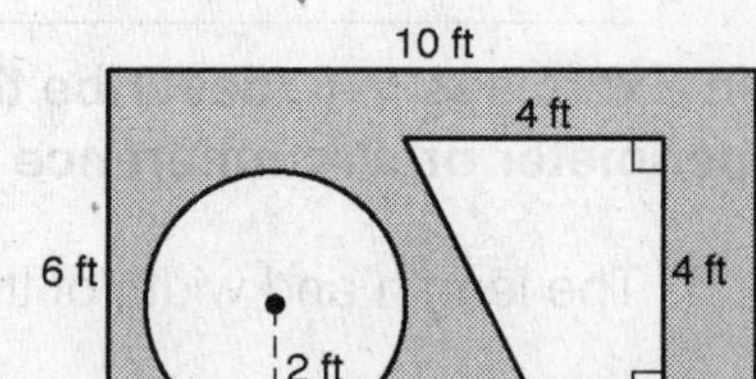

9. the circle ____________
10. the trapezoid ____________
11. the circle or the trapezoid ____________
12. not the circle and the trapezoid ____________

Barb is practicing her chip shots on the chipping green at the local golf club. Suppose Barb's ball drops randomly on the chipping green. The figure shows the chipping green in a grid whose squares have 1-yard sides. There are 18 different 4.5-inch diameter holes on the chipping green.

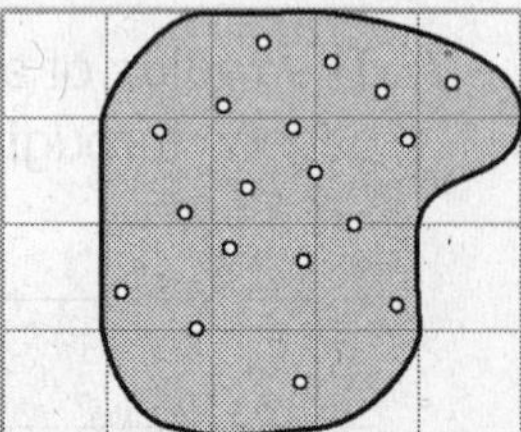

13. Estimate the probability that Barb will chip her ball into any hole. Round to the nearest thousandth. ____________
14. Estimate the probability that Barb will chip her ball into the one hole she is aiming for. Round to the nearest thousandth. ____________
15. Estimate how many chip shots Barb will have to take to ensure that one goes into a randomly selected hole. ____________
16. Barb is getting frustrated, so her shots are even worse. Now the ball drops randomly anywhere in the grid shown in the figure. Estimate the probability that Barb will miss the chipping green. Round to the nearest thousandth. ____________

Name ______________________ Date ____________ Class ____________

LESSON 11-1

Practice

Solid Geometry

Classify each figure. Name the vertices, edges, and bases.

1. 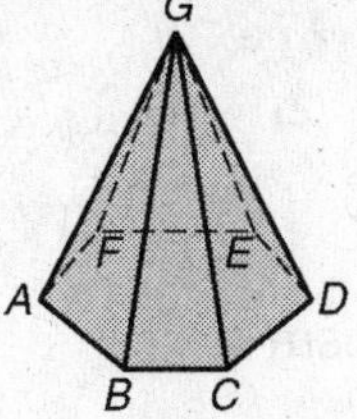

2. 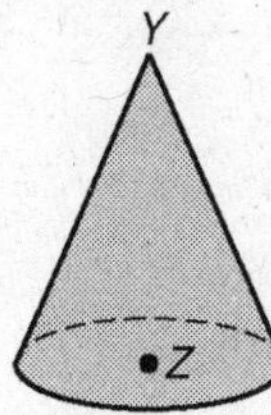

Name the type of solid each object is and sketch an example.

3. a shoe box

4. a can of tuna

Describe the three-dimensional figure that can be made from the given net.

5. 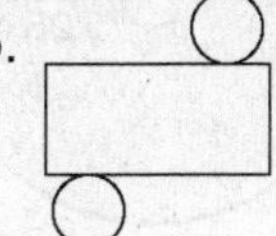

6. 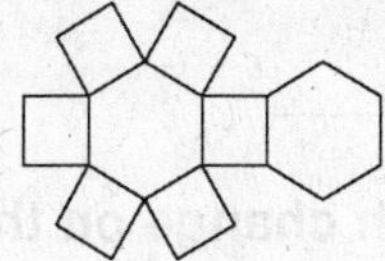

7. Two of the nets below make the same solid. Tell which one does not. ____________

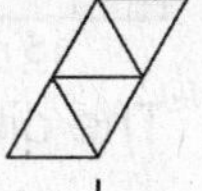
I

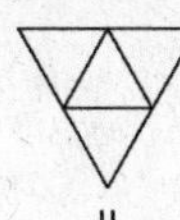
II

III

Describe each cross section.

8. 

9. 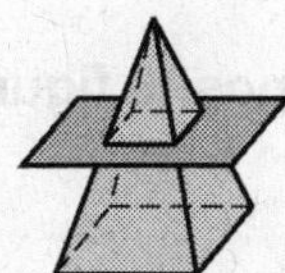

10. After completing Exercises 8 and 9, Lloyd makes a conjecture about the shape of any cross section parallel to the base of a solid. Write your own conjecture.

Name ______________________ Date ______________ Class ______________

LESSON 11-2

Practice

Volume of Prisms and Cylinders

Find the volume of each prism. Round to the nearest tenth if necessary.

1. 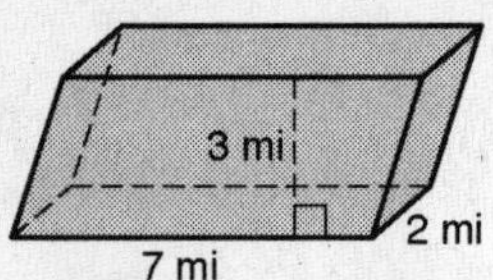

the oblique rectangular prism

____

2. 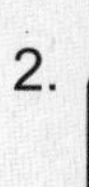 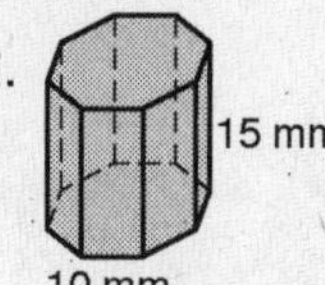

the regular octagonal prism

____

3. a cube with edge length 0.75 m ______________________

Find the volume of each cylinder. Give your answers both in terms of π and rounded to the nearest tenth.

4. 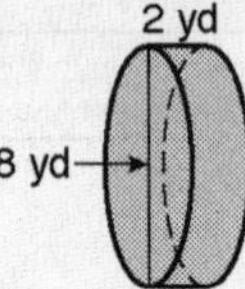

____

5. 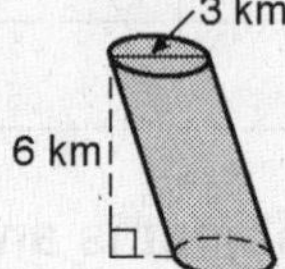

____

6. a cylinder with base circumference 18π ft and height 10 ft ______________________

7. CDs have the dimensions shown in the figure. Each CD is 1 mm thick. Find the volume in cubic centimeters of a stack of 25 CDs. Round to the nearest tenth.

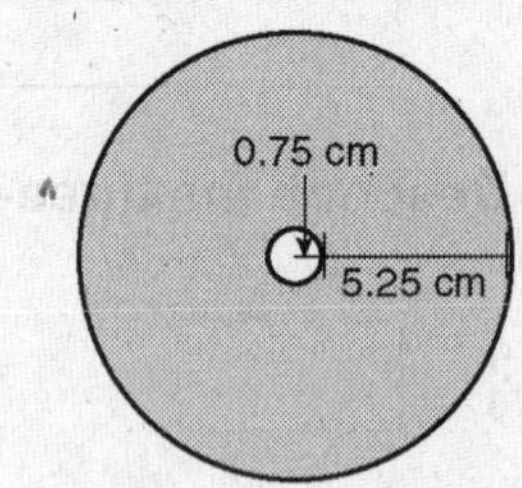

____

Describe the effect of each change on the volume of the given figure.

8. 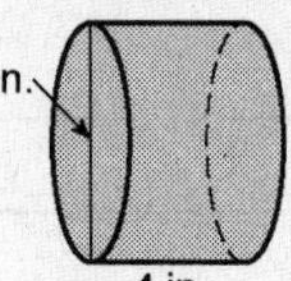

The dimensions are halved.

____

9. 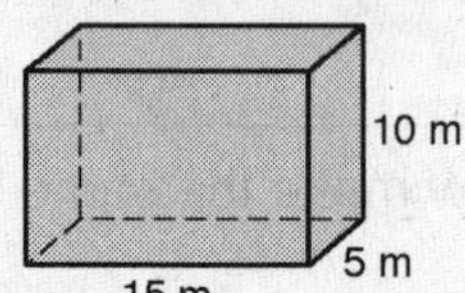

The dimensions are divided by 5.

____

Find the volume of each composite figure. Round to the nearest tenth.

10. 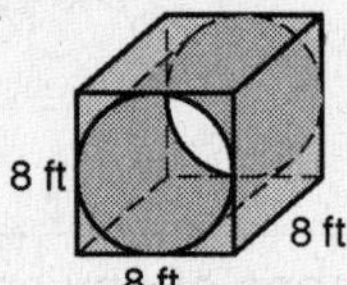

____

11. 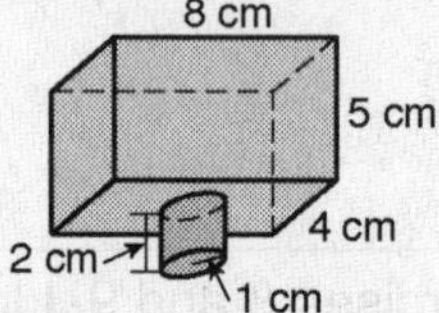

____

Name ______________________ Date ______________ Class ______________

LESSON 11-3

Practice

Volume of Pyramids and Cones

Find the volume of each pyramid. Round to the nearest tenth if necessary.

1. 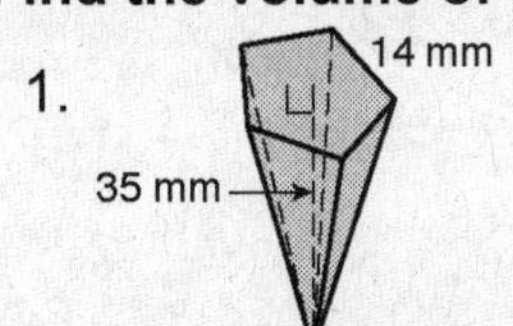

the regular pentagonal pyramid

____

2. 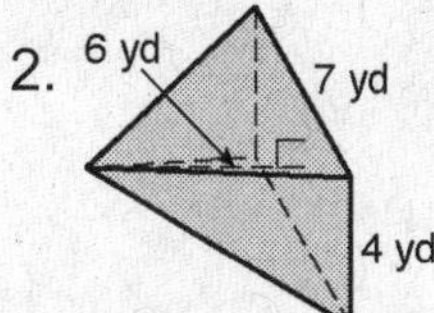

the rectangular right pyramid

____

3. Giza in Egypt is the site of the three great Egyptian pyramids. Each pyramid has a square base. The largest pyramid was built for Khufu. When first built, it had base edges of 754 feet and a height of 481 feet. Over the centuries, some of the stone eroded away and some was taken for newer buildings. Khufu's pyramid today has base edges of 745 feet and a height of 471 feet. To the nearest cubic foot, find the difference between the original and current volumes of the pyramid.

____

Find the volume of each cone. Give your answers both in terms of π and rounded to the nearest tenth.

4. 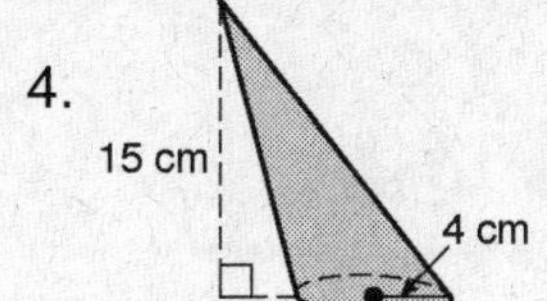

____

5. 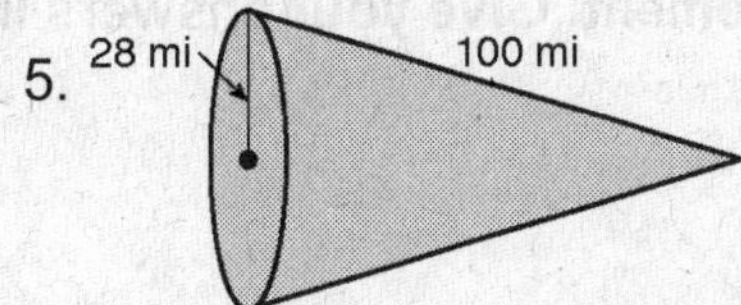

____

6. a cone with base circumference 6π m and a height equal to half the radius

____

7. Compare the volume of a cone and the volume of a cylinder with equal height and base area.

____

Describe the effect of each change on the volume of the given figure.

8. 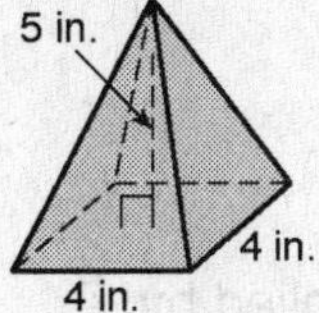

The dimensions are multiplied by $\frac{2}{3}$.

____

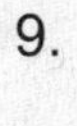

9. 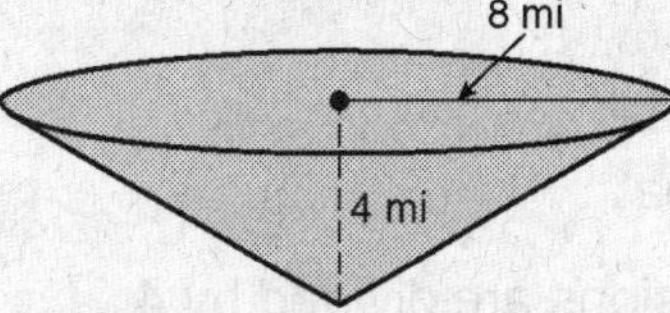

The dimensions are tripled.

____

Find the volume of each composite figure. Round to the nearest tenth.

10. 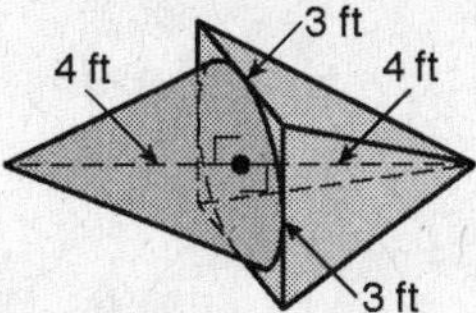

____

11. 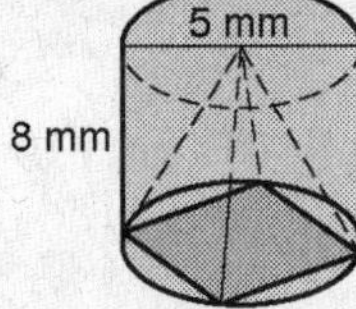

____

Name ______________________ Date ______________ Class ______________

LESSON 11-4

Practice

Spheres

Find each measurement. Give your answers in terms of π.

1. 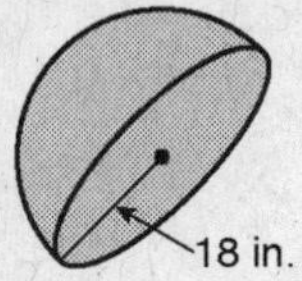

the volume of the hemisphere

____

2. 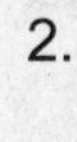 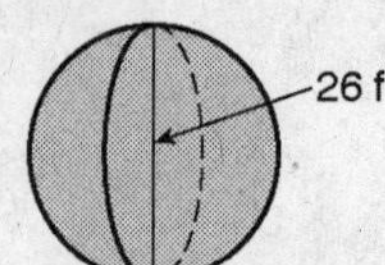

the volume of the sphere

____

3. the diameter of a sphere with volume $\frac{500\pi}{3}$ m^3 ________________________

4. The figure shows a grapefruit half. The radius to the outside of the rind is 5 cm. The radius to the inside of the rind is 4 cm. The edible part of the grapefruit is divided into 12 equal sections. Find the volume of the half grapefruit and the volume of one edible section. Give your answers in terms of π.

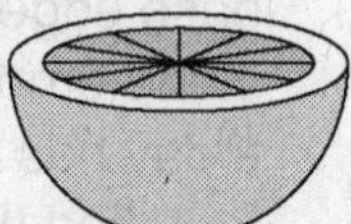

____

Find each measurement. Give your answers in terms of π.

5. 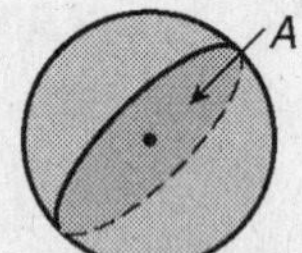

the surface area of the sphere

____

6. 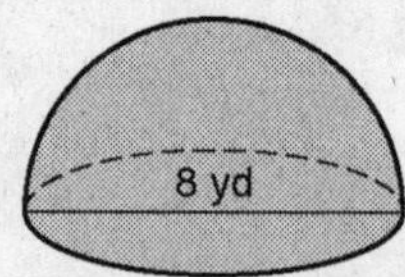

the surface area of the closed hemisphere and its circular base

____

7. the volume of a sphere with surface area 196π km^2 ________________________

Describe the effect of each change on the given measurement of the figure.

8. 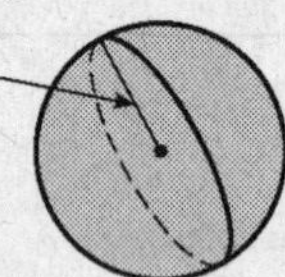

surface area

The dimensions are divided by 4.

____

9. 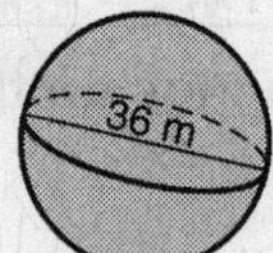

volume

The dimensions are multiplied by $\frac{2}{5}$.

____

Find the surface area and volume of each composite figure. Round to the nearest tenth.

10. 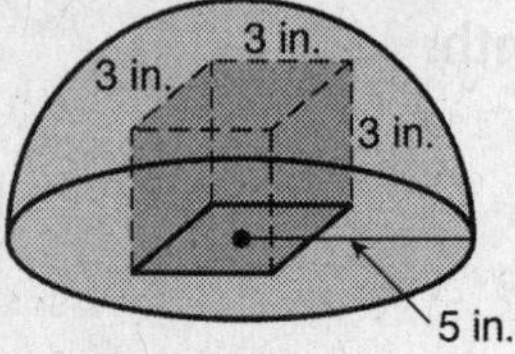

____

11. 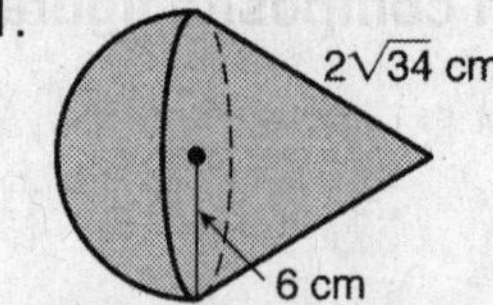

____

Name ______________________ Date ______________ Class ______________

LESSON 12-1

Practice

Lines That Intersect Circles

Identify each line or segment that intersects each circle.

1. 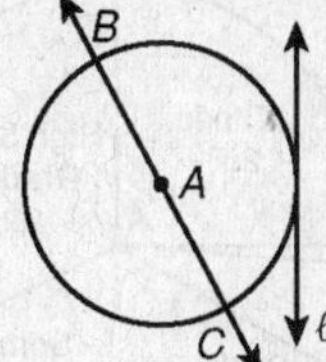

2. 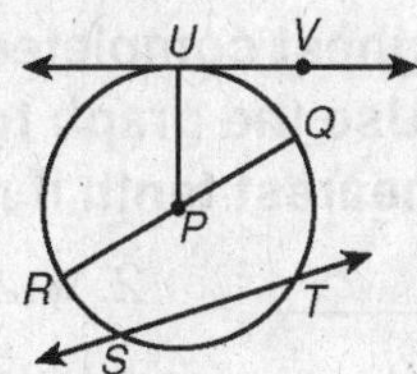

Find the length of each radius. Identify the point of tangency and write the equation of the tangent line at this point.

3. 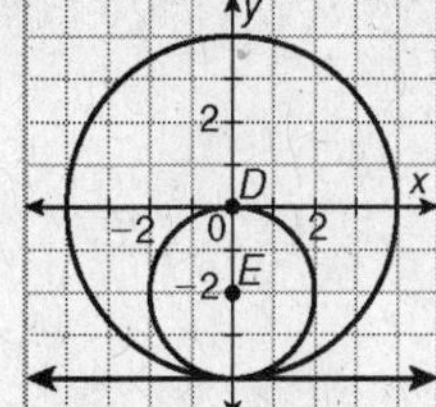

4. 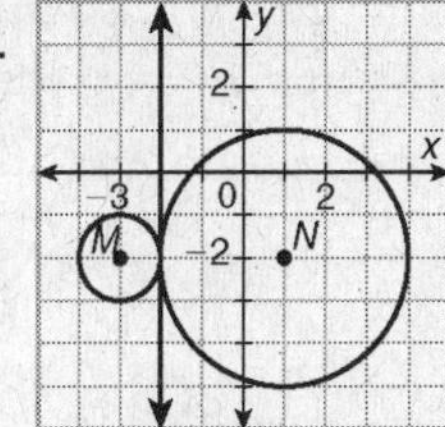

5. The Moon's orbit is not exactly circular, but the average distance from its surface to Earth's surface is 384,000 kilometers. The diameter of the Moon is 3476 kilometers. Find the distance from the surface of Earth to the visible edge of the Moon if the Moon is directly above the observer. Round to the nearest kilometer. (*Note:* The figure is not drawn to scale.)

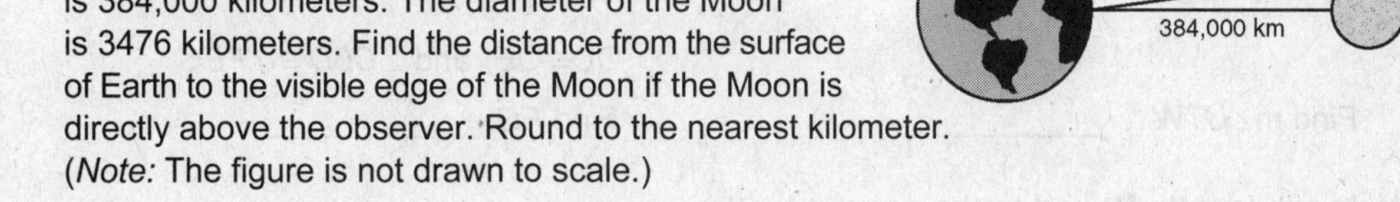

In Exercises 6 and 7, $\overline{EF}$ and $\overline{EG}$ are tangent to ⊙*H*. Find *EF*.

6. 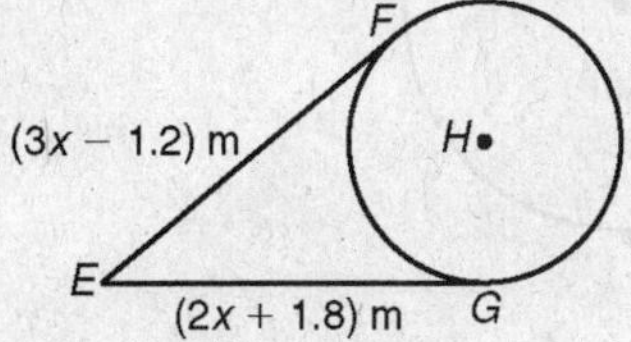

7. 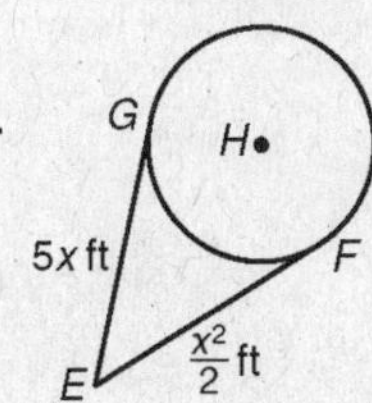

Name ______________________ Date ______________ Class ______________

LESSON 12-2

Practice

Arcs and Chords

The circle graph shows data collected by the U.S. Census Bureau in 2004 on the highest completed educational level for people 25 and older. Use the graph to find each of the following. Round to the nearest tenth if necessary.

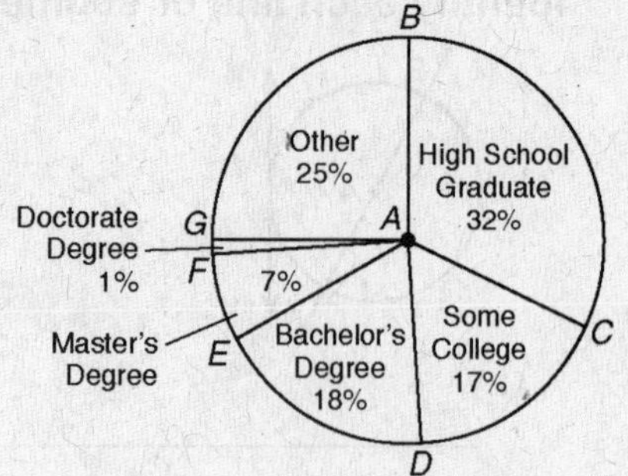

1. $m\angle CAB$ ______________
2. $m\angle DAG$ ______________
3. $m\angle EAC$ ______________
4. $m\overset{\frown}{BG}$ ______________
5. $m\overset{\frown}{GF}$ ______________
6. $m\overset{\frown}{BDE}$ ______________

Find each measure.

7.

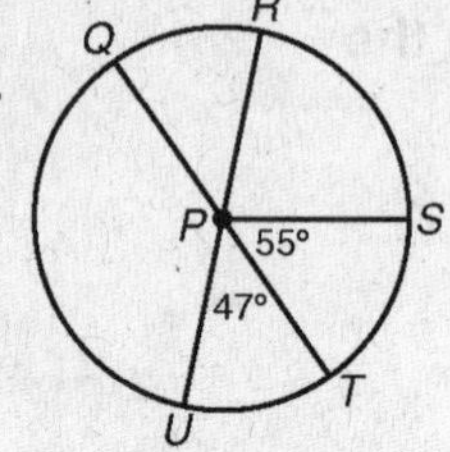

$m\overset{\frown}{QS}$ ______________

$m\overset{\frown}{RQT}$ ______________

8.

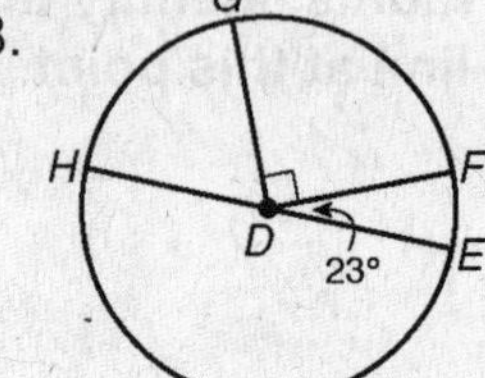

$m\overset{\frown}{HG}$ ______________

$m\overset{\frown}{FEH}$ ______________

9.

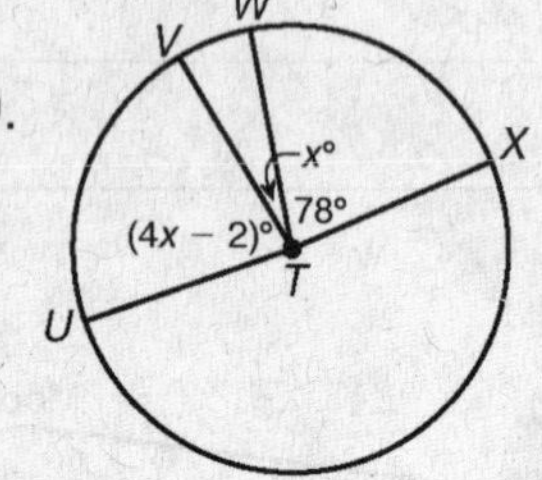

Find $m\angle UTW$. ______________

10.

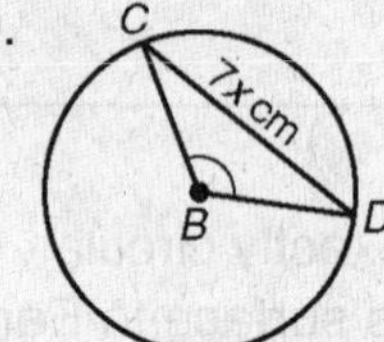

$\odot L \cong \odot E$, and $\angle CBD \cong \angle FEG$.

Find FG. ______________

Find each length. Round to the nearest tenth.

11.

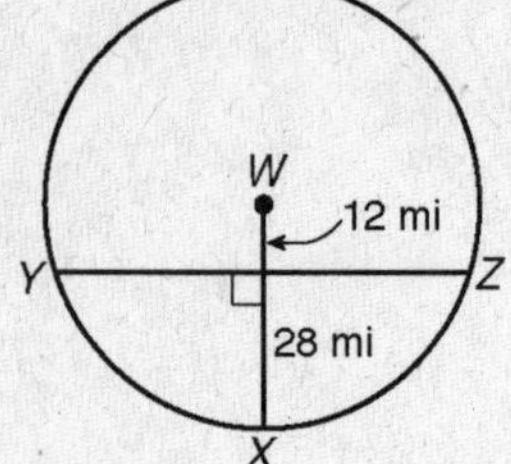

ZY ______________

12.

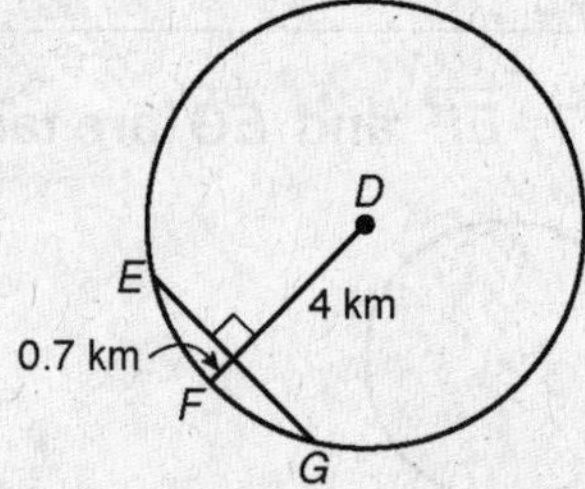

EG ______________

Name ______________________ Date ______________ Class ______________

LESSON 12-3

Practice

Sector Area and Arc Length

Find the area of each sector. Give your answer in terms of π and rounded to the nearest hundredth.

1.
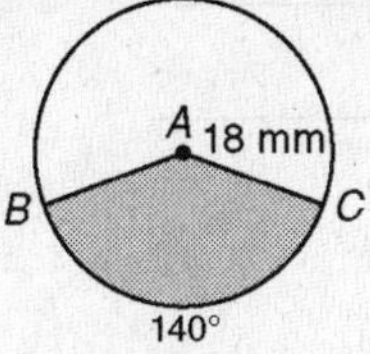

sector *BAC* ______________

2.
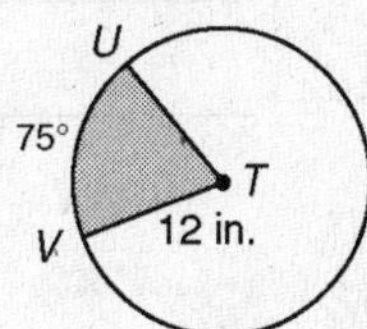

sector *UTV* ______________

3.
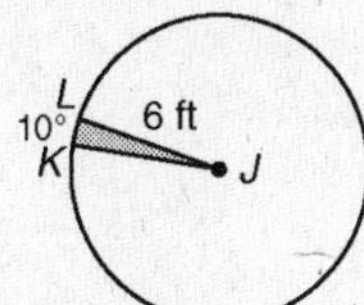

sector *KJL* ______________

4.
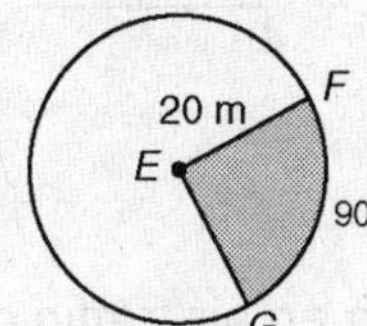

sector *FEG* ______________

5. The speedometer needle in Ignacio's car is 2 inches long. The needle sweeps out a 130° sector during acceleration from 0 to 60 mi/h. Find the area of this sector. Round to the nearest hundredth. ______________

Find the area of each segment to the nearest hundredth.

6.
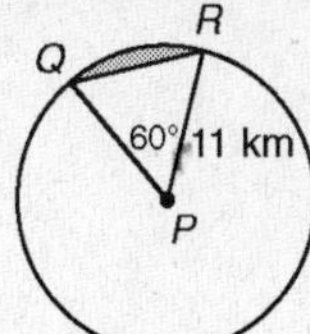

____

7.
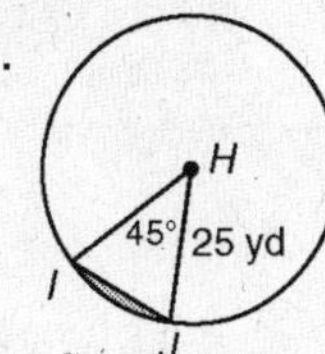

____

8.
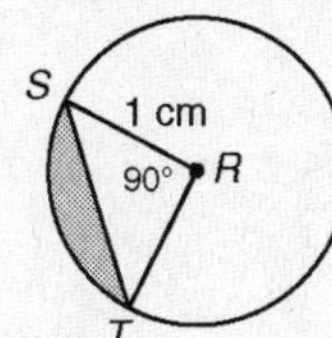

____

9.
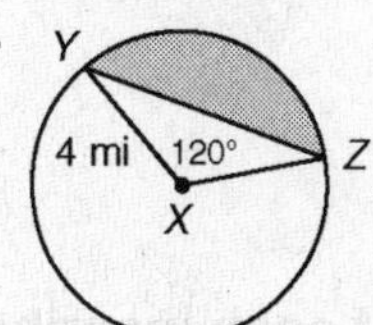

____

Find each arc length. Give your answer in terms of π and rounded to the nearest hundredth.

10.
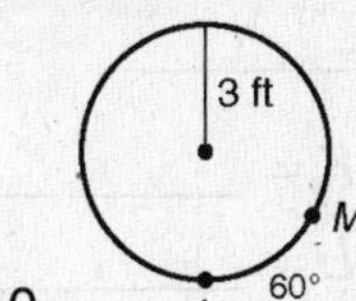

____

11.
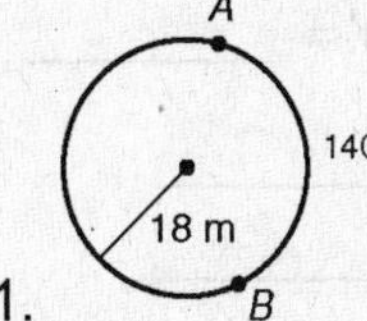

____

12. an arc with measure 45° in a circle with radius 2 mi ______________

13. an arc with measure 120° in a circle with radius 15 mm ______________

Name ______________________ Date ______________ Class ______________

LESSON 12-4

Practice

Inscribed Angles

Find each measure.

1. m∠*CED* = ________ m$\widehat{DEA}$ = ________

2. m∠*FGI* = ________ m$\widehat{GH}$ = ________

3. m$\widehat{QRS}$ = ________ m$\widehat{TSR}$ = ________

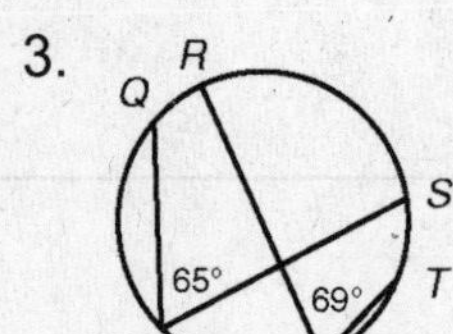

4. m∠*XVU* = ________ m∠*VXW* = ________

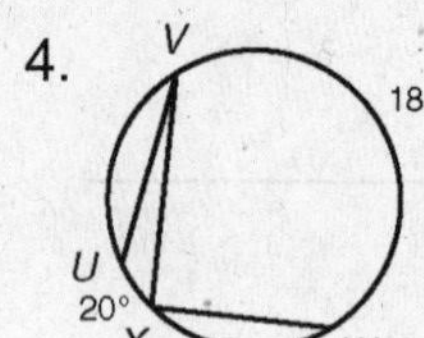

5. A circular radar screen in an air traffic control tower shows these flight paths. Find m∠*LNK*. ________

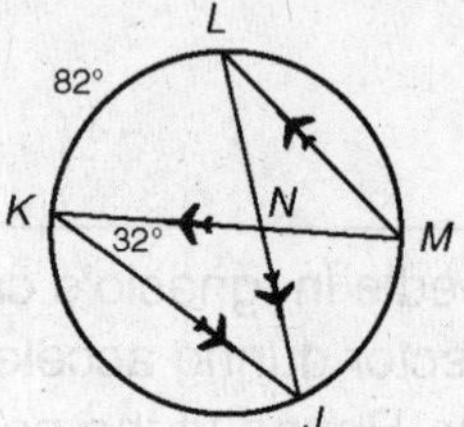

Find each value.

6.

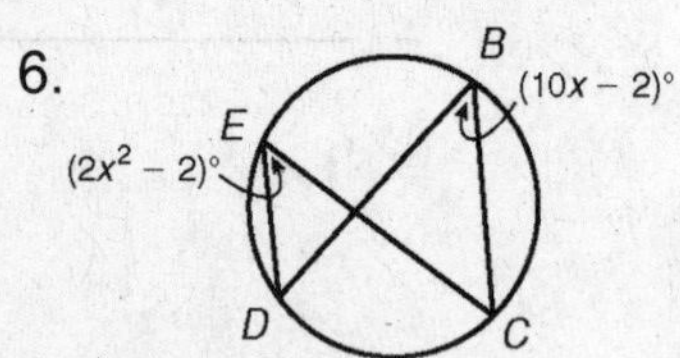

m∠*CED* = ________

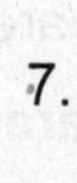

7.

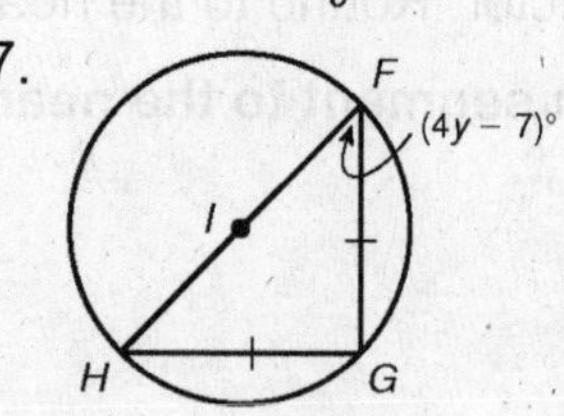

y = ________

8. *a* = ________

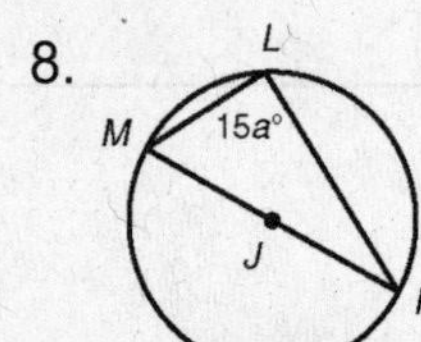

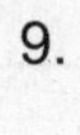

9. m∠*SRT* = ________

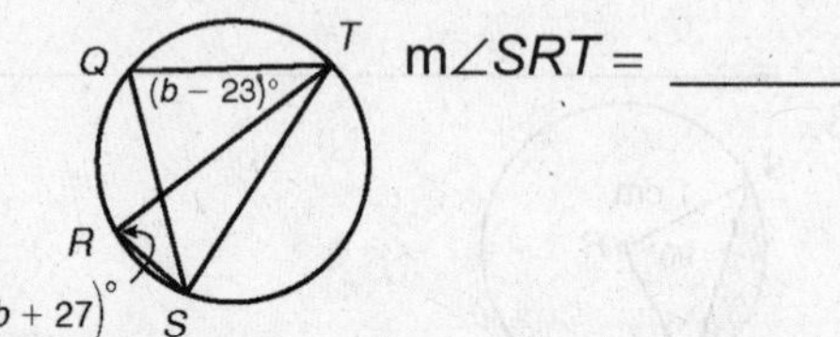

Find the angle measures of each inscribed quadrilateral.

10. m∠*X* = ________ m∠*Y* = ________ m∠*Z* = ________ m∠*W* = ________

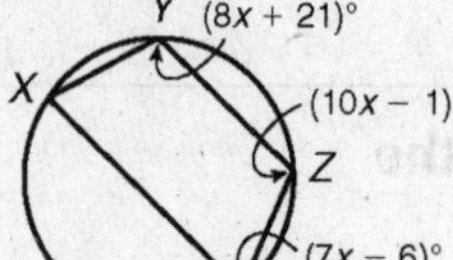

11. m∠*C* = ________ m∠*D* = ________ m∠*E* = ________ m∠*F* = ________

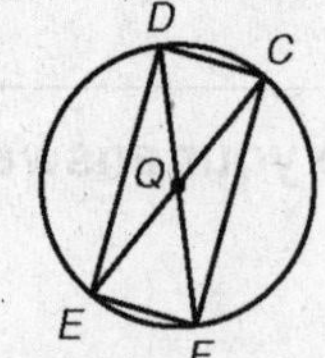

12. m∠*T* = ________ m∠*U* = ________ m∠*V* = ________ m∠*W* = ________

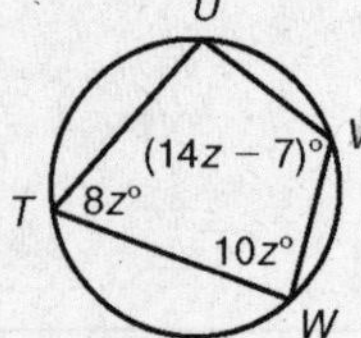

13. m∠*K* = ________ m∠*L* = ________ m∠*M* = ________ m∠*N* = ________

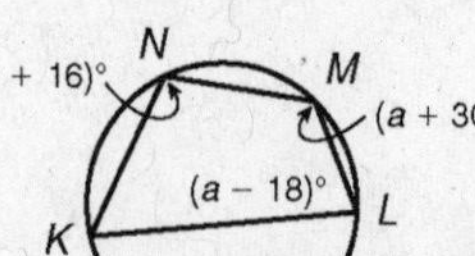

Name ______________________ Date ______________ Class ______________

LESSON 12-5

Practice

Angle Relationships in Circles

Find each measure.

1.
128° E D A 68° B C

$m\angle ABE$ = ________

$m\widehat{BC}$ = ________

2. 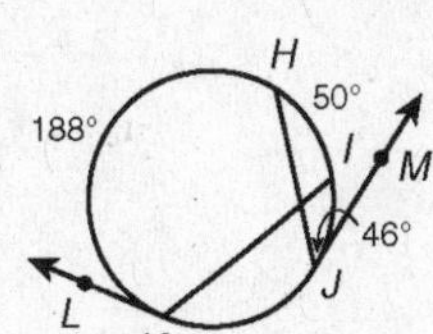

$m\angle LKI$ = ________

$m\widehat{IJ}$ = ________

3.
59° Q T P S R 201°

$m\angle RPS$ = ________

4. 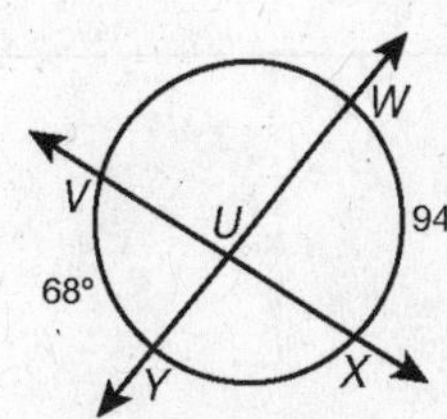

$m\angle YUX$ = ________

Find the value of *x*.

5. 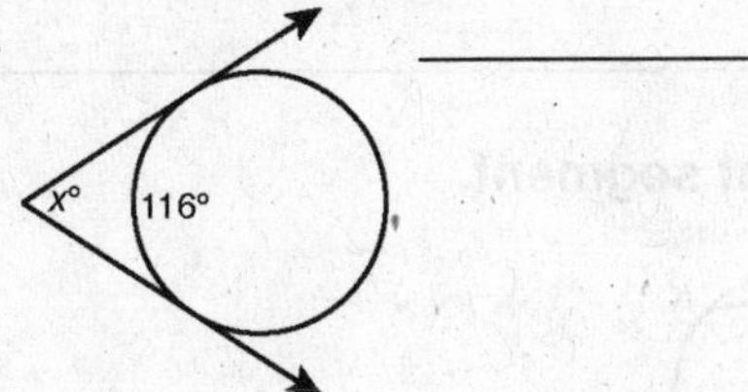

____

6. 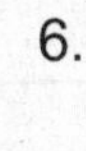 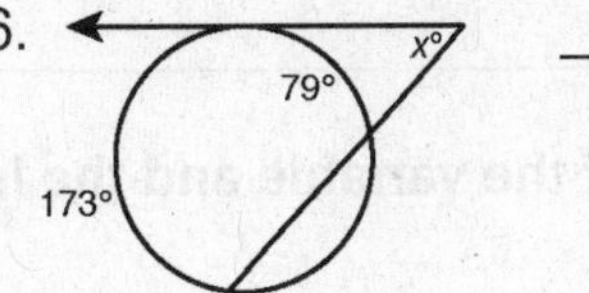

____

7. 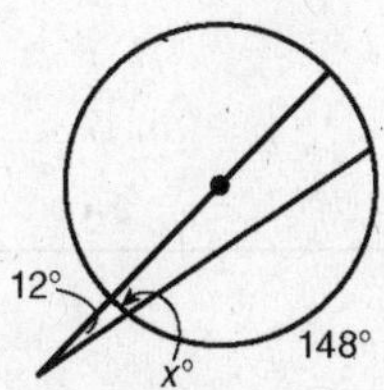

____

8. 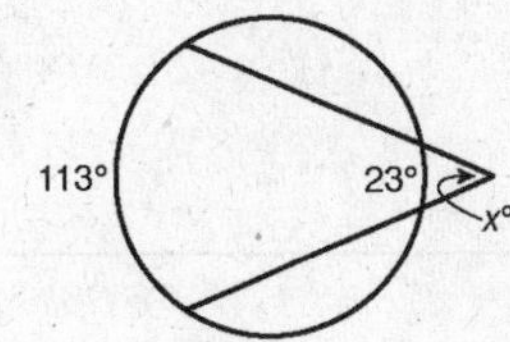

____

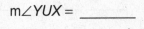

9. The figure shows a spinning wheel. The large wheel is turned by hand or with a foot trundle. A belt attaches to a small bobbin that turns very quickly. The bobbin twists raw materials into thread, twine, or yarn. Each pair of spokes intercepts a 30° arc. Find the value of *x*.

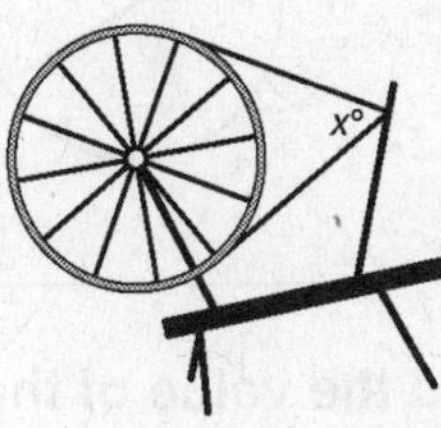

____

Find each measure.

10. 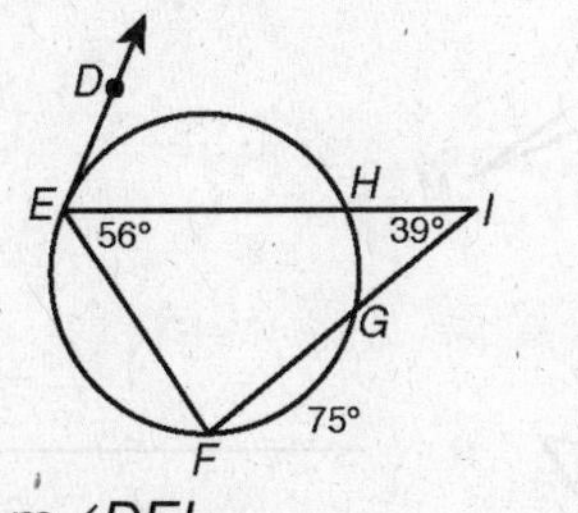

$m\angle DEI$ = ________

$m\widehat{EF}$ = ________

11. 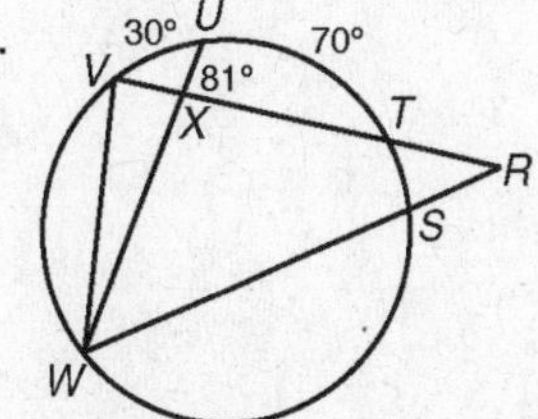

$m\angle WVR$ = ________

$m\widehat{TUW}$ = ________

Name ______________________ Date ______________ Class ______________

LESSON 12-6

Practice

Segment Relationships in Circles

Find the value of the variable and the length of each chord.

1.

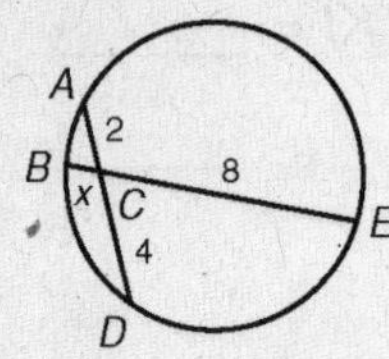

2.

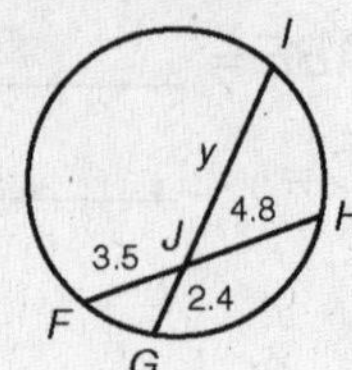

3.

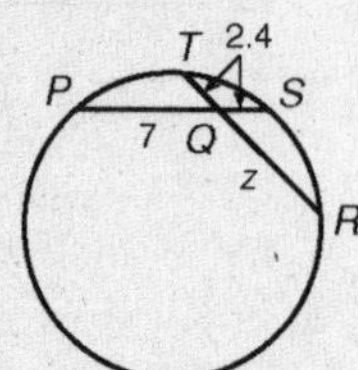

4.

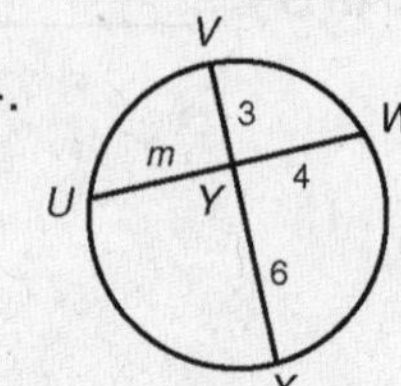

Find the value of the variable and the length of each secant segment.

5.

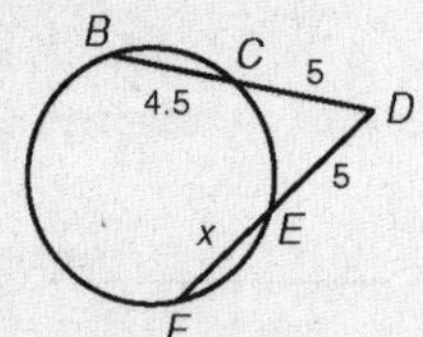

6.

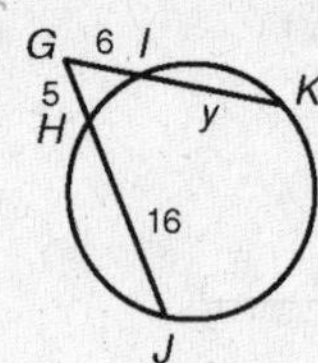

7.

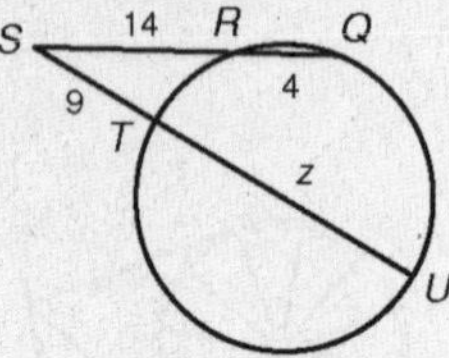

8.

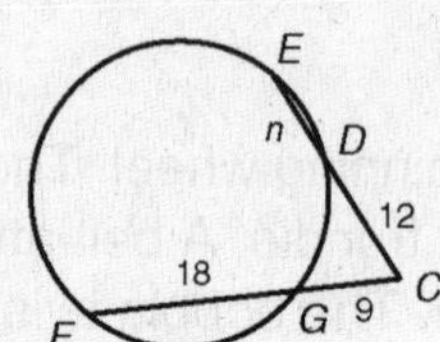

Find the value of the variable. Give answers in simplest radical form if necessary.

9.

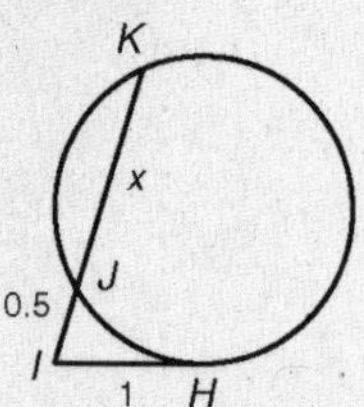

____

10.

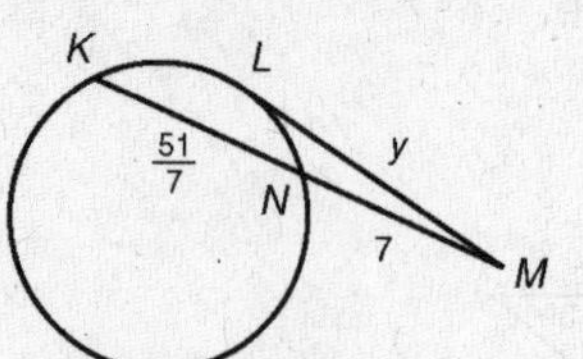

____

11.

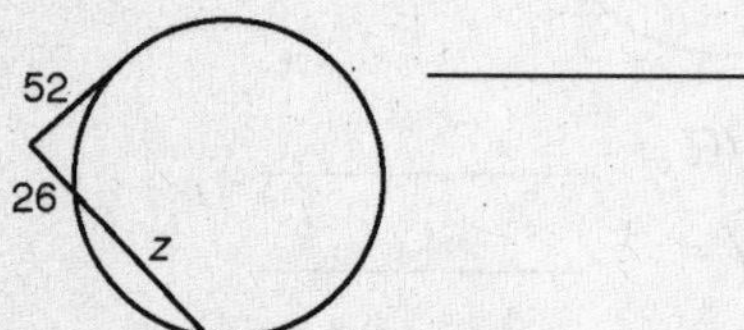

____

12.

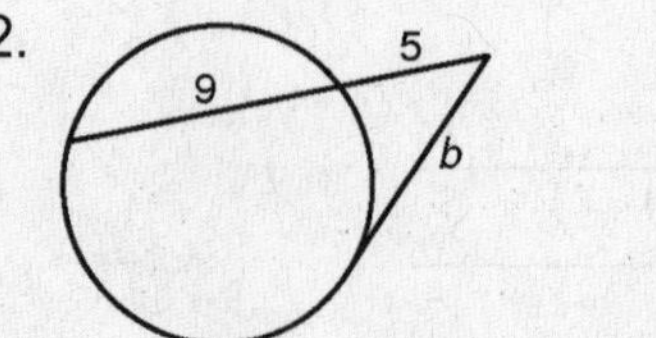

____

Name ______________________ Date ______________ Class ______________

LESSON 12-7

Practice

Circles in the Coordinate Plane

Write the equation of each circle.

1. $\odot X$ centered at the origin with radius 10 ________________
2. $\odot R$ with center $R(-1, 8)$ and radius 5 ________________
3. $\odot P$ with center $P(-5, -5)$ and radius $2\sqrt{5}$ ________________
4. $\odot O$ centered at the origin that passes through $(9, -2)$ ________________
5. $\odot B$ with center $B(0, -2)$ that passes through $(-6, 0)$ ________________
6. $\odot F$ with center $F(11, 4)$ that passes through $(-2, 5)$. ________________

Graph each equation.

7. $x^2 + y^2 = 25$

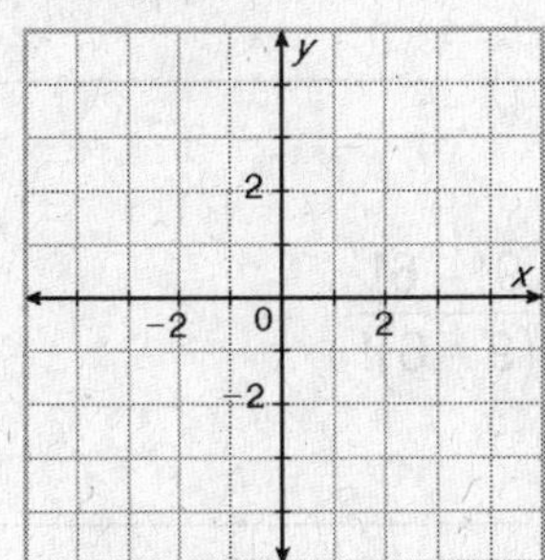

8. $(x + 2)^2 + (y - 1)^2 = 4$

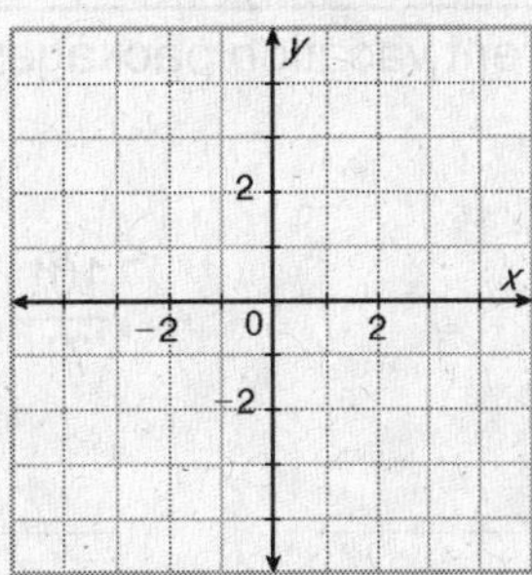

9. $x^2 + (y + 3)^2 = 1$

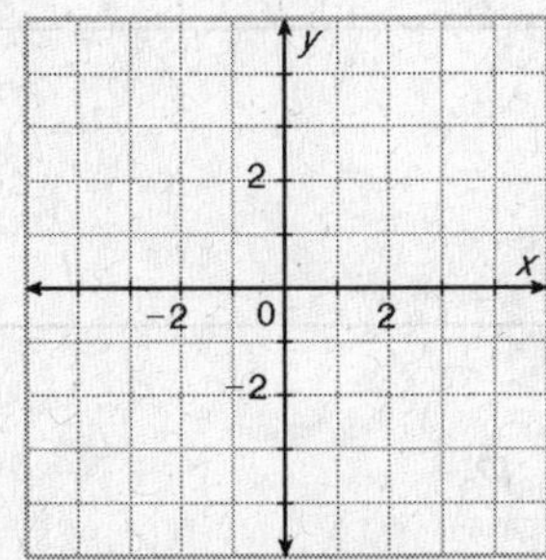

10. $(x - 1)^2 + (y - 1)^2 = 16$

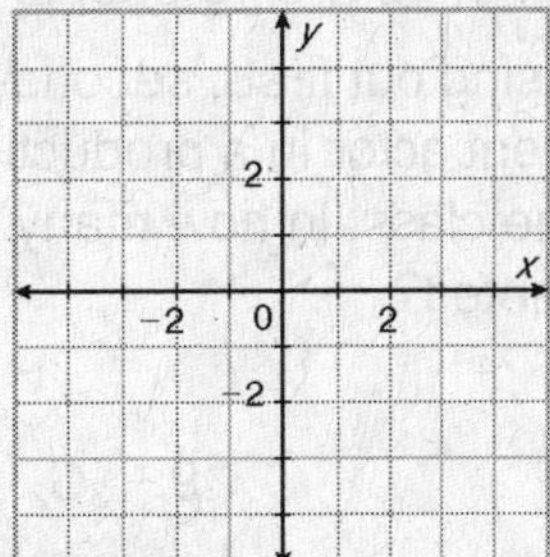

Crater Lake in Oregon is a roughly circular lake. The lake basin formed about 7000 years ago when the top of a volcano exploded in an immense explosion. Hillman Peak, Garfield Peak, and Cloudcap are three mountain peaks on the rim of the lake. The peaks are located in a coordinate plane at *H*(−4, 1), *G*(−2, −3), and *C*(5, −2).

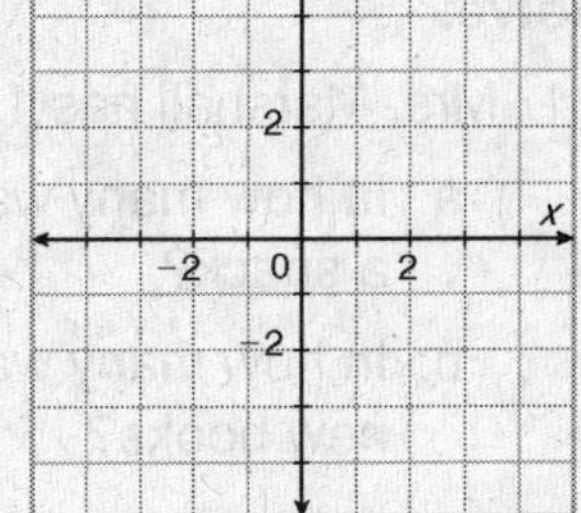

11. Find the coordinates of the center of the lake.

____

12. Each unit of the coordinate plane represents $\frac{3}{5}$ mile.

Find the diameter of the lake. ________________

Name ______________________ Date ______________ Class ______________

LESSON 13-1

Practice

Permutations and Combinations

Use the Fundamental Counting Principle.

1. The soccer team is silk-screening T-shirts. They have 4 different colors of T-shirts and 2 different colors of ink. How many different T-shirts can be made using one ink color on a T-shirt? ____________

2. A travel agent is offering a vacation package. Participants choose the type of tour, a meal plan, and a hotel class from the table below.

Tour	Meal	Hotel
Walking	Restaurant	4-Star
Boat	Picnic	3-Star
Bicycle		2-Star
		1-Star

How many different vacation packages are offered? ____________

Evaluate.

3. $\frac{3!6!}{3!}$ ____________

4. $\frac{10!}{7!}$ ____________

5. $\frac{9!-6!}{(9-6)!}$ ____________

Solve.

6. In how many ways can the debate team choose a president and a secretary if there are 10 people on the team? ____________

7. A teacher is passing out first-, second-, and third-place prizes for the best student actor in a production of *Hamlet*. If there are 14 students in the class, in how many different ways can the awards be presented? ____________

Evaluate.

8. ${}_5P_4$ ____________

9. ${}_3C_2$ ____________

10. ${}_8P_3$ ____________

Solve.

11. Mrs. Marshall has 11 boys and 14 girls in her kindergarten class this year.

   a. In how many ways can she select 2 girls to pass out a snack? ____________

   b. In how many ways can she select 5 boys to pass out new books? ____________

   c. In how many ways can she select 3 students to carry papers to the office? ____________

Name ________________ Date ____________ Class ____________

LESSON 13-2

Practice

Theoretical and Experimental Probability

Solve.

1. A fruit bowl contains 4 green apples and 7 red apples. What is the probability that a randomly selected apple will be green? ________

2. When two number cubes labeled 1–6 are rolled, what is the probability that the result will be two 4's? ________

3. Joanne is guessing which day in November is Bess's birthday. Joanne knows that Bess's birthday does not fall on an odd-numbered day. What is the probability that Joanne will guess the correct day on her first try? ________

4. Tom has a dollar's worth of dimes and a dollar's worth of nickels in his pocket.

   a. What is the probability he will randomly select a nickel from his pocket? ________

   b. What is the probability he will randomly select a dime from his pocket? ________

5. Clarice has 7 new CDs; 3 are classical music and the rest are pop music. If she randomly grabs 3 CDs to listen to in the car on her way to school, what is the probability that she will select only classical music? ________

6. Find the probability that a point chosen at random inside the larger circle shown here will also fall inside the smaller circle.

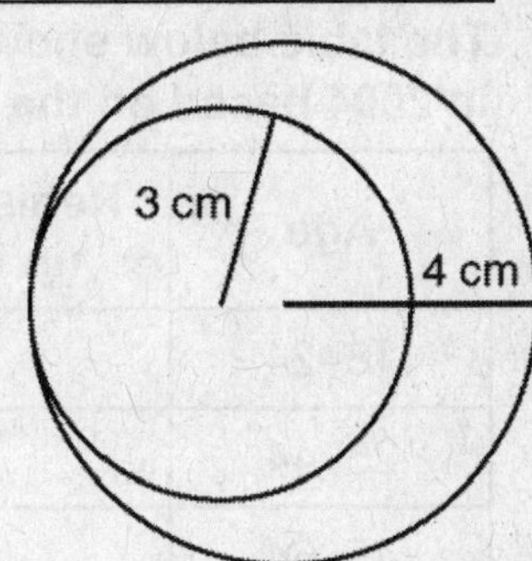

____

Frank is playing darts. The results of his throws are shown in the table below. Assume that his results continue to follow this trend.

Color Hit	Number of Throws
Blue	12
Red	5
White	2

Find the experimental probability of each event.

7. Frank's next throw will hit white. ________

8. Frank's next throw will hit blue. ________

9. Frank's next throw will hit either red or white. ________

10. Frank's next throw will NOT hit red. ________

Name ______________________ Date ______________ Class ______________

LESSON 13-3

Practice

Independent and Dependent Events

Find each probability.

1. A bag contains 5 red, 3 green, 4 blue, and 8 yellow marbles. Find the probability of randomly selecting a green marble, and then a yellow marble if the first marble is replaced. ______________
2. A sock drawer contains 5 rolled-up pairs of each color of socks, white, green, and blue. What is the probability of randomly selecting a pair of blue socks, replacing it, and then randomly selecting a pair of white socks? ______________

Two 1–6 number cubes are rolled—one is black and one is white.

3. The sum of the rolls is greater than or equal to 6 and the black cube shows a 3.
   a. Explain why the events are dependent.
   ____
   b. Find the probability. ______________
4. The white cube shows an even number, and the sum is 8.
   a. Explain why the events are dependent.
   ____
   b. Find the probability. . ______________

The table below shows numbers of registered voters by age in the United States in 2004 based on the census. Find each probability in decimal form.

Age	Registered Voters (in thousands)	Not Registered to Vote (in thousands)
18–24	14,334	13,474
25–44	49,371	32,763
45–64	51,659	19,355
65 and over	26,706	8,033

5. A randomly selected person is registered to vote, given that the person is between the ages of 18 and 24. ______________
6. A randomly selected person is between the ages of 45 and 64 and is not registered to vote. ______________
7. A randomly selected person is registered to vote and is at least 65 years old. ______________

A bag contains 12 blue cubes, 12 red cubes, and 20 green cubes. Determine whether the events are independent or dependent, and find each probability.

8. A green cube and then a blue cube are chosen at random with replacement. ______________
9. Two blue cubes are chosen at random without replacement. ______________

Name ______________________ Date ______________ Class ______________

LESSON 13-4

Practice

Two-Way Tables

1. The table shows the results of a customer satisfaction survey of 100 randomly selected shoppers at the mall who were asked if they would shop at an earlier time if the mall opened earlier. Make a table of joint and marginal relative frequencies.

	Ages 10–20	Ages 21–45	Ages 46–65	65 and Older
Yes	13	2	8	24
No	25	10	15	3

	Ages 10–20	Ages 21–45	Ages 46–65	65 and Older	Total
Yes					
No					
Total					

2. Jerrod collected data on 100 randomly selected students, and summarized the results in a table.

Owns a Smart phone		Owns an MP3 Player: Yes	No
	Yes	28	12
	No	34	26

a. Make a table of the joint relative frequencies and marginal relative frequencies. Round to the nearest hundredth where appropriate.

Owns a Smart Phone		Owns an MP3 player: Yes	No	Total
	Yes			
	No			
	Total			

b. If you are given that a student owns an MP3 player, what is the probability that the student also owns a smart phone? Round your answer to the nearest hundredth.

____

c. If you are given that a student owns a smart phone, what is the probability that the student also owns an MP3 player? Round your answer to the nearest hundredth.

____

Name ________________________ Date ______________ Class ______________

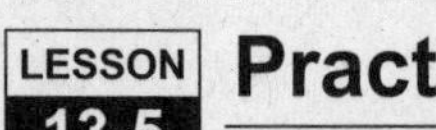

Practice

Compound Events

A can of vegetables with no label has a $\frac{1}{8}$ chance of being green beans and a $\frac{1}{5}$ chance of being corn.

1. Explain why the events “green beans” or “corn” are mutually exclusive.

____

2. What is the probability that an unlabeled can of vegetables is either green beans or corn? ______________

Ben rolls a 1–6 number cube. Find each probability.

3. Ben rolls a 3 or a 4. ______________

4. Ben rolls a number greater than 2 or an even number. ______________

5. Ben rolls a prime number or an odd number. ______________

Of the 400 doctors who attended a conference, 240 practiced family medicine and 130 were from countries outside the United States. One-third of the family medicine practitioners were not from the United States.

6. What is the probability that a doctor practices family medicine or is from the United States? ______________

7. What is the probability that a doctor practices family medicine or is not from the United States? ______________

8. What is the probability that a doctor does not practice family medicine or is from the United States? ______________

Use the data to fill in the Venn diagram. Then solve.

9. Of the 220 people who came into the Italian deli on Friday, 104 bought pizza and 82 used a credit card. Half of the people who bought pizza used a credit card. What is the probability that a customer bought pizza or used a credit card?

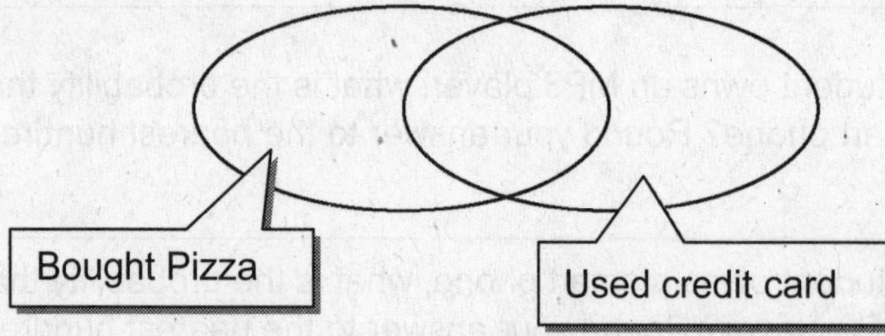

____

Solve.

10. There are 6 people in a gardening club. Each gardener orders seeds from a list of 11 different types of seeds available. What is the probability that 2 gardeners will order the same type of seeds? ______________

Name ______________________ Date ______________ Class ______________

LESSON 1-1

Problem Solving

Understanding Points, Lines, and Planes

Use the map of part of San Antonio for Exercises 1 and 2.

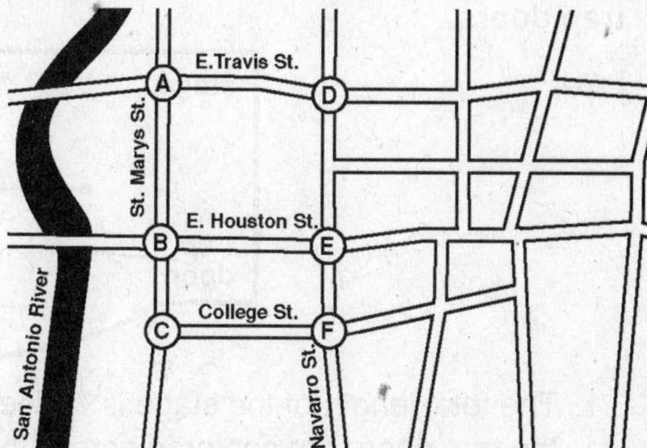

1. Name a point that appears to be collinear with $\overline{EF}$. Which streets intersect at this point?

____

____

2. Explain why point *A* is NOT collinear with $\overline{BE}$.

____

____

3. Suppose $\overline{UV}$ represents the pencil that you are using to do your homework and plane P represents the paper that you are writing on. Describe the relationship between $\overline{UV}$ and plane P.

____

____

4. Two cyclists start at the same point, but travel along two straight streets in different directions. If they continue, how many times will their paths cross again? Explain.

____

____

Choose the best answer.

5. In a building, planes W, X, and Y represent each of the three floors; planes Q and R represent the front and back of the building; planes S and T represent the sides. Which is a true statement?

   A Planes W and Y intersect in a line.

   B Planes Q and X intersect in a line.

   C Planes W, X, and T intersect in a point.

   D Planes Q, R, and S intersect in a point.

6. Suppose point *G* represents a duck flying over a lake, points *H* and *J* represent two ducks swimming on the lake, and plane L represents the lake. Which is a true statement?

   F There are two lines through *G* and *J*.

   G The line containing *G* and *H* lies in plane L.

   H *G*, *H*, and *J* are noncoplanar.

   J There is exactly one plane containing points *G*, *H*, and *J*.

Use the figure for Exercise 7.

7. A frame holding two pictures sits on a table. Which is NOT a true statement?

   A $\overline{PN}$ and $\overline{NM}$ lie in plane T.

   B $\overline{PN}$ and $\overline{NM}$ intersect in a point.

   C $\overline{LM}$ and *N* intersect in a line.

   D *P* and $\overline{NM}$ are coplanar.

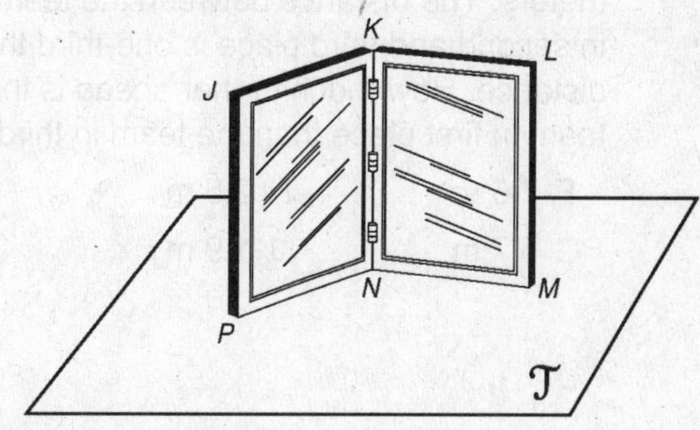

Name ________________ Date ____________ Class ____________

LESSON 1-2

Problem Solving

Measuring and Constructing Segments

For Exercises 1 and 2, use the figure. It shows the top view of a stage that has three trap doors.

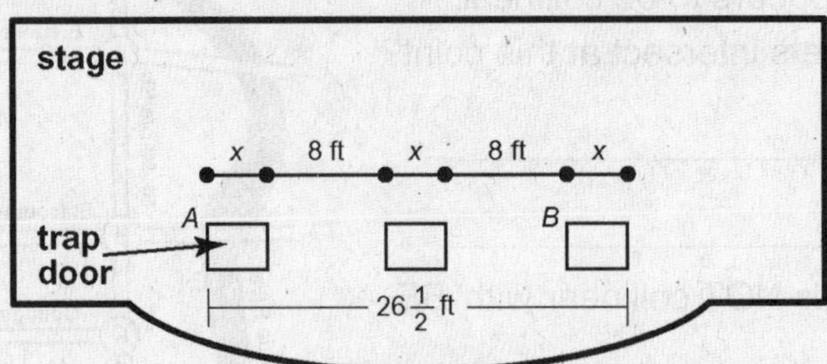

1. The total length of the stage is 76 feet. If the trap doors are centered across the stage, what is the distance from the left side of the stage to the first trap door?

____

2. An actor starts at point *A*, walks across the stage, and then stops at point *B* before disappearing through the trap door. How far does he walk across the stage?

____

3. Anna is 26 feet high on a rock-climbing wall. She descends to the 15-foot mark, rests, and then climbs down until she reaches her friend, who is 8 feet from the ground. How many feet has Anna descended?

____

4. Jamilla has a piece of ribbon that is 48.5 centimeters long. For her scrapbook, she cuts it into two pieces so that one piece is 4 times as long as the other. What are the lengths of the pieces?

____

Choose the best answer.

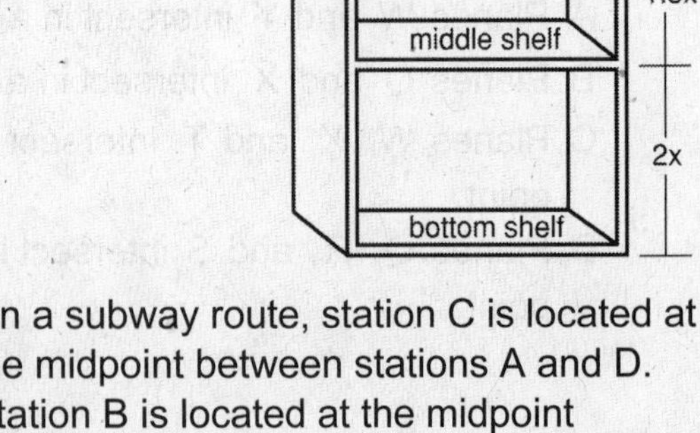

5. Jordan wants to adjust the shelves in his bookcase so that there is twice as much space on the bottom shelf as on the top shelf, and one and a half times more space on the middle shelf as on the top shelf. If the total height of the bookcase is 0.9 meter, how much space is the middle shelf on?

   A 0.2 m C 0.4 m

   B 0.3 m D 0.5 m

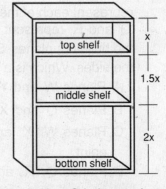

6. In a rowing race, the distance between the teams in first and second place is 5.7 meters. The distance between the teams in second and third place is one-third that distance. How much farther ahead is the team in first place than the team in third?

   F 7.6 m H 2.5 m

   G 5.7 m J 1.9 m

7. On a subway route, station C is located at the midpoint between stations A and D. Station B is located at the midpoint between stations A and C. If the distance between stations A and D is 2.4 kilometers, what is the distance between stations B and D?

   A 0.3 km C 1.2 km

   B 0.6 km D 1.8 km

Name ______________________ Date ______________ Class ______________

LESSON 1-3

Problem Solving

Measuring and Constructing Angles

Projection drawings are often used to represent three-dimensional molecules. The projection drawing of a methane molecule is shown below, along with the angles that are formed in the drawing.

Methane Molecule

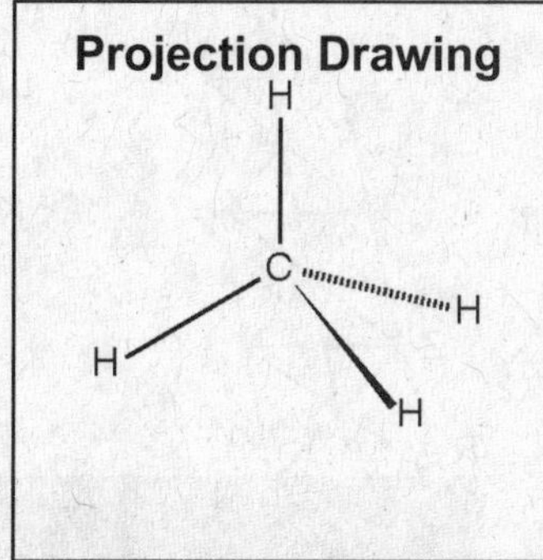

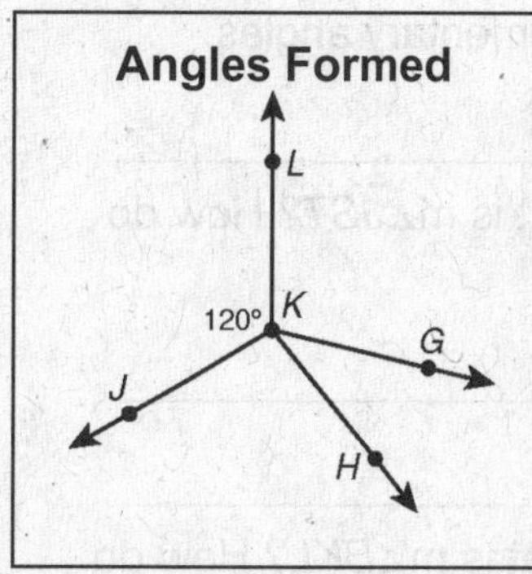

1. Name five different angles that are formed in the drawing.

____

2. If $m\angle LKH = m\angle JKL + 20°$ and $m\angle HKG = 37°$, what is $m\angle GKL$? ______________

3. Find $m\angle JKH$. ______________

The figure shows the proper way to sit at a computer to avoid straining your back or eyes. Use the figure for Exercises 4 and 5.

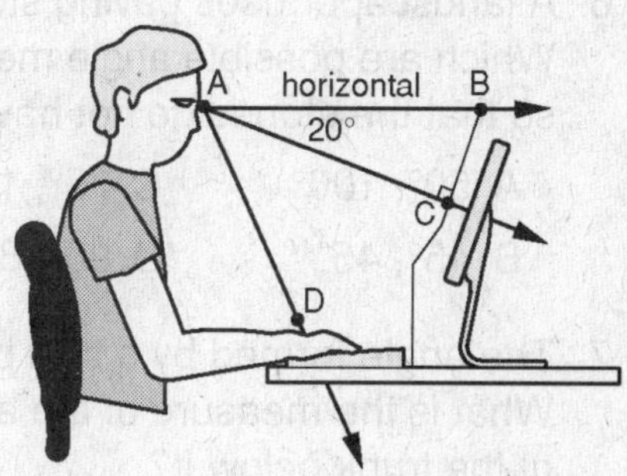

4. The *total viewing angle* is $\angle DAB$. If $m\angle DAC = \frac{1}{2}(m\angle ACB)$, what is the measure of the total viewing angle?

____

5. The *optimum viewing angle* is 38° below the horizontal. If $\overrightarrow{AV}$ is drawn to form this angle with $\overrightarrow{AB}$ and $\angle DAB$ measures 65°, what is the measure of $\angle DAV$?

____

Choose the best answer.

6. $\overrightarrow{QR}$ is in the interior of obtuse $\angle PQS$, and $\angle PQR$ is a right angle. Classify $\angle SQR$.

   A acute   B right   C obtuse   D straight

7. $\overrightarrow{VX}$ bisect $\angle WVY$, $m\angle WVX = (6x)°$, and $m\angle WVY = (16x - 42)°$. What is the value of x?

   F $\frac{21}{11}$ G $\frac{42}{13}$ H 4.2   J 10.5

Name ______________________ Date ______________ Class ______________

LESSON 1-4

Problem Solving

Pairs of Angles

Use the drawing of part of the Eiffel Tower for Exercises 1–5.

1. Name a pair of angles that appear to be complementary.

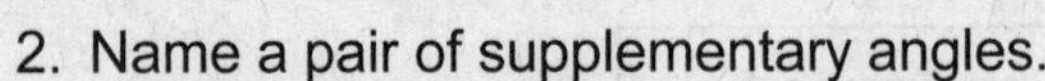

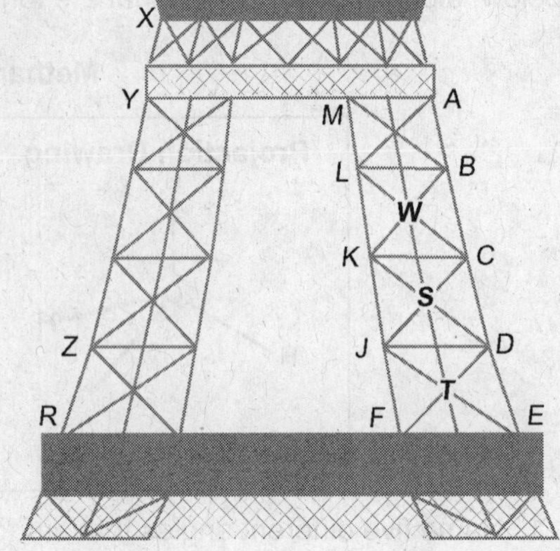

2. Name a pair of supplementary angles.

____

3. If m∠*CSW* = 45°, what is m∠*JST*? How do you know?

____

____

4. If m∠*FKB* = 135°, what is m∠*BKL*? How do you know?

____

____

5. Name three angles whose measures sum to 180°.

____

Choose the best answer.

6. A landscaper uses paving stones for a walkway. Which are possible angle measures for *a*° and *b*° so that the stones do not have space between them?

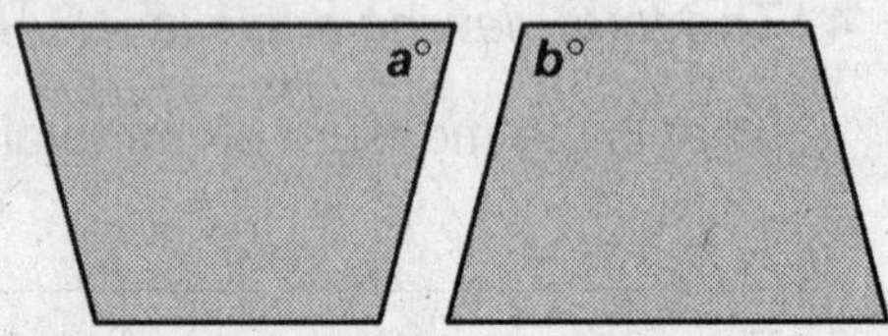

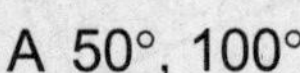

A 50°, 100°   C 75°, 105°

B 45°, 45°   D 90°, 80°

7. The angle formed by a tree branch and the part of the trunk above it is 68°. What is the measure of the angle that is formed by the branch and the part of the trunk below it?

F 22°   H 158°

G 112°   J 180°

8. ∠*R* and ∠*S* are complementary. If m∠*R* = $(7 + 3x)°$ and m∠*S* = $(2x + 13)°$, which is a true statement?

A ∠*R* is acute.   C ∠*R* and ∠*S* are right angles.

B ∠*R* is obtuse.   D m∠*S* > m∠*R*

Name ______________________ Date ______________ Class ______________

LESSON 1-5

Problem Solving

Using Formulas in Geometry

Use the table for Exercises 1–6.

Figure	Perimeter or Circumference	Area
rectangle	$P = 2\ell + 2w$ or $2(\ell + w)$	$A = \ell w$
triangle	$P = a + b + c$	$A = \frac{1}{2}bh$
circle	$C = 2\pi r$	$A = \pi r^2$

Use the diagram of a hockey field for Exercises 1–4.

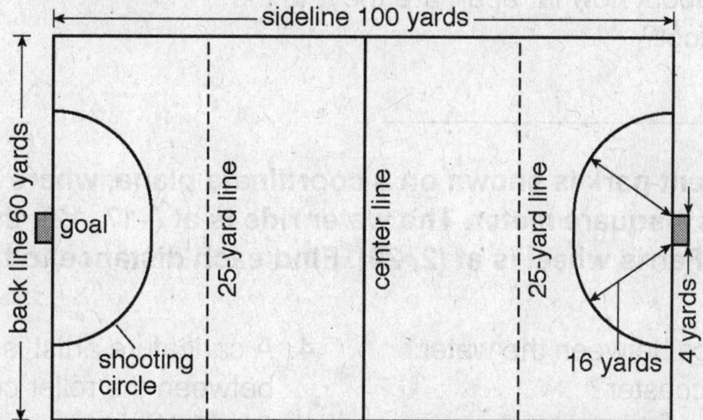

1. What is the perimeter of the field?

____

2. What is the area of the field?

____

3. What is the area of each of the shooting circles? Use 3.14 for π.

____

4. What is the area of the field between the two 25-yard lines?

____

Choose the best answer.

5. A rectangular counter 3 feet wide and 5 feet long has a circle cut out of it in order to have a sink installed. The circle has a diameter of 18 inches. What is the approximate area of the remaining countertop surface? Use 3.14 for π.

   A 13.2 ft^2 C 18.9 ft^2

   B 15.0 ft^2 D 29.5 ft^2

6. The base of a triangular garden measures 5.5 feet. Its height is 3 feet. If 4 pounds of mulch are needed to cover a square foot, how many pounds of mulch will be needed to cover the garden?

   F 8.25 lb H 16.5 lb

   G 33 lb J 66 lb

Name ______________________ Date ______________ Class ______________

LESSON 1-6

Problem Solving

Midpoint and Distance in the Coordinate Plane

For Exercises 1 and 2, use the diagram of a tennis court.

1. A singles tennis court is a rectangle 27 feet wide and 78 feet long. Suppose a player at corner *A* hits the ball to her opponent in the diagonally opposite corner *B*. Approximately how far does the ball travel, to the nearest tenth of a foot?

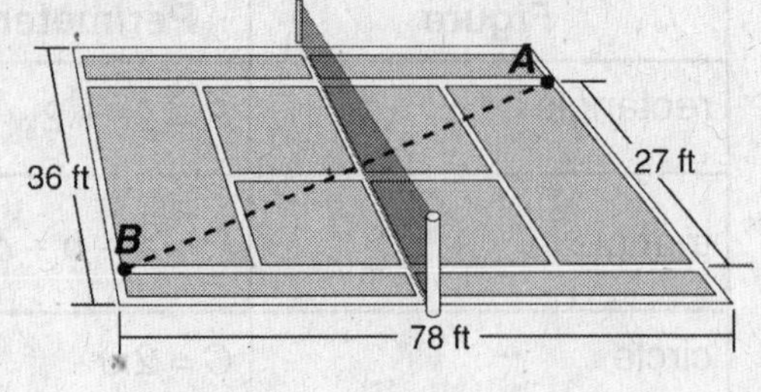

____

2. A doubles tennis court is a rectangle 36 feet wide and 78 feet long. If two players are standing in diagonally opposite corners, about how far apart are they, to the nearest tenth of a foot?

____

A map of an amusement park is shown on a coordinate plane, where each square of the grid represents 1 square meter. The water ride is at (–17, 12), the roller coaster is at (26, –8), and the Ferris wheel is at (2, 20). Find each distance to the nearest tenth of a meter.

3. What is the distance between the water ride and the roller coaster?

____

4. A caricature artist is at the midpoint between the roller coaster and the Ferris wheel. What is the distance from the artist to the Ferris wheel?

____

Use the map of the Sacramento Zoo on a coordinate plane for Exercises 5–7. Choose the best answer.

Sacramento Zoo

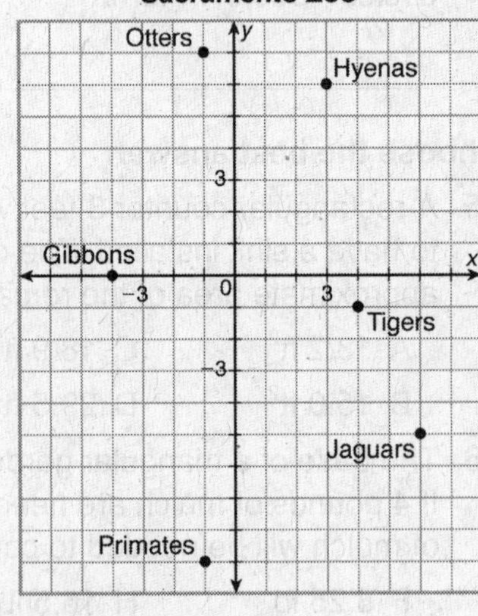

5. To the nearest tenth of a unit, how far is it from the tigers to the hyenas?

   A 5.1 units C 9.9 units

   B 7.1 units D 50.0 units

6. Between which of these exhibits is the distance the least?

   F tigers and primates

   G hyenas and gibbons

   H otters and gibbons

   J tigers and otters

7. Suppose you walk straight from the jaguars to the tigers and then to the otters. What is the total distance to the nearest tenth of a unit?

   A 11.4 units C 13.9 units

   B 13.0 units D 14.2 units

Name ______________________ Date ______________ Class ______________

LESSON 1-7

Problem Solving

Transformations in the Coordinate Plane

Use the diagram of the starting positions of five basketball players for Exercises 1 and 2.

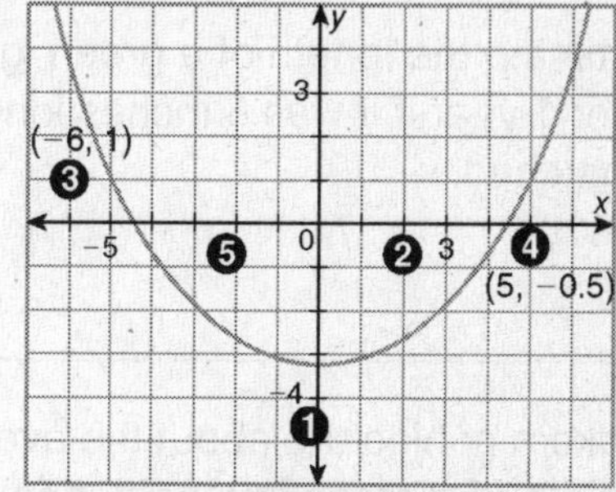

1. After the first step of a play, player 3 is at (−1.5, 0) and player 4 is at (1, 0.5). Write a rule to describe the translations of players 3 and 4 from their starting positions to their new positions.

____

____

2. For the second step of the play, player 3 is to move to a position described by the rule $(x, y) \rightarrow (x - 4, y - 2)$ and player 4 is to move to a position described by the rule $(x, y) \rightarrow (x + 3, y - 2)$. What are the positions of these two players after this step of the play?

____

Use the diagram for Exercises 3–5.

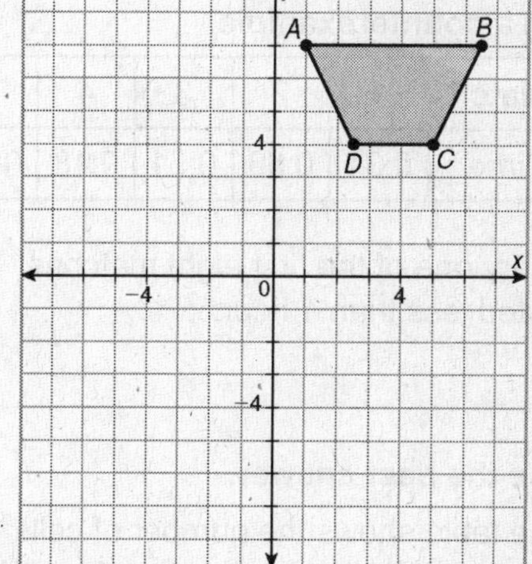

3. Find the coordinates of the image of *ABCD* after it is moved 6 units left and 2 units up.

____

4. The original image is moved so that its new coordinates are $A'(-1, 7)$, $B'(-6\frac{1}{2}, 7)$, $C'(-5, 4)$, and $D'(-2\frac{1}{2}, 4)$. Identify the transformation.

____

5. The original image is translated so that the coordinates of B' are $(11\frac{1}{2}, 17)$. What are the coordinates of the other three vertices of the image after this translation?

____

6. Triangle *HJK* has vertices $H(0, -9)$, $J(-1, -5)$, and $K(7, 8)$. What are the coordinates of the vertices after the translation $(x, y) \rightarrow (x - 1, y - 3)$?

   A $H'(-1, 12)$, $J'(-2, 8)$, $K'(6, -5)$
   C $H'(-1, -12)$, $J'(-2, -8)$, $K'(6, 5)$
   B $H'(1, -12)$, $J'(2, -8)$, $K'(-6, 5)$
   D $H'(1, 12)$, $J'(2, 8)$, $K'(-6, -5)$

7. A segment has endpoints at $S(2, 3)$ and $T(-2, 8)$. After a transformation, the image has endpoints at $S'(2, 3)$ and $T'(6, 8)$. Which best describes the transformation?

   F reflection across the *y*-axis
   H rotation about the origin
   G translation $(x, y) \rightarrow (x + 8, y)$
   J rotation about the point (2, 3)

Name _______________ Date _______________ Class _______________

LESSON 2-1

Problem Solving

Using Inductive Reasoning to Make Conjectures

The table shows the lengths of five green iguanas after birth and then after 1 year.

Iguana	Length after Hatching (in.)	Length after 1 Year (in.)
1	10	36
2	9	34
3	11	35
4	12	35
5	10	37

1. Estimate the length of a green iguana after 1 year if it was 8 inches long when it hatched.

____

2. Make a conjecture about the average growth of a green iguana during the first year.

____

The times for the first eight matches of the Santa Barbara Open women's volleyball tournament are shown. Show that each conjecture is false by finding a counterexample.

Match	1	2	3	4	5	6	7	8
Time	0:31	0:56	0:51	0:18	0:50	0:34	1:03	0:36

3. Every one of the first eight matches lasted less than 1 hour.

____

4. These matches were all longer than a half hour.

____

Choose the best answer.

Sample	Number of Cells		
	Interphase	Prophase	Metaphase
1	86	22	5
2	70	28	3
3	76	32	3
4	91	25	5
5	65	16	4
6	89	34	6

5. The table shows the number of cells present during three phases of mitosis. If a sample contained 80 cells during interphase, which is the best prediction for the number of cells present during prophase?

   A 18 cells C 40 cells
   B 24 cells D 80 cells

6. About 75% of the students at Jackson High School volunteer to clean up a half-mile stretch of road every year. If there are 408 students in the school this year, about how many are expected to volunteer for the clean-up?

   F 102 students H 306 students
   G 204 students J 333 students

7. Mara earned \$25, \$25, \$20, and \$28 in the last 4 weeks for walking her neighbor's dogs. If her earnings continue in this way, which is the best estimate for her average weekly earnings for next month?

   A \$20.50 C \$24.50
   B \$23.33 D \$25.00

Name ______________________ Date ______________ Class ______________

LESSON 2-2

Problem Solving

Conditional Statements

1. Write the converse, inverse, and contrapositive of the conditional statement. Find the truth value of each.

If it is April, then there are 30 days in the month.

____

____

____

2. Write a conditional statement from the diagram. Then write the converse, inverse, and contrapositive. Find the truth value of each.

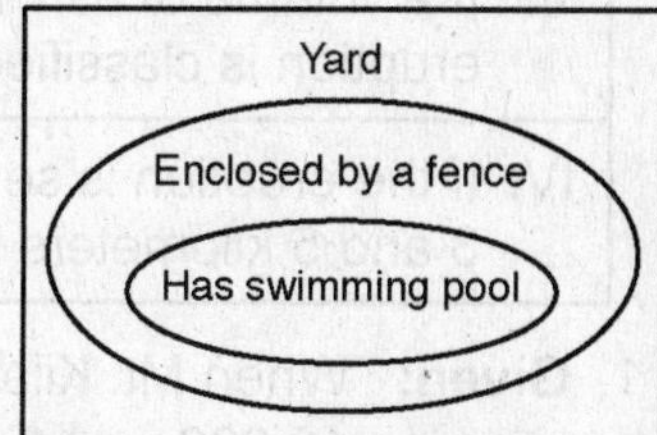

____

____

____

____

____

Use the table and the statements listed. Write each conditional and find its truth value.

U.S. Flag	
Year	**Number of Stars**
1777	13
1818	20
1848	30
1959	50

p: 1777 *q*: 30 stars *r*: after 1818 *s*: less than 50 stars

3. $p \rightarrow q$ ____

____

4. $r \rightarrow s$ ____

5. $q \rightarrow s$ ____

Choose the best answer.

6. What is the converse of "If you saw the movie, then you know how it ends"?
   - A If you know how the movie ends, then you saw the movie.
   - B If you did not see the movie, then you do not know how it ends.
   - C If you do not know how the movie ends, then you did not see the movie.
   - D If you do not know how the movie ends, then you saw the movie.

7. What is the inverse of "If you received a text message, then you have a cell phone"?
   - F If you have a cell phone, then you received a text message.
   - G If you do not have a cell phone, then you did not receive a text message.
   - H If you did not receive a text message, then you do not have a cell phone.
   - J If you received a text message, then you do not have a cell phone.

Name ______________________ Date ______________ Class ______________

LESSON 2-3

Problem Solving

Using Deductive Reasoning to Verify Conjectures

Use the information in the table and the given statement to draw a valid conclusion for each. If a valid conclusion cannot be made, explain why not.

Volcanic Eruptions
I. A category 2 eruption produces a plume of ash 1–5 kilometers high.
II. An explosive volcano produces a volume of ash between 1 million and 10 million cubic meters.
III. If a volume of ash 10,000–1,000,000 cubic meters is produced, the eruption is classified as a category 1 eruption.
IV. If the eruption is severe, then it produces a plume of ash between 3 and 5 kilometers high.

1. **Given:** When Mt. Kilauea in Hawaii erupted, it produced a volume of ash between 10,000 and 1 million cubic meters.

____

____

2. **Given:** The eruption of a volcano in Unzen, Japan, was not explosive.

____

____

3. **Given:** The eruption of a volcano in Stromboli, Italy, was a category 2 eruption.

____

____

Choose the best answer.

4. A sports store has running shoes 25% off original prices. Andrea sees a pair of running shoes that she likes for $65.00. Which is a valid conclusion?

   A The sale price of the shoes is $40.00.

   B The sale price of the shoes is $48.75.

   C Andrea will buy the shoes.

   D Andrea will not buy the shoes.

5. If Zack makes $1\frac{1}{2}$ quarts of lemonade, then he uses 6 lemons. If Zack makes $1\frac{1}{2}$ quarts of lemonade, then he makes 4 servings. Zack uses 5 lemons. Which is a valid conclusion?

   F Zack makes 3 servings.
   H Zack makes 1 quart.

   G Zack makes 2 servings.
   J Zack does not make $1\frac{1}{2}$ quarts.

Name ______________________ Date ______________ Class ______________

LESSON 2-4

Problem Solving

Biconditional Statements and Definitions

Use the table for Exercises 1–4. Determine if a true biconditional statement can be written from each conditional. If so, then write a biconditional. If not, then explain why not.

Mountain Bike Races	Characteristics
Cross-country	A massed-start race. Riders must carry their own tools to make repairs.
Downhill	Riders start at intervals. The rider with the lowest time wins.
Freeride	Courses contain cliffs, drops, and ramps. Scoring depends on the style and the time.
Marathon	A massed-start race that covers more than 250 kilometers.

1. If a mountain bike race is mass-started, then it is a cross-country race.

2. If a mountain bike race is downhill, then time is a factor in who wins.

3. If a mountain bike race covers more than 250 kilometers, then it is a marathon race.

4. If a race course contains cliffs, drops, and ramps, then it is not a marathon race.

Choose the best answer.

5. The cat is the only species that can hold its tail vertically while it walks.
   - A The converse of this statement is false.
   - B The biconditional of this statement is false.
   - C The biconditional of this statement is true.
   - D This statement cannot be written as a biconditional.

6. Which conditional statement can be used to write a true biconditional?
   - F If you travel 2 miles in 4 minutes, then distance is a function of time.
   - G If the distance depends on the time, then distance is a function of time.
   - H If y increases as x increases, then y is a function of x.
   - J If y is not a function of x, then y does not increase as x increases.

Name ____________________ Date ____________ Class ____________

LESSON 2-5

Problem Solving

Algebraic Proof

1. Because of a recent computer glitch, an airline mistakenly sold tickets for round-trip flights at a discounted price. The equation $n(p + t) = 3298.75$ relates the number of discounted tickets sold n, the price of each ticket p, and the tax per ticket t. What was the discounted price of each ticket if 1015 tickets were sold and the tax per ticket was \$1.39? Solve the equation for p. Justify each step.

2. The equation $C = 7.25s + 15.95a$ describes the total cost of admission C to the aquarium. How many student tickets were sold if the total cost for the entire class and 6 adults was \$298.70? Solve the equation for s. Justify each step.

s = number of student tickets
a = number of adult tickets
C = total cost of admission

Refer to the figure. Choose the best answer.

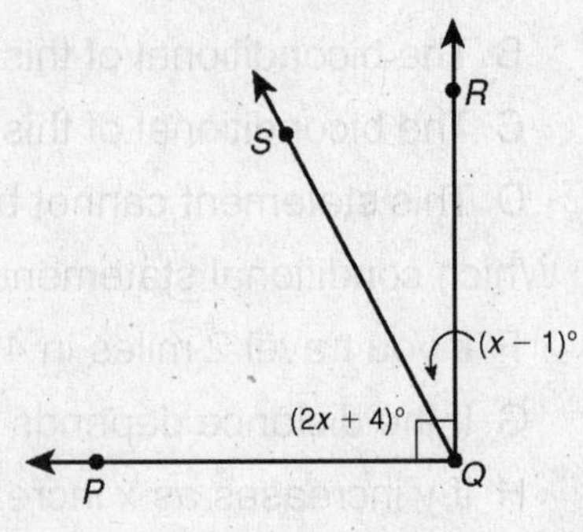

3. Which could be used to find the value of x?
   - A Segment Addition Postulate
   - B Angle Addition Postulate
   - C Transitive Property of Congruence
   - D Definition of supplementary angles

4. What is $m\angle SQR$?
   - F 28°
   - G 29°
   - H 61°
   - J 62°

Name ______________________ Date ______________ Class ______________

LESSON 2-6

Problem Solving

Geometric Proof

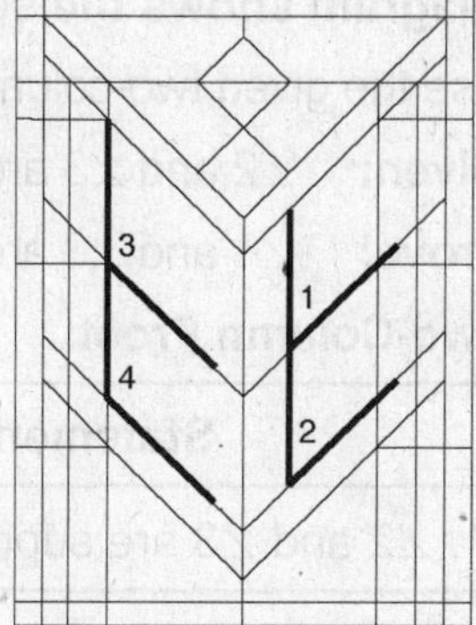

1. Refer to the diagram of the stained-glass window and use the given plan to write a two-column proof.

   Given: ∠1 and ∠3 are supplementary.
   ∠2 and ∠4 are supplementary.
   ∠3 ≅ ∠4

   Prove: ∠1 ≅ ∠2

   Plan: Use the definition of supplementary angles to write the given information in terms of angle measures. Then use the Substitution Property of Equality and the Subtraction Property of Equality to conclude that ∠1 ≅ ∠2.

The position of a sprinter at the starting blocks is shown in the diagram. Which statement can be proved using the given information? Choose the best answer.

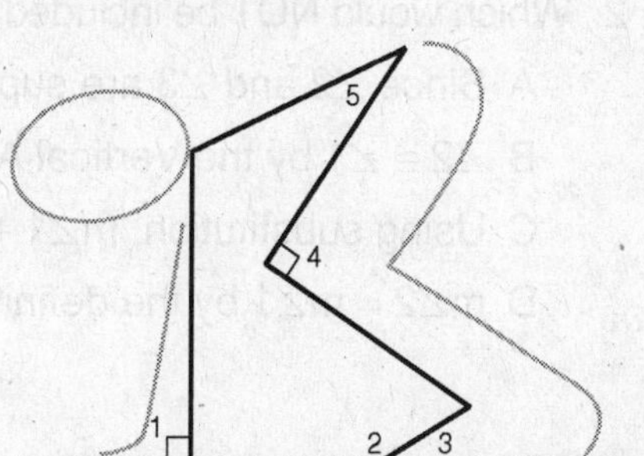

2. **Given:** ∠1 and ∠4 are right angles.

   A ∠3 ≅ ∠5 C m∠1 + m∠4 = 90°

   B ∠1 ≅ ∠4 D m∠3 + m∠5 = 180°

3. **Given:** ∠2 and ∠3 are supplementary.
   ∠2 and ∠5 are supplementary.

   F ∠3 ≅ ∠5 H ∠3 and ∠5 are complementary.

   G ∠2 ≅ ∠5 J ∠1 and ∠2 are supplementary.

Name ______________________ Date ______________ Class ______________

LESSON 2-7

Problem Solving

Flowchart and Paragraph Proofs

The diagram shows the second-floor glass railing at a mall.

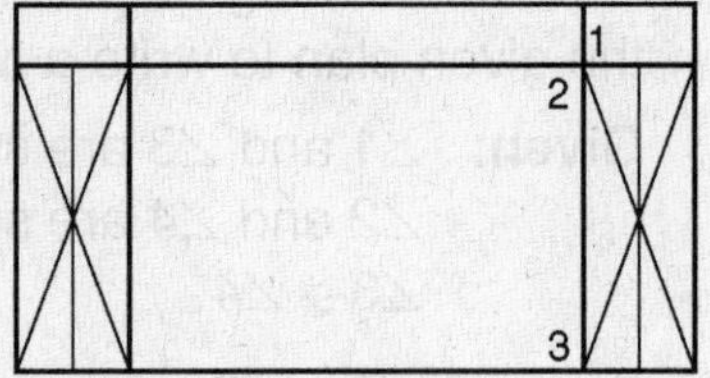

1. Use the given two-column proof to write a flowchart proof.

   Given: $\angle 2$ and $\angle 3$ are supplementary.

   Prove: $\angle 1$ and $\angle 3$ are supplementary.

   Two-Column Proof:

Statements	Reasons
1. $\angle 2$ and $\angle 3$ are supplementary.	1. Given
2. $m\angle 2 + m\angle 3 = 180°$	2. Def. of supp. $\angle$s
3. $\angle 2 \cong \angle 1$	3. Vert. $\angle$s Thm.
4. $m\angle 2 = m\angle 1$	4. Def. of $\cong$ $\angle$s
5. $m\angle 1 + m\angle 3 = 180°$	5. Subst.
6. $\angle 1$ and $\angle 3$ are supplementary.	6. Def. of supp. $\angle$s

Choose the best answer.

2. Which would NOT be included in a paragraph proof of the two-column proof above?

   A Since $\angle 2$ and $\angle 3$ are supplementary, $m\angle 2 = m\angle 3$.

   B $\angle 2 \cong \angle 1$ by the Vertical Angles Theorem.

   C Using substitution, $m\angle 1 + m\angle 3 = 180°$.

   D $m\angle 2 = m\angle 1$ by the definition of congruent angles.

Name ______________________ Date ______________ Class ______________

LESSON 3-1

Problem Solving

Lines and Angles

Use the diagram of the rectangular box for Exercises 1 and 2. Refer to the diagram to help justify your answer.

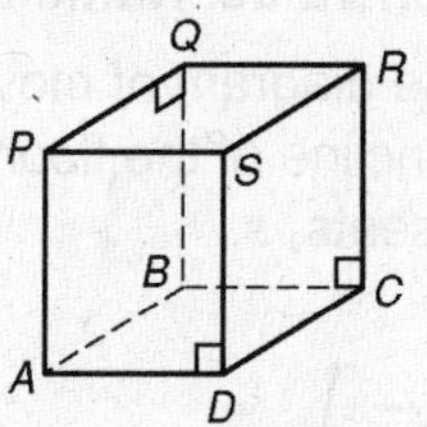

1. Is the relationship "is skew to" transitive?

____

____

2. If a segment is skew to one of two parallel segments, must it be skew to the other?

____

Use the flag of Puerto Rico for Exercises 3 and 4.

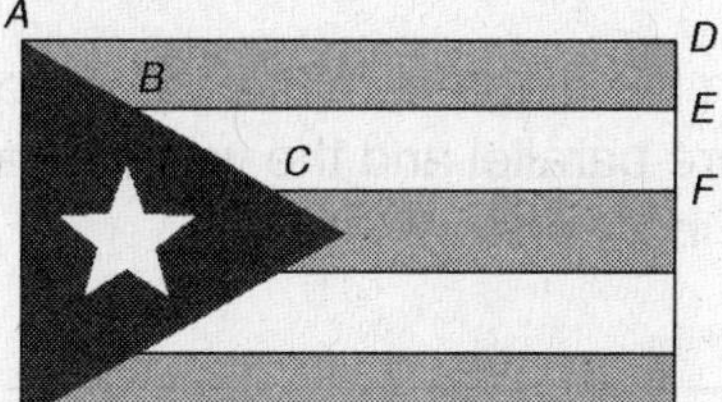

3. If $\angle DFC$ and $\angle ACF$ are same-side interior angles, identify the transversal.

____

4. Name a pair of alternate interior angles if the transversal is $\overline{BE}$.

____

Choose the best answer.

5. Describe the type of lines suggested by the two skis of a person water skiing.
   A intersecting lines
   B parallel lines
   C perpendicular lines
   D skew lines

6. Describe the type of lines suggested by the paths of two people at a fair when one person is riding the aerial ride from one end of the fair to the other, and the other person is walking in a different direction on the ground.
   F intersecting   H perpendicular
   G parallel   J skew

7. In the quilt pattern, which is a true statement about the angles formed by the transversal $\overline{HK}$ and $\overline{HM}$ and $\overline{JL}$?
   A $\angle LSK$ and $\angle PHQ$ are corresponding angles.
   B $\angle JSQ$ and $\angle JQH$ are corresponding angles.
   C $\angle LSK$ and $\angle QSJ$ are same-side interior angles.
   D $\angle PHQ$ and $\angle RLS$ are same-side interior angles.

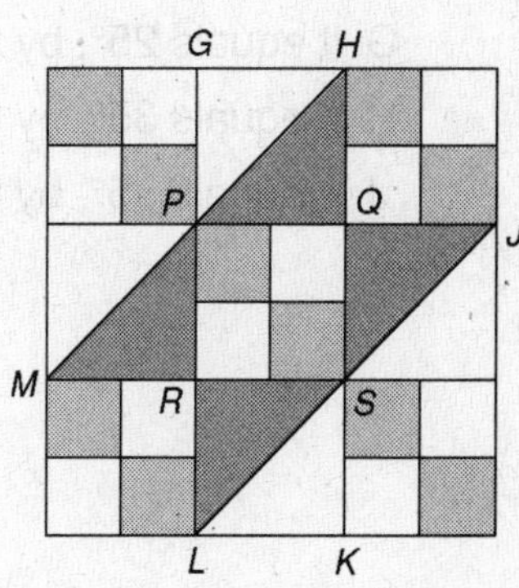

Name ______________________ Date ______________ Class ______________

LESSON 3-2

Problem Solving

Angles Formed by Parallel Lines and Transversals

Find each value. Name the postulate or theorem that you used to find the values.

1. In the diagram of movie theater seats, the incline of the floor, *f*, is parallel to the seats, *s*.

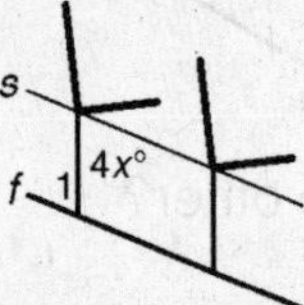

If m∠1 = 68°, what is *x*?

____

2. In the diagram, roads *a* and *b* are parallel.

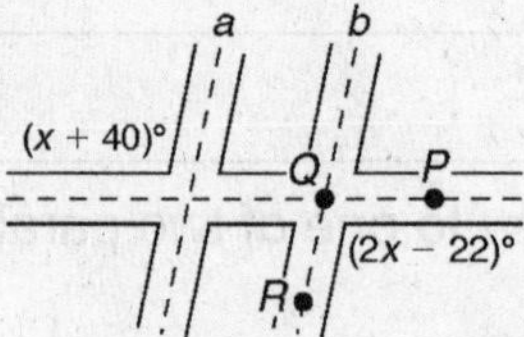

What is the measure of ∠*PQR*?

____

3. In the diagram of the gate, the horizontal bars are parallel and the vertical bars are parallel. Find *x* and *y*.

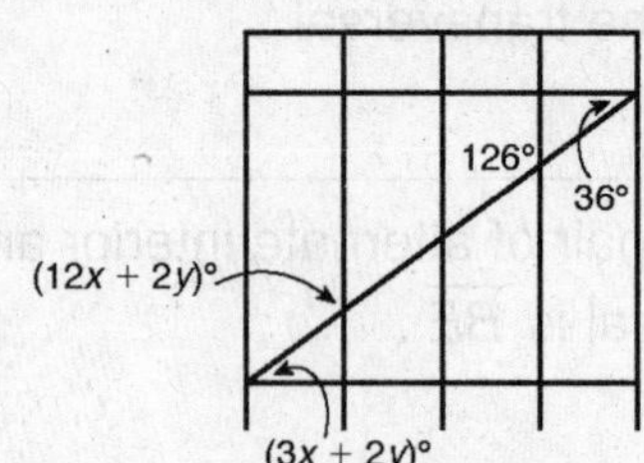

____

____

____

Use the diagram of a staircase railing for Exercises 4 and 5. $\overline{AG} \parallel \overline{CJ}$ and $\overline{AD} \parallel \overline{FJ}$. Choose the best answer.

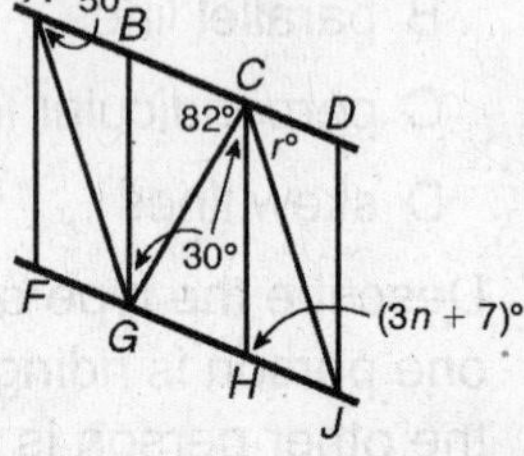

4. Which is a true statement about the measure of ∠*DCJ*?

A It equals 30°, by the Alternate Interior Angles Theorem.

B It equals 30°, by the Corresponding Angles Postulate.

C It equals 50°, by the Alternate Interior Angles Theorem.

D It equals 50°, by the Corresponding Angles Postulate.

5. Which is a true statement about the value of *n*?

F It equals 25°, by the Alternate Interior Angles Theorem.

G It equals 25°, by the Same-Side Interior Angles Theorem.

H It equals 35°, by the Alternate Interior Angles Theorem.

J It equals 35°, by the Same-Side Interior Angles Theorem.

Name _______________ Date _______________ Class _______________

LESSON 3-3

Problem Solving

Proving Lines Parallel

1. A bedroom has sloping ceilings as shown. Marcel is hanging a shelf below a rafter. If $m\angle 1 = (8x - 1)°$, $m\angle 2 = (6x + 7)°$, and $x = 4$, show that the shelf is parallel to the rafter above it.

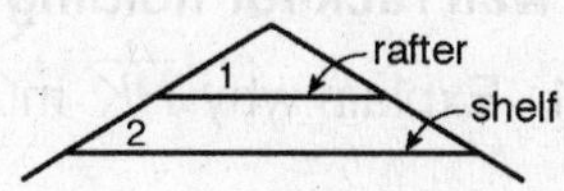

2. In the sign, $m\angle 3 = (3y + 7)°$, $m\angle 4 = (5y + 5)°$, and $y = 21$. Show that the sign posts are parallel.

Choose the best answer.

3. In the bench, $m\angle EFG = (4n + 16)°$, $m\angle FJL = (3n + 40)°$, $m\angle GKL = (3n + 22)°$, and $n = 24$. Which is a true statement?

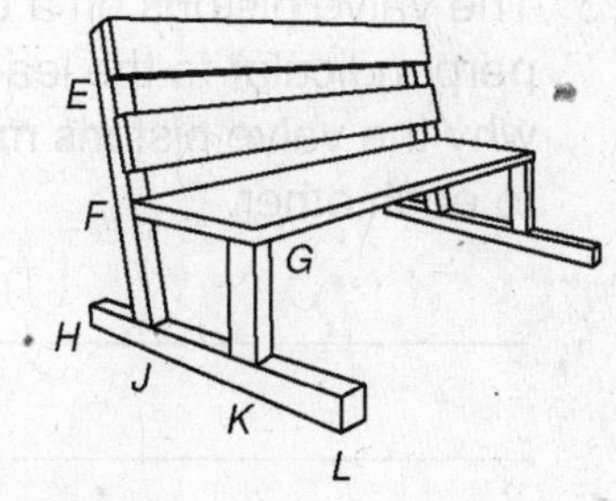

A $\overline{FG} \parallel \overline{HK}$ by the Converse of the Corr. ∠s Post.

B $\overline{FG} \parallel \overline{HK}$ by the Converse of the Alt. Int. ∠s Thm.

C $\overline{EJ} \parallel \overline{GK}$ by the Converse of the Corr. ∠s Post.

D $\overline{EJ} \parallel \overline{GK}$ by the Converse of the Alt. Int. ∠s Thm.

4. In the windsurfing sail, $m\angle 5 = (7c + 1)°$, $m\angle 6 = (9c - 1)°$, $m\angle 7 = 17c°$, and $c = 6$. Which is a true statement?

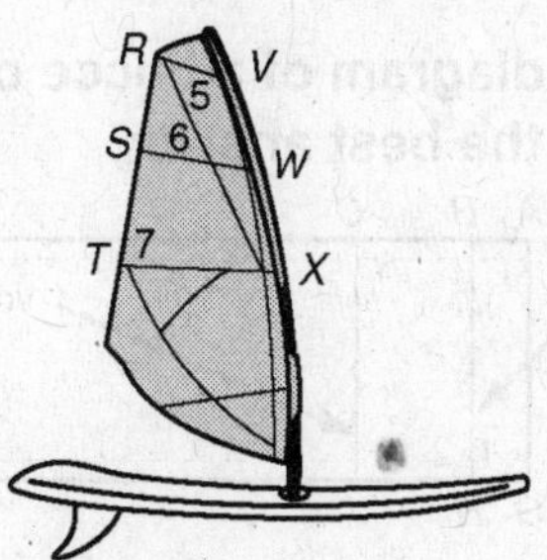

F $\overline{RV}$ is parallel to $\overline{SW}$.

G $\overline{SW}$ is parallel to $\overline{TX}$.

H $\overline{RT}$ is parallel to $\overline{VX}$.

J Cannot conclude that two segments are parallel

The figure shows Natalia's initials, which are monogrammed on her duffel bag. Use the figure for Exercises 5 and 6.

5. If $m\angle 1 = (4x - 24)°$, $m\angle 2 = (2x + 8)°$, and $x = 16$, show that the sides of the letter N are parallel.

6. If $m\angle 3 = (7x + 13)°$, $m\angle 4 = (5x + 35)°$, and $x = 11$, show that the sides of the letter H are parallel.

Name ______________________ Date ______________ Class ______________

LESSON 3-4

Problem Solving

Perpendicular Lines

A wall rack for holding CDs is shown. Use the figure for Exercises 1 and 2.

1. Explain why $\overline{HK}$ must be perpendicular to $\overline{KL}$.

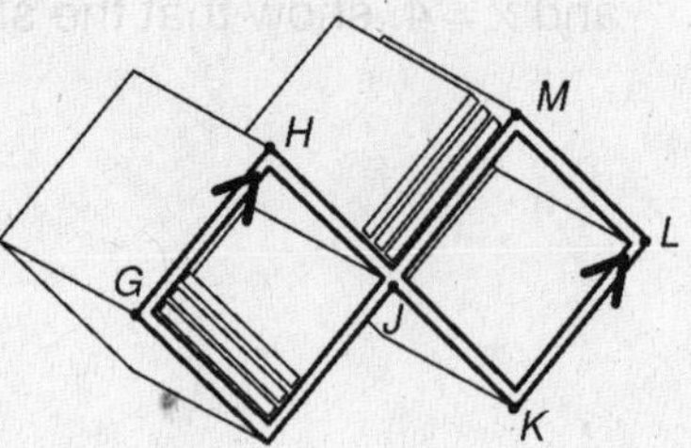

2. If $\overline{JM} \perp \overline{HK}$, explain why $\overline{JM} \parallel \overline{GH}$.

3. The valve pistons on a trumpet are all perpendicular to the lead pipe. Explain why the valve pistons must be parallel to each other.

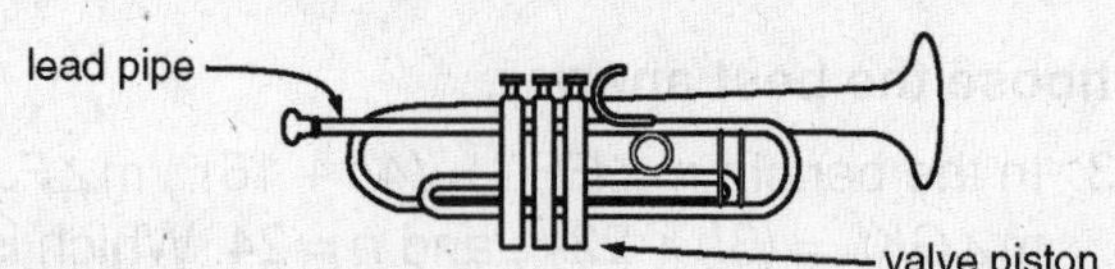

Use the diagram of a bocce court for Exercises 4 and 5. Choose the best answer.

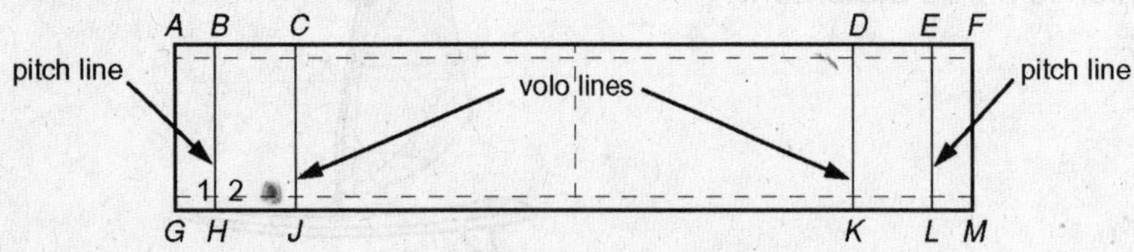

4. If $m\angle 1 = m\angle 2$, what can you conclude?

   A $\overline{BH} \perp \overline{GJ}$ C $\overline{BH} \parallel \overline{CJ}$

   B $\overline{AC} \perp \overline{BH}$ D $\overline{AC} \parallel \overline{GJ}$

5. The pitch lines are parallel, and the first pitch line is perpendicular to the long sides of the court. Which is a correct conclusion?

   F $BH = CJ$ H $\overline{EL} \perp \overline{AF}$

   G $\overline{BH} \parallel \overline{CJ}$ J $\overline{DK} \perp \overline{AF}$

Name ______________________ Date ______________ Class ______________

LESSON 3-5

Problem Solving

Slopes of Lines

Graph the line that represents each situation. Then find and interpret the slope of the line.

1. Mara is jogging at a constant speed. She jogs 2 miles in 14 minutes. After 35 minutes, she has jogged 5 miles. Graph the line that represents Mara's distance traveled.

2. A turtle swimming at a constant speed travels 12 miles by 3:00 P.M. and 28 miles by 7:00 P.M. Graph the line that represents the turtle's distance traveled.

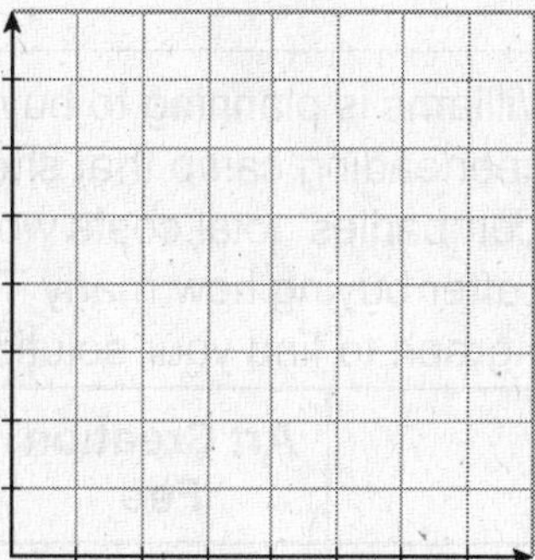

Choose the best answer.

3. A hang glider who started at 7:55 A.M. has traveled at a constant speed as shown in the table.

Time	Distance Traveled
8:00 A.M.	2 mi
8:30 A.M.	14 mi

If the line that represents the hang glider's distance traveled is graphed, which is a true interpretation of the slope?

A The hang glider is traveling at an average speed of 24 miles per hour.

B The hang glider is traveling at an average speed of 16 miles per hour.

C The hang glider is traveling at an average speed of 12 miles per minute.

D The hang glider is traveling at an average speed of 7 miles per minute.

4. The line represents the distance traveled by an in-line skater traveling at a constant speed. What is the rate of change represented in the graph?

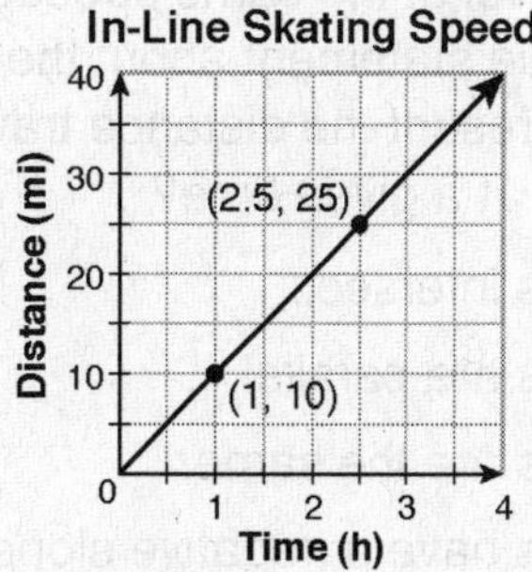

F 25 mi/h

G 15 mi/h

H 10 mi/h

J 0.1 mi/h

Name ______________________ Date ______________ Class ______________

LESSON 3-6

Problem Solving

Lines in the Coordinate Plane

Use the following information for Exercises 1 and 2. Josh can order 1 color ink cartridge and 2 black ink cartridges for his printer for $78. He can also order 1 color ink cartridge and 1 black ink cartridge for $53.

1. Let x equal the cost of a color ink cartridge and y equal the cost of a black ink cartridge. Write a system of equations to represent this situation.

____

2. What is the cost of each cartridge?

____

3. Ms. Williams is planning to buy T-shirts for the cheerleading camp that she is running. Both companies' total costs would be the same after buying how many T-shirts? Use a graph to find your solution.

	Art Creation Fee	Cost per T-shirt
Company A	$70	$10
Company B	$50	$12

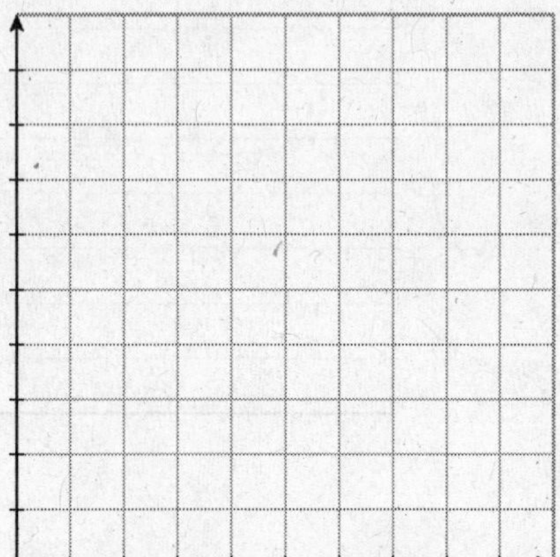

____

____

Choose the best answer.

4. Two floats begin a parade at different times, but travel at the same speeds. Which is a true statement about the lines that represent the distance traveled by each float at a given time?

   A The lines intersect.

   B The lines are parallel.

   C The lines are the same.

   D The lines have a negative slope.

5. A piano teacher charges $20 for each half hour lesson, plus an initial fee of $50. Another teacher charges $40 per hour, plus a fee of $50. Which is a true statement about the lines that represent the total cost by each piano teacher?

   F The lines intersect.

   G The lines are parallel.

   H The lines are the same.

   J The lines have a negative slope.

6. Serina is trying to decide between two similar packages for starting her own Web site. Which is a true statement?

   A Both packages cost $235.50 for 5 months.

   B Both packages cost $295 for 10 months.

   C Both packages cost $355 for 15 months.

   D The packages will never have the same cost.

	Design and Setup	Monthly Fee to Host
Package A	$150.00	$14.50
Package B	$175.00	$12.00

Name ______________________ Date ______________ Class ______________

LESSON 4-1

Problem Solving

Congruence and Transformations

1. Irena is designing a quilt. She made this diagram to follow when making her quilt. What transformation(s) are used on the triangles to create the pattern in the quilt design?

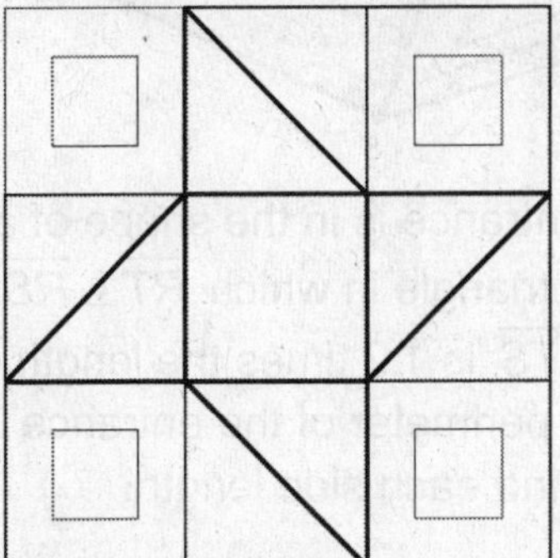

____

2. An architect used this design for a stained glass window. What frieze transformation(s) is used to create the pattern in the window?

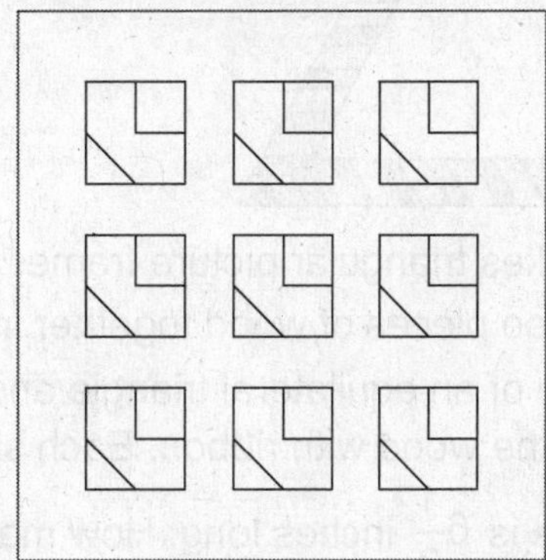

____

3. A graphic artist incorporated the universal symbol for radiation for one of his designs. Describe the transformation(s) he used.

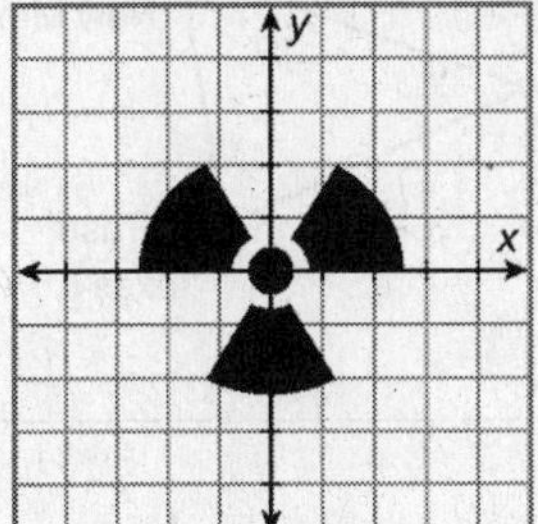

____

4. Richard developed a tessellating shape for floor tile. Describe the series of transformations he used to create the design.

____

Choose the best answer.

5. A team flag is made using a fabric with the design shown. What transformation is used?

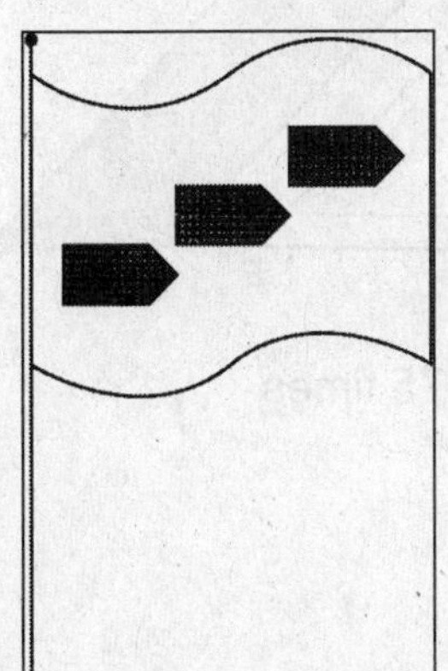

A translation

B reflection

C rotation

D dilation

6. An art student used transformations in all her art. What transformation did she use for her design shown?

F translation

G reflection

H rotation

J dilation

Name ______________________ Date ____________ Class ____________

LESSON 4-2

Problem Solving

Classifying Triangles

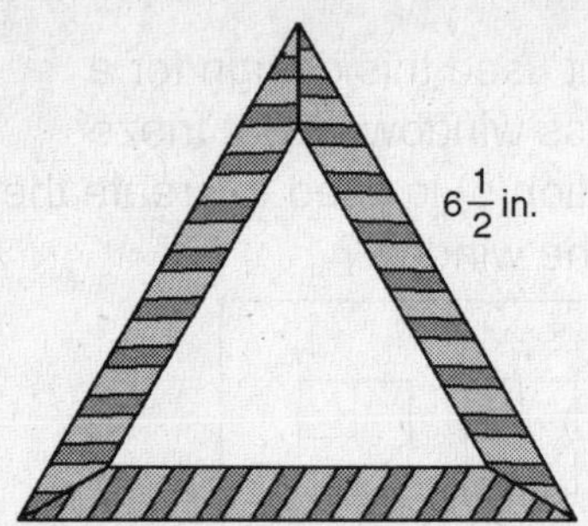

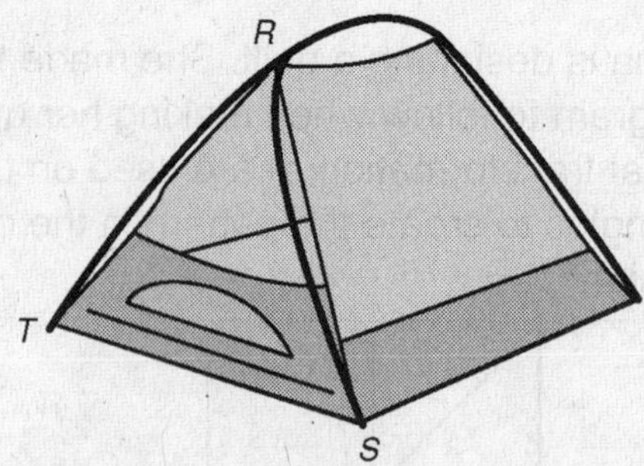

1. Aisha makes triangular picture frames by gluing three pieces of wood together in the shape of an equilateral triangle and covering the wood with ribbon. Each side of a frame is $6\frac{1}{2}$ inches long. How many frames can she cover with 2 yards of ribbon?

____

2. A tent's entrance is in the shape of an isosceles triangle in which $\overline{RT} \cong \overline{RS}$. The length of $\overline{TS}$ is 1.2 times the length of a side. The perimeter of the entrance is 14 feet. Find each side length.

____

Use the figure and the following information for Exercises 3 and 4.

The distance "as the crow flies" between Santa Fe and Phoenix is 609 kilometers. This is 245 kilometers less than twice the distance between Santa Fe and El Paso. Phoenix is 48 kilometers closer to El Paso than it is to Santa Fe.

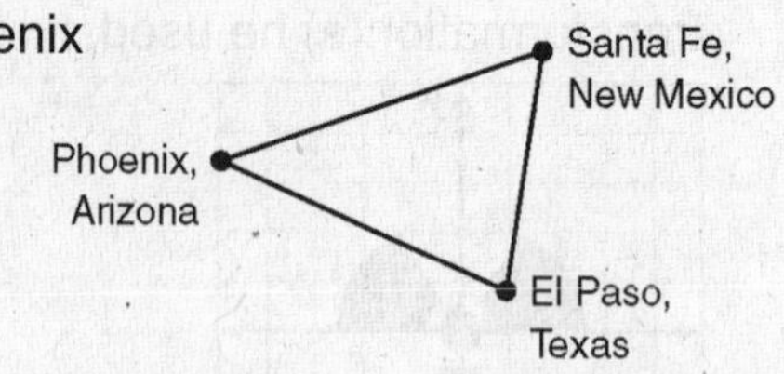

3. What is the distance between each pair of cities?

____

____

4. Classify the triangle that connects the cities by its side lengths. _______________

Choose the best answer.

A *gable*, as shown in the diagram, is the triangular portion of a wall between a sloping roof.

5. Triangle *ABC* is an isosceles triangle. The length of $\overline{CB}$ is 12 feet 4 inches and the congruent sides are each $\frac{3}{4}$ this length. What is the perimeter of $\triangle ABC$?

   A 31 ft 4 in.   C 21 ft 7 in.

   B 30 ft 10 in.   D 18 ft 6 in.

A
D
C F E B

6. In $\triangle DEF$, $\overline{DE}$ and $\overline{DF}$ are each 6 feet 3 inches long. This length is 0.75 times the length of $\overline{FE}$. What is the perimeter of $\triangle DEF$?

   F 12 ft 4 in.   H 17 ft 2 in.

   G 14 ft 7 in.   J 20 ft 10 in.

Name ______________________ Date ______________ Class ______________

LESSON 4-3

Problem Solving

Angle Relationships in Triangles

1. The locations of three food stands on a fair's midway are shown. What is the measure of the angle labeled $x°$?

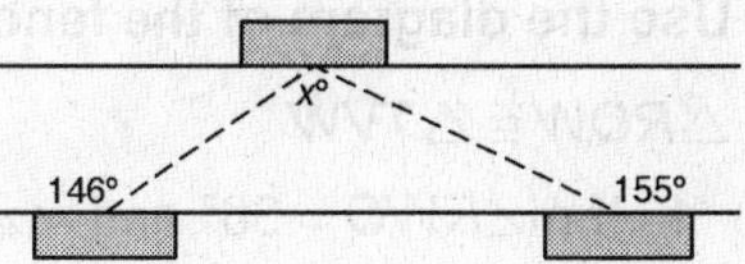

____

2. A large triangular piece of plywood is to be painted to look like a mountain for the spring musical. The angles at the base of the plywood measure 76° and 45°. What is the measure of the top angle that represents the mountain peak?

____

Use the figure of the banner for Exercises 3 and 4.

3. What is the value of n?

____

4. What is the measure of each angle in the banner?

____

Use the figure of the athlete pole vaulting for Exercises 5 and 6.

5. What is $x°$, the measure of the angle that the pole makes when it first touches the ground?

____

6. At takeoff, $a° = 23°$. What is $c°$, the measure of the angle the pole makes with the athlete's body?

____

The figure shows a path through a garden. Choose the best answer.

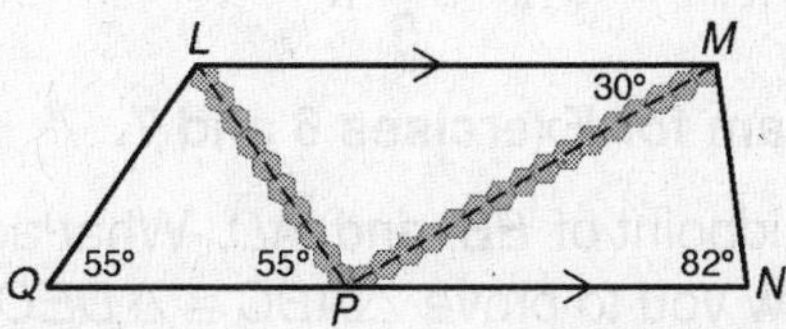

7. What is the measure of $\angle QLP$?

A 20° C 110°

B 70° D 125°

8. What is the measure of $\angle LPM$?

F 85° H 95°

G 90° J 125°

9. What is the measure of $\angle PMN$?

A 98° C 60°

B 68° D 55°

Name ______________________ Date ______________ Class ______________

LESSON 4-4

Problem Solving

Congruent Triangles

Use the diagram of the fence for Exercises 1 and 2.

$\triangle RQW \cong \triangle TVW$

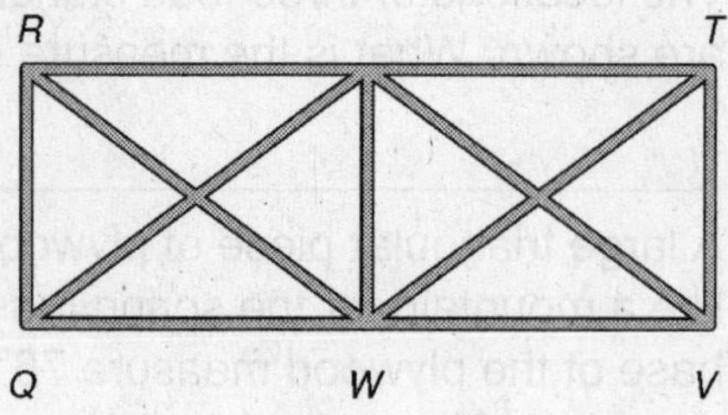

1. If $m\angle RWQ = 36°$ and $m\angle TWV = (2x + 5)°$, what is the value of x?

____

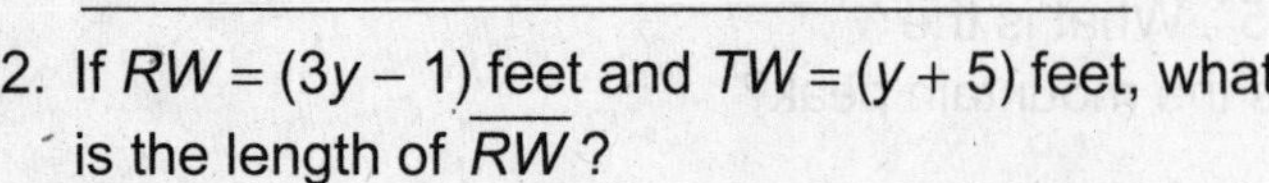

2. If $RW = (3y - 1)$ feet and $TW = (y + 5)$ feet, what is the length of $\overline{RW}$?

____

Use the diagram of a section of the Bank of China Tower for Exercises 3 and 4.

$\triangle JKL \cong \triangle LHJ$

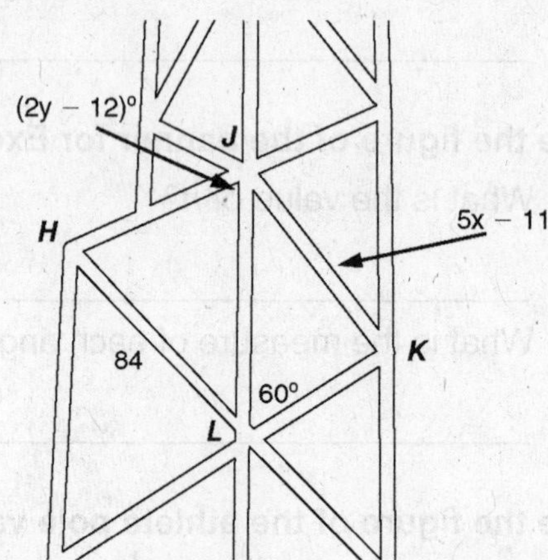

3. What is the value of x?

____

4. Find $m\angle JHL$.

____

Choose the best answer.

5. Chairs with triangular seats were popular in the Middle Ages. Suppose a chair has a seat that is an isosceles triangle and the congruent sides measure $1\frac{1}{2}$ feet. A second chair has a triangular seat with a perimeter of $5\frac{1}{10}$ feet, and it is congruent to the first seat. What is a side length of the second seat?

A $1\frac{4}{5}$ ft C 3 ft

B $2\frac{1}{10}$ ft D $3\frac{3}{5}$ ft

Use the diagram for Exercises 6 and 7.

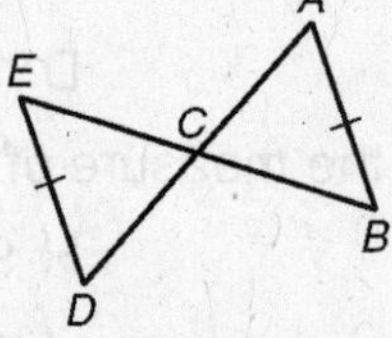

6. C is the midpoint of $\overline{EB}$ and $\overline{AD}$. What additional information would allow you to prove $\triangle ABC \cong \triangle DEC$ by the definition of congruent triangles?

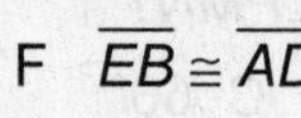

F $\overline{EB} \cong \overline{AD}$ H $\angle ECD \cong \angle ACB$

G $\overline{DE} \cong \overline{AB}$ J $\angle A \cong \angle D, \angle B \cong \angle E$

7. If $\triangle ABC \cong \triangle DEC$, $ED = 4y + 2$, and $AB = 6y - 4$, what is the length of $\overline{AB}$?

A 3 C 14

B 12 D 18

Name ______________________ Date ______________ Class ______________

LESSON 4-5

Problem Solving

Triangle Congruence: SSS and SAS

Use the diagram for Exercises 1 and 2.

A shed door appears to be divided into congruent right triangles.

1. Suppose $\overline{AB} \cong \overline{CD}$. Use SAS to show $\triangle ABD \cong \triangle DCA$.

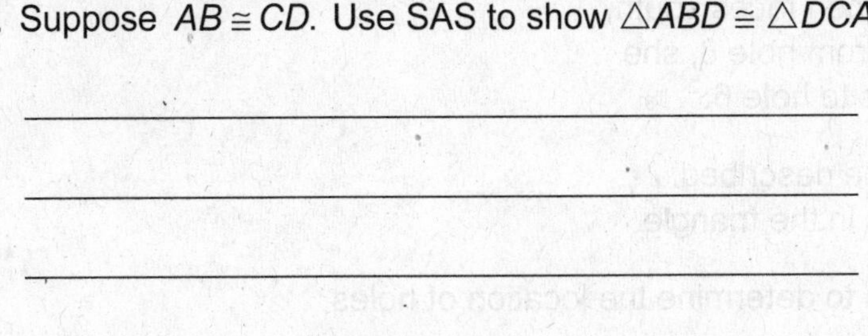

2. J is the midpoint of AB and $\overline{AK} \cong \overline{BK}$. Use SSS to explain why $\triangle AKJ \cong \triangle BKJ$.

3. A *balalaika* is a Russian stringed instrument. Show that the triangular parts of the two balalaikas are congruent for $x = 6$.

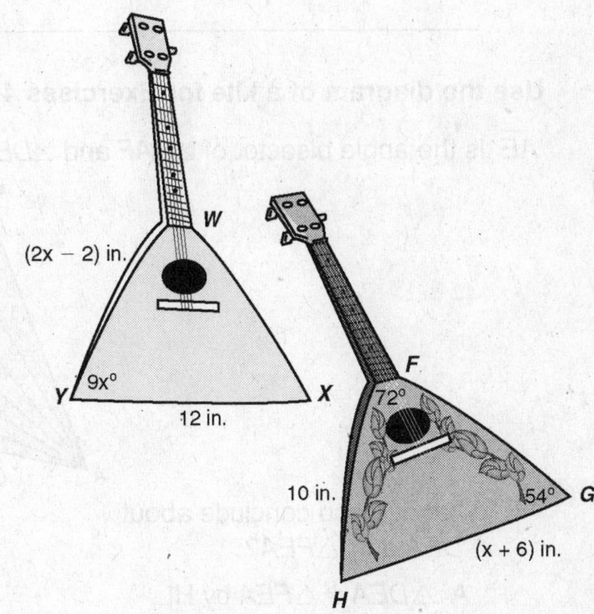

A quilt pattern of a dog is shown.
Choose the best answer.

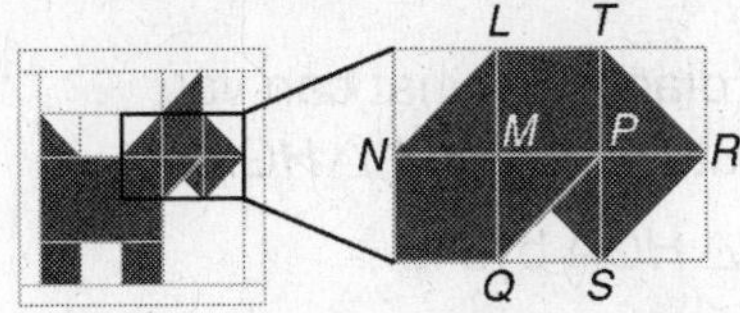

4. $ML = MP = MN = MQ = 1$ inch. Which statement is correct?

   A $\triangle LMN \cong \triangle QMP$ by SAS.

   B $\triangle LMN \cong \triangle QMP$ by SSS.

   C $\triangle LMN \cong \triangle MQP$ by SAS.

   D $\triangle LMN \cong \triangle MQP$ by SSS.

5. P is the midpoint of $\overline{TS}$ and $TR = SR = 1.4$ inches. What can you conclude about ΔTRP and ΔSRP?

   F $\triangle TRP \cong \triangle SRP$ by SAS.

   G $\triangle TRP \cong \triangle SRP$ by SSS.

   H $\triangle TRP \cong \triangle SPR$ by SAS.

   J $\triangle TRP \cong \triangle SPR$ by SSS.

Name ______________________ Date ______________ Class ______________

LESSON 4-6

Problem Solving

Triangle Congruence: ASA, AAS, and HL

Use the following information for Exercises 1 and 2.

Melanie is at hole 6 on a miniature golf course. She walks east 7.5 meters to hole 7. She then faces south, turns 67° west, and walks to hole 8. From hole 8, she faces north, turns 35° west, and walks to hole 6.

1. Draw the section of the golf course described. Label the measures of the angles in the triangle.

2. Is there enough information given to determine the location of holes 6, 7, and 8? Explain.

____

3. A section of the front of an English Tudor home is shown in the diagram. If you know that $\overline{KN} \cong \overline{LN}$ and $\overline{JN} \cong \overline{MN}$, can you use HL to conclude that $\triangle JKN \cong \triangle MLN$? Explain.

____

____

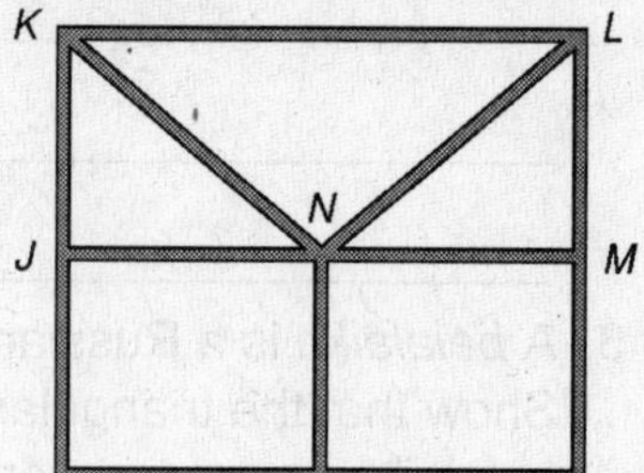

Use the diagram of a kite for Exercises 4 and 5.

$\overline{AE}$ is the angle bisector of $\angle DAF$ and $\angle DEF$.

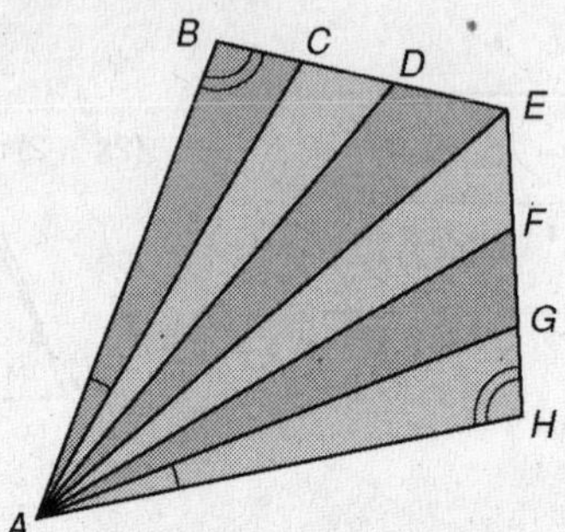

4. What can you conclude about $\triangle DEA$ and $\triangle FEA$?

   A $\triangle DEA \cong \triangle FEA$ by HL.

   B $\triangle DEA \cong \triangle FEA$ by AAA.

   C $\triangle DEA \cong \triangle FEA$ by ASA.

   D $\triangle DEA \cong \triangle FEA$ by SAS.

5. Based on the diagram, what can you conclude about $\triangle BCA$ and $\triangle HGA$?

   F $\triangle BCA \cong \triangle HGA$ by HL.

   G $\triangle BCA \cong \triangle HGA$ by AAS.

   H $\triangle BCA \cong \triangle HGA$ by ASA.

   J It cannot be shown using the given information that $\triangle BCA \cong \triangle HGA$.

Name ______________________ Date ______________ Class ______________

LESSON 4-7

Problem Solving

Triangle Congruence: CPCTC

1. Two triangular plates are congruent. The area of one of the plates is 60 square inches. What is the area of the other plate? Explain.

____

____

2. An archaeologist draws the triangles to find the distance *XY* across a ravine. What is *XY*? Explain.

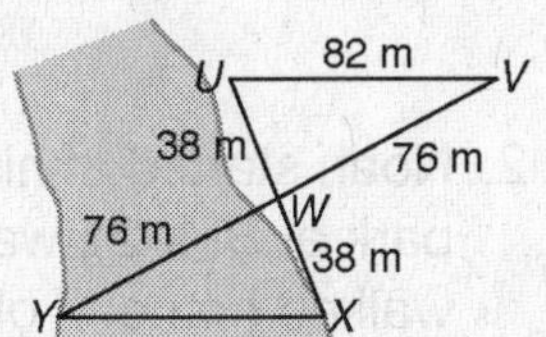

____

____

3. A city planner sets up the triangles to find the distance *RS* across a river. Describe the steps that she can use to find *RS*.

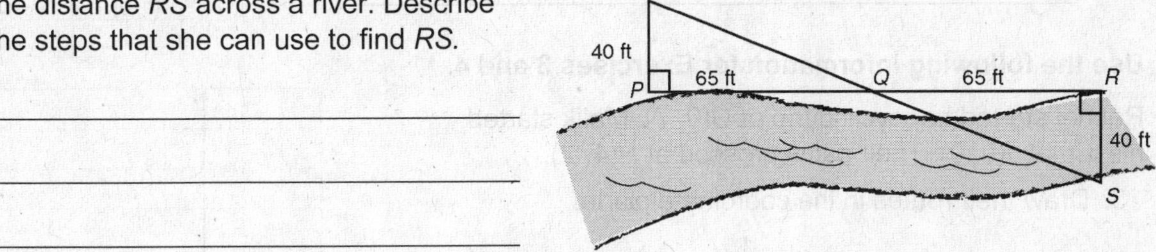

____

____

____

____

____

Choose the best answer.

4. A lighthouse and the range of its shining light are shown. What can you conclude?

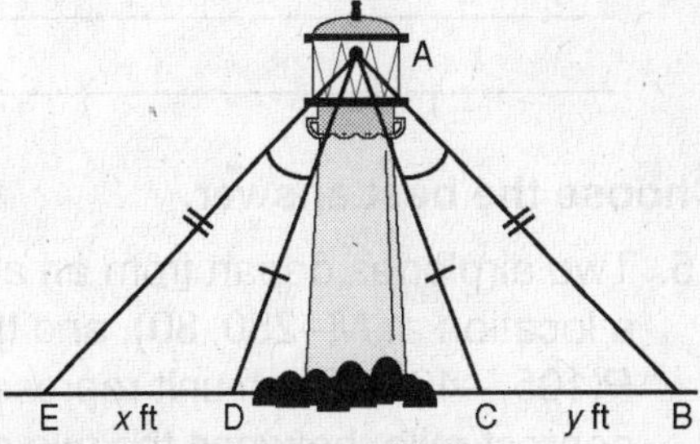

A $x = y$ by CPCTC
C $\angle AED \cong \angle ADE$ by CPCTC
B $x = 2y$
D $\angle AED \cong \angle ACB$

5. A rectangular piece of cloth 15 centimeters long is cut along a diagonal to form two triangles. One of the triangles has a side length of 9 centimeters. Which is a true statement?

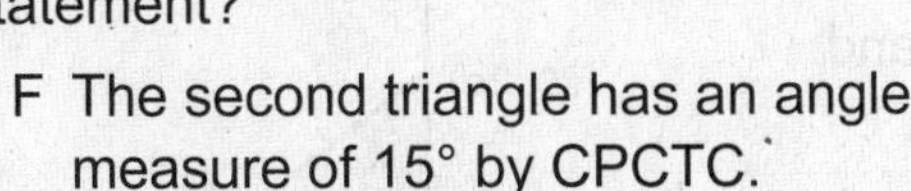

F The second triangle has an angle measure of 15° by CPCTC.

G The second triangle has a side length of 9 centimeters by CPCTC.

H You cannot make a conclusion about the side length of the second triangle.

J The triangles are not congruent.

6. Small sandwiches are cut in the shape of right triangles. The longest sides of all the sandwiches are 3 inches. One sandwich has a side length of 2 inches. Which is a true statement?

A All the sandwiches have a side length of 2 inches by CPCTC.

B All the sandwiches are isosceles triangles with side lengths of 2 inches.

C None of the other sandwiches have side lengths of 2 inches.

D You cannot make a conclusion using CPCTC.

Name ______________________ Date ______________ Class ______________

LESSON 4-8

Problem Solving

Introduction to Coordinate Proof

Round to the nearest tenth for Exercises 1 and 2.

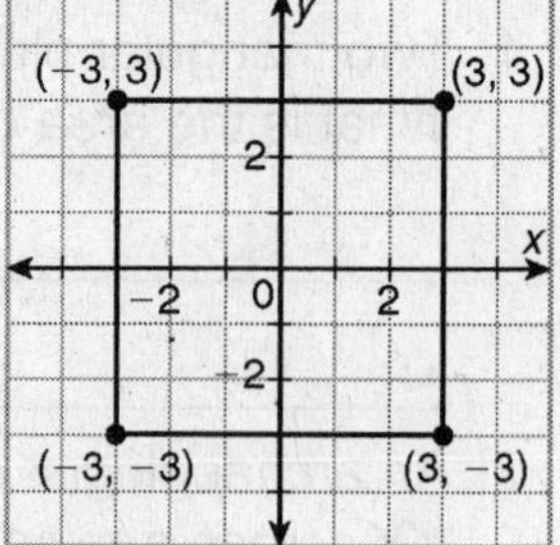

1. A fountain is at the center of a square courtyard. If one grid unit represents one yard, what is the distance from the fountain at (0, 0) to each corner of the courtyard?

____

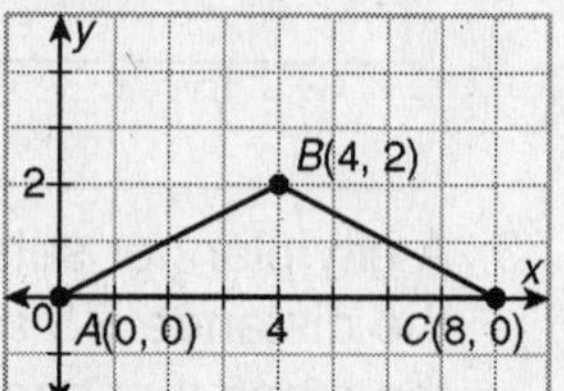

2. Noah started at his home at $A(0, 0)$, walked with his dog to the park at $B(4, 2)$, walked to his friend's house at $C(8, 0)$, then walked home. If one grid unit represents 20 meters, what is the distance that Noah and his dog walked?

____

Use the following information for Exercises 3 and 4.

Rachel started her cycling trip at $G(0, 7)$. Malik started his trip at $J(0, 0)$. Their paths crossed at $H(4, 2)$.

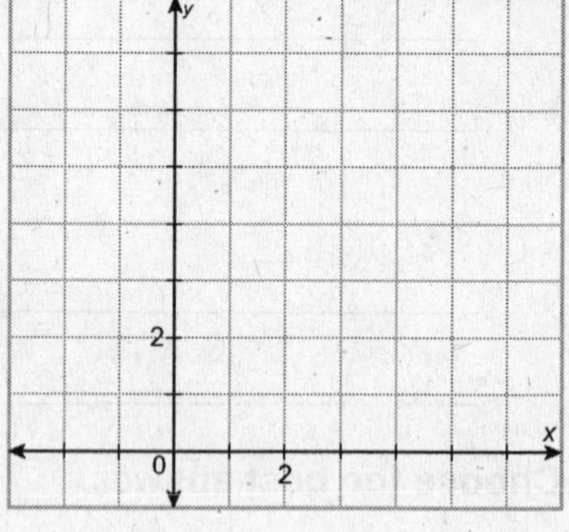

3. Draw their routes in the coordinate plane.

4. If one grid unit represents $\frac{1}{2}$ mile, who had ridden farther when their paths crossed? Explain.

____

____

Choose the best answer.

5. Two airplanes depart from an airport at $A(9, 11)$. The first airplane travels to a location at $N(-250, 80)$, and the second airplane travels to a location at $P(105, -400)$. Each unit represents 1 mile. What is the distance, to the nearest mile, between the two airplanes?

   A 335.3 mi   C 490.3 mi

   B 477.9 mi   D 597.0 mi

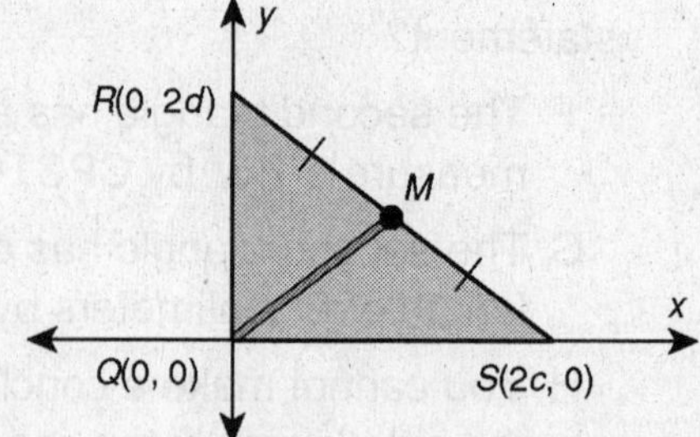

6. A corner garden has vertices at $Q(0, 0)$, $R(0, 2d)$, and $S(2c, 0)$. A brick walkway runs from point Q to the midpoint M of $\overline{RS}$. What is QM?

   F (c, d) H $\sqrt{c+d}$

   G $c^2 + d^2$ J $\sqrt{c^2 + d^2}$

Name ______________________ Date ____________ Class ____________

LESSON 4-9

Problem Solving

Isosceles and Equilateral Triangles

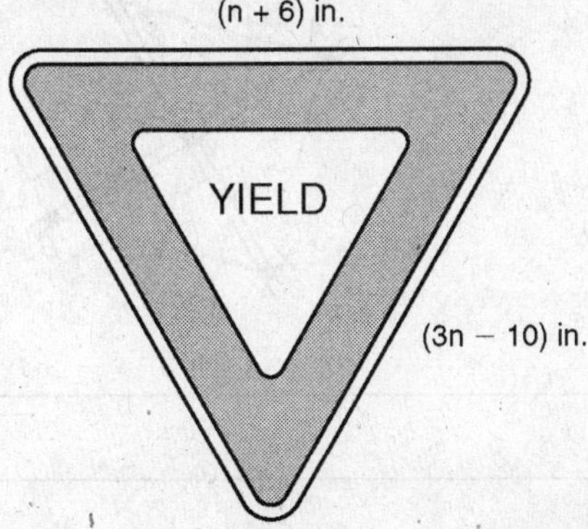

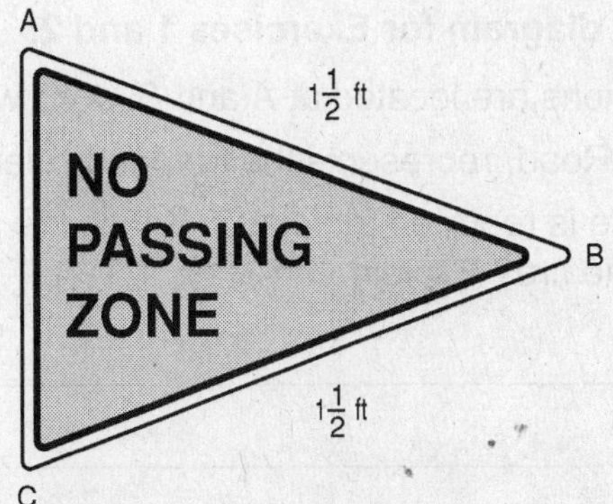

1. A "Yield" sign is an equiangular triangle. What are the lengths of the sides?

   ____

2. The measure of $\angle C$ is 70°. What is the measure of $\angle B$?

   ____

3. Samantha is swimming along $\overline{HF}$. When she is at point *H*, she sees a necklace straight ahead of her but on the bottom of the pool at point *J*. Then she swims 11 more feet to point *G*. Use the diagram to find *GJ*, the distance Samantha is from the necklace. Explain.

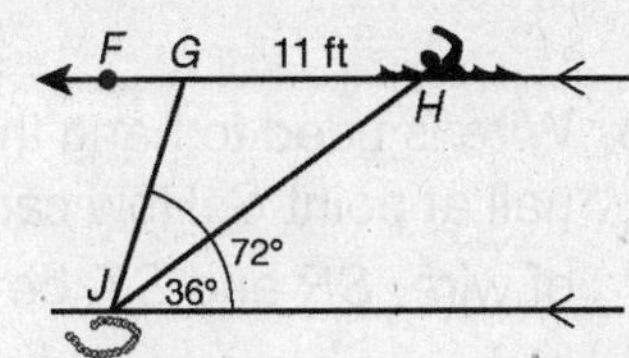

   ____

   ____

Choose the best answer.

4. A billiards triangle is equiangular. What is the perimeter?

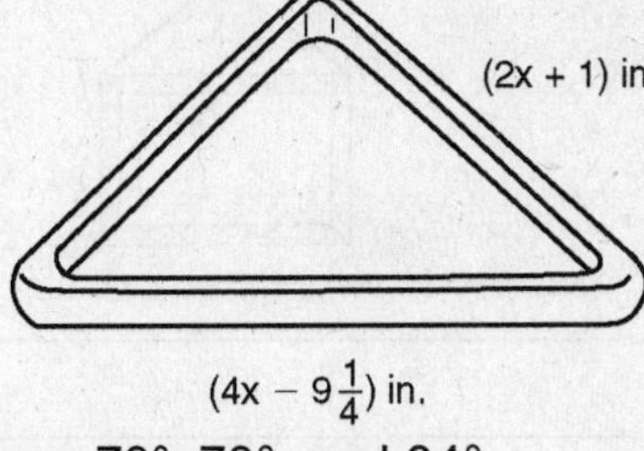

   A $5\frac{1}{8}$ in. C $11\frac{1}{4}$ in.

   B $10\frac{1}{4}$ in. D $33\frac{3}{4}$ in.

5. A triangular shaped trellis has angles *R*, *S*, and *T* that measure 73°, 73°, and 34°, respectively. If $ST = 4y + 6$ and $TR = 7y - 21$, what is the value of *y*?

   F 5 H 11

   G 9 J 15

6. Two triangular tiles each have two sides measuring 4 inches. Which is a true statement?

   A Their corresponding angles are congruent. C The triangles may be congruent.

   B The triangles are congruent. D The triangles cannot be congruent.

7. What is the value of *x* in the figure?

   F 42° H 96°

   G 90° J 106°

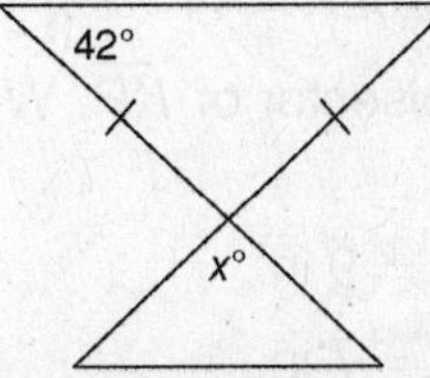

Name ______________________ Date ______________ Class ______________

LESSON 5-1

Problem Solving

Perpendicular and Angle Bisectors

Use the diagram for Exercises 1 and 2.

Fire stations are located at A and B. $\overleftrightarrow{XY}$, which contains Havens Road, represents the perpendicular bisector of $\overline{AB}$.

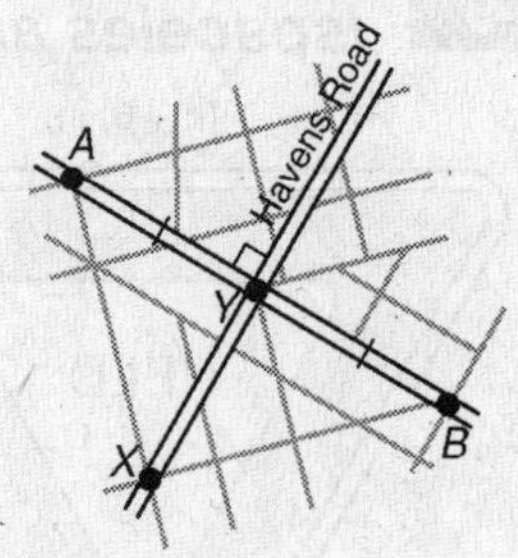

1. A fire is reported at point X. Which fire station is closer to the fire? Explain.

____

____

____

2. The city wants to build a third fire station so that it is the same distance from the stations at A and B. How can the city be sure that this is the case?

____

____

3. Wire is used to hang the picture on a nail at point S. How can the two lengths of wire, SR and ST, be used so that the picture is straight and centered under the nail?

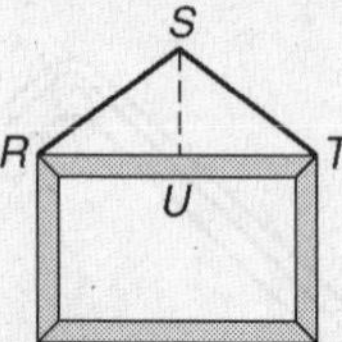

____

____

____

____

4. A piece of wood for a birdhouse is shown. Point H is the center of a ventilation hole that is to be drilled 2 inches from $\overline{FE}$ and $\overline{FG}$. If you drew $\overrightarrow{FH}$, what would be $m\angle EFH$? Explain.

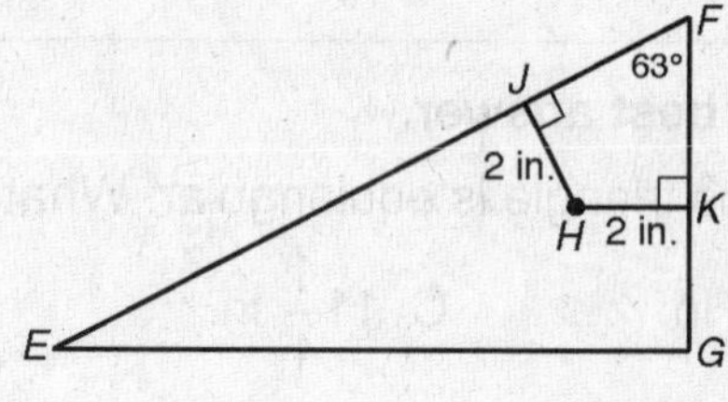

____

____

____

____

Choose the best answer.

The design at the right was made by wrapping string around nails.

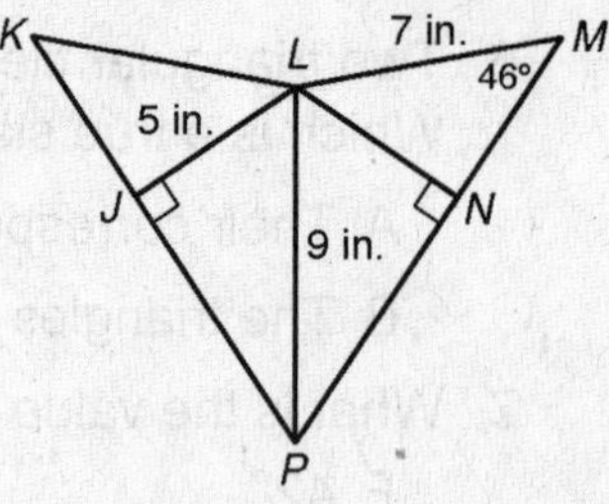

5. $\overline{PL}$ is the angle bisector of $\angle KPM$. Which can you conclude from this statement?

   A $LN = 5$ in. C $m\angle K = 46°$

   B $LK = 7$ in. D $m\angle JLK = 44°$

6. $\overline{LJ}$ is the perpendicular bisector of $\overline{KP}$. Which can you conclude?

   F $m\angle K = 46°$ H $KL = 9$ in.

   G $m\angle K = 44°$ J $KL = 7$ in.

Name ______________________ Date ______________ Class ______________

LESSON 5-2

Problem Solving

Bisectors of Triangles

1. A new dog park is being planned. Describe how to find a location for the park so that it is the same distance from three suburbs.

____

____

____

____

____

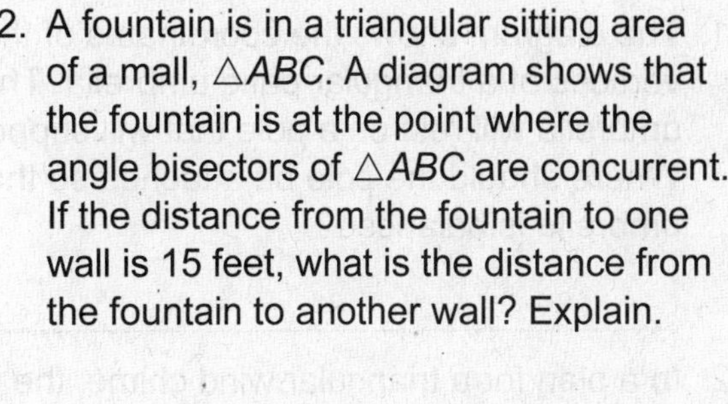

2. A fountain is in a triangular sitting area of a mall, △*ABC*. A diagram shows that the fountain is at the point where the angle bisectors of △*ABC* are concurrent. If the distance from the fountain to one wall is 15 feet, what is the distance from the fountain to another wall? Explain.

____

____

____

3. A water tower is to be built so that it is the same distance from the cities at *X*, *Y*, and *Z*. Draw a sketch on △*XYZ* to show the location *W* where the water tower should be built. Justify your sketch.

____

____

____

____

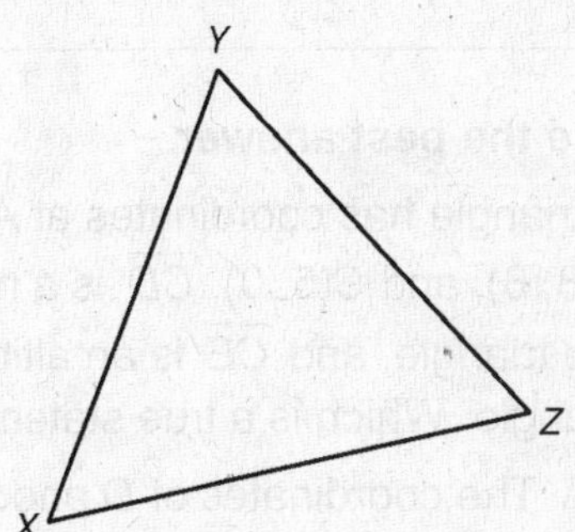

Choose the best answer.

4. The circumcenter of △*FGH* is at (4, –5). If *G* is at (0, 0), which of the following are possible coordinates of *F* and *H*?

   A *F*(0, –8), *H*(10, 0)
   B *F*(0, 8), *H*(–10, 0)
   C *F*(0, –10), *H*(8, 0)
   D *F*(0, 10), *H*(–8, 0)

5. A triangle has vertices *Q*(–9, 10), *R*(0, 1), and *S*(8, 4). Which is a correct statement about the incenter and circumcenter of △*QRS*?

   F Both points are on △*QRS*.
   G Both points are inside △*QRS*.
   H Both points are outside △*QRS*.
   J One point is inside △*QRS*, and one point is outside △*QRS*.

6. $\overline{RT}$ and $\overline{TS}$ are perpendicular bisectors of △*ABC*. What is the perimeter of △*ATC*?

   A 17.2 units
   B 19.4 units
   C 20.9 units
   D 22.4 units

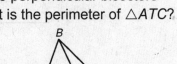

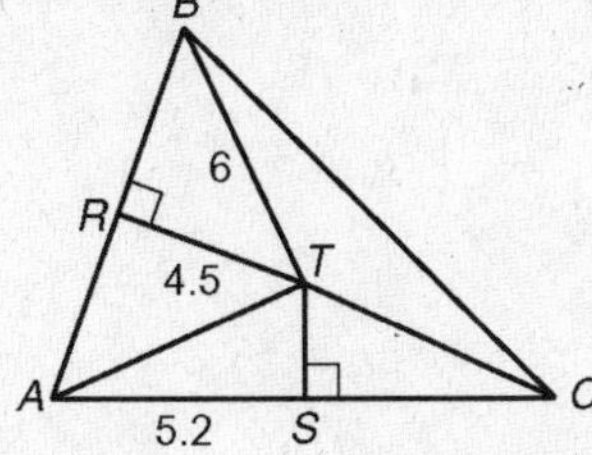

7. If m∠*KPN* = 44°, find m∠*JLP*.

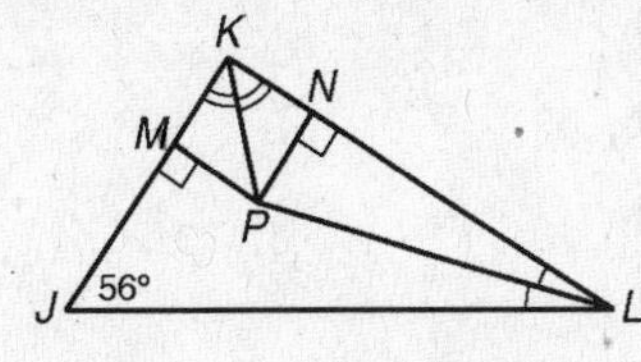

   F 16°
   G 18°
   H 23°
   J 32°

Name ________________________ Date ______________ Class ______________

LESSON 5-3

Problem Solving

Medians and Altitudes of Triangles

1. The diagram shows the coordinates of the vertices of a triangular patio umbrella. The umbrella will rest on a pole that will support it. Where should the pole be attached so that the umbrella is balanced?

____

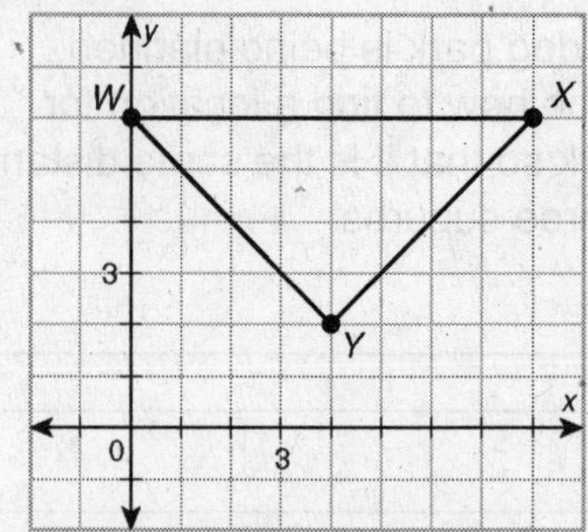

2. In a plan for a triangular wind chime, the coordinates of the vertices are $J(10, 2)$, $K(7, 6)$, and $L(12, 10)$. At what coordinates should the manufacturer attach the chain from which it will hang in order for the chime to be balanced?

3. Triangle PQR has vertices at $P(-3, 5)$, $Q(-1, 7)$, and $R(3, 1)$. Find the coordinates of the orthocenter and the centroid.

____

Choose the best answer.

4. A triangle has coordinates at $A(0, 6)$, $B(8, 6)$, and $C(5, 0)$. $\overline{CD}$ is a median of the triangle, and $\overline{CE}$ is an altitude of the triangle. Which is a true statement?

   A The coordinates of *D* and *E* are the same.

   B The distance between *D* and *E* is 1 unit.

   C The distance between *D* and *E* is 2 units.

   D *D* is on the triangle, and *E* is outside the triangle.

5. Lines *j* and *k* contain medians of $\triangle DEF$. Find *y* and *z*.

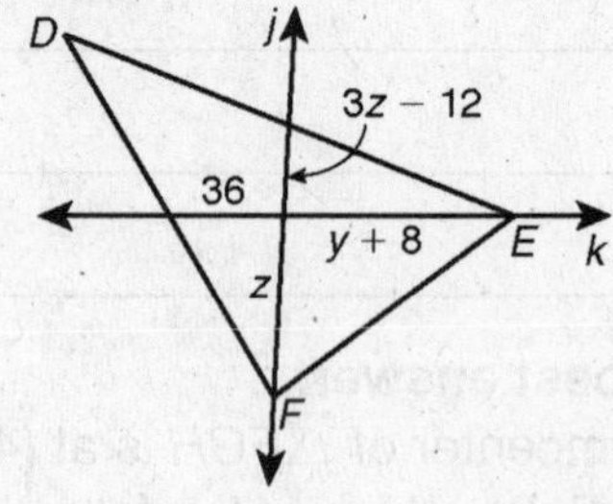

   F $y = 16$; $z = 4$ H $y = 64$; $z = 4.8$

   G $y = 32$; $z = 4$ J $y = 108$; $z = 8$

6. An inflatable triangular raft is towed behind a boat. The raft is an equilateral triangle. To maintain balance, the seat is at the centroid *B* of the triangle. What is *AB*, the distance from the seat to the tow rope? Round to the nearest tenth.

   A 18.7 in.

   B 37.4 in.

   C 43.1 in.

   D 56.0 in.

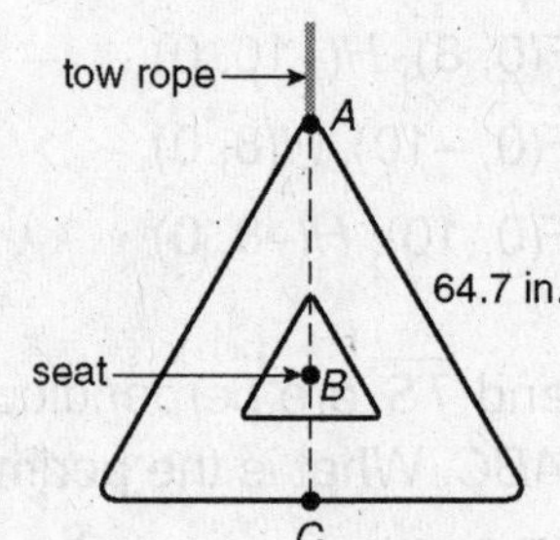

Name ______________________ Date ______________ Class ______________

LESSON 5-4

Problem Solving

The Triangle Midsegment Theorem

1. The vertices of $\triangle JKL$ are $J(-9, 2)$, $K(10, 1)$, and $L(5, 6)$. $\overline{CD}$ is the midsegment parallel to $\overline{JK}$. What is the length of $\overline{CD}$? Round to the nearest tenth.

____

2. In $\triangle QRS$, $QR = 2x + 5$, $RS = 3x - 1$, and $SQ = 5x$. What is the perimeter of the midsegment triangle of $\triangle QRS$?

____

3. Is XY a midsegment of $\triangle LMN$ if its endpoints are $X(8, 2.5)$ and $Y(6.5, -2)$? Explain.

____

____

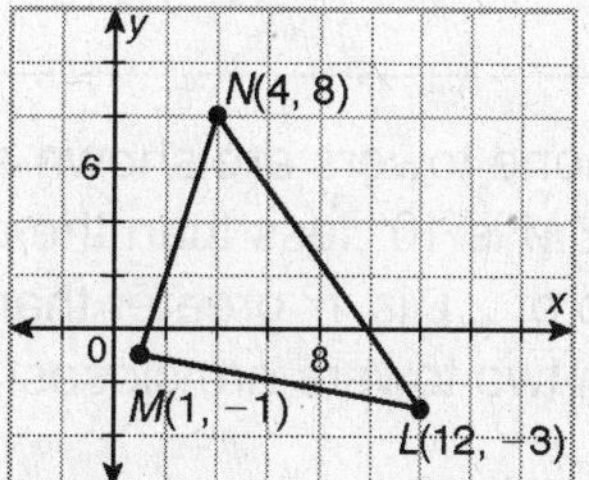

4. The diagram at right shows horseback riding trails. Point B is the halfway point along path $\overline{AC}$. Point D is the halfway point along path $\overline{CE}$. The paths along $\overline{BD}$ and $\overline{AE}$ are parallel. If riders travel from A to B to D to E, and then back to A, how far do they travel?

____

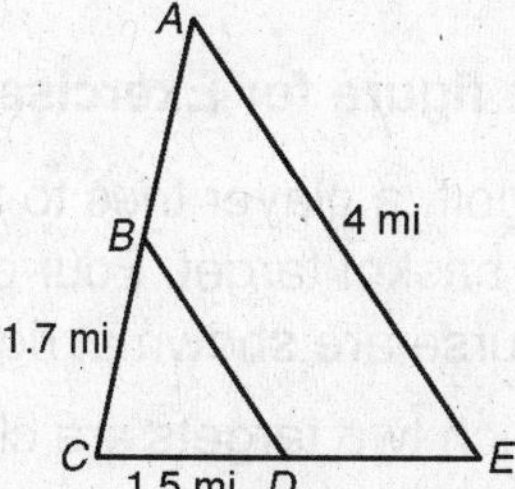

Choose the best answer.

5. Right triangle FGH has midsegments of length 10 centimeters, 24 centimeters, and 26 centimeters. What is the area of $\triangle FGH$?

A 60 cm^2 C 240 cm^2

B 120 cm^2 D 480 cm^2

6. In triangle HJK, $m\angle H = 110°$, $m\angle J = 30°$, and $m\angle K = 40°$. If R is the midpoint of $\overline{JK}$, and S is the midpoint of $\overline{HK}$, what is $m\angle JRS$?

F 150° H 110°

G 140° J 30°

Use the diagram for Exercises 7 and 8.

On the balance beam, V is the midpoint of $\overline{AB}$, and W is the midpoint of $\overline{YB}$.

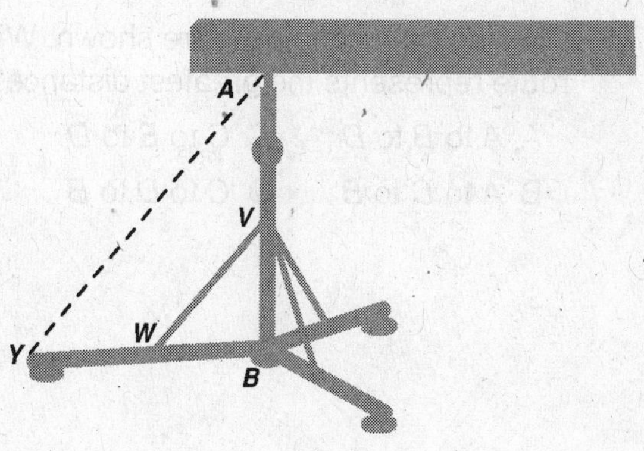

7. The length of $\overline{VW}$ is $1\frac{7}{8}$ feet. What is AY?

A $\frac{7}{8}$ ft C $3\frac{3}{4}$ ft

B $\frac{15}{16}$ ft D $7\frac{1}{2}$ ft

8. The measure of $\angle AYW$ is 50°. What is the measure of $\angle VWB$?

F 45° H 90°

G 50° J 130°

Name ______________________ Date ______________ Class ______________

LESSON 5-5

Problem Solving

Indirect Proof and Inequalities in One Triangle

1. A charter plane travels from Barrow, Alaska, to Fairbanks. From Fairbanks, it flies to Nome, and then back to its starting point in Barrow. Which of the three legs of the trip is the longest?

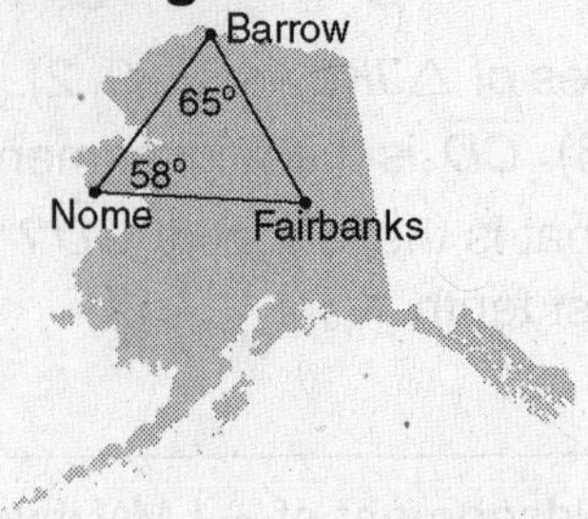

____

2. Three cell phone towers are shown at the right. The measure of $\angle M$ is 10° less than the measure of $\angle K$. The measure of $\angle L$ is 1° greater than the measure of $\angle K$. Which two towers are closest together?

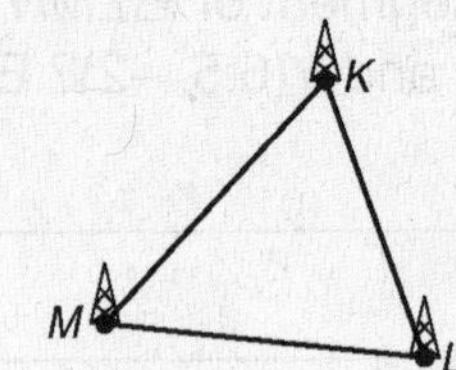

____

Use the figure for Exercises 3 and 4.

In disc golf, a player tries to throw a disc into a metal basket target. Four disc golf targets on a course are shown at right.

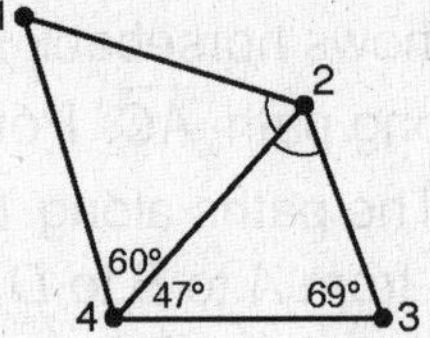

3. Which two targets are closest together?

____

4. Which two targets are farthest apart?

____

Choose the best answer.

5. The distance from Jacksonville to Tampa is 171 miles. The distance from Tampa to Miami is 206 miles. Use the Triangle Inequality Theorem to find the range for the distance from Jacksonville to Miami.

A 0 mi < d < 35 mi

B 0 mi < d < 377 mi

C 35 mi < d < 377 mi

D –35 mi < d < 377 mi

6. In Jessica's room, the distance from the door D to the closet C is 4 feet. The distance from the closet to the window W is 6 feet. The distance from the window to the door is 8 feet. On a floor plan of her room, $\triangle CDW$ is drawn. Order the angles from least to greatest measure.

F $\angle C, \angle D, \angle W$ H $\angle W, \angle C, \angle D$

G $\angle D, \angle C, \angle W$ J $\angle W, \angle D, \angle C$

7. Walking paths at a park are shown. Which route represents the greatest distance?

A A to B to D C C to B to D

B A to D to B D C to D to B

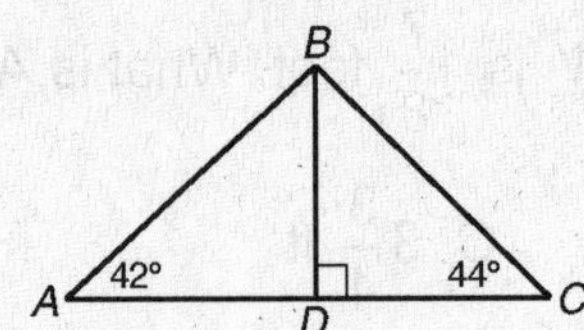

Name ______________________ Date ______________ Class ______________

LESSON 5-6

Problem Solving

Inequalities in Two Triangles

1. The angle that a person makes as he or she is sitting changes with the task. The diagram shows the position of a student at his desk. In which position is the angle measure $a°$ at which he is sitting the greatest? The least? Explain.

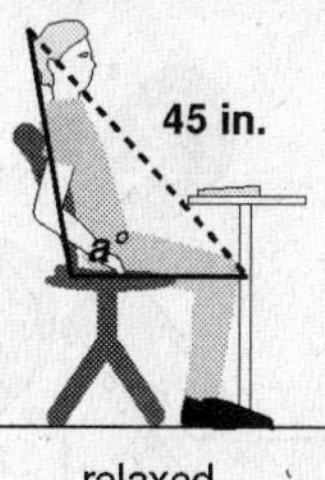

relaxed

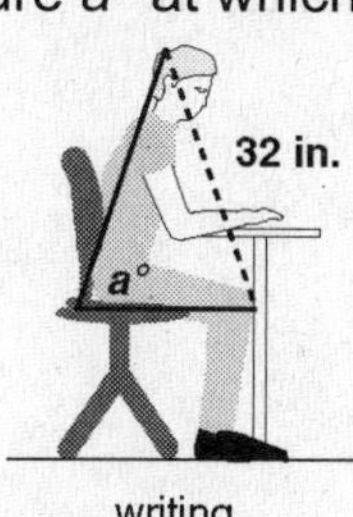

writing

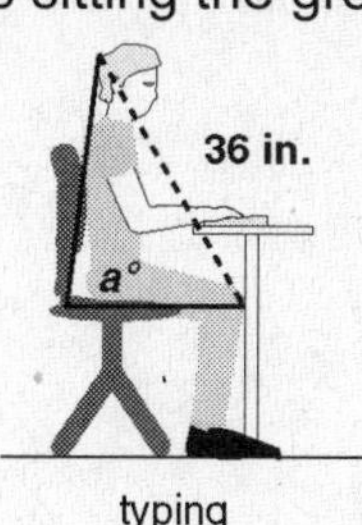

typing

____

____

____

____

2. Two cyclists start from the same location and travel in opposite directions for 2 miles each. Then the first cyclist turns right 90° and continues for another mile. At the same time, the second cyclist turns 45° left and continues for another mile. At this point, which cyclist is closer to the original starting point?

____

____

3. A compass is used to draw a circle. Then the compass is opened wider and another circle is drawn. Explain how this illustrates the Hinge Theorem.

____

____

____

____

____

Choose the best answer.

4. Two sides of each triangle in the circle are formed from the radii of the circle. Compare *EF* and *FG*.

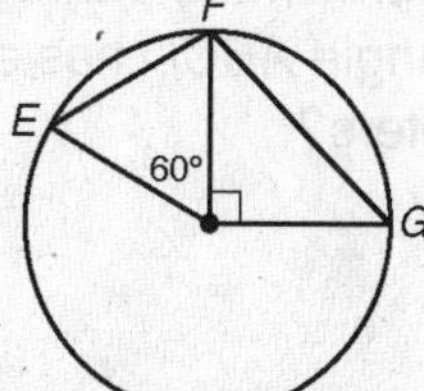

A $EF = FG$

B $EF < FG$

C $EF > FG$

D Not enough information is given.

5. Compare $m\angle Y$ and $m\angle M$.

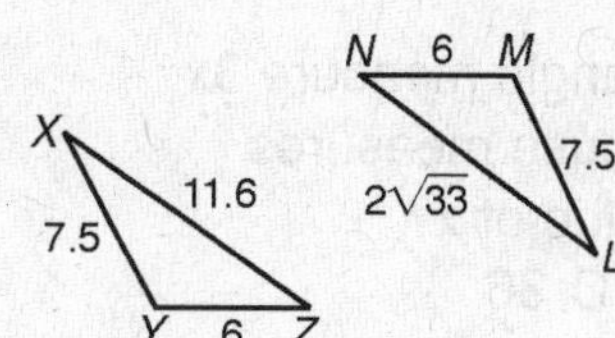

F $m\angle Y = m\angle M$

G $m\angle Y > m\angle M$

H $m\angle Y < m\angle M$

J Not enough information is given.

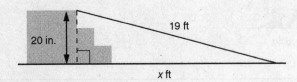

Name ______________________ Date ____________ Class ____________

LESSON 5-7

Problem Solving

The Pythagorean Theorem

1. It is recommended that for a height of 20 inches, a wheelchair ramp be 19 feet long. What is the value of x to the nearest tenth?

20 in. 19 ft x ft

____

2. Find x, the length of the weight-lifting incline bench. Round to the nearest tenth.

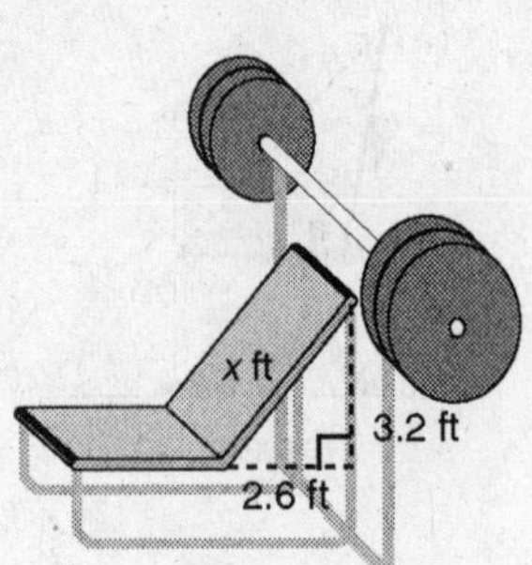

____

3. A ladder 15 feet from the base of a building reaches a window that is 35 feet high. What is the length of the ladder to the nearest foot?

____

4. In a wide-screen television, the ratio of width to height is 16 : 9. What are the width and height of a television that has a diagonal measure of 42 inches? Round to the nearest tenth.

____

Choose the best answer.

5. The distance from Austin to San Antonio is about 74 miles, and the distance from San Antonio to Victoria is about 102 miles. Find the approximate distance from Austin to Victoria.

   A 28 mi　　C 126 mi
   B 70 mi　　D 176 mi

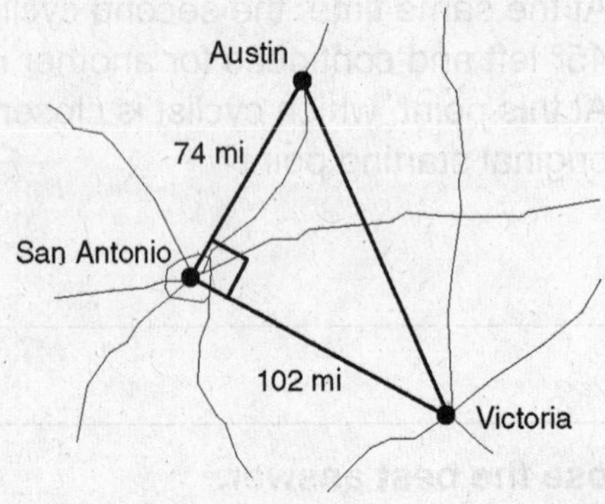

6. What is the approximate perimeter of $\triangle DEC$ if rectangle $ABCD$ has a length of 4.6 centimeters?

   F 5.1 cm
   G 6.5 cm
   H 9.8 cm
   J 11.1 cm

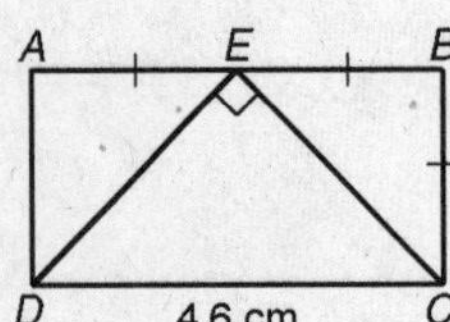

7. The legs of a right triangle measure $3x$ and 15. If the hypotenuse measures $3x + 3$, what is the value of x?

   A 12　　C 36
   B 16　　D 221

8. A cube has edge lengths of 6 inches. What is the approximate length of a diagonal d of the cube?

   F 6 in.　　H 10.4 in.
   G 8.4 in.　　J 12 in.

Name ______________________ Date ______________ Class ______________

LESSON 5-8

Problem Solving

Applying Special Right Triangles

For Exercises 1–6, give your answers in simplest radical form.

1. In bowling, the pins are arranged in a pattern based on equilateral triangles. What is the distance between pins 1 and 5?

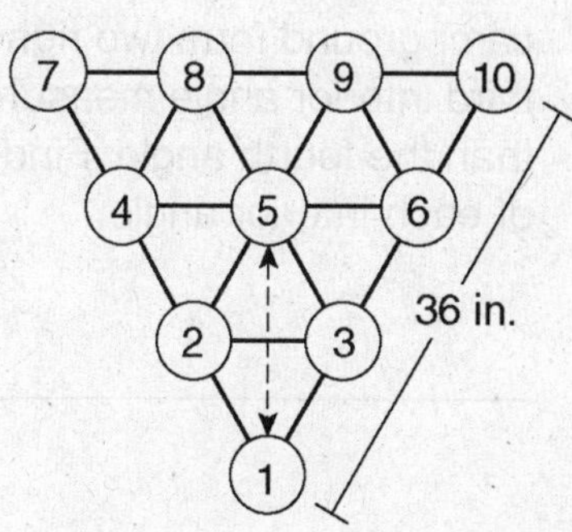

____

2. To secure an outdoor canopy, a 64-inch cord is extended from the top of a vertical pole to the ground. If the cord makes a 60° angle with the ground, how tall is the pole?

____

Find the length of $\overline{AB}$ in each quilt pattern.

3. 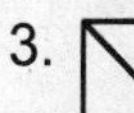 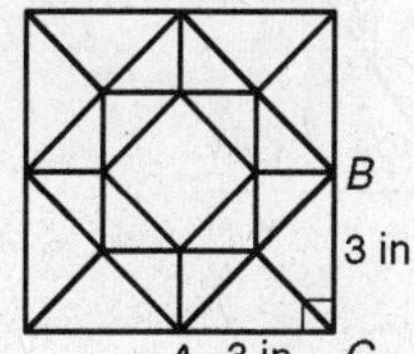

4. 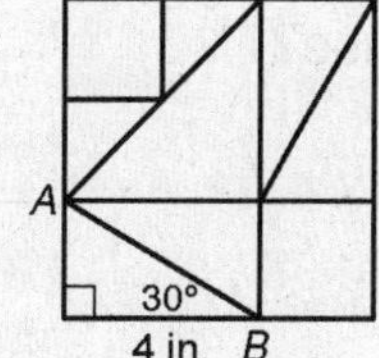

_______________________ _______________________

Choose the best answer.

5. An equilateral triangle has an altitude of 21 inches. What is the side length of the triangle?

____

6. A shelf is an isosceles right triangle, and the longest side is 38 centimeters. What is the length of each of the other two sides?

____

Use the figure for Exercises 7 and 8.

Assume $\triangle JKL$ is in the first quadrant, with $m\angle K = 90°$.

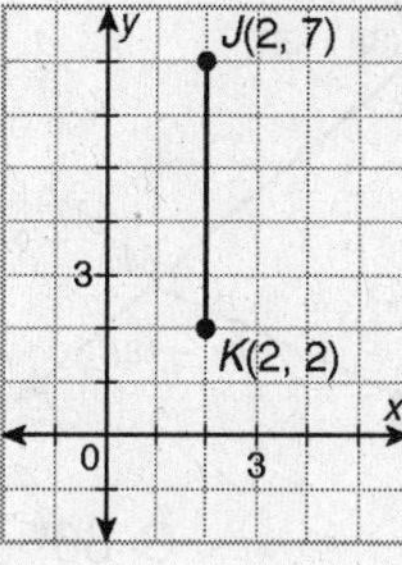

7. Suppose that $\overline{JK}$ is a leg of $\triangle JKL$, a 45°-45°-90° triangle. What are possible coordinates of point L?

A (6, 4.5) C (6, 2)

B (7, 2) D (8, 7)

8. Suppose $\triangle JKL$ is a 30°-60°-90° triangle and $\overline{JK}$ is the side opposite the 60° angle. What are the approximate coordinates of point L?

F (4.9, 2) H (8.7, 2)

G (4.5, 2) J (7.1, 2)

Name ______________________ Date ______________ Class ______________

LESSON 6-1

Problem Solving

Properties and Attributes of Polygons

1. A campground site is in the shape of a convex quadrilateral. Three sides of the campground form two right angles. The third interior angle measures 10° less than the fourth angle. Find the measure of each interior angle.

____

2. A pentagon has two exterior angles that measure $(3x)°$, two exterior angles that measure $(2x + 22)°$, and an exterior angle that measures $(x + 41)°$. If all of these angles have different vertices, what are the measures of the exterior angles of the pentagon?

____

3. The top view of a hexagonal greenhouse is shown at the right. What is the measure of $\angle PQR$, the acute angle formed by the house and the greenhouse?

____

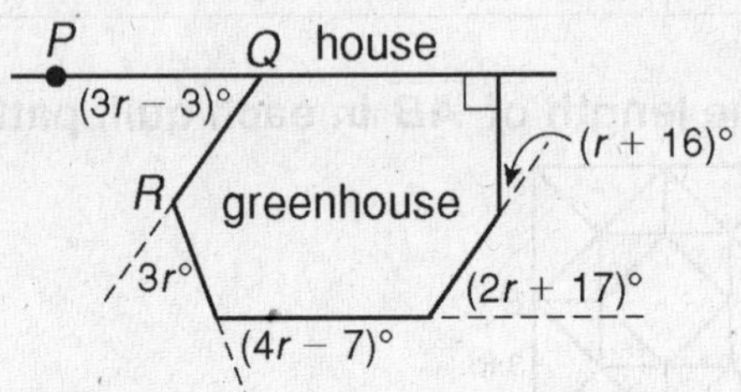

Choose the best answer.

4. A figure is an equiangular 18-gon. What is the measure of each exterior angle of the polygon?

A 10°
B 18°
C 20°
D 36°

5. Three interior angles of a convex heptagon measure 125°, and two of the interior angles measure 143°. Which are possible measures for the other two interior angles of the heptagon?

F 48° and 48° H 100° and 116°
G 39° and 100° J 89° and 150°

6. Find the measure of $\angle RKL$.

A 34° C 86°
B 68° D 148°

7. What is the measure of $\angle GCD$?

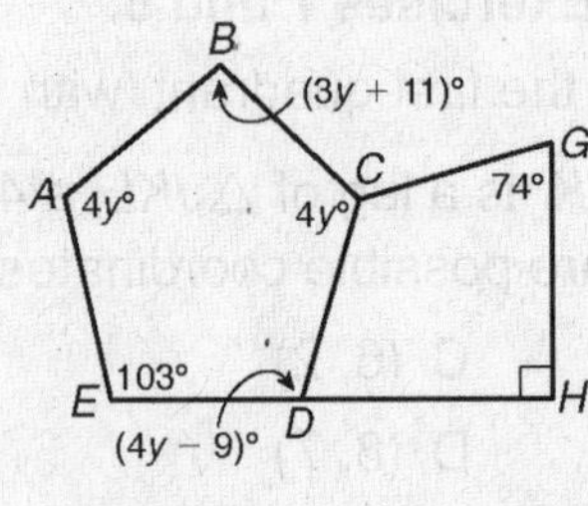

F 123° H 73°
G 116° J 29°

Name ______________________ Date ______________ Class ______________

LESSON 6-2

Problem Solving

Properties of Parallelograms

Use the diagram for Exercises 1 and 2.

The wall frames on the staircase wall form parallelograms *ABCD* and *EFGH*.

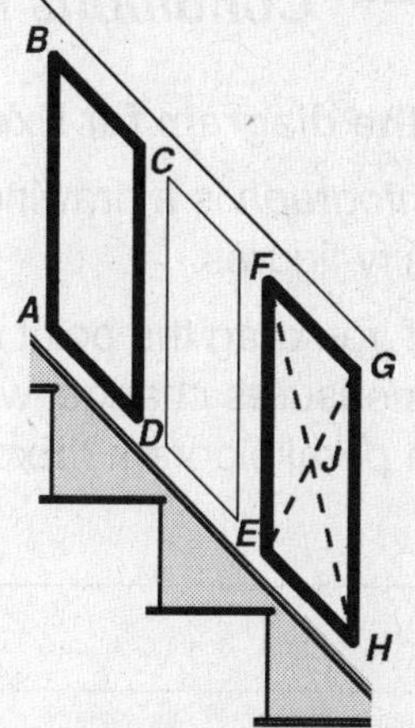

1. In ▱*ABCD*, the measure of ∠*A* is three times the measure of ∠*B*. What are the measures of ∠*C* and ∠*D*?

____

2. In ▱*EFGH*, *FH* = 5*x* inches, *EG* = (2*x* + 4) inches, and *JG* = 8 inches. What is the length of *JH*?

____

3. The diagram shows a section of the support structure of a roller coaster. In ▱*JKLM*, *JK* = (3*z* – 0.9) feet, and *LM* = (*z* + 2.7) feet. Find *JK*.

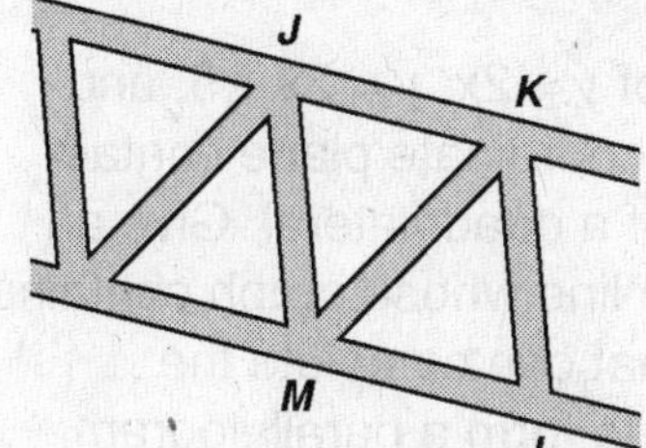

____

4. In ▱*TUVW*, part of a ceramic tile pattern, m∠*TUV* = (8*x* + 1)° and m∠*UVW* = (12*x* + 19)°. Find m∠*TUV*.

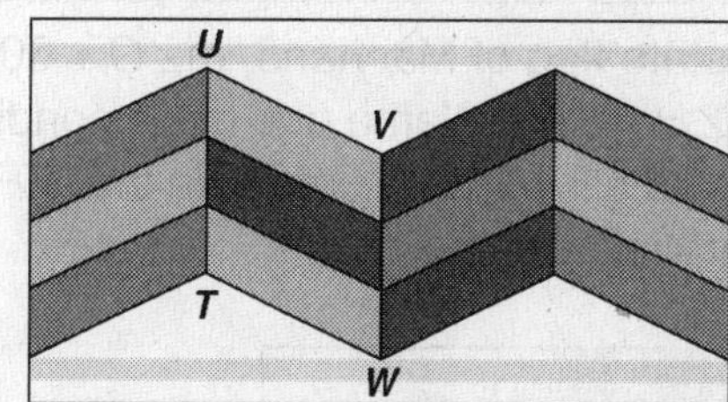

____

Choose the best answer.

5. What is the measure of ∠*Z* in parallelogram *WXYZ*?

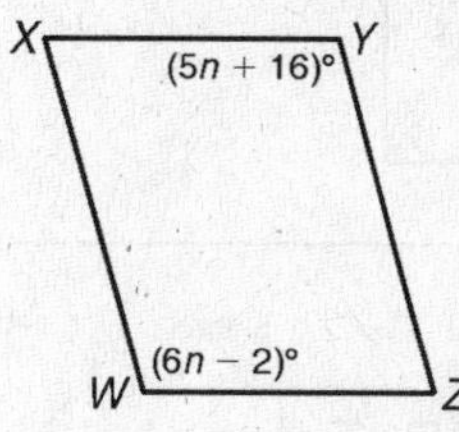

A 18°

B 74°

C 106°

D 108°

6. The perimeter of ▱*CDEF* is 54 centimeters. Find the length of $\overline{FC}$ if $\overline{DE}$ is 5 centimeters longer than $\overline{EF}$.

F 11 cm

G 14 cm

H 16 cm

J 44 cm

7. In ▱*PQRS*, *QT* = 7*x*, *TS* = 2*x* + 2.5, *RT* = 2*y*, and *TP* = *y* + 3. Find the perimeter of Δ*PTS*.

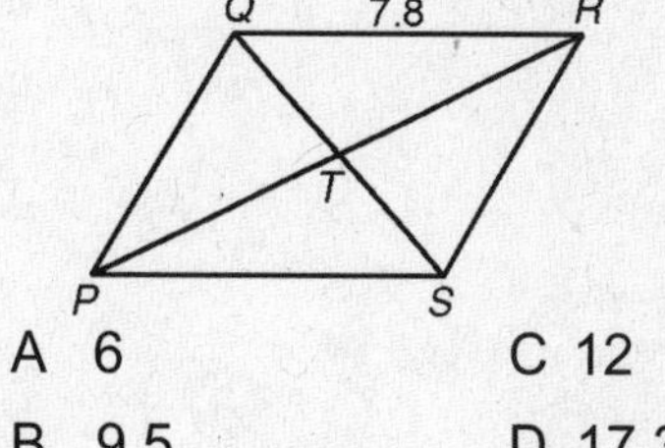

A 6

B 9.5

C 12

D 17.3

Name ______________________ Date ______________ Class ______________

LESSON 6-3

Problem Solving

Conditions for Parallelograms

Use the diagram for Exercises 1 and 2.

A *pantograph* is a drawing instrument used to magnify figures.

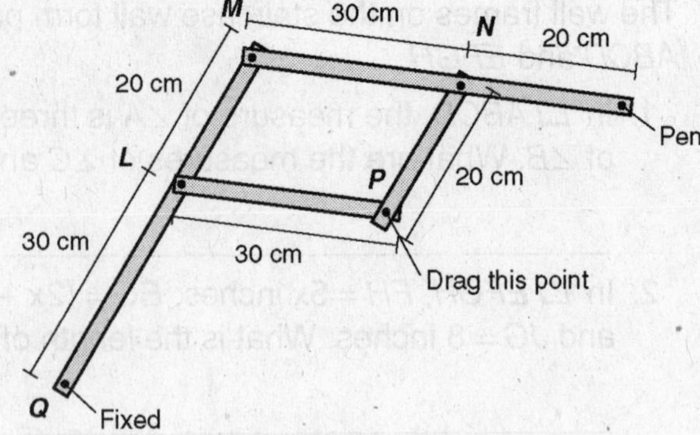

1. If you drag the point at P so that the angle measures change, will $LMNP$ continue to be a parallelogram? Explain.

____

____

____

2. If you drag the point at P so that $m\angle LMN = 56°$, what will be the measure of $\angle QLP$?

____

3. In the state flag of Maryland, $m\angle G = 60°$ and $m\angle H = 120°$. Name one more condition that would allow you to conclude that $EFGH$ is a parallelogram.

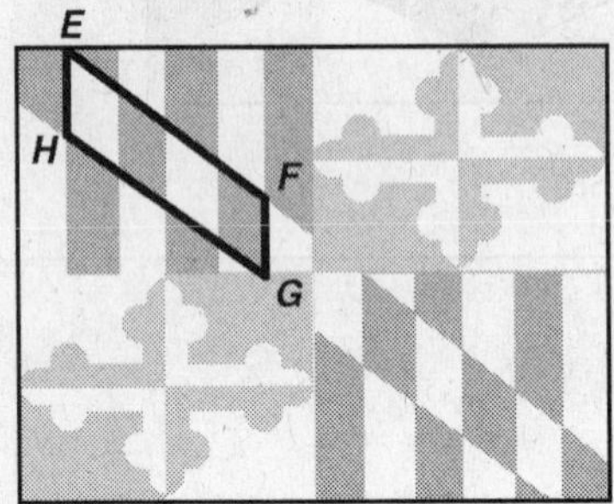

____

4. The graphs of $y = 2x$, $y = 2x - 5$, and $y = -x$ in the coordinate plane contain three sides of a quadrilateral. Give an equation of a line whose graph contains a segment that can complete the quadrilateral to form a parallelogram. Explain.

____

____

____

Choose the best answer.

5. For which value of n is $QRST$ a parallelogram?

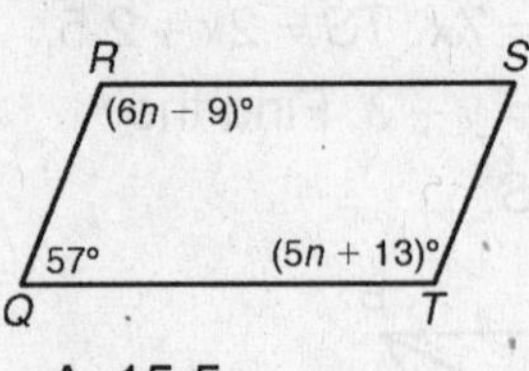

A 15.5

B 20.6

C 22

D 25

6. Under what conditions must $ABCD$ be a parallelogram?

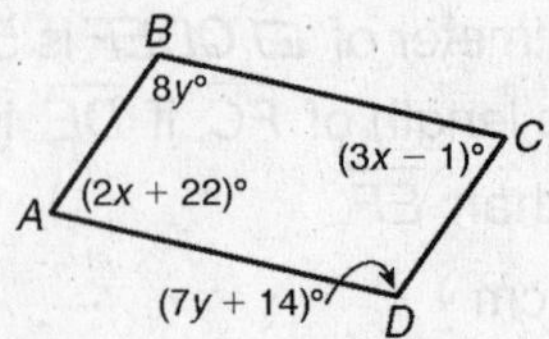

F $x = 23$

G $y = 14$

H $x = 23$ and $y = 14$

J $x = 14$ and $y = 23$

Name ______________________ Date ______________ Class ______________

LESSON 6-4

Problem Solving

Properties of Special Parallelograms

Use the diagram for Exercises 1 and 2.

The soccer goalposts determine rectangle *ABCD*.

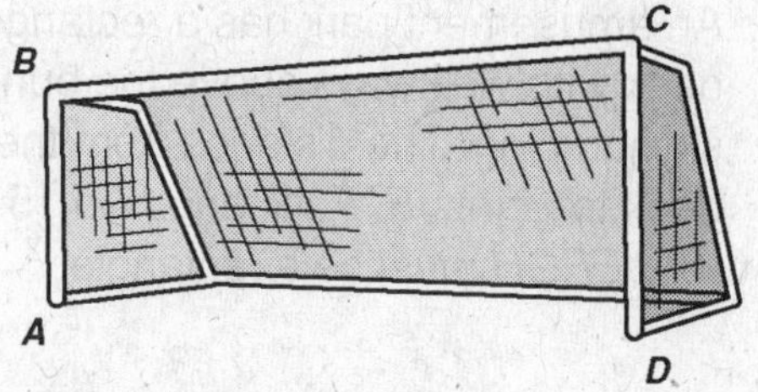

1. The distance between goalposts, *BC*, is three times the distance from the top of the goalpost to the ground. If the perimeter of *ABCD* is $21\frac{1}{3}$ yards, what is the length of $\overline{BC}$?

____

2. The distance from *B* to *D* is approximately $(x + 10)$ feet, and the distance from *A* to *C* is approximately $(2x - 5.3)$ feet. What is the approximate distance from *A* to *C*?

____

3. *MNPQ* is a rhombus. The measure of $\angle MRQ$ is $(13t - 1)°$, and the measure of $\angle PQR$ is $(7t + 4)°$. What is the measure of $\angle PQM$?

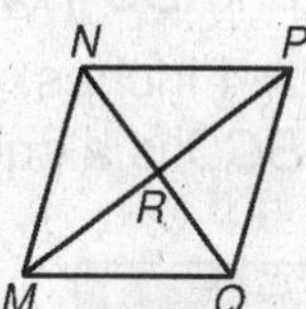

____

4. The *scissor lift* forms rhombus *PQRS* with $PQ = (7b - 5)$ meters and $QR = (2b - 0.5)$ meters. If *S* is the midpoint of $\overline{RT}$, what is the length of $\overline{RT}$?

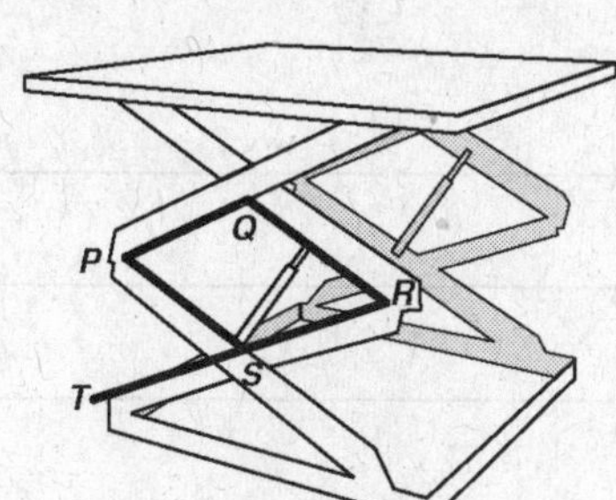

____

5. The diagram shows the lid of a rectangular case that holds 80 CDs. What are the dimensions of the case?

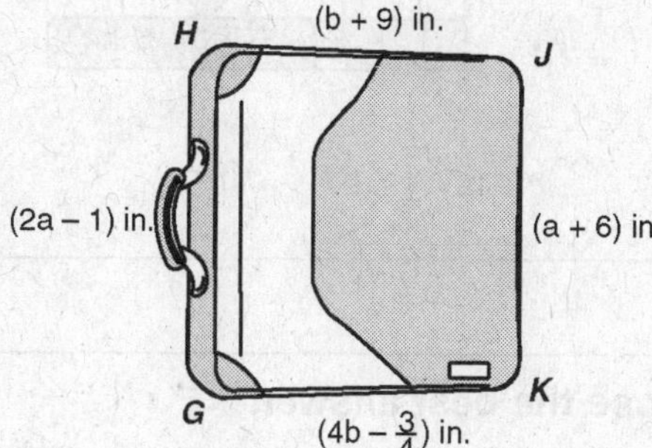

____

Choose the best answer.

6. What is the measure of $\angle 1$ in the rectangle?

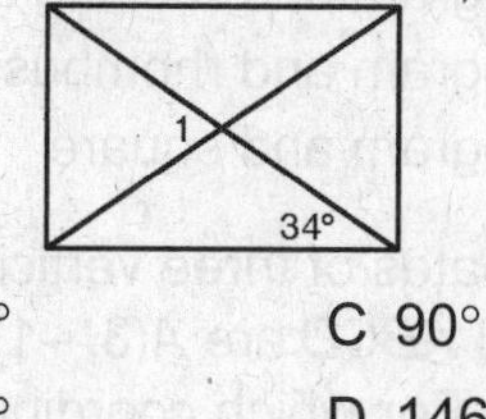

A 34°
B 68°
C 90°
D 146°

7. A square graphed on the coordinate plane has a diagonal with endpoints *E*(2, 3) and *F*(0, –3). What are the coordinates of the endpoints of the other diagonal?

F (4, –1) and (–2, 1)
G (4, 0) and (–2, 1)
H (4, –1) and (–3, 1)
J (3, –1) and (–2, 1)

Name ______________________ Date ______________ Class ______________

LESSON 6-5

Problem Solving

Conditions for Special Parallelograms

1. An amusement park has a rectangular observation deck with walkways above the bungee jumping and sky jumping. The distance from the center of the deck to points *E*, *F*, *G*, and *H* is 15 meters. Explain why *EFGH* must be a rectangle.

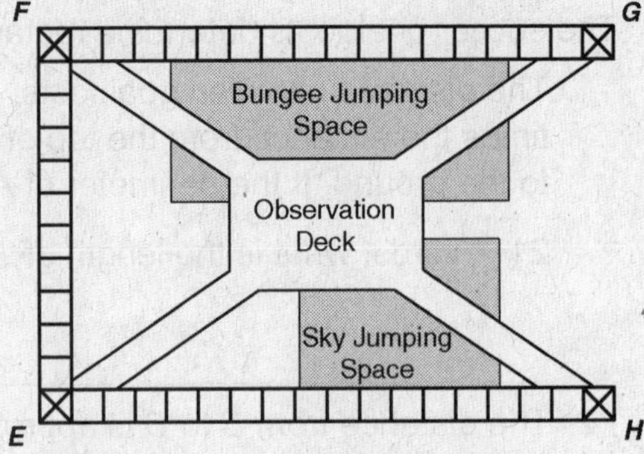

____

____

____

____

2. In the mosaic, $\overline{AB} \parallel \overline{CD}$ and $\overline{BC} \parallel \overline{DA}$. If $AB = 4$ inches and $BC = 4$ inches, can you conclude that *ABCD* is a square? Explain.

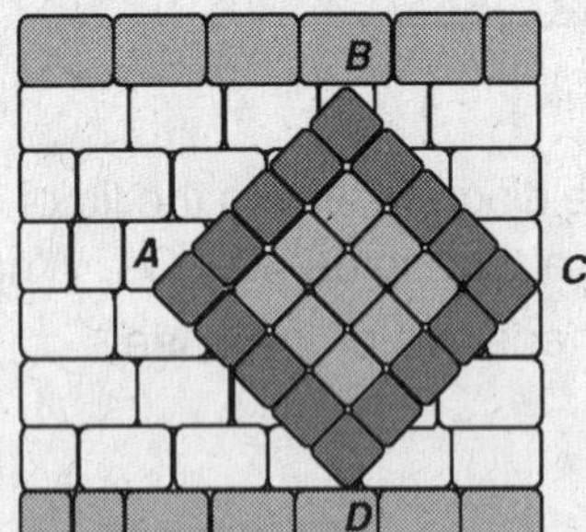

____

____

3. If $\overline{TV} \cong \overline{US}$, explain why the basketball backboard must be a rectangle.

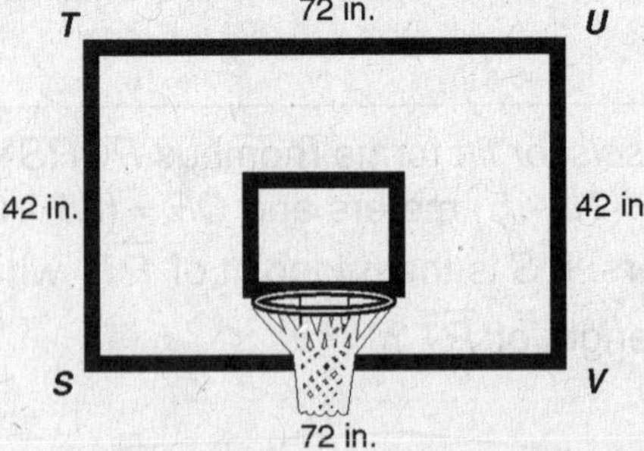

____

____

____

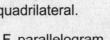

Choose the best answer.

4. The vertices of a parallelogram are *N*(0, –4), *P*(6, –1), *Q*(4, 3), and *R*(–2, 0). Classify the parallelogram as specifically as possible.

   A rectangle only

   B square

   C rhombus only

   D quadrilateral

5. Choose the best description for the quadrilateral.

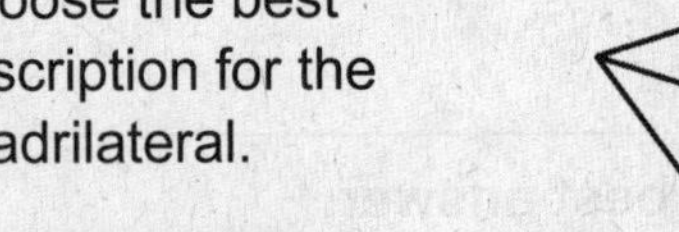

   F parallelogram

   G parallelogram and rectangle

   H parallelogram and rhombus

   J parallelogram and square

6. In parallelogram *KLMN*, $m\angle L = (4w + 5)°$. Choose the value of *w* that makes *KLMN* a rectangle.

   A 90   C 43.75

   B 85   D 21.25

7. The coordinates of three vertices of quadrilateral *ABCD* are *A*(3, –1), *B*(10, 0), and *C*(5, 5). For which coordinates of *D* will the quadrilateral be a rhombus?

   F (–1, 4)   H (–1, 3)

   G (–2, 4)   J (–2, 3)

Name ______________________ Date ______________ Class ______________

LESSON 6-6

Problem Solving

Properties of Kites and Trapezoids

Use the figure of the kite for Exercises 1 and 2.

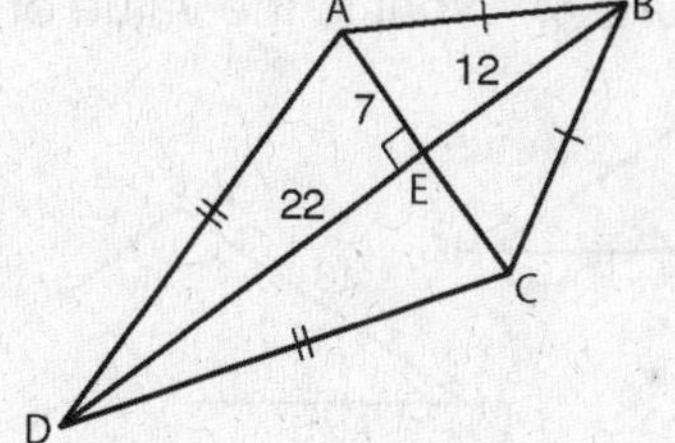

1. What is AD to the nearest tenth?

____

2. What is the perimeter of the kite to the nearest tenth?

____

3. In kite $STUV$, $m\angle TUW = 35°$ and $m\angle WSV = 21°$. What is the measure of $\angle UVS$?

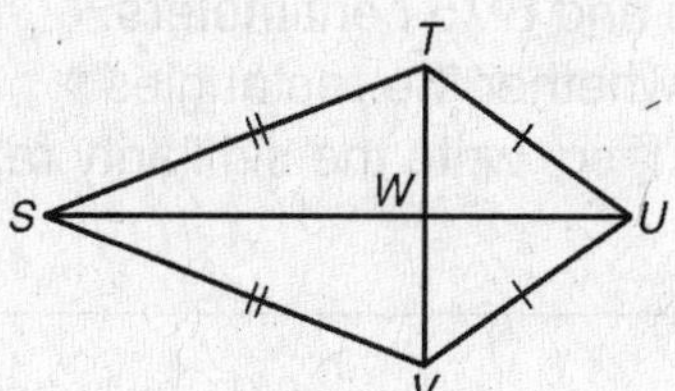

____

4. A car window is in the shape of a trapezoid. When the window is halfway down, the top is $\overline{KL}$, the midsegment of $FGHJ$. If $KL = 23$ inches, what is GH?

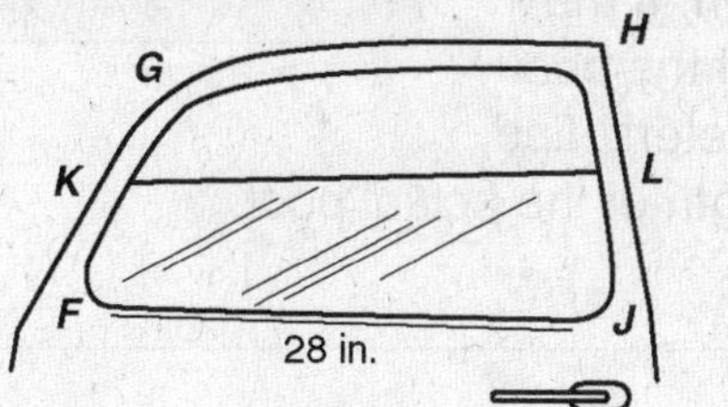

____

Choose the best answer.

5. Trapezoid $PQRS$ has base angles that measure $(9r + 21)°$ and $(15r - 21)°$. Find the value of r so that $PQRS$ is isosceles.

   A 3

   B 5

   C 7

   D 14

6. In kite $KLMN$, find the measure of $\angle M$.

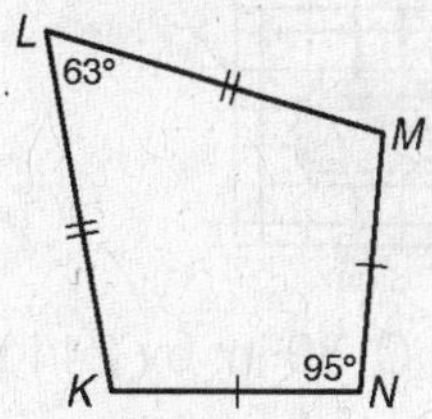

   F 100.5°   H 122°

   G 101°   J 130°

7. In the design, eight isosceles trapezoids surround a regular octagon. What is the measure of $\angle B$ in trapezoid $ABCD$?

   A 35°

   B 45°

   C 55°

   D 65°

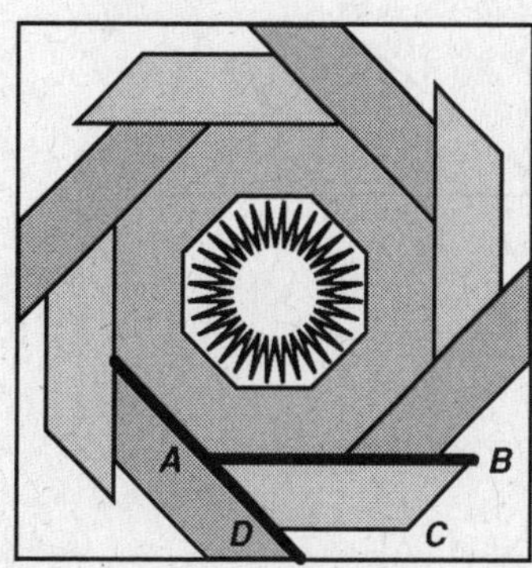

Name ________________________ Date ______________ Class ______________

LESSON 7-1

Problem Solving

Ratios in Similar Polygons

1. $EFGH \sim JKLM$. What is the value of x?

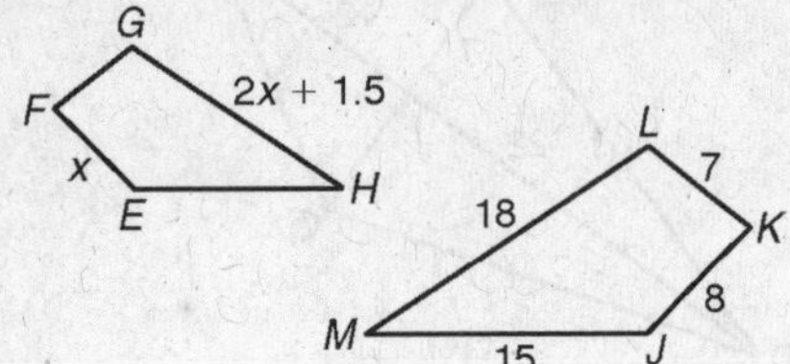

____

2. The ratio of a model scale die cast motorcycle is 1 : 18. The model is $5\frac{1}{4}$ inches long. What is the length of the actual motorcycle in feet and inches?

____

3. A diagram of a new competition swimming pool is shown. If the width of the pool is 25 meters, find the length of the actual pool.

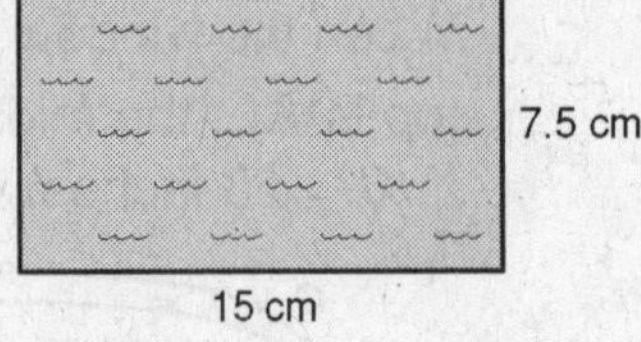

____

4. Rectangle A has side lengths 16.4 centimeters and 10.8 centimeters. Rectangle B has side lengths 10.25 centimeters and 6.75 centimeters. Determine whether the rectangles are similar. If so, write the similarity ratio.

____

Choose the best answer.

5. A pet store has various sizes of guinea pig cages. A diagram of the top view of one of the cages is shown. What are possible dimensions of this cage?

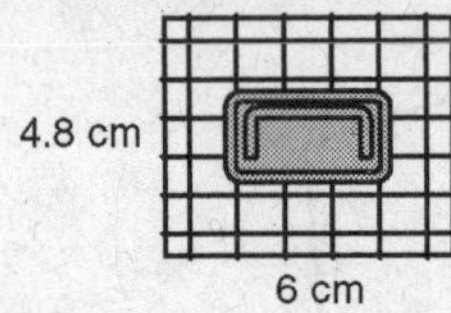

A 28 in. by 24 in. C 30 in. by 24 in.

B 28 in. by 18 in. D 30 in. by 18 in.

6. A gymnasium is 96 feet long and 75 feet wide. On a blueprint, the gymnasium is 5.5 inches long. To the nearest tenth of an inch, what is the width of the gymnasium on the blueprint?

F 3.7 in. H 7.0 in.

G 4.3 in. J 13.6 in.

7. $\triangle QRS \sim \triangle TUV$. Find the value of y.

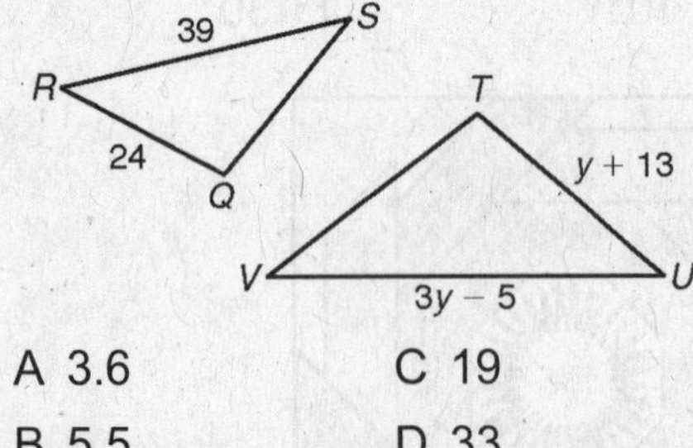

A 3.6 C 19

B 5.5 D 33

8. $\triangle ABC$ has side lengths 14, 8, and 10.4. What are possible side lengths of $\triangle DEF$ if $\triangle ABC \sim \triangle DEF$?

F 28, 20, 20.8

G 35, 16, 20.8

H 28, 20, 26

J 35, 20, 26

Name ______________________ Date ______________ Class ______________

LESSON 7-2

Problem Solving

Similarity and Transformations

1. Irena is designing a quilt. She started with a large square and then made this diagram to follow when making her quilt. Describe how she used dilations to make the pattern.

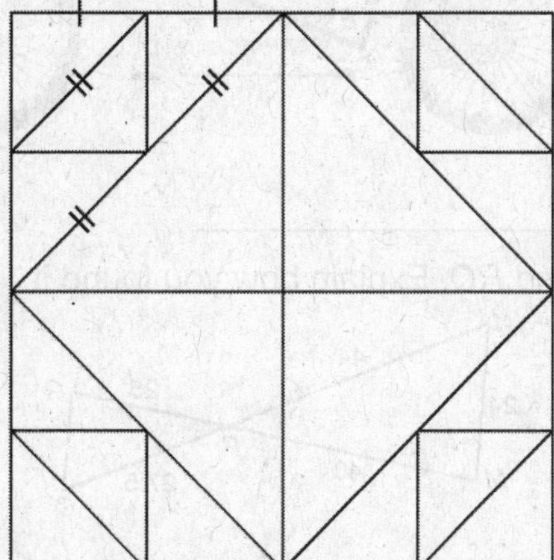

____

2. A crop circle is a large pattern formed by flattening or cutting crops so the design is apparent when viewed from above. Every year, Hector puts a crop circle into his corn field. This year's design is shown below. Describe how he used dilations to complete his design.

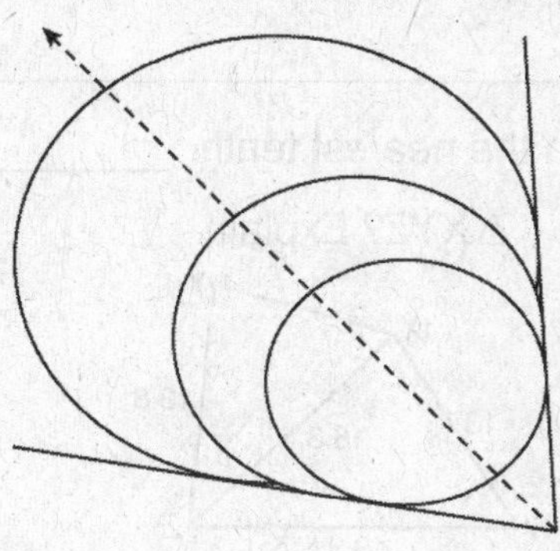

____

3. A graphic artist incorporated two similar right triangles into a logo with one triangle twice the size of the other. He used a computer graphics program to draw the first triangle and then used the enlargement tool of the program to draw the other triangle. How can he verify that the two triangles are similar?

____

4. A toy designer is planning to create a doll house. The design includes two similar rectangles with one being three times the size of the other. She cuts and traces the small rectangle onto grid paper first. Describe how she can use the tracing to make a pattern for the larger rectangle.

____

Choose the best answer.

5. Circle *A* with radius 4 and center (3, 0) is drawn in the coordinate plane. What is the scale factor that maps the circle with radius 3 and center (2, 3) onto circle *A*?

A $\frac{4}{3}$ C $\frac{7}{3}$

B $\frac{3}{4}$ D $\frac{3}{7}$

6. An art student uses dilations in all her art. She first plans the art piece on a coordinate grid. Determine the vertices of the image of the triangle with vertices *A*(1, 1), *B*(2, 4), and *C*(3, 9) after a dilation with scale factor 1.5.

F *A*′(1.5, 1.5), *B*′(3, 5), *C*′(4.5, 13.5)

G *A*′ (2.5, 2.5), *B*′(5, 10), *C*′(7.5, 22.5)

H *A*′ (1.5, 1.5), *B*′(4, 8), *C*′(6, 18)

J *A*′ (1.5, 1.5), *B*′(3, 6), *C*′(4.5, 13.5)

LESSON 7-3

Problem Solving

Triangle Similarity: AA, SSS, and SAS

Use the diagram for Exercises 1 and 2.

In the diagram of the tandem bike, $\overline{AE} \parallel \overline{BD}$.

1. Explain why $\triangle CBD \sim \triangle CAE$.

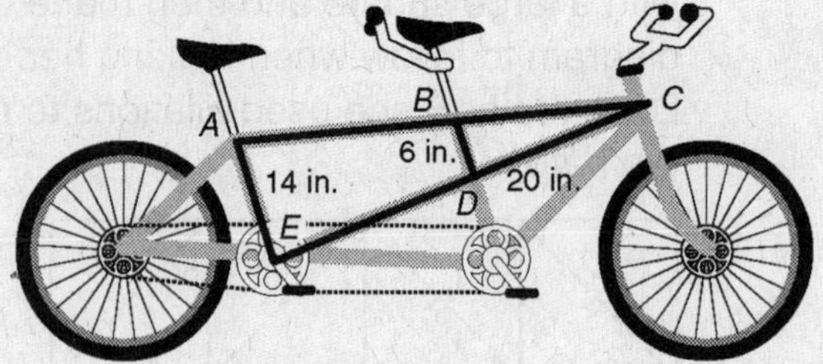

2. Find *CE* to the nearest tenth. ______________________

3. Is $\triangle WXZ \sim \triangle XYZ$? Explain.

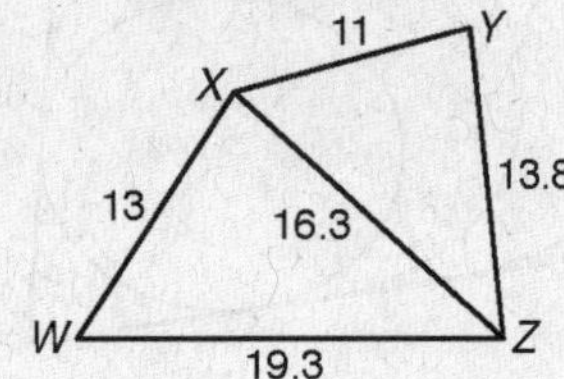

____

4. Find *RQ*. Explain how you found it.

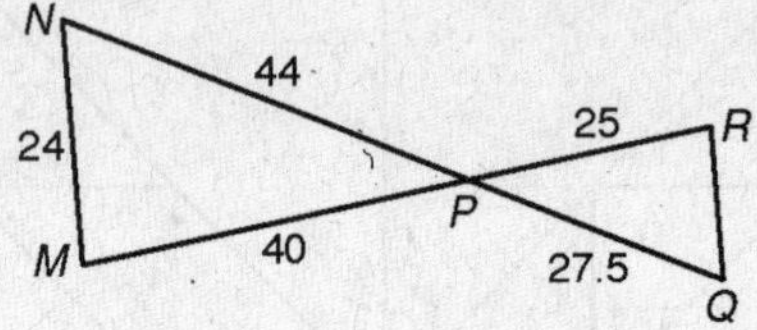

____

____

____

Choose the best answer.

5. Find the value of *x* that makes $\triangle FGH \sim \triangle JKL$.

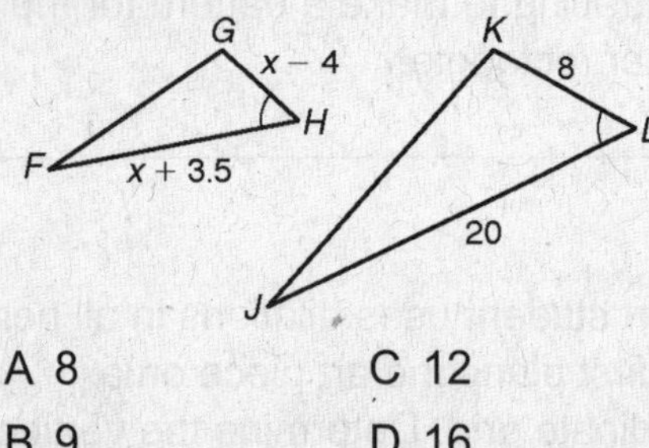

A 8 C 12

B 9 D 16

6. Triangle *STU* has vertices at *S*(0, 0), *T*(2, 6), and *U*(8, 2). If $\triangle STU \sim \triangle WXY$ and the coordinates of *W* are (0, 0), what are possible coordinates of *X* and *Y*?

F *X*(1, 3) and *Y*(4, 1)

G *X*(1, 3) and *Y*(2, 0)

H *X*(3, 1) and *Y*(2, 4)

J *X*(0, 3) and *Y*(4, 0)

7. To measure the distance *EF* across the lake, a surveyor at *S* locates points *E*, *F*, *G*, and *H* as shown. What is *EF*?

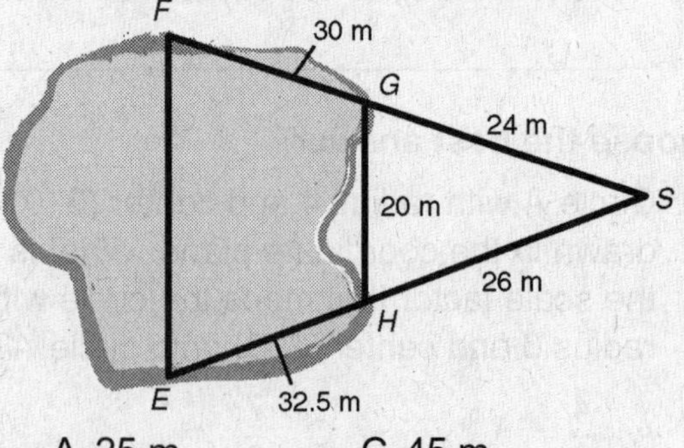

A 25 m C 45 m

B 36 m D 90 m

LESSON 7-4

Problem Solving

Applying Properties of Similar Triangles

1. Is $\overline{GF} \parallel \overline{HJ}$ if $x = 5$? Explain.

____

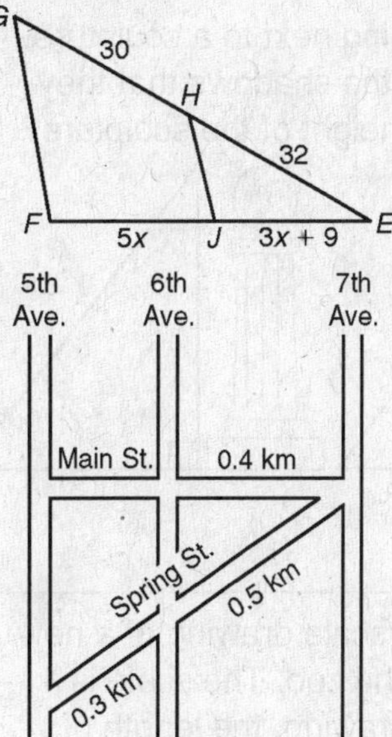

2. On the map, 5th Ave., 6th Ave., and 7th Ave. are parallel. What is the length of Main St. between 5th Ave. and 6th Ave.?

____

3. Find the length of $\overline{BC}$.

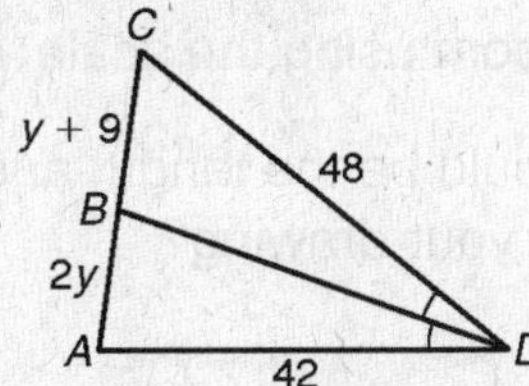

____

4. The figure shows three lots in a housing development. If the boundary lines separating the lots are parallel, what is *GF* to the nearest tenth?

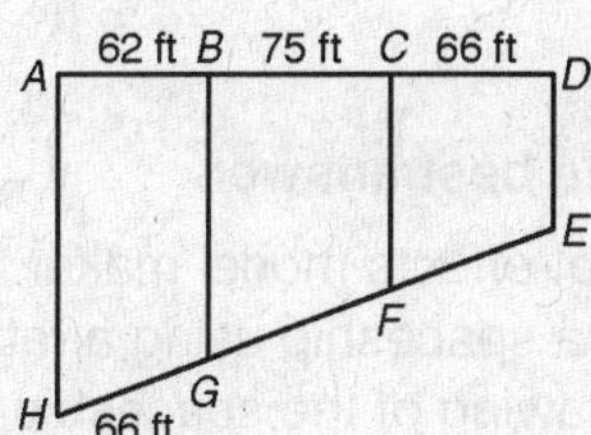

____

Choose the best answer.

5. If $LM = 22$, what is *PM*?

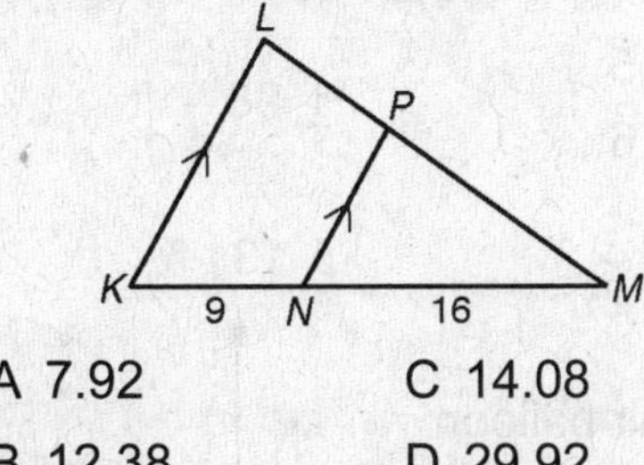

A 7.92 C 14.08

B 12.38 D 29.92

6. In $\triangle QRS$, the bisector of $\angle R$ divides $\overline{QS}$ into segments with lengths 2.1 and 2.8. If $RQ = 3$, which is the length of $\overline{RS}$?

F 2 H 4

G 2.25 J 4.5

7. In $\triangle CDE$, the bisector of $\angle C$ divides $\overline{DE}$ into segments with lengths $4x$ and $x + 13$. If $CD = 24$ and $CE = 32$, which is the length of $\overline{DE}$?

A 20 C 26

B 24 D 28

Name ______________________ Date ______________ Class ______________

LESSON 7-5

Problem Solving

Using Proportional Relationships

1. A student is standing next to a sculpture. The figure shows the shadows that they cast. What is the height of the sculpture?

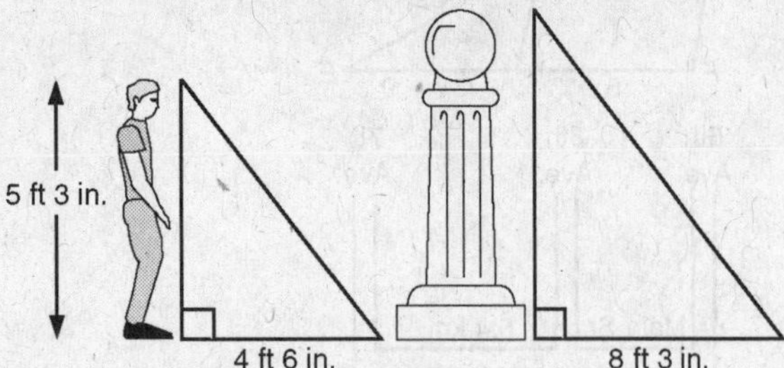

____

2. At the halftime show during a football game, a marching band is to form a rectangle 50 yards by 16 yards. The conductor wants to plan out the band members' positions using a 14- by 8.5-in. sheet of paper. What scale should she use to fit both dimensions of the rectangle on the page? (Use whole inches and yards.)

____

3. An artist makes a scale drawing of a new lion enclosure at the zoo. The scale is 1 in : 25 ft. On the drawing, the length of the enclosure is $7\frac{1}{4}$ inches. What is the actual length of the lion enclosure?

____

4. A room is 14 feet long and 11 feet wide. If you made a scale drawing of the top view of the room using the scale $\frac{1}{2}$ in = 2 ft, what would be the length and width of the room in your drawing?

____

Choose the best answer.

5. A visual-effects model maker for a movie draws a spaceship using a ratio of 1 : 24. The drawing of the spaceship is 22 inches long. What is the length of the spaceship in the movie?

A 4 ft C 44 ft
B 8 ft D 528 ft

6. A free-fall ride at an amusement park casts a shadow $43\frac{2}{3}$ feet long. At the same time, a 6-foot-tall person standing in line casts a shadow 2 feet long. What is the height of the ride?

F $21\frac{5}{6}$ ft H $98\frac{1}{4}$ ft
G $65\frac{1}{2}$ ft J 131 ft

7. The scale of the park map is 1.5 cm = 60 m. Which is the best estimate for the actual distance between the horse stables and the picnic area?

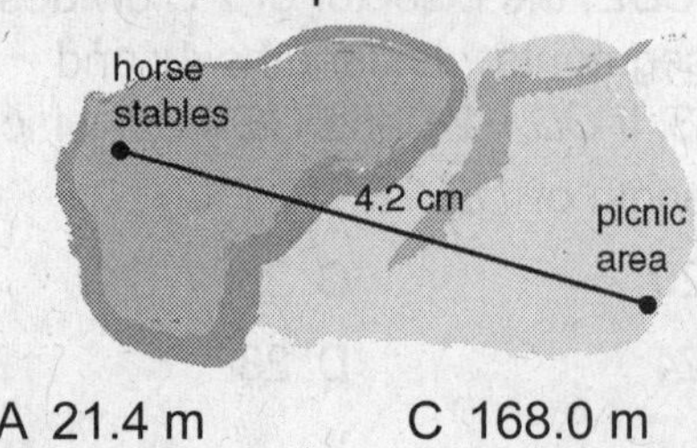

A 21.4 m C 168.0 m
B 90.0 m D 288.0 m

8. A hot-air balloon is 26.8 meters tall. Use the scale drawing to find the actual distance across the hot-air balloon.

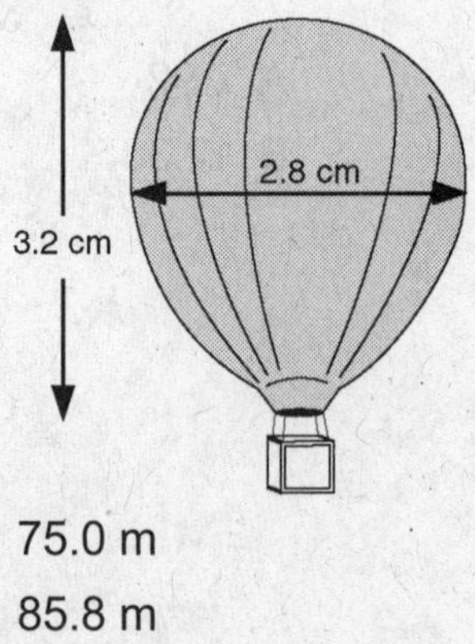

3.2 cm
2.8 cm

F 23.45 m H 75.0 m
G 30.6 m J 85.8 m

Name ______________________ Date ______________ Class ______________

LESSON 7-6

Problem Solving

Dilations and Similarity in the Coordinate Plane

1. The figure shows a photograph on grid paper. What are the coordinates of C' if the photograph is enlarged with scale factor $\frac{4}{3}$?

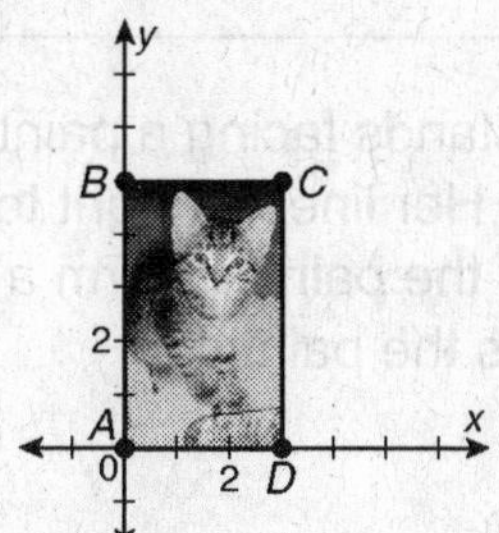

____

2. In the figure, $\triangle HFJ \sim \triangle EFG$. Find the coordinates of G and the scale factor.

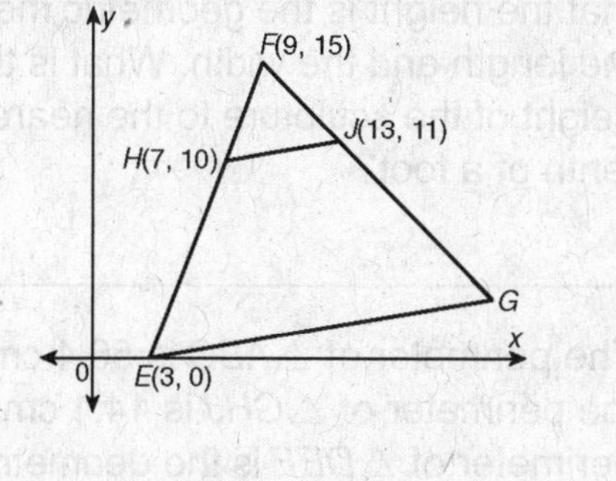

____

3. Triangle LMN has vertices $L(-10, 2)$, $M(-4, 11)$, and $N(6, -6)$. Find the vertices of the image of $\triangle LMN$ after a dilation with scale factor $\frac{5}{2}$.

____

____

4. Triangle HJM has vertices $H(-36, 0)$, $J(0, 20)$, and $M(0, 0)$. Triangle $H'J'M'$ has two vertices at $H'(-27, 0)$ and $M'(0, 0)$, and $\triangle H'J'M'$ is a dilation image of $\triangle HJM$. Find the coordinates of J' and the scale factor.

____

Choose the best answer.

5. The arrow is cut from a logo. The artist needs to make a copy five times as large for a sign. If the coordinates of T are $T(3, 4.5)$, what are the coordinates of T' after the arrow is dilated with scale factor 5?

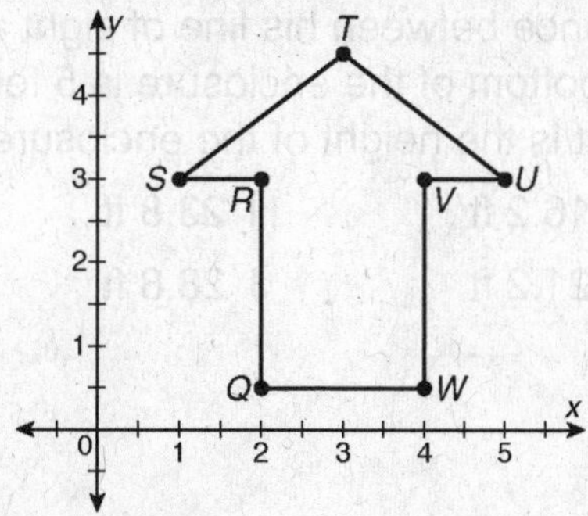

A $T'(15, 22.5)$
B $T'(7.5, 9)$
C $T'(4.5, 6.75)$
D $T'(2.5, 20)$

6. Triangle QRS has vertices $Q(-7, 3)$, $R(9, 8)$, and $S(2, 16)$. What is the scale factor if the vertices after a dilation are $Q'(-10.5, 4.5)$, $R'(13.5, 15)$, and $S'(3, 24)$?

F $\frac{1}{3}$

G $\frac{1}{2}$

H $\frac{2}{3}$

J $\frac{3}{2}$

7. A triangle has vertices $H(-4, 2)$, $J(-8, 6)$, and $K(0, 6)$. If $\triangle ABC \sim \triangle HJK$, what are possible vertices of $\triangle ABC$?

A $A(-4, 3)$, $B(-2, 1)$, $C(0, 3)$
B $A(-2, 1)$, $B(-4, 3)$, $C(0, 3)$
C $A(-2, 4)$, $B(0, 6)$, $C(-2, 8)$
D $A(-2, 4)$, $B(-8, 6)$, $C(-4, 2)$

Name ______________________ Date ______________ Class ______________

LESSON 8-1

Problem Solving

Similarity in Right Triangles

1. A sculpture is 10 feet long and 6 feet wide. The artist made the sculpture so that the height is the geometric mean of the length and the width. What is the height of the sculpture to the nearest tenth of a foot?

____

2. The altitude to the hypotenuse of a right triangle divides the hypotenuse into two segments that are 12 mm long and 27 mm long. What is the area of the triangle?

____

3. The perimeter of $\triangle ABC$ is 56.4 cm, and the perimeter of $\triangle GHJ$ is 14.1 cm. The perimeter of $\triangle DEF$ is the geometric mean of these two perimeters. What is the perimeter of $\triangle DEF$?

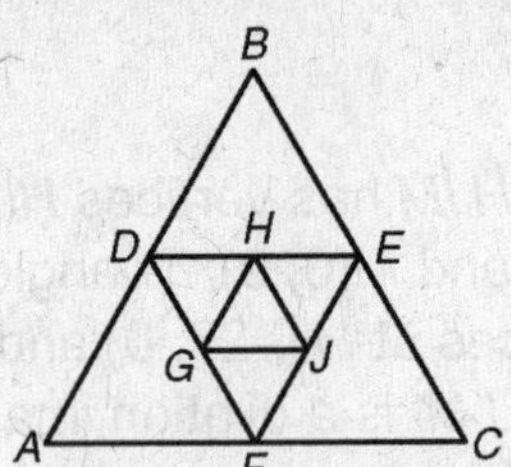

____

4. Tamara stands facing a painting in a museum. Her lines of sight to the top and bottom of the painting form a 90° angle. How tall is the painting?

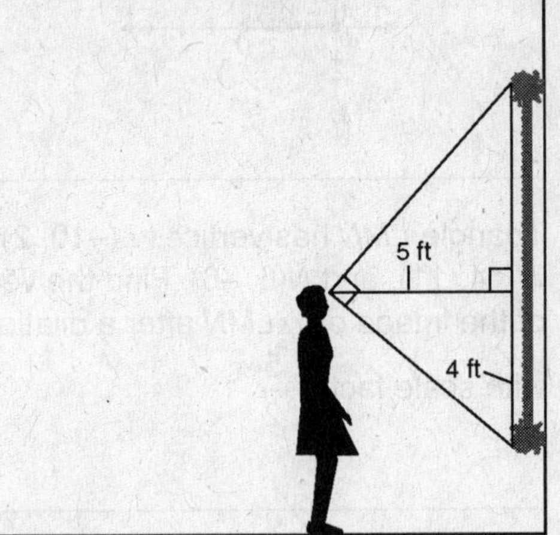

____

Choose the best answer.

5. The altitude to the hypotenuse of a right triangle divides the hypotenuse into two segments that are *x* cm and 4*x* cm, respectively. What is the length of the altitude?

A 2*x* C 5*x*

B 2.5*x* D $4x^2$

6. Jack stands 9 feet from the primate enclosure at the zoo. His lines of sight to the top and bottom of the enclosure form a 90° angle. When he looks straight ahead at the enclosure, the vertical distance between his line of sight and the bottom of the enclosure is 5 feet. What is the height of the enclosure?

F 16.2 ft H 23.8 ft

G 21.2 ft J 28.8 ft

7. A surveyor sketched the diagram at right to calculate the distance across a ravine. What is *x*, the distance across the ravine, to the nearest tenth of a meter?

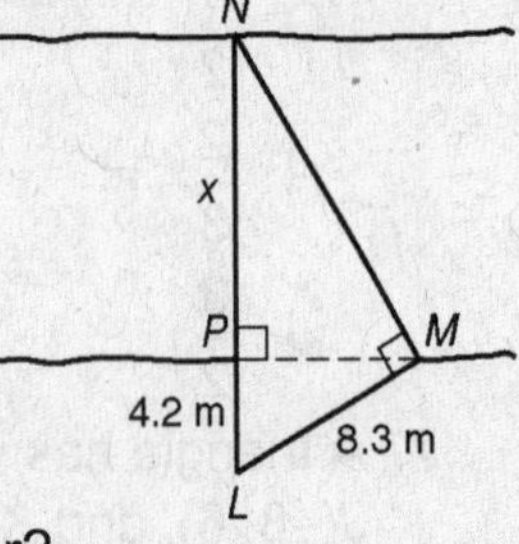

A 7.2 m C 16.4 m

B 12.2 m D 64.7 m

Name ______________________ Date ______________ Class ______________

LESSON 8-2

Problem Solving

Trigonometric Ratios

1. A ramp is used to load a 4-wheeler onto a truck bed that is 3 feet above the ground. The angle that the ramp makes with the ground is 32°. What is the horizontal distance covered by the ramp? Round to the nearest hundredth.

____

2. Find the perimeter of the triangle. Round to the nearest hundredth.

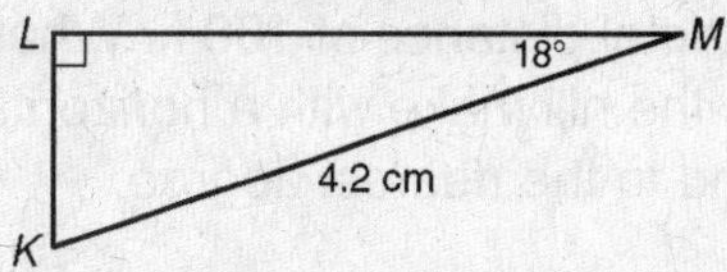

____

3. A right triangle has an angle that measures 55°. The leg adjacent to this angle has a length of 43 cm. What is the length of the other leg of the triangle? Round to the nearest tenth.

____

4. The hypotenuse of a right triangle measures 9 inches, and one of the acute angles measures 36°. What is the area of the triangle? Round to the nearest square inch.

____

Choose the best answer.

5. A 14-foot ladder makes a 62° angle with the ground. To the nearest foot, how far up the house does the ladder reach?

   A 6 ft

   B 7 ft

   C 12 ft

   D 16 ft

6. To the nearest inch, what is the length of the springboard shown below?

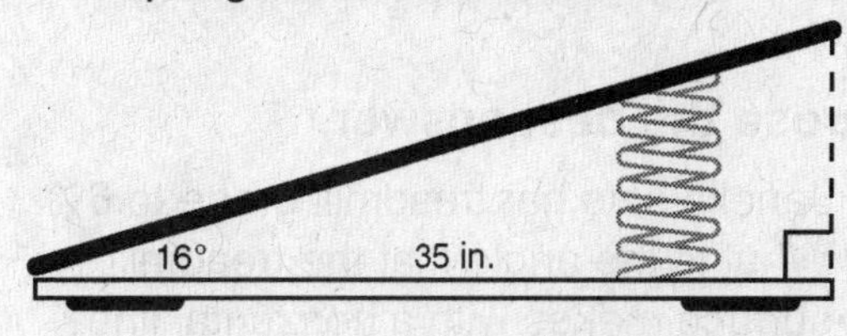

   F 24 in. H 38 in.

   G 36 in. J 127 in.

7. What is *EF*, the measure of the longest side of the sail on the model? Round to the nearest inch.

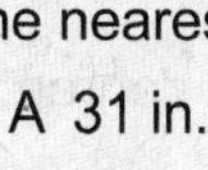

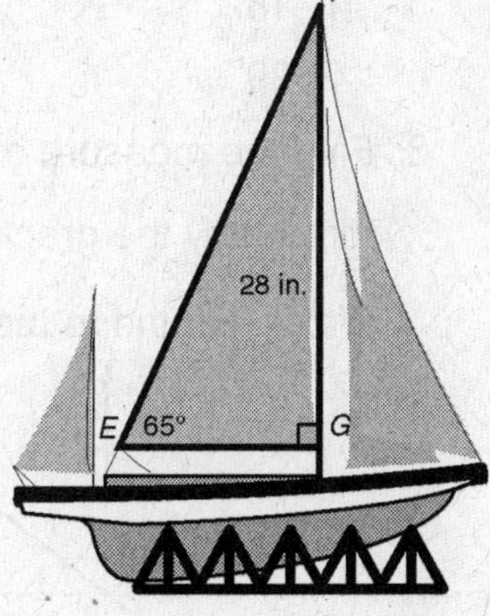

   A 31 in.

   B 35 in.

   C 40 in.

   D 60 in.

8. Right triangle *ABC* is graphed on the coordinate plane and has vertices at *A*(–1, 3), *B*(0, 5), and *C*(4, 3). What is the measure of ∠*C* to the nearest degree?

   F 27°

   G 29°

   H 32°

   J 43°

Name ______________________ Date ______________ Class ______________

LESSON 8-3

Problem Solving

Solving Right Triangles

1. A road has a grade of 28.4%. This means that the road rises 28.4 ft over a horizontal distance of 100 ft. What angle does the hill make with a horizontal line? Round to the nearest degree.

____

2. Pet ramps for loading larger dogs into vehicles usually have slopes between $\frac{2}{5}$ and $\frac{1}{2}$. What is the range of angle measures that most pet ramps make with a horizontal line? Round to the nearest degree.

____

Use the side view of a water slide for Exercises 3 and 4.

The ladder, represented by $\overline{AB}$, is 17 feet long.

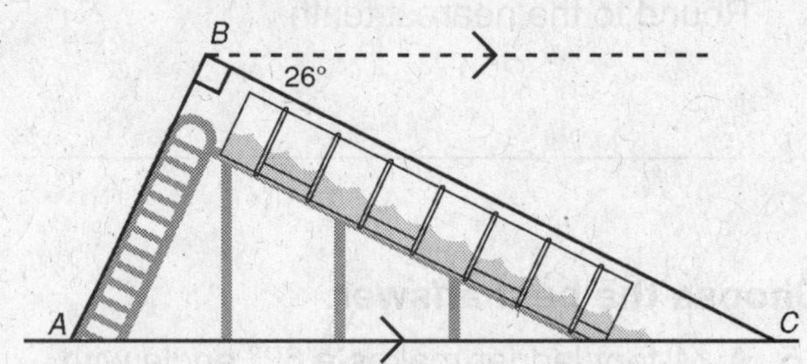

3. What is the measure of angle *A*, the angle that the ladder makes with a horizontal line?

____

4. What is *BC*, the length of the slide? Round to the nearest tenth of a foot.

____

Choose the best answer.

5. Janelle sets her treadmill grade to 6%. What is the angle that the treadmill surface makes with a horizontal line? Round to the nearest degree.

   A 3° C 12°
   B 4° D 31°

6. The coordinates of the vertices of $\triangle RST$ are *R*(3, 3), *S*(8, 3), and *T*(8, –6). What is the measures of angle *T*? Round to the nearest degree.

   F 18° H 61°
   G 29° J 65°

7. If cos $A = 0.28$, which angle in the triangles below is $\angle A$?

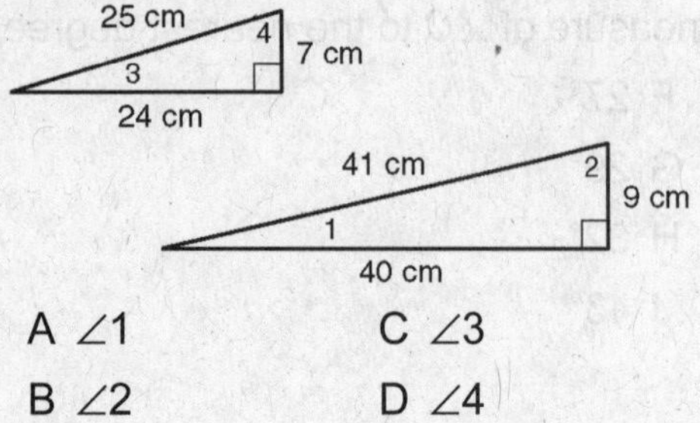

   A $\angle 1$ C $\angle 3$
   B $\angle 2$ D $\angle 4$

8. Find the measure of the acute angle formed by the graph of $y = \frac{3}{4}x$ and the *x*-axis. Round to the nearest degree.

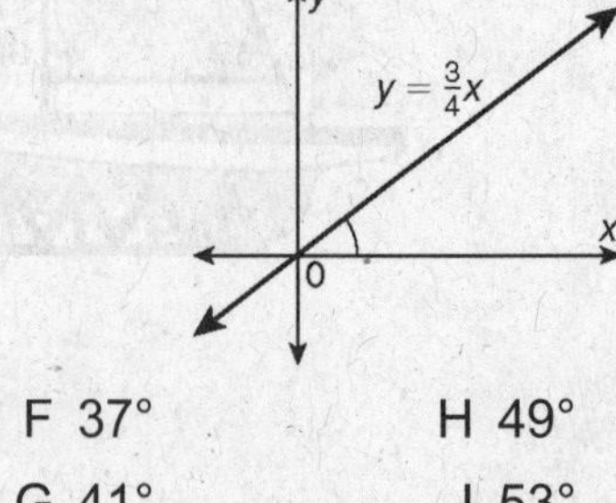

   F 37° H 49°
   G 41° J 53°

Name ______________________ Date ______________ Class ______________

LESSON 8-4

Problem Solving

Angles of Elevation and Depression

1. Mayuko is sitting 30 feet high in a football stadium. The angle of depression to the center of the field is 14°. What is the horizontal distance between Mayuko and the center of the field? Round to the nearest foot.

____

2. A surveyor 50 meters from the base of a cliff measures the angle of elevation to the top of the cliff as 72°. What is the height of the cliff? Round to the nearest meter.

____

3. Shane is 61 feet high on a ride at an amusement park. The angle of depression to the park entrance is 42°, and the angle of depression to his friends standing below is 80°. How far from the entrance are his friends standing? Round to the nearest foot.

____

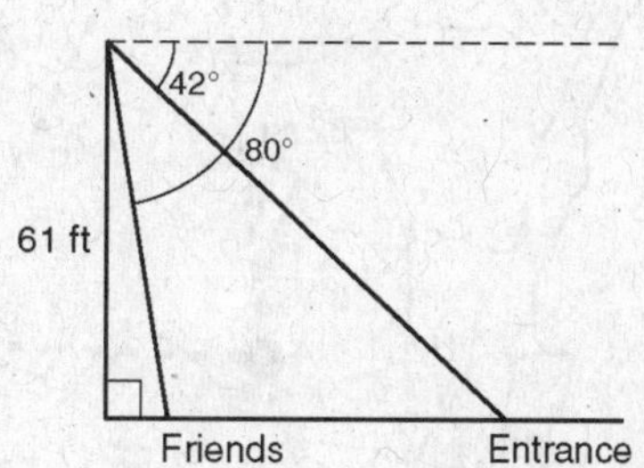

Choose the best answer.

4. The figure shows a person parasailing. What is x, the height of the parasailer, to the nearest foot?

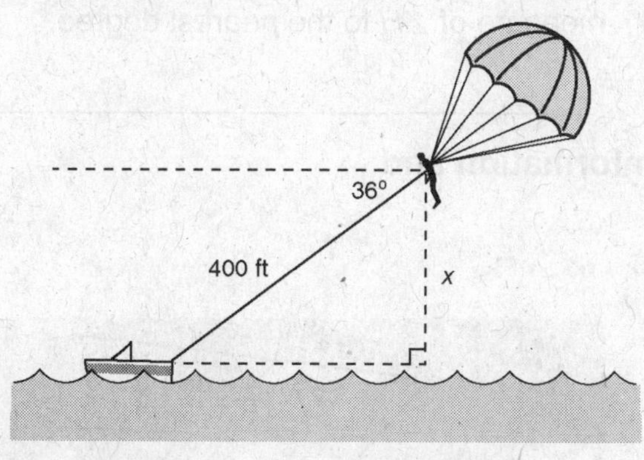

A 235 ft C 290 ft

B 245 ft D 323 ft

5. The elevation angle from the ground to the object to which the satellite dish is pointed is 32°. If $x = 2.5$ meters, which is the best estimate for y, the height of the satellite stand?

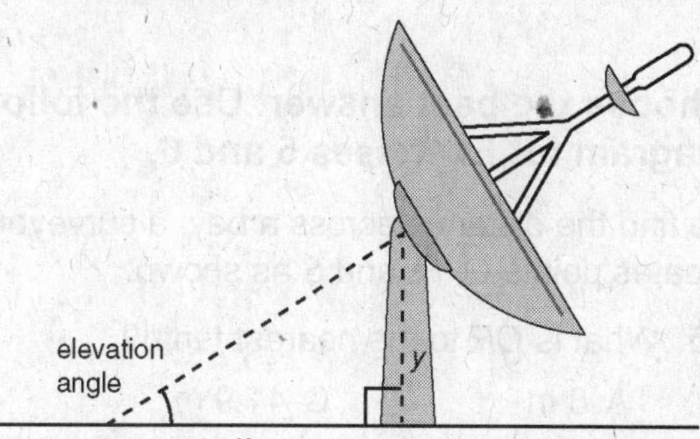

F 0.8 m H 1.6 m

G 1.3 m J 2.1 m

6. A lifeguard is in an observation chair and spots a person who needs help. The angle of depression to the person is 22°. The eye level of the lifeguard is 10 feet above the ground. What is the horizontal distance between the lifeguard and the person? Round to the nearest foot.

A 4 ft C 25 ft

B 11 ft D 27 ft

7. At a topiary garden, Emily is 8 feet from a shrub that is shaped like a dolphin. From where she is looking, the angle of elevation to the top of the shrub is 46°. If she is 5 feet tall, which is the best estimate for the height of the shrub?

F 6 ft H 10 ft

G 8 ft J 13 ft

Name ________________________ Date ______________ Class ______________

LESSON 8-5

Problem Solving

Law of Sines and Law of Cosines

1. The map shows three earthquake centers for one week in California. How far apart were the earthquake centers at points *A* and *C*? Round to the nearest tenth.

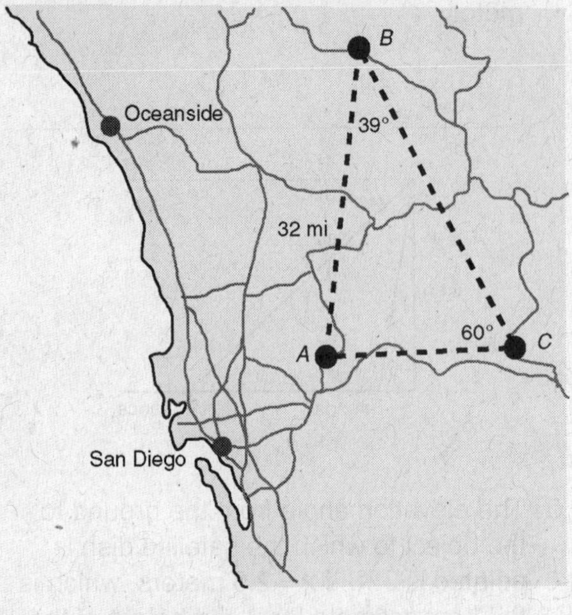

____

2. A BMX track has a starting hill as shown in the diagram. What is the length of the hill, *WY*? Round to the nearest tenth.

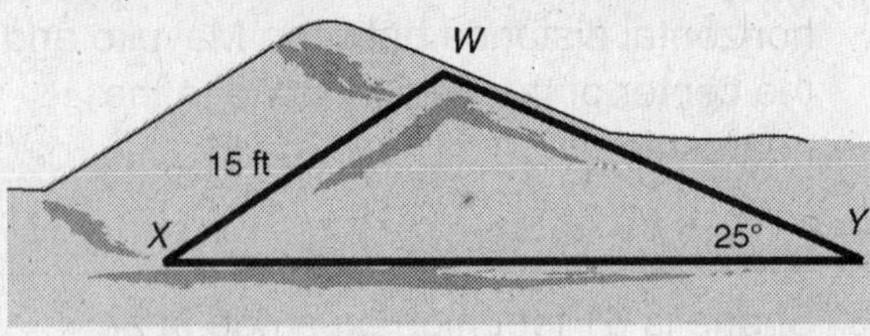

____

3. The edges of a triangular cushion measure 8 inches, 3 inches, and 6 inches. What is the measure of the largest angle of the cushion to the nearest degree?

____

4. The coordinates of the vertices of $\triangle HJK$ are $H(0, 4)$, $J(5, 7)$, and $K(9, -1)$. Find the measure of $\angle H$ to the nearest degree.

____

Choose the best answer. Use the following information and diagram for Exercises 5 and 6.

To find the distance across a bay, a surveyor locates points *Q*, *R*, and *S* as shown.

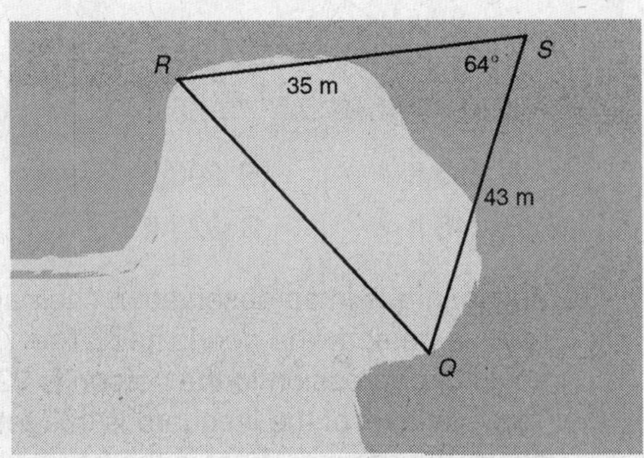

5. What is *QR* to the nearest tenth?

   A 8 m C 41.9 m

   B 35.2 m D 55.4 m

6. What is $m\angle Q$ to the nearest degree?

   F 43° H 67°

   G 49° J 107°

7. Two angles of a triangle measure 56° and 77°. The side opposite the 56° angle is 29 cm long. What is the measure of the shortest side? Round to the nearest tenth.

   A 23.4 cm C 32.9 cm

   B 25.6 cm D 34.1 cm

8. Which is the best estimate for the perimeter of a triangle if two sides measure 7 inches and 10 inches, and the included angle between the two sides is 82°?

   F 11.4 in. H 28.4 in.

   G 12.2 in. J 39.9 in.

Name ____________________ Date ____________ Class ____________

LESSON 8-6

Problem Solving

Vectors

1. The velocity of a wave is given by the vector ⟨7, 3⟩. Find the direction of the vector to the nearest degree.

____

2. Hikers set out on a course given by the vector ⟨6, 11⟩. What is the length of the trip to the nearest unit?

____

Use the following information for Exercises 3 –5.

A sailboat is traveling in water with a current shown in the table.

	Direction	Rate
sailboat	due east	4 mi/h
current	N 60° E	1 mi/h

3. What is the resultant vector in component form? Round to the nearest tenth.

____

4. What is the sailboat's actual speed to the nearest tenth?

____

5. What is the sailboat's actual direction? Round to the nearest degree.

____

Choose the best answer. Use the following information for Exercises 6 and 7.

A small plane is flying with the conditions shown in the table.

	Direction	Rate
plane	due north	200 mi/h
wind	due east	28 mi/h

6. What is the plane's actual speed to the nearest mile per hour?

A 172 mi/h C 202 mi/h

B 198 mi/h D 228 mi/h

7. What is the direction of the plane to the nearest degree?

F 82° H 16°

G 41° J 8°

8. Find the direction of the resultant vector when you add the given vectors. Round to the nearest degree.

$\vec{u} = \langle -4, 3\rangle$ and $\vec{v} = \langle 1, 3\rangle$

A N 63° E C N 27° W

B N 63° W D N 27° E

9. A person in a canoe leaves shore at a bearing of N 45° W and paddles at a constant speed of 2 mi/h. There is a 1.5 mi/h current moving due west. What is the canoe's actual speed?

F 0.5 mi/h H 3.2 mi/h

G 0.8 mi/h J 3.5 mi/h

Name ______________________ Date ______________ Class ______________

LESSON 9-1

Problem Solving

Reflections

1. Quadrilateral *JLKM* has vertices *J*(7, 9), *K*(0, –4), *L*(2, 2), and *M*(5, –3). If the figure is reflected across the line $y = x$, what are the coordinates of *M′*?

____

2. In the drawing, the left side of a structure is shown with its line of reflection. Draw the right side of the structure.

3. The function $y = -3^x$ passes through the point *P*(6, –729). If the graph is reflected across the *y*-axis, what are the coordinates of the image of *P*?

____

Choose the best answer.

4. A park planner is designing two paths that connect picnic areas *E* and *F* to a point on the park road. Which point on the park road will make the total length of the paths as small as possible? (*Hint:* Use a reflection. What is the shortest distance between two points?)

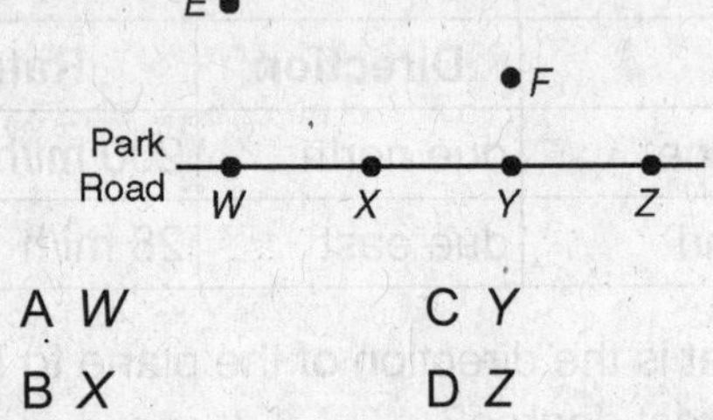

A *W* C *Y*

B *X* D *Z*

5. △*RST* is reflected across a line so that *T′* has coordinates (1, 3). What are the coordinates of *S′*?

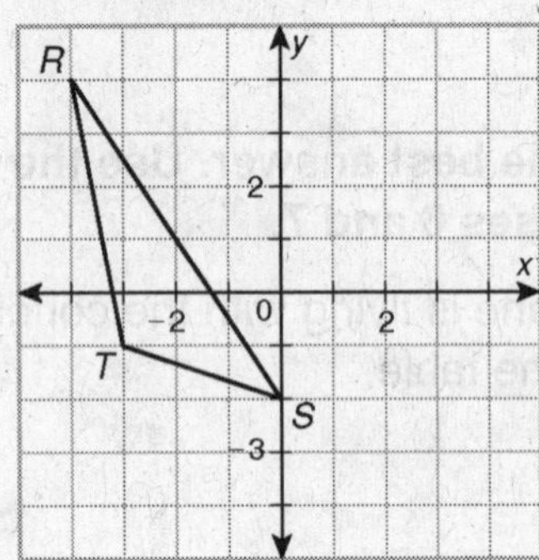

F (0, 2) H (2, 0)

G (0, –2) J (–2, 0)

6. △*MNP* with vertices *M*(1, 5), *N*(0, –3), and *P*(–2, 2) is reflected across a line. The coordinates of the reflection image are *M′*(7, 5), *N′*(8, –3), and *P′*(10, 2). Over which line was △*MNP* reflected?

A $y = 2$

B $x = 2$

C $y = 4$

D $x = 4$

7. Sarah is using a coordinate plane to design a rug. The rug is to have a triangle with vertices at (8, 13), (2, –13), and (14, –13). She wants the rug to have a second triangle that is the reflection of the first triangle across the *x*-axis. Which is a vertex of the second triangle?

F (–13, 14) H (–2, –13)

G (–14, 13) J (2, 13)

Name ________________________ Date ______________ Class ______________

LESSON 9-2

Problem Solving

Translations

1. A checker player's piece begins at *K* and, through a series of moves, lands on *L*. What translation vector represents the path from *K* to *L*?

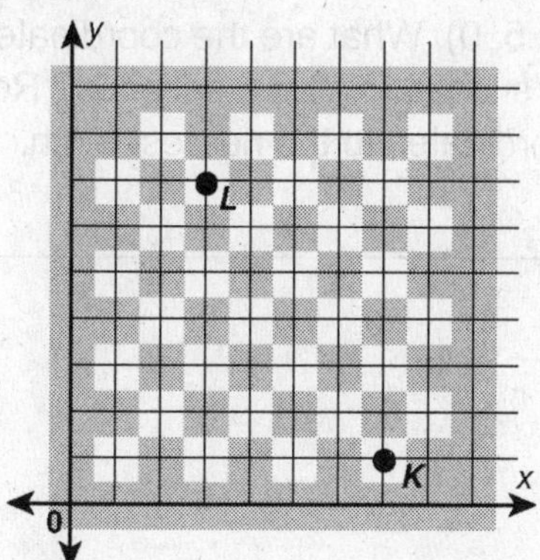

____

2. The preimage of *M′* has coordinates (–6, 5). What is the vector that translates $\triangle MNP$ to $\triangle M'N'P'$?

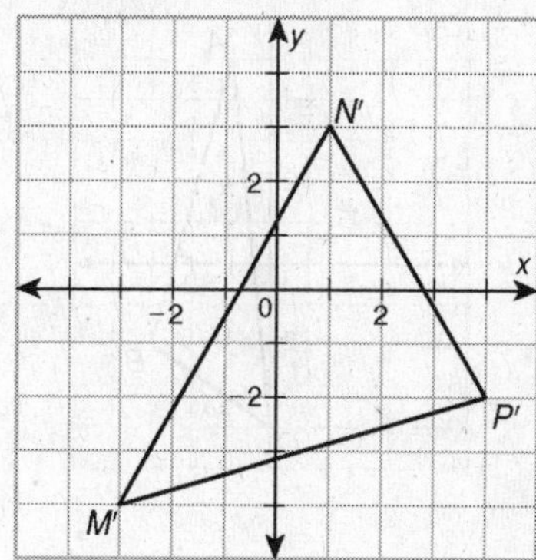

____

3. In a quilt pattern, a polygon with vertices (3, –2), (7, –1), (9, –5), and (5, –6) is translated repeatedly along the vector ⟨4, 5⟩. What are the coordinates of the third polygon in the pattern?

____

4. A group of hikers walks 2 miles east and then 1 mile north. After taking a break, they then hike 4 miles east and set up camp. What vector describes their hike from their starting position to their camp? Let 1 unit represent 1 mile.

____

Choose the best answer.

5. In a video game, a character at (8, 3) moves three times, as described by the translations shown at right. What is the final position of the character after the three moves?

Move 1: ⟨2, 7⟩
Move 2: ⟨–10, –4⟩
Move 3: ⟨1, –5⟩

A (–8, 3) C (1, 1)

B (–7, –2) D (9, 2)

6. The logo is translated along the vector ⟨8, 15⟩. What are the coordinates of *R′*?

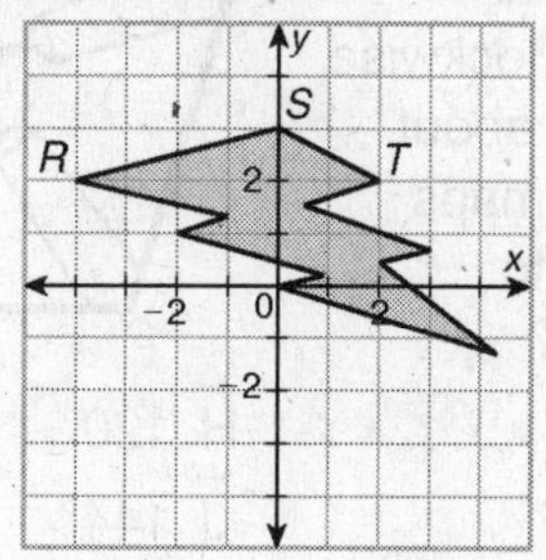

F (4, 17) H (15, 18)

G (12, 17) J (11, 19)

7. $\triangle DEF$ is translated so that the image of *E* has coordinates (0, 3). What is the image of *F* after this translation?

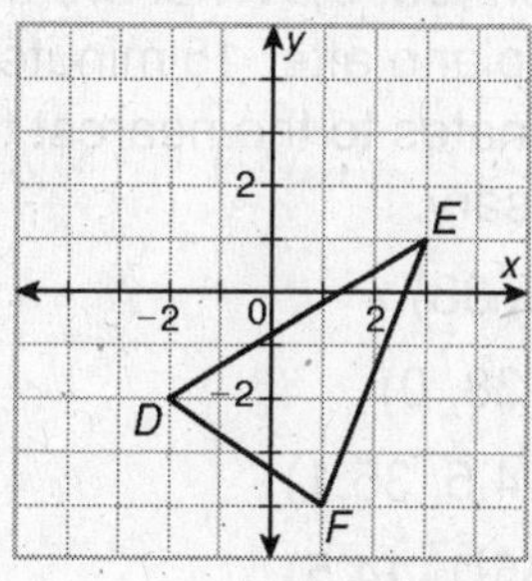

A (1, –1) C (–2, –2)

B (4, –2) D (–2, 6)

Name ______________________ Date ______________ Class ______________

LESSON 9-3

Problem Solving

Rotations

1. △*ABC* is rotated about the origin so that *A′* has coordinates (–1, –5). What are the coordinates of *B′*?

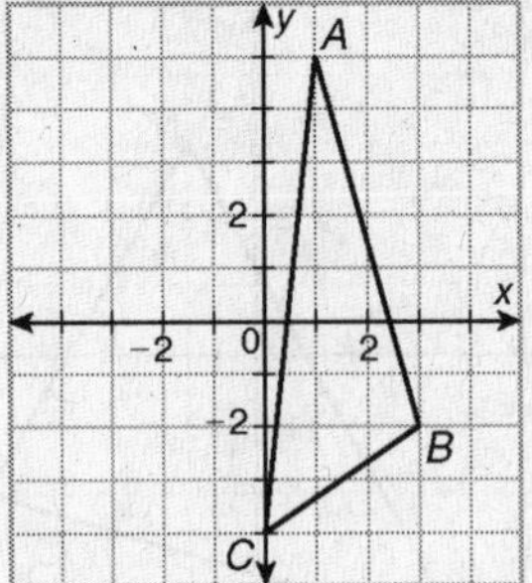

____

2. A spinning ride at an amusement park is a wheel that has a radius of 21.5 feet and rotates counterclockwise 12 times per minute. A car on the ride starts at position (21.5, 0). What are the coordinates of the car's location after 6 seconds? Round coordinates to the nearest tenth.

____

3. To make a design, Trent rotates the figure 120° about point *P*, and then rotates that image 120° about point *P*. Draw the final design.

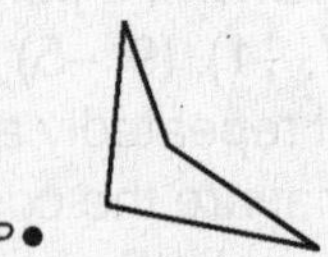

Choose the best answer.

4. Point *K* has coordinates (6, 8). After a counterclockwise rotation about the origin, the image of point *K* lies on the *y*-axis. What are the coordinates of *K′*?

   A (0, 5) C (0, 8)
   B (0, 6) D (0, 10)

5. △*NPQ* has vertices *N*(–6, –4), *P*(–3, 4), and *Q*(1, 1). If the triangle is rotated 90° counterclockwise about the origin, what are the coordinates of *P′*?

   F (–4, –3) H (3, 4)
   G (–4, 3) J (3, –4)

6. The Top of the World Restaurant in Las Vegas, Nevada, revolves 360° in 1 hour and 20 minutes. A piano that is 38 feet from the center of the restaurant starts at position (38, 0). What are the coordinates of the piano after 15 minutes? Round coordinates to the nearest tenth if necessary.

   A (0, 38)
   B (–38, 0)
   C (14.5, 35.1)
   D (35.1, 14.5)

7. The five blades of a ceiling fan form a regular pentagon. Which clockwise rotation about point *P* maps point *B* to point *D*?

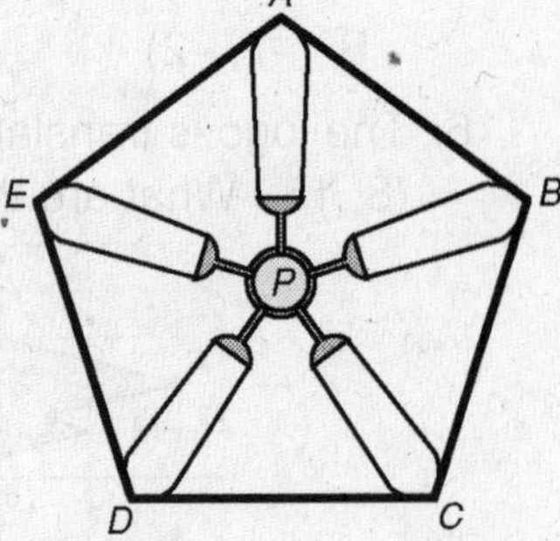

   F 60° H 120°
   G 72° J 144°

Name ______________________ Date ______________ Class ______________

LESSON 9-4

Problem Solving

Compositions of Transformations

1. A pattern for a new fabric is made by rotating the figure 90° counterclockwise about the origin and then translating along the vector ⟨–1, 2⟩. Draw the resulting figure in the pattern.

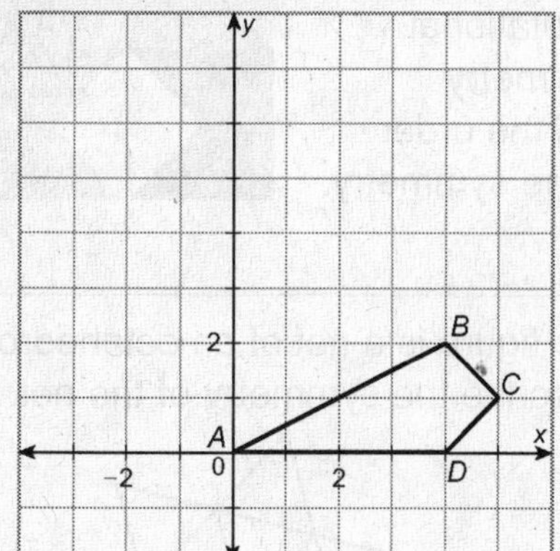

2. △*LMN* is reflected across the line $y = x$ and then reflected across the *y*-axis. What are the coordinates of the final image of △*LMN*?

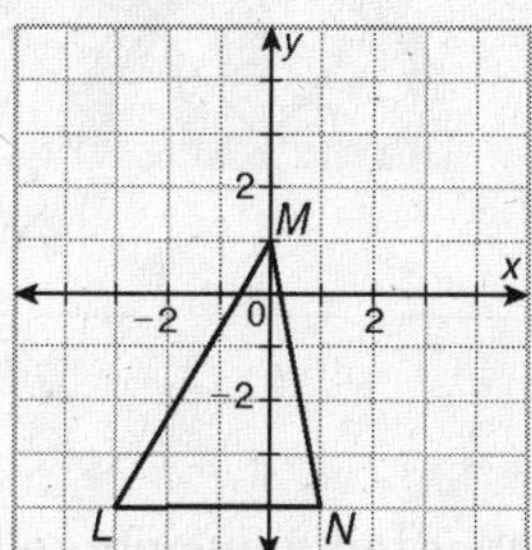

____

Choose the best answer.

3. △*EFG* has vertices *E*(1, 5), *F*(0, –3), and *G*(–1, 2). △*EFG* is translated along the vector ⟨7, 1⟩, and the image is reflected across the *x*-axis. What are the coordinates of the final image of *G*?

   A (6, –3) C (–6, 3)

   B (6, 3) D (–6, –3)

4. △*KLM* with vertices *K*(8, –1), *L*(–1, –4), and *M*(2, 3) is rotated 180° about the origin. The image is then translated. The final image of *K* has coordinates (–2, –3). What is the translation vector?

   F ⟨6, 4⟩ H ⟨–1, –11⟩

   G ⟨6, –4⟩ J ⟨–10, –2⟩

5. To create a logo for new sweatshirts, a designer reflects the letter *T* across line *h*. That image is then reflected across line *j*. Describe a single transformation that moves the figure from its starting position to its final position.

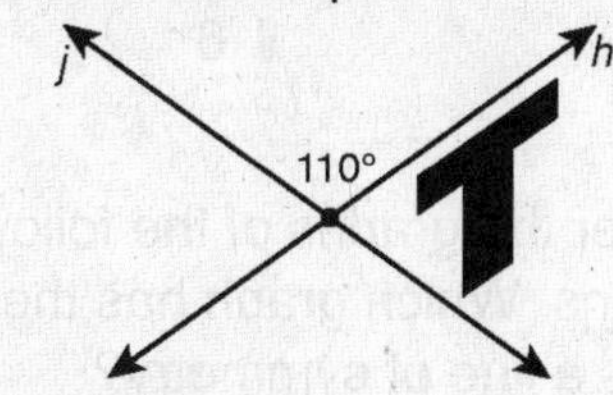

   A translation

   B rotation of 110°

   C rotation of 220°

   D reflection across vertical line

6. Which composition of transformations maps △*QRS* into Quadrant III?

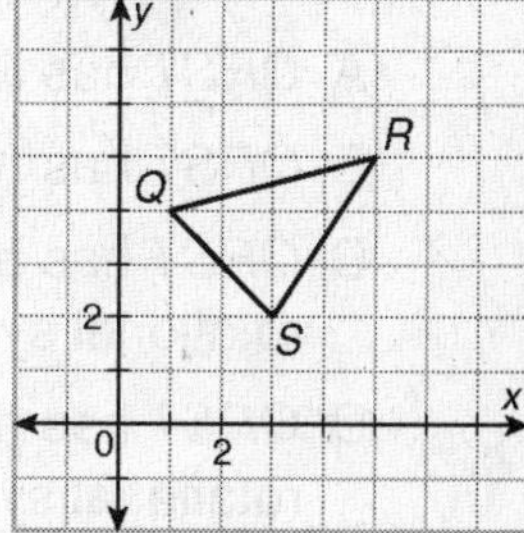

   F Translate along the vector ⟨–6, 4⟩ and then reflect across the *y*-axis.

   G Rotate by 90° about the origin and then reflect across the *x*-axis.

   H Reflect across the *y*-axis and then rotate by 180° about the origin.

   J Translate along the vector ⟨1, 2⟩ and then rotate 90° about the origin.

Name ______________________ Date ______________ Class ______________

LESSON 9-5

Problem Solving

Symmetry

1. Tell whether the window has line symmetry. If so, draw all the lines of symmetry.

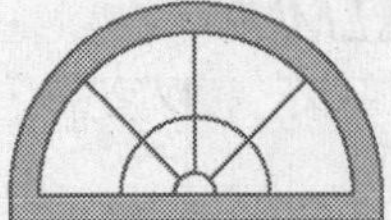

____

2. Tell whether the quilt block design has rotational symmetry. If so, give the angle of rotational symmetry and the order of the symmetry.

____

3. Tell whether the hemisphere has plane symmetry, symmetry about an axis, both, or neither.

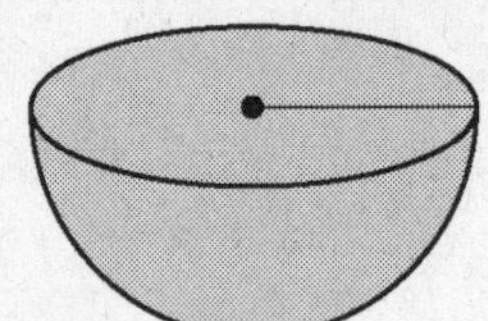

____

4. The figure is a net of an octahedron. Describe the symmetry of the net.

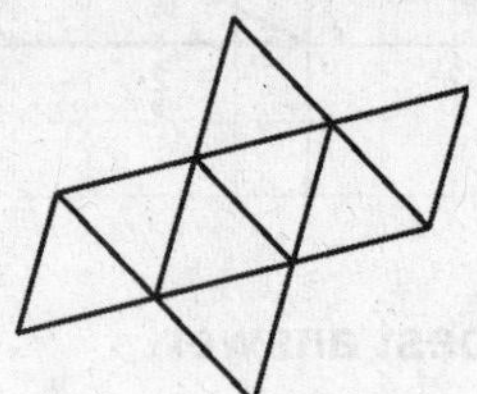

____

Choose the best answer.

5. Which is a true statement about the figure with vertices $Q(-2, -4)$, $R(0, 1)$, $S(8, 1)$, and $T(5, -4)$?

   A *QRST* has line symmetry only.

   B *QRST* has rotational symmetry only.

   C *QRST* has both line symmetry and rotational symmetry.

   D *QRST* has neither line symmetry nor rotational symmetry.

6. What is the order of rotational symmetry for the figure shown?

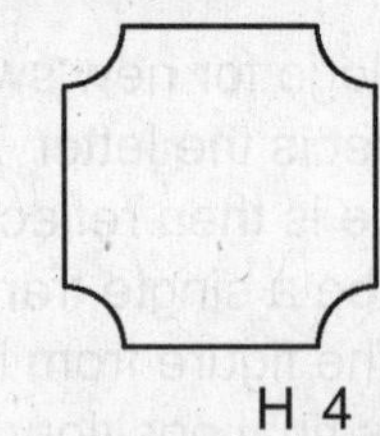

   F 2 H 4

   G 3 J 6

7. Which of these figures has exactly three lines of symmetry?

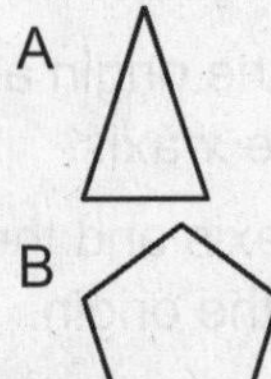

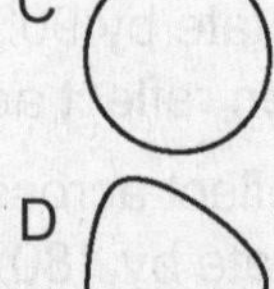

8. Consider the graphs of the following equations. Which graph has the line $x = 3$ as a line of symmetry?

   F $y = x^2 + 3$

   G $y = (x + 3)^2$

   H $y = (x - 3)^2$

   J $y = x^3$

Name ______________________ Date ______________ Class ______________

LESSON 9-6

Problem Solving

Tessellations

1. Identify all the types of symmetry (translation, reflection, or rotation) in the pattern.

____

2. Mara made the beaded bracelet shown below. Identify the symmetry in the main pattern of the bracelet.

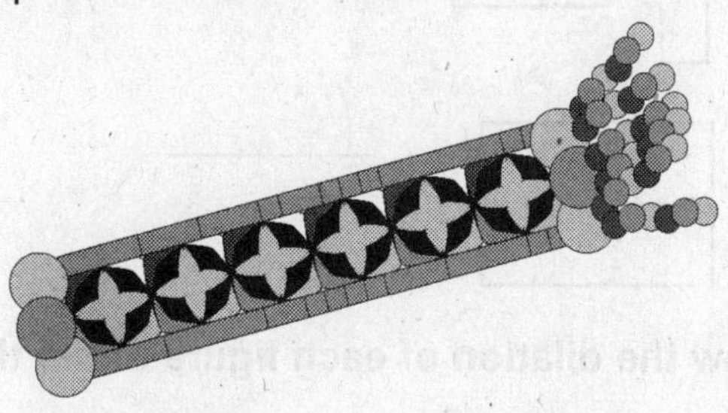

____

Choose the best answer.

3. Classify the tessellation.

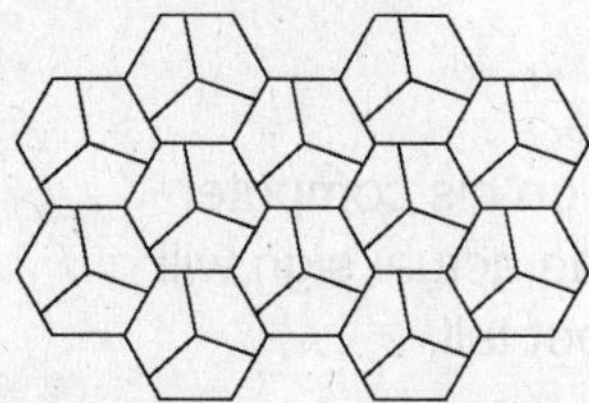

A regular

B semiregular

C neither regular nor semiregular

D part regular and part semiregular

4. The square tile below is formed from a tessellation of polygons. Which of the following types of symmetry is in the tile?

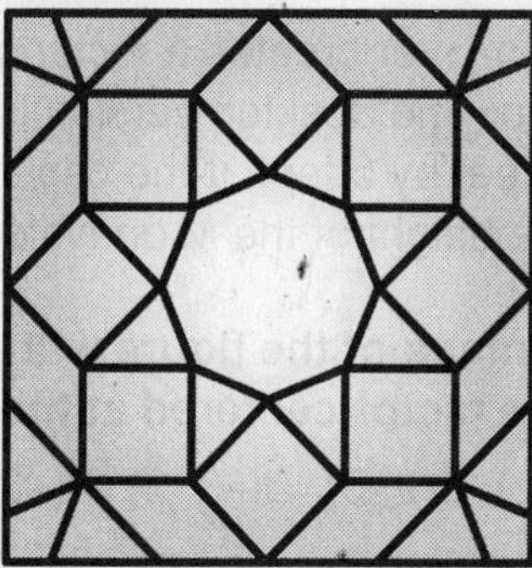

F rotation

G glide reflection

H translation

J no symmetry

5. Which is a true statement about the pattern?

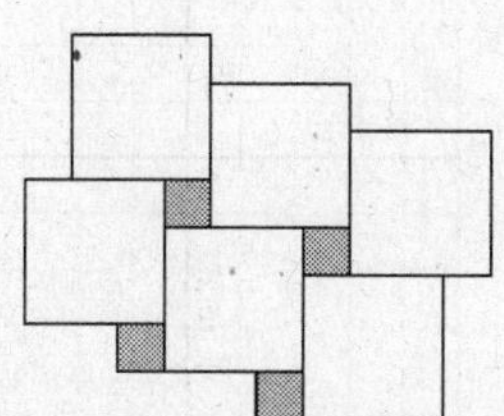

A It is a regular tessellation because it is made from squares.

B It is a semiregular tessellation because the squares are not congruent.

C It is a tessellation that is neither regular nor semiregular.

D The pattern does not form a tessellation.

6. Which is a true statement about the parallelograms shown below?

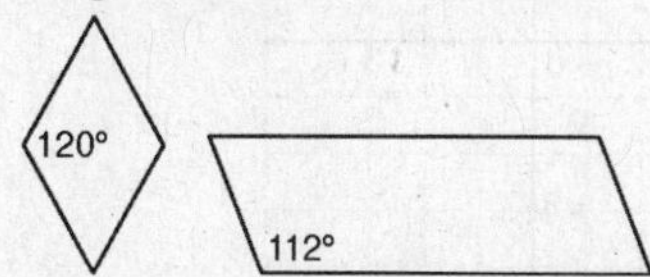

F They can be used to form a semiregular tessellation.

G They can be used to form a tessellation that is neither regular nor semiregular.

H They cannot be used to form a tessellation.

J It is impossible to tell whether the figures can form a tessellation.

Name ______________________ Date ______________ Class ______________

LESSON 9-7

Practice

Dilations

Tell whether each transformation appears to be a dilation.

1. 

2. 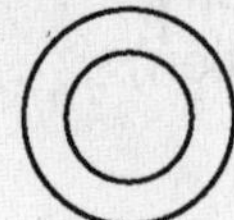

3. 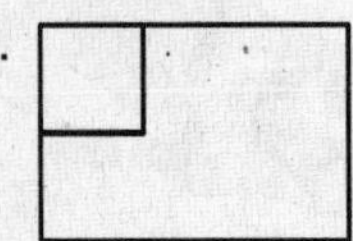 ____________

4. 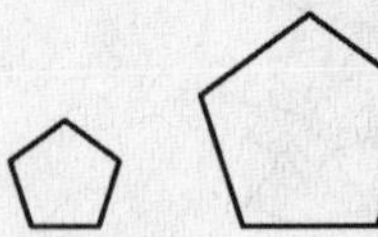 ____________

Draw the dilation of each figure under the given scale factor with center of dilation *P*.

5. scale factor: $\frac{1}{2}$

P•

6. scale factor: –2

P•

7. A sign painter creates a rectangular sign for Mom's Diner on his computer desktop. The desktop version is 12 inches by 4 inches. The actual sign will be 15 feet by 5 feet. If the capital *M* in "Mom's" will be 4 feet tall, find the height of the *M* on his desktop version. ____________

Draw the image of the figure with the given vertices under a dilation with the given scale factor centered at the origin.

8. $A(2, -2)$, $B(2, 3)$, $C(-3, 3)$, $D(-3, -2)$;
scale factor: $\frac{1}{2}$

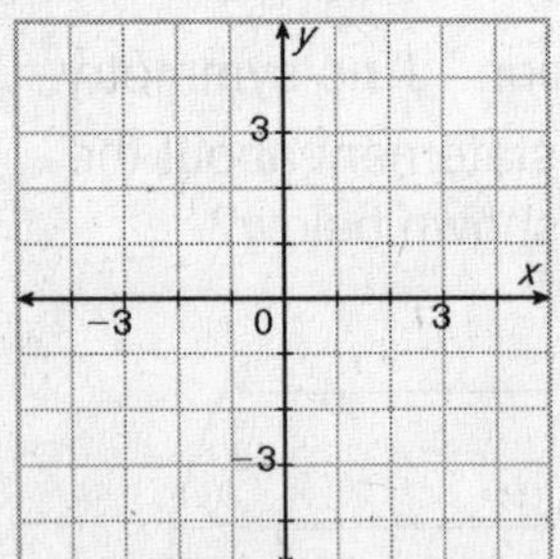

9. $P(-4, 4)$, $Q(-3, 1)$, $R(2, 3)$;
scale factor: –1

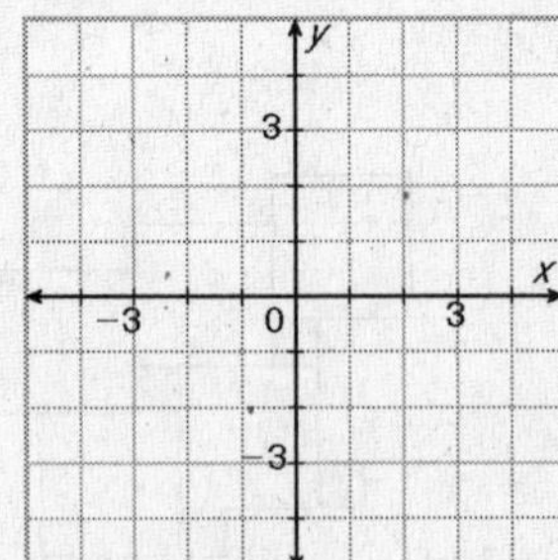

10. $J(0, 2)$, $K(-2, 1)$, $L(0, -2)$, $M(2, -1)$;
scale factor: 2

11. $D(0, 0)$, $E(-1, 0)$, $F(-1, -1)$;
scale factor: –2

Name ______________________ Date ______________ Class ______________

LESSON 10-1

Problem Solving

Developing Formulas for Triangles and Quadrilaterals

1. The area of trapezoid *HJKL* is 385 mm^2. Find *LM* to the nearest tenth.

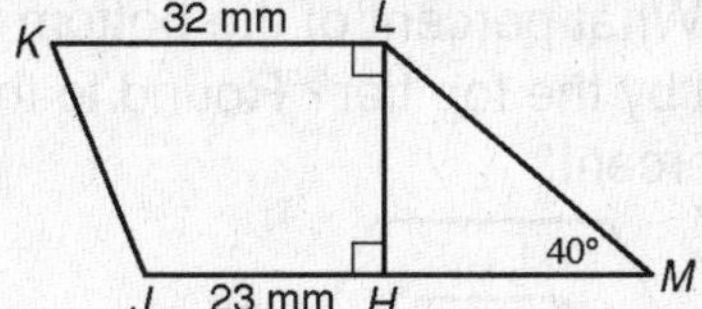

____

2. Samantha is buying stones for a 16 foot by 3 foot walkway. She needs to buy 10% extra for cutting stones for the corners and ends. The stones are rectangles 7 inches long and 4 inches wide and cost $0.97 each. About how much will the stones cost for her walkway?

____

3. The length of a rectangular pool is 2 feet less than twice the width. If the area of the pool is 264 ft^2, what are the dimensions of the pool?

____

4. Find the area of the kite. Round to the nearest tenth.

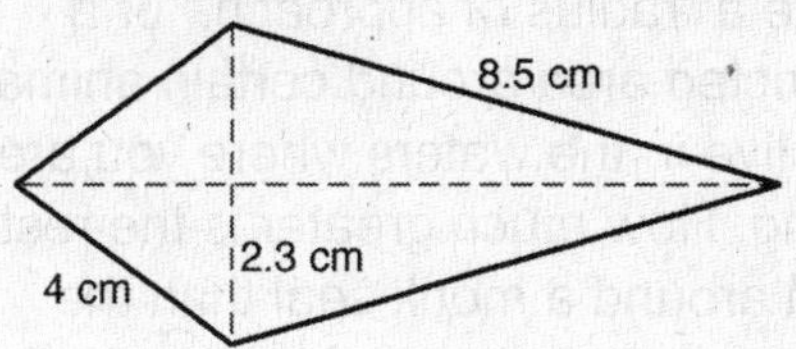

____

Choose the best answer.

5. A parallelogram has sides of length 30 centimeters and 18 centimeters.. One of its angles measures 58°. Which is the best estimate for the area of the parallelogram?

   A 274.8 cm^2

   B 286.2 cm^2

   C 457.9 cm^2

   D 540.0 cm^2

6. Jamie is cutting out 32 right triangles from fabric for her quilt. The shortest side of each triangle is 2 inches, and the longest side is 5 inches. How much fabric will she use to cut out all the triangles?

   F 146.6 in^2 H 366.6 in^2

   G 293.3 in^2 J 672 in^2

7. In rhombus *ABCD*, the length of diagonal $\overline{BD}$ is $\frac{2}{3}$ the length of diagonal $\overline{AC}$. If the area of the figure is 75 cm^2, find *BD*.

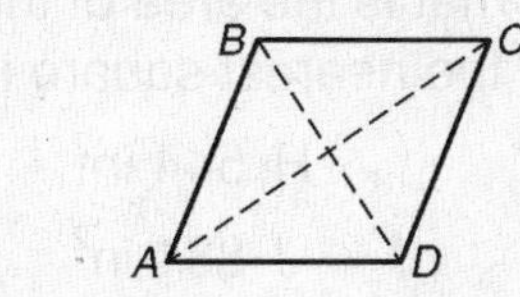

   A 7.1 cm C 10.6 cm

   B 10 cm D 15 cm

8. The house is made from 7 puzzle pieces. The pieces are triangles and parallelograms. If the area of the chimney is $\frac{1}{8}$ in^2, what is the area of △*LMN*?

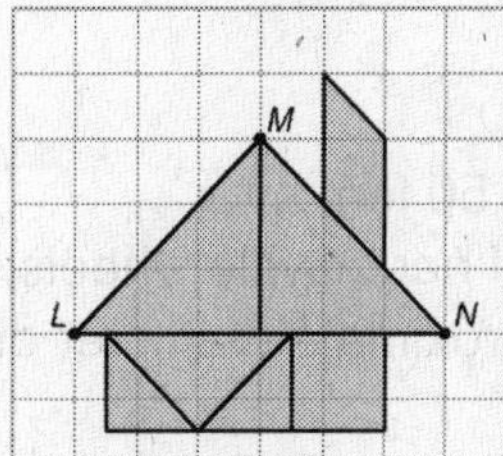

   F $\frac{9}{32}$ in^2 H $\frac{9}{2}$ in^2

   G $\frac{9}{16}$ in^2 J 9 in^2

Name ______________________ Date ______________ Class ______________

LESSON 10-2

Problem Solving

Developing Formulas for Circles and Regular Polygons

1. What is the area of the regular nonagon? Round to the nearest tenth.

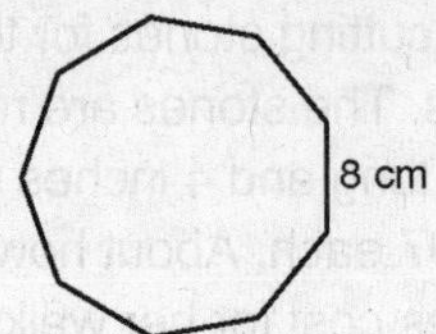

2. The top view of a two-tiered wedding cake is shown. Each tier is a regular hexagon. What percent of the bottom tier is covered by the top tier? Round to the nearest percent.

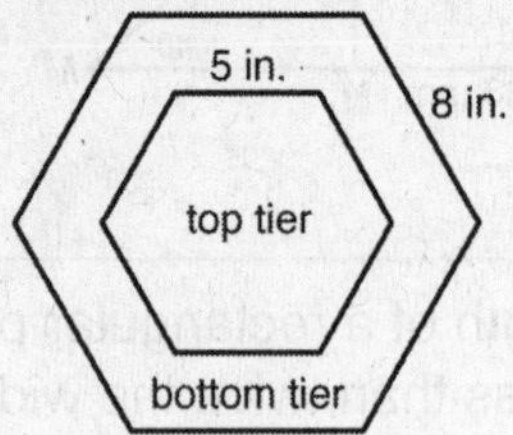

3. When diving and snorkeling, you should leave a "radius of approach," or a restricted area around certain animals that live in the waters where you are diving. How much greater is the restricted area around a monk seal than the restricted area around a sea turtle? Give your answer in terms of π.

Animal	Radius of Approach
sea turtle	20 ft
monk seal	100 ft

4. A yield sign is a regular triangle and is available in two sizes: 30 inches or 36 inches. Find how much more metal is needed to make a 36 inch sign than a 30 inch sign. Answer to the nearest percent.

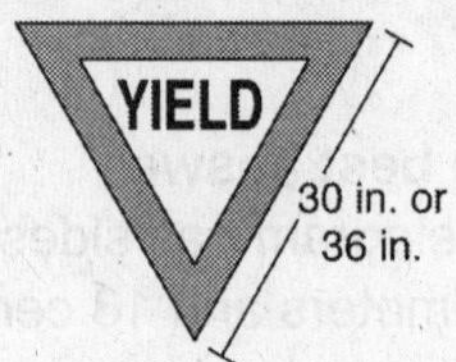

Choose the best answer.

5. A regular hexagon has an apothem of 4.6 centimeters. Which is the best estimate for the area of the hexagon?

   A 36.7 cm^2

   B 63.5 cm^2

   C 73.3 cm^2

   D 146.6 cm^2

6. An amusement park ride is made up of a large circular frame that holds 50 riders. The circumference of the frame is about 138 feet. What is the diameter of the ride to the nearest foot?

   F 22 ft H 69 ft

   G 44 ft J 138 ft

7. A cyclist travels 50 feet after 7.34 rotations of her bicycle wheels. What is the approximate diameter of the wheels?

   A 13 in. C 26 in.

   B 24 in. D 28 in.

8. A regular pentagon has side length of 16 inches. What is the area of the pentagon to the nearest square inch?

   F 440 in^2 H 544 in^2

   G 369 in^2 J 881 in^2

Name ______________________ Date ______________ Class ______________

LESSON 10-3

Problem Solving

Composite Figures

1. Find the shaded area. Round to the nearest tenth.

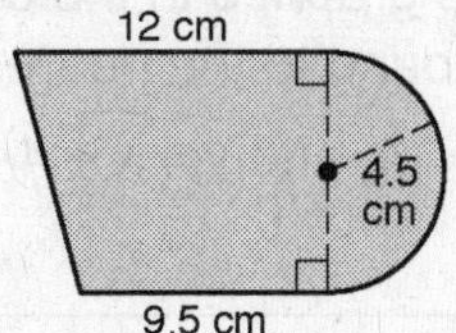

____

2. Jessica is painting a bedroom wall shown by the shaded area below. The cost of paint is $6.90 per quart, and each quart covers 65 square feet. What is the total cost of the paint if she applies two coats of paint to the wall?

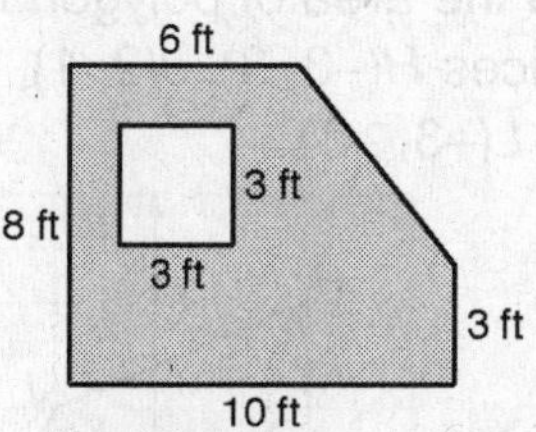

____

Choose the best answer.

3. Enchanted Rock State Natural Area in Fredericksburg, Texas, has a primitive camping area called Moss Lake. Which is the best estimate for this area if the length of each grid square is 10 meters?

A 1600 m^2

B 3200 m^2

C 6400 m^2

D 8000 m^2

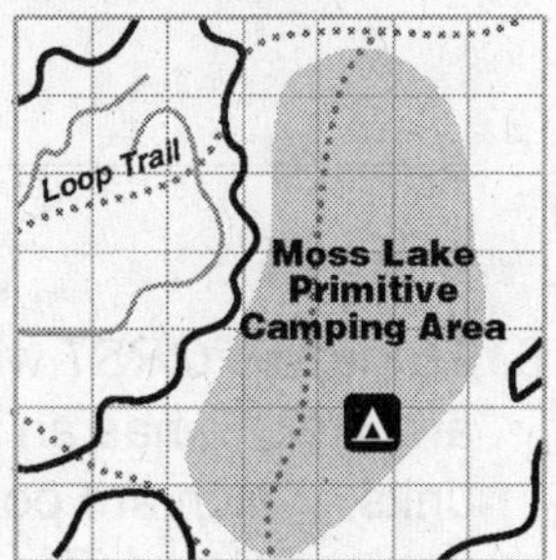

4. Find the area of the section of basketball court that is shown. Round to the nearest tenth.

F 612.7 ft^2

G 820.1 ft^2

H 1225.4 ft^2

J 2450.8 ft^2

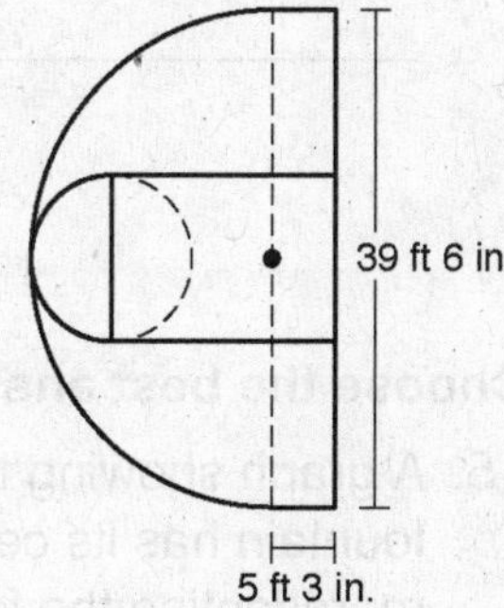

5. Find the shaded area. Round to the nearest tenth.

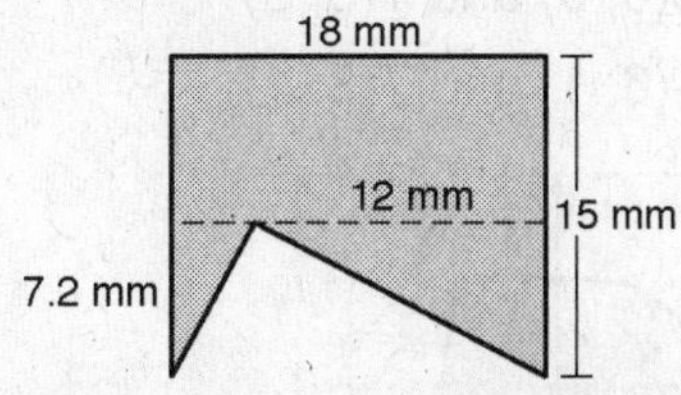

A 183.6 mm^2

B 194.4 mm^2

C 205.2 mm^2

D 216.0 mm^2

6. Which is the best estimate for the area of the pond? Each grid square represents 4 square feet.

F 24 ft^2

G 48 ft^2

H 96 ft^2

J 120 ft

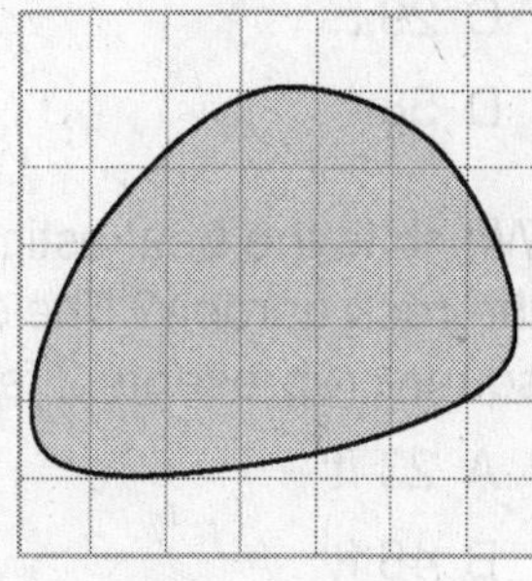

Name ______________________ Date ______________ Class ______________

LESSON 10-4

Problem Solving

Perimeter and Area in the Coordinate Plane

1. Find the perimeter and area of a polygon with vertices $A(-3, -2)$, $B(2, 4)$, $C(5, 2)$, and $D(0, -4)$. Round to the nearest tenth.

____

2. What are the perimeter and area of the triangle that is formed when the lines below are graphed in the coordinate plane? Round to the nearest tenth.

   $y = 2x$, $y = 4$, and $y = x + 4$

____

3. Find the area of polygon *HJKL* with vertices $H(-3, 3)$, $J(2, 1)$, $K(4, -4)$, and $L(-3, -3)$.

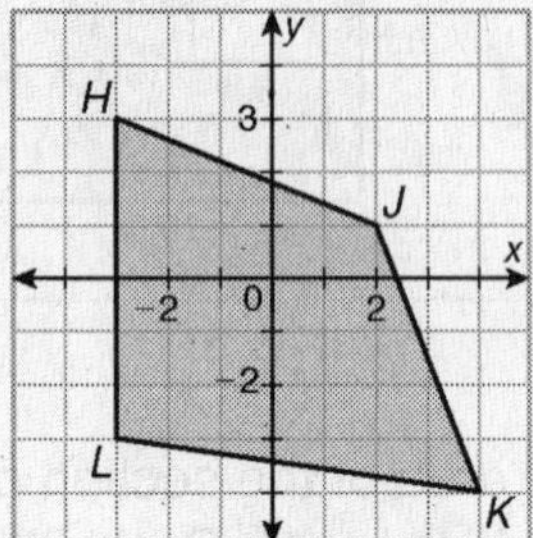

____

4. The diagram represents train tracks in the children's area of a zoo. Estimate the area enclosed by the tracks. The side length of each square represents 1 meter.

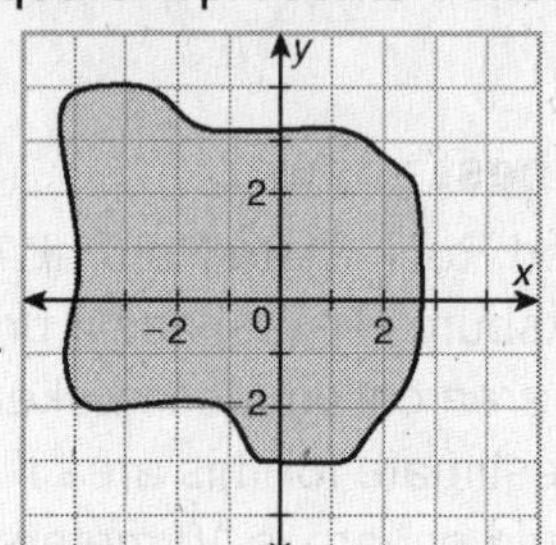

____

Choose the best answer.

5. A graph showing the top view of a circular fountain has its center at (4, 6). The circle representing the fountain passes through (2, 1). What is the area of the space covered by the fountain?

   A $\sqrt{29}\,\pi$

   B $2\sqrt{29}\,\pi$

   C 29π

   D 58π

6. Trapezoid *QRST* with vertices $Q(1, 5)$ and $R(9, 5)$ has an area of 12 square units. Which are possible locations for vertices *S* and *T*?

   F $S(6, 7)$ and $T(2, 7)$

   G $S(4, 7)$ and $T(2, 7)$

   H $S(6, 8)$ and $T(3, 8)$

   J $S(6, 1)$ and $T(3, 1)$

7. Which is the best estimate for the area of the rock garden? The side length of each square represents 2 feet.

   A 23 ft^2

   B 46 ft^2

   C 69 ft^2

   D 92 ft^2

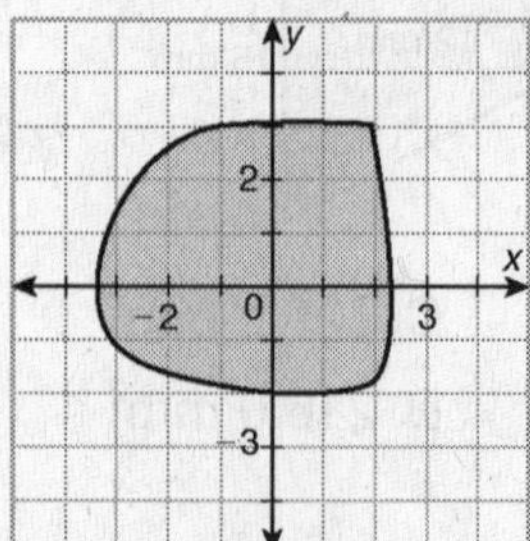

Name ______________________ Date ______________ Class ______________

LESSON 10-5

Problem Solving

Effects of Changing Dimensions Proportionally

1. Mara has a photograph 5 inches by 7 inches. She wants to enlarge the photo so that the length and width are each tripled. Describe how the area of the photo will change.

____

2. On a map, 1 inch = 2 miles. On the map, the area of a wildlife preserve is about 3 square inches. Estimate the actual area of the preserve in acres. (*Hint:* 1 square mile = 640 acres)

____

3. A triangle has vertices $N(3, 5)$, $P(7, 2)$, and $Q(3, 1)$. Point P is moved to be twice as far from $\overline{NQ}$ as in the original triangle. Describe the effect on the area.

____

4. The length of each base of a trapezoid is divided by 2. How does the area change?

____

Use the information below for Exercises 5 and 6.

Steven's dog is on a chain 6 feet long with one end of the chain attached to the ground as shown in the diagram. Steven replaces the chain with one that is $1\frac{1}{2}$ times as long.

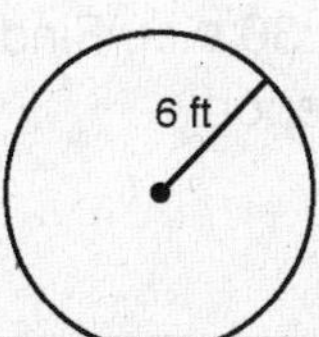

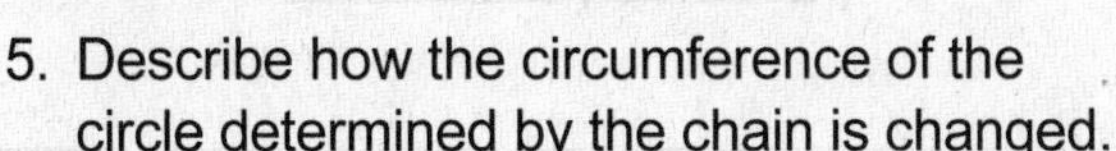

5. Describe how the circumference of the circle determined by the chain is changed.

____

6. Describe how the area of the circle determined by the chain is changed.

____

Choose the best answer.

7. In kite $RSTU$, $RT = 2.5$ centimeters and $SU = 4.3$ centimeters. Both diagonals of the kite are doubled. What happens to the area of the kite?

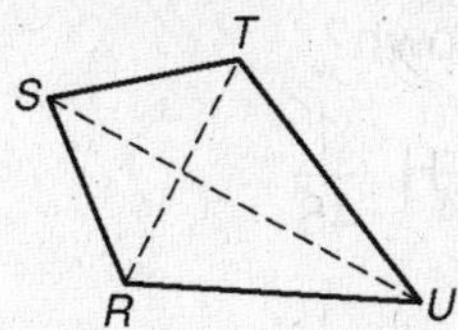

A The area is doubled.

B The area is tripled.

C The area is 4 times as great.

D The area is 8 times as great.

8. The side length of the regular hexagon is divided by 3. Which is a true statement?

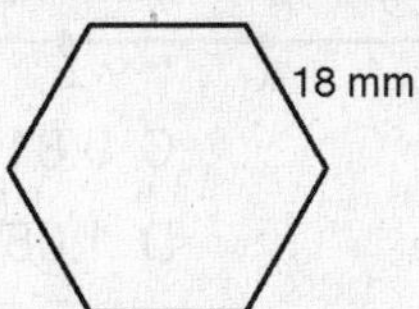

F The perimeter is divided by 9, and the area is divided by 3.

G The perimeter is divided by 3, and the area is divided by 9.

H The perimeter and area are both divided by 3.

J The perimeter and area are both divided by 9.

Name ______________________ Date ______________ Class ______________

LESSON 10-6

Problem Solving

Geometric Probability

Use the diagram of a spinner for Exercises 1 and 2.

1. Find the probability of the pointer landing on the 120° section.

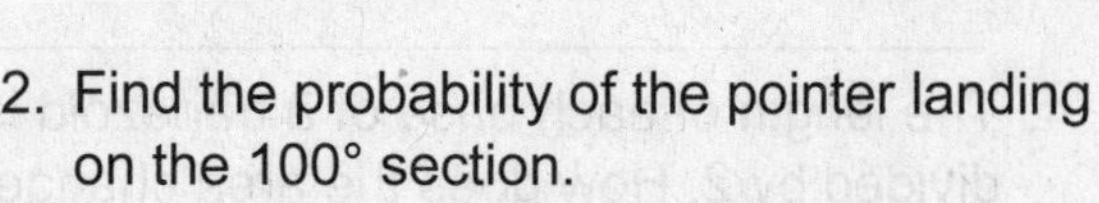

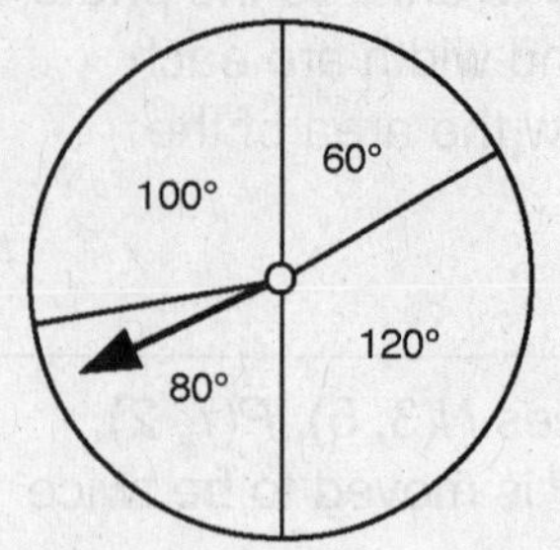

____

2. Find the probability of the pointer landing on the 100° section.

____

3. Between 4:00 P.M. and 6:30 P.M., a radio station gives a traffic report every 20 minutes. This report lasts 15 seconds. Suppose you turn on the radio between 4:00 P.M. and 6:30 P.M. Find the probability that a traffic report will be on.

____

4. Find the probability that a point chosen randomly inside the rectangle is in the triangle. Round to the nearest hundredth.

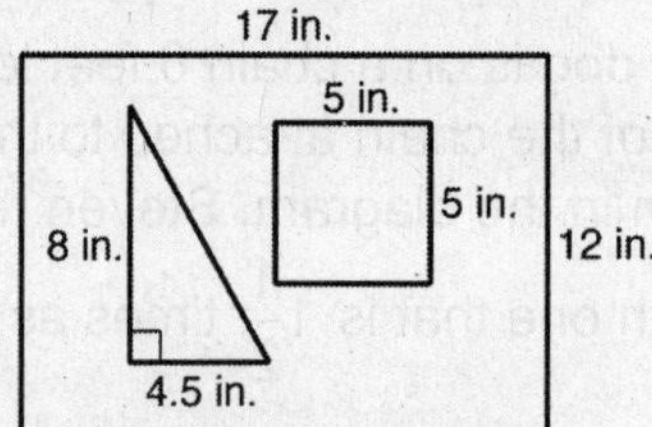

Choose the best answer.

5. A point is chosen randomly on $\overline{JM}$. Find the probability that the point is on $\overline{JK}$ or $\overline{JL}$. Round to the nearest hundredth.

2 2 1.5
J K L M

A 0.41 C 0.81

B 0.73 D 1.08

6. A train crosses at a railroad crossing 6 times a day—once every 4 hours. It takes an average of 5 minutes for the railroad gates to go down and then come up again. If you are approaching the railroad crossing, what is the probability that the gates are down?

F $\frac{1}{360}$ H $\frac{1}{48}$

G $\frac{1}{120}$ J $\frac{1}{30}$

7. On the dart board, the center circle has a diameter of 2 inches. What is the probability of hitting the shaded ring? Round to the nearest hundredth.

A 0.01

B 0.29

C 0.30

D 0.45

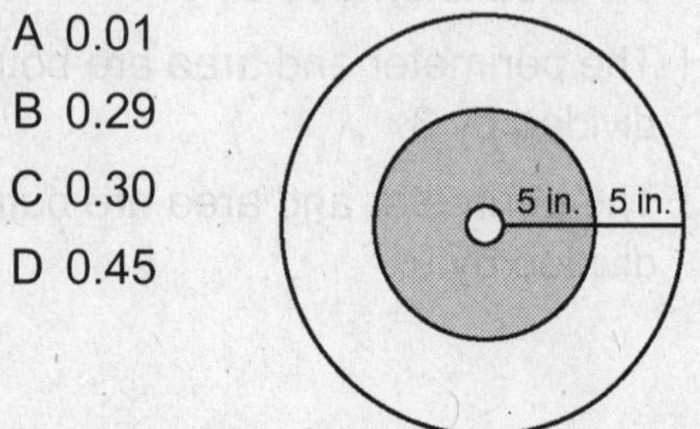

8. What is the probability that a coin randomly tossed into the rectangular fountain lands on one of the square "islands"? The "islands" are all the same size.

F 0.03

G 0.05

H 0.15

J 0.17

9 ft
5 ft
1.5 ft

Name ______________________ Date ______________ Class ______________

LESSON 11-1

Problem Solving

Solid Geometry

1. A slice of cheese is cut from the cylinder-shaped cheese as shown. Describe the cross section.

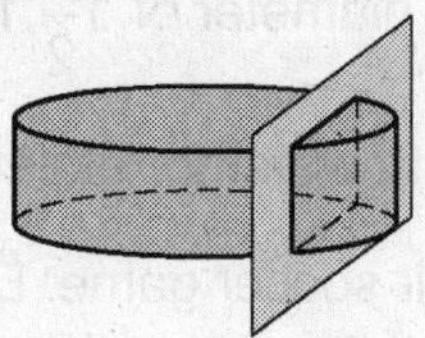

____

2. Mara has cut out five pieces of fabric to sew together to form a pillow. There are three rectangular pieces and two triangles. Describe the solid that will be formed.

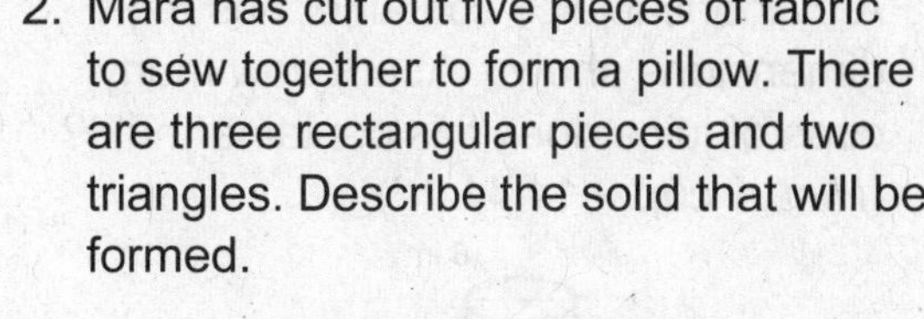

____

3. A square pyramid is intersected by a plane as shown. Describe the cross section.

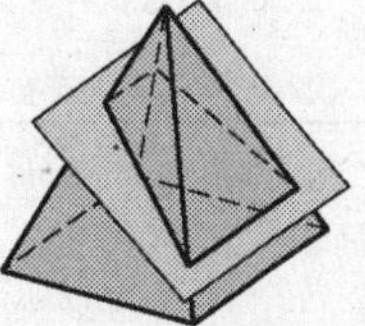

____

Choose the best answer.

4. A gift box is in the shape of a pentagonal prism. How many faces, edges, and vertices does the box have?

   A 6 faces, 10 edges, 6 vertices

   B 7 faces, 12 edges, 10 vertices

   C 7 faces, 15 edges, 10 vertices

   D 8 faces, 18 edges, 12 vertices

5. Which two solids have the same number of vertices?

   F rectangular prism and triangular pyramid

   G triangular prism and rectangular pyramid

   H rectangular prism and pentagonal pyramid

   J triangular prism and pentagonal pyramid

6. Which three-dimensional figure does the net represent?

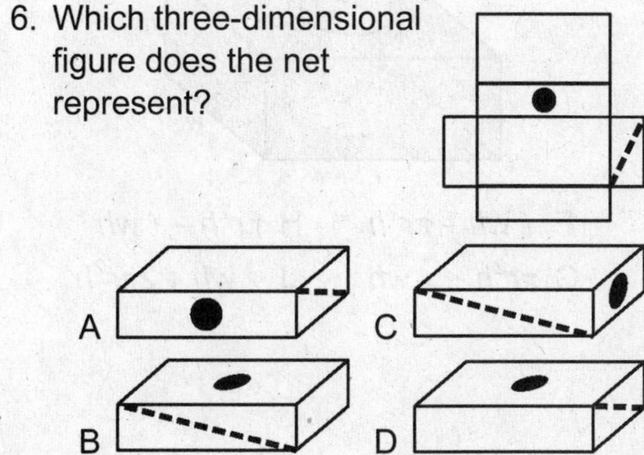

7. Which can be a true statement about the triangular prism whose net is shown?

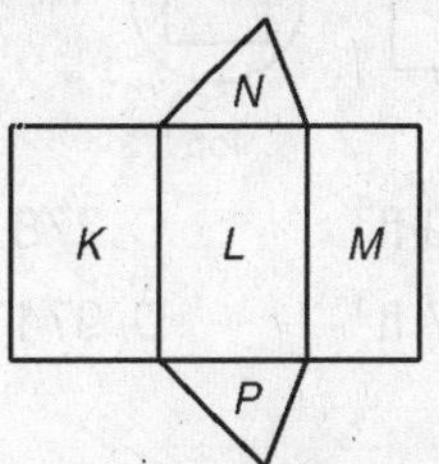

   F Faces *L* and *M* are perpendicular.

   G Faces *N* and *P* are perpendicular.

   H Faces *K* and *L* are parallel.

   J Faces *N* and *P* are parallel.

Name ______________________ Date ______________ Class ______________

LESSON 11-2

Problem Solving

Volume of Prisms and Cylinders

1. A cylindrical juice container has the dimensions shown. About how many cups of juice does this container hold? (*Hint:* 1 cup ≈ 14.44 in^3)

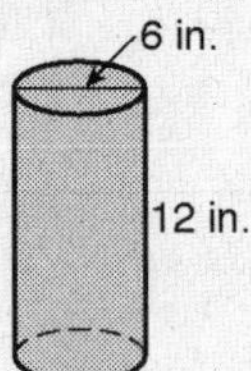

____

2. A large cylindrical cooler is $2\frac{1}{2}$ feet high and has a diameter of $1\frac{1}{2}$ feet. It is filled $\frac{3}{4}$ high with water for athletes to use during their soccer game. Estimate the volume of the water in the cooler in gallons. (*Hint:* 1 gallon ≈ 231 in^3)

____

Choose the best answer.

3. How many 3-inch cubes can be placed inside the box?

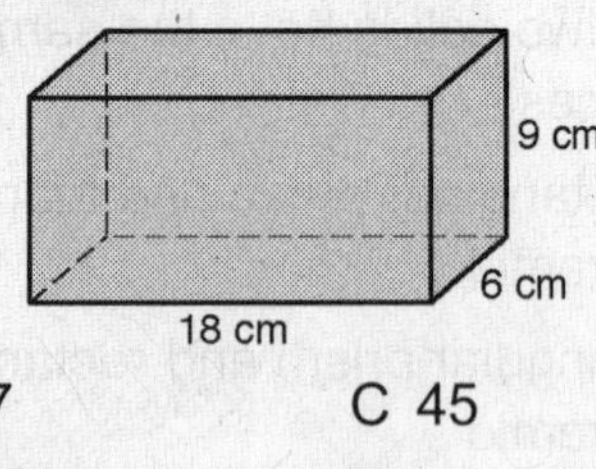

A 27 C 45

B 36 D 72

4. A cylinder has a volume of 4π cm^3. If the radius and height are each tripled, what will be the new volume of the cylinder?

F 12π cm^3 H 64π cm^3

G 36π cm^3 J 108π cm^3

5. What is the volume of the composite figure with the dimensions shown in the three views? Round to the nearest tenth.

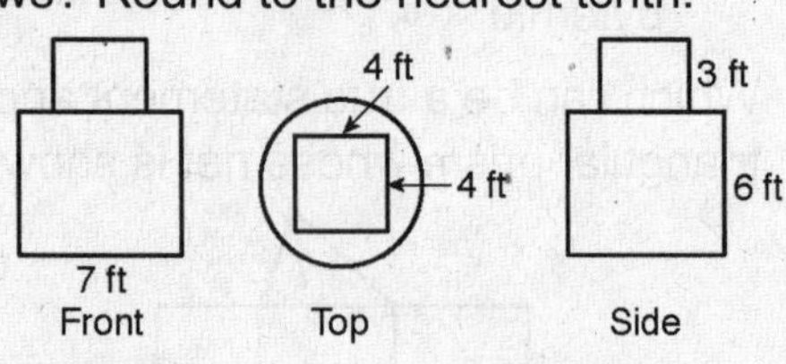

A 182.9 ft^3 C 278.9 ft^3

B 205.7 ft^3 D 971.6 ft^3

6. Find the expression that can be used to determine the volume of the composite figure shown.

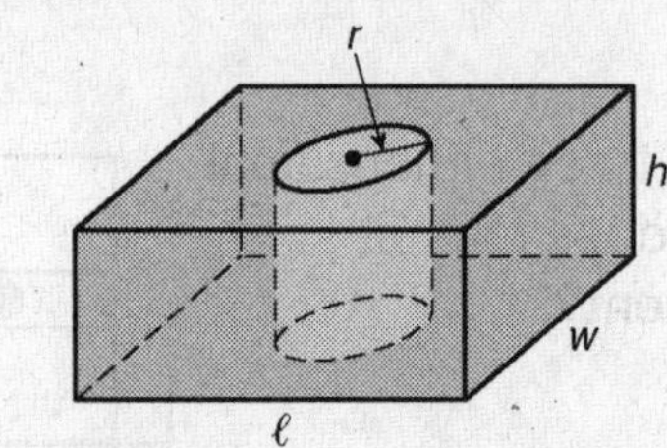

F $\ell wh - \pi r^2 h$ H $\pi r^2 h - \ell wh$

G $\pi r^2 h + \ell wh$ J $\ell wh + 2\pi r^2 h$

Name ______________________ Date ______________ Class ______________

LESSON 11-3

Problem Solving

Volume of Pyramids and Cones

1. A regular square pyramid has a base area of 196 meters and a lateral area of 448 square meters. What is the volume of the pyramid? Round your answer to the nearest tenth.

____

2. A paper cone for serving roasted almonds has a volume of 406π cubic centimeters. A smaller cone has half the radius and half the height of the first cone. What is the volume of the smaller cone? Give your answer in terms of π.

____

3. The hexagonal base in the pyramid is a regular polygon. What is the volume of the pyramid if its height is 9 centimeters? Round to the nearest tenth.

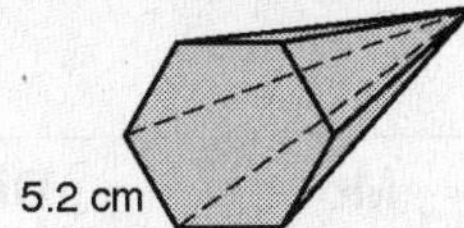

____

4. Find the volume of the shaded solid in the figure shown. Give your answer in terms of π.

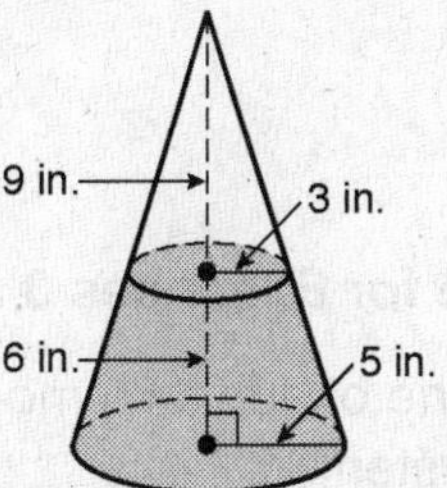

____

Choose the best answer.

5. The diameter of the cone equals the width of the cube, and the figures have the same height. Find the expression that can be used to determine the volume of the composite figure.

A $4(4)(4) - \frac{1}{3}\pi(2^2)(4)$

B $4(4)(4) + \frac{1}{3}\pi(2^2)(4)$

C $4(4)(4) - \pi(2^2)(4)$

D $4(4)(4) + \frac{1}{3}\pi(2^2)$

4 ft
4 ft
4 ft

6. Approximately how many fluid ounces of water can the paper cup hold? (*Hint:* 1 fl oz $\approx$ 1.805 in^3)

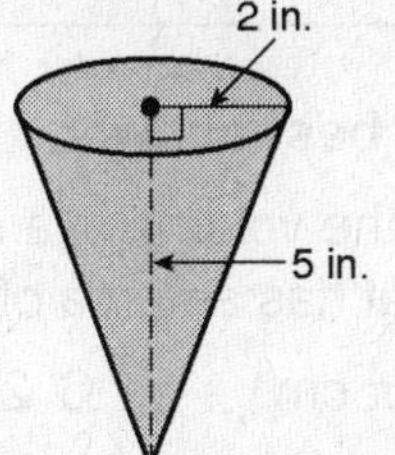

F 10.9 fl oz H 32.7 fl oz

G 11.6 fl oz J 36.3 fl oz

7. The Step Pyramid of Djoser in Lower Egypt was the first pyramid in the history of architecture. Its original height was 204 feet, and it had a rectangular base measuring 411 feet by 358 feet. Which is the best estimate for the volume of the pyramid in cubic yards?

A 370,570 yd^3 C 3,335,128 yd^3

B 1,111,709 yd^3 D 10,005,384 yd^3

Name ______________________ Date ______________ Class ______________

LESSON 11-4

Problem Solving

Spheres

1. A globe has a volume of 288π in^3. What is the surface area of the globe? Give your answer in terms of π.

____

2. Eight bocce balls are in a box 18 inches long, 9 inches wide, and 4.5 inches deep. If each ball has a diameter of 4.5 inches, what is the volume of the space around the balls? Round to the nearest tenth.

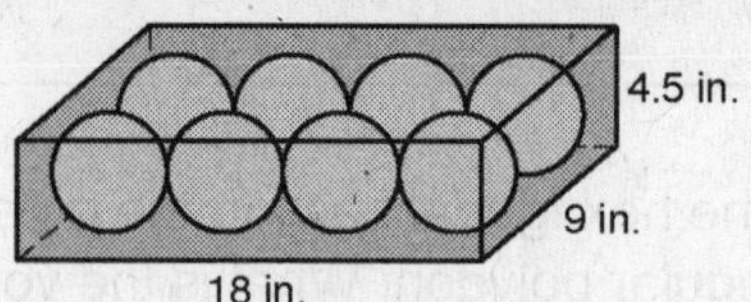

____

Use the table for Exercises 3 and 4.

Ganymede, one of Jupiter's moons, is the largest moon in the solar system.

Moon	Diameter
Earth's moon	2160 mi
Ganymede	3280 mi

3. Approximately how many times as great as the volume of Earth's moon is the volume of Ganymede?

____

4. Approximately how many times as great is the surface area of Ganymede than the surface area of Earth's moon?

____

Choose the best answer.

5. What is the volume of a sphere with a great circle that has an area of 225π cm^2?

A 300π cm^3 C 2500π cm^3

B 900π cm^3 D 4500π cm^3

6. A hemisphere has a surface area of 972π cm^2. If the radius is multiplied by $\frac{1}{3}$, what will be the surface area of the new hemisphere?

F 36π cm^2 H 162π cm^2

G 108π cm^2 J 324π cm^2

7. Which expression represents the volume of the composite figure formed by the hemisphere and cone?

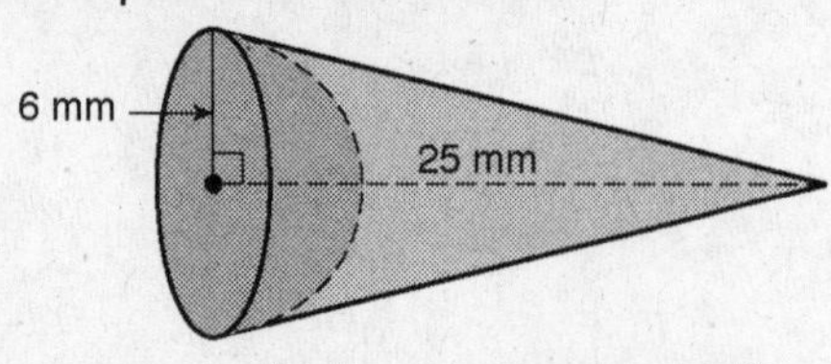

A 52π mm^3 C 276π mm^3

B 156π mm^3 D 288π mm^3

8. Which best represents the surface area of the composite figure?

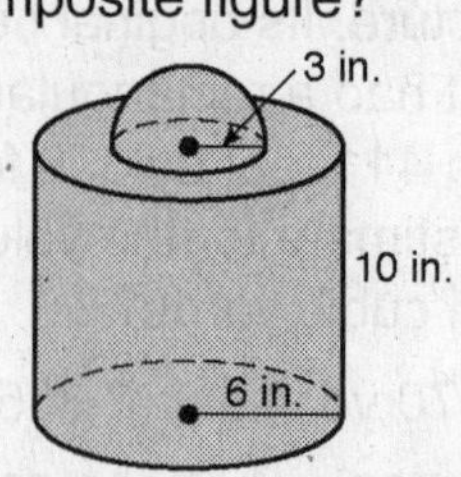

F 129π in^2 H 201π in^2

G 138π in^2 J 210π in^2

Name ______________________ Date ______________ Class ______________

LESSON 12-1

Problem Solving

Lines That Intersect Circles

1. The cruising altitude of a commercial airplane is about 9000 meters. Use the diagram to find AB, the distance from an airplane at cruising altitude to Earth's horizon. Round to the nearest kilometer.

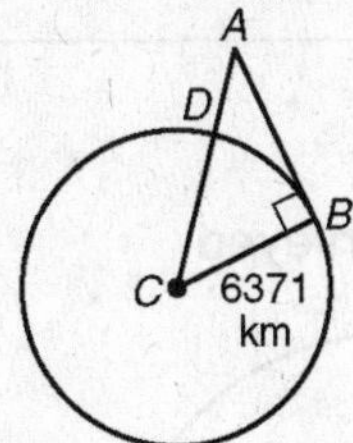

____

2. In the figure, segments that appear to be tangent are tangent. Find QS.

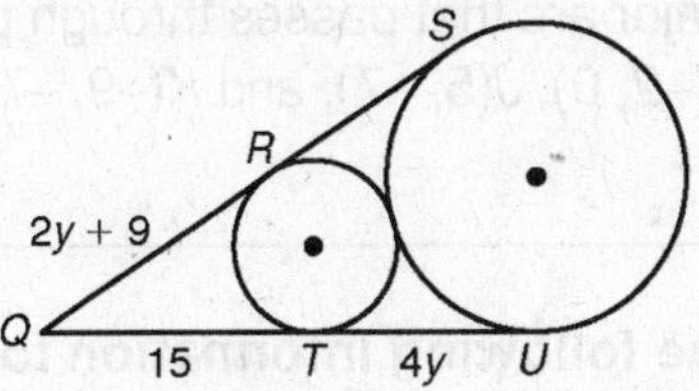

____

3. The area of $\odot H$ is 100π, and $HF = 26$ centimeters. What is the perimeter of quadrilateral $EFGH$?

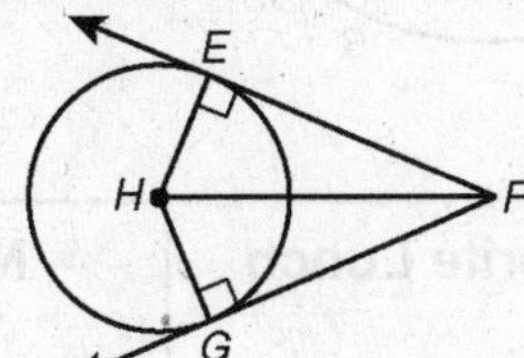

____

4. $\overrightarrow{IH}$, $\overline{IK}$, and $\overrightarrow{KL}$ are tangent to $\odot A$. What is IK?

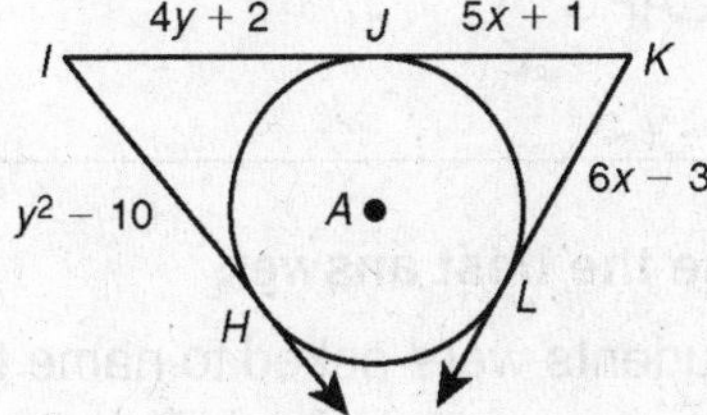

____

Choose the best answer.

5. A teardrop-shaped roller coaster loop is a section of a spiral in which the radius is constantly changing. The radius at the bottom of the loop is much larger than the radius at the top of the loop, as shown in the figure. Which is a true statement?

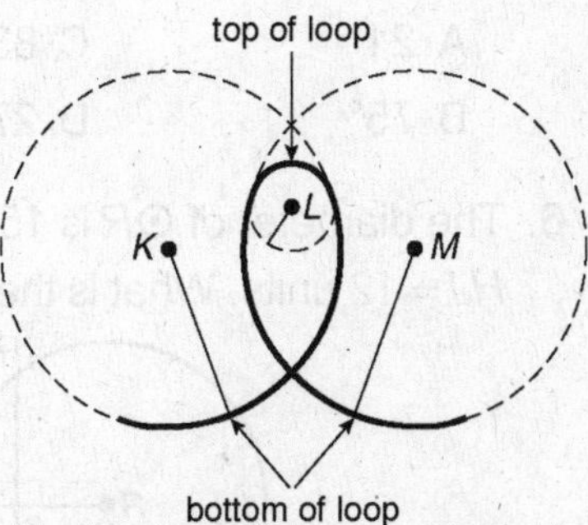

A $\odot K$ and $\odot M$ have two points of tangency.

B $\odot K$, $\odot L$, and $\odot M$ have one point of tangency.

C $\odot L$ is internally tangent to $\odot K$ and $\odot M$.

D $\odot L$ is externally tangent to $\odot K$ and $\odot M$.

6. $\odot G$ has center (2, 5) and radius 3. $\odot H$ has center (2, 0). If the circles are tangent, which line could be tangent to both circles?

F $x = 2$ H $y = 2$

G $x = 0$ J $y = 5$

7. The Hubble Space Telescope orbits 353 miles above Earth, and Earth's radius is about 3960 miles. Which is closest to the distance from the telescope to Earth's horizon?

A 1634 mi C 3976 mi

B 1709 mi D 5855 mi

Name ______________________ Date ______________ Class ______________

LESSON 12-2

Problem Solving

Arcs and Chords

1. Circle D has center $(-2, -7)$ and radius 7. What is the measure, in degrees, of the major arc that passes through points $H(-2, 0)$, $J(5, -7)$, and $K(-9, -7)$?

____

2. A circle graph is composed of sectors with central angles that measure $3x°$, $3x°$, $4x°$, and $5x°$. What is the measure, in degrees, of the smallest minor arcs?

____

Use the following information for Exercises 3 and 4.

The circle graph shows the results of a survey in which teens were asked what says the most about them at school. Find each of the following.

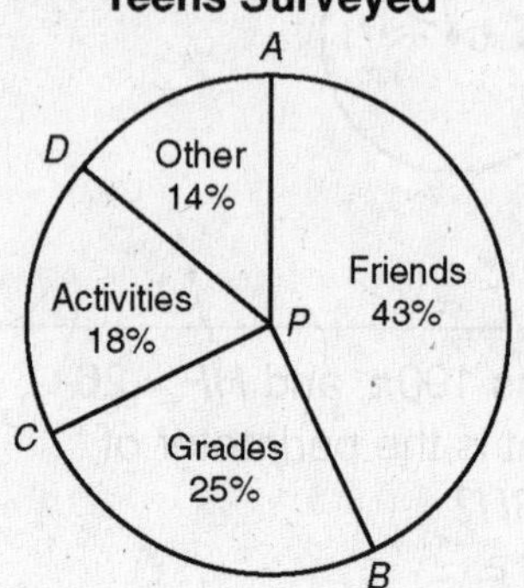

3. $m\overset{\frown}{AB}$

____

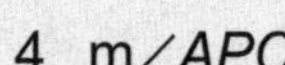

4. $m\angle APC$

____

Choose the best answer.

5. Students were asked to name their favorite cafeteria food. The results of the survey are shown in the table. In a circle graph showing these results, which is closest to the measure of the central angle for the section representing chicken tenders?

Favorite Lunch	Number of Students
Pizza	108
Chicken tenders	75
Taco salad	90
Other	54

A 21° C 83°

B 75° D 270°

6. The diameter of $\odot R$ is 15 units, and $HJ = 12$ units. What is the length of $\overline{ST}$?

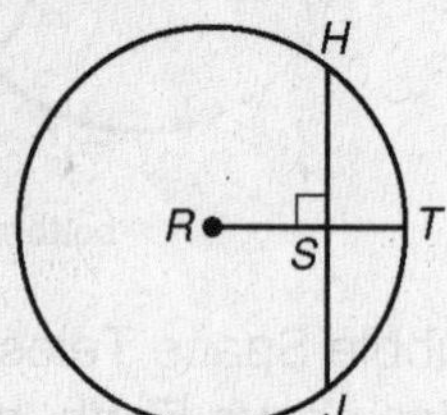

F 2.1 units H 4.5 units

G 3 units J 9.6 units

7. In the stained glass window, $\overline{AB} \cong \overline{CD}$ and $\overline{AB} \parallel \overline{CD}$. What is $m\overset{\frown}{CBD}$?

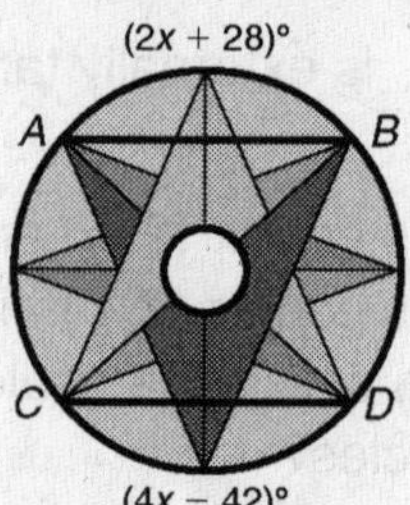

A 35° C 98°

B 70° D 262°

Name ______________________ Date ______________ Class ______________

LESSON 12-3

Problem Solving

Sector Area and Arc Length

1. A circle with a radius of 20 centimeters has a sector that has an arc measure of 105°. What is the area of the sector? Round to the nearest tenth.

____

2. A sector whose central angle measures 72° has an area of 16.2π square feet. What is the radius of the circle?

____

3. The archway below is to be painted. What is the area of the archway to the nearest tenth?

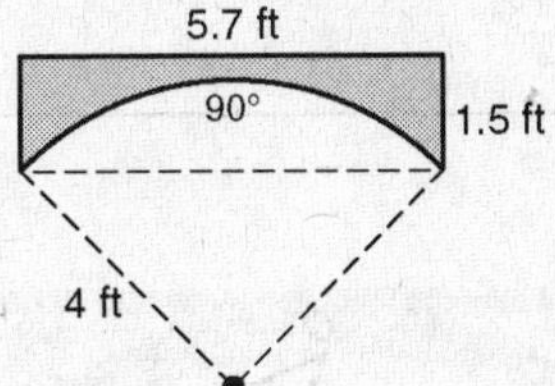

____

4. Circle *N* has a circumference of 16π millimeters. What is the area of the shaded region to the nearest tenth?

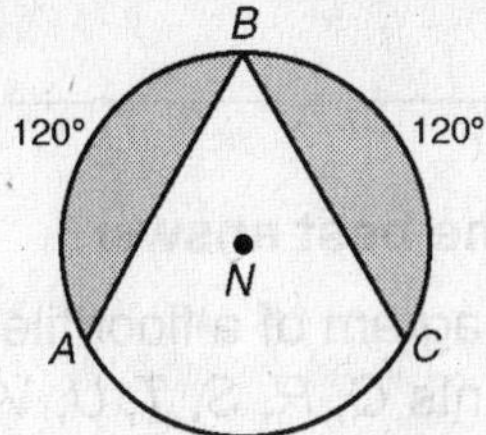

____

Choose the best answer.

5. The circular shelves in diagram are each 28 inches in diameter. The "cut-out" portion of each shelf is 90°. Approximately how much shelf paper is needed to cover both shelves?

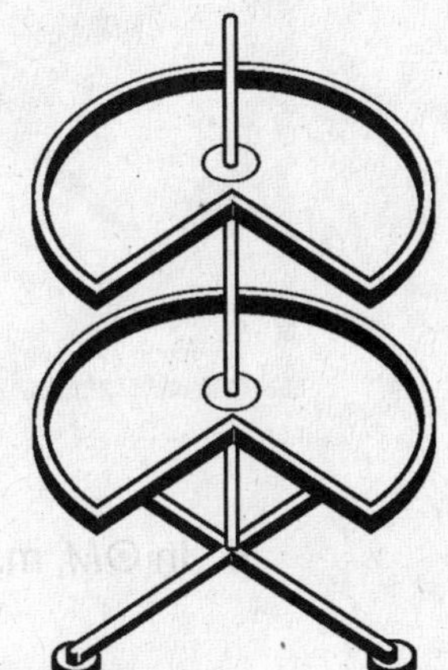

A 154 in^2
B 308 in^2
C 462 in^2
D 924 in^2

6. Find the area of the shaded region. Round to the nearest tenth.

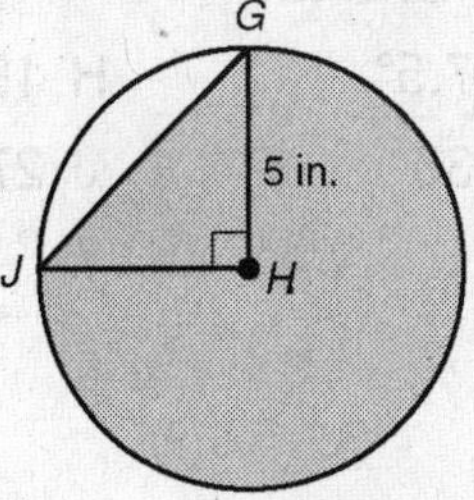

F 8.2 in^2 H 71.4 in^2
G 19.6 in^2 J 78.5 in^2

7. A semicircular garden with a diameter of 6 feet is to have 2 inches of mulch spread over it. To the nearest tenth, what is the volume of mulch that is needed?

A 2.4 ft^3 C 14.1 ft^3
B 4.8 ft^3 D 28.3 ft^3

8. A round cheesecake 12 inches in diameter and 3 inches high is cut into 8 equal-sized pieces. If five pieces have been taken, what is the approximate volume of the cheesecake that remains?

F 42.4 in^3 H 127.2 in^3
G 70.7 in^3 J 212.1 in^3

Name ________________________ Date ______________ Class ______________

LESSON 12-4

Problem Solving

Inscribed Angles

1. Find $m\widehat{AB}$.

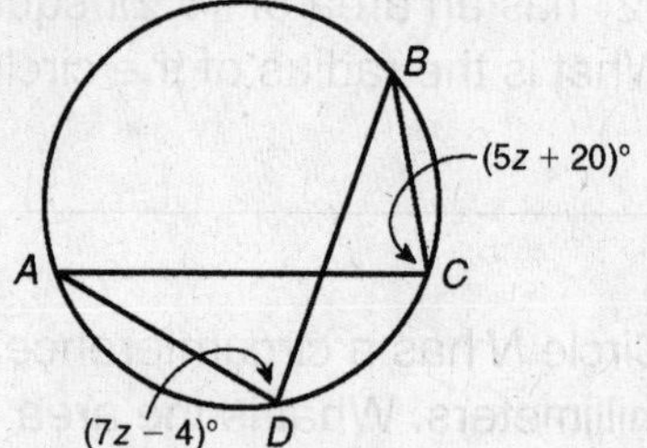

____

2. Find the angle measures of *RSTU*.

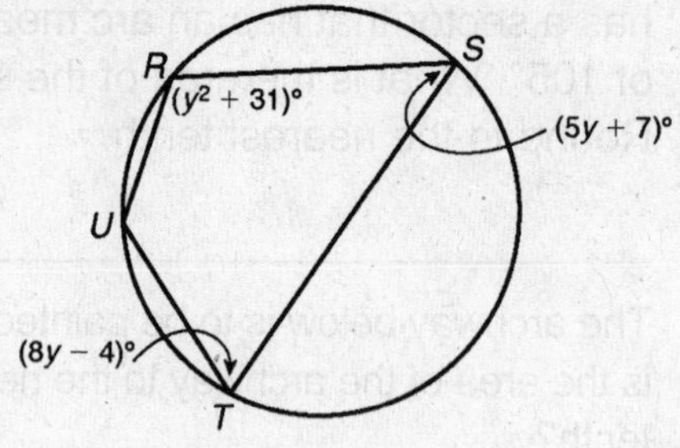

____

Choose the best answer.

Use the diagram of a floor tile for Exercises 3 and 4. Points *Q*, *R*, *S*, *T*, *U*, *V*, *W*, and *X* are equally spaced around ⊙*L*.

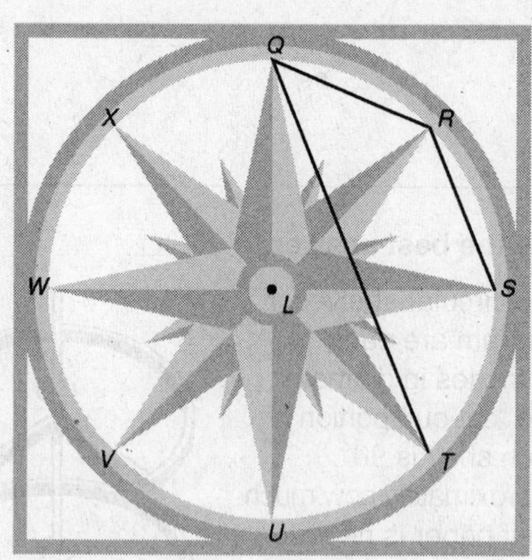

3. Find m∠*RQT*.

A 15° C 45°

B 30° D 60°

4. Find m∠*QRS*.

F 67.5° H 180°

G 135° J 270°

5. If m∠*KLM* = 20° and $m\widehat{MP} = 30°$, what is m∠*KNP*?

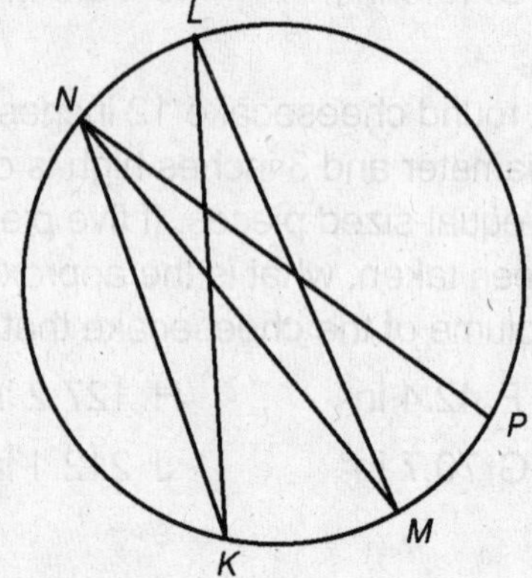

A 25° C 50°

B 35° D 70°

6. In ⊙*M*, m∠*AMB* = 74°. What is m∠*CDB*?

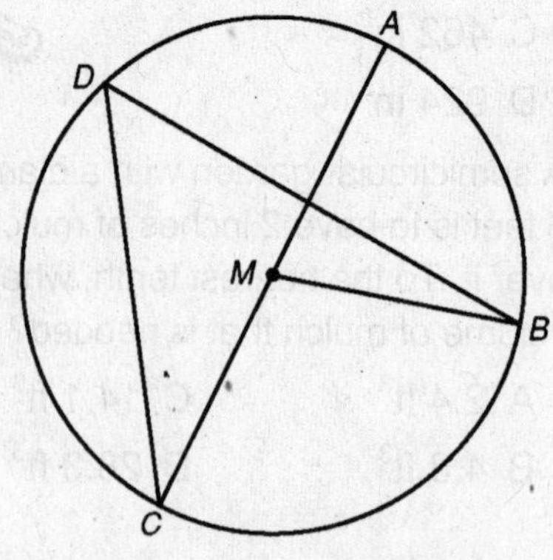

F 37° H 74°

G 53° J 106°

Name ______________________ Date ______________ Class ______________

LESSON 12-5

Problem Solving

Angle Relationships in Circles

1. What is $m\overparen{LM}$?

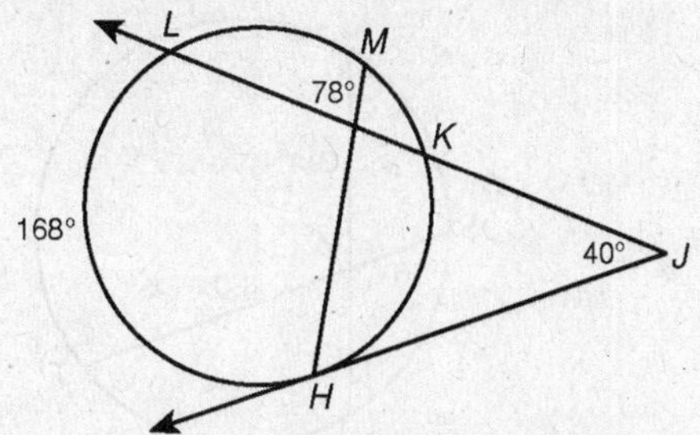

____

2. An artist painted the design shown below. What is the value of *x*?

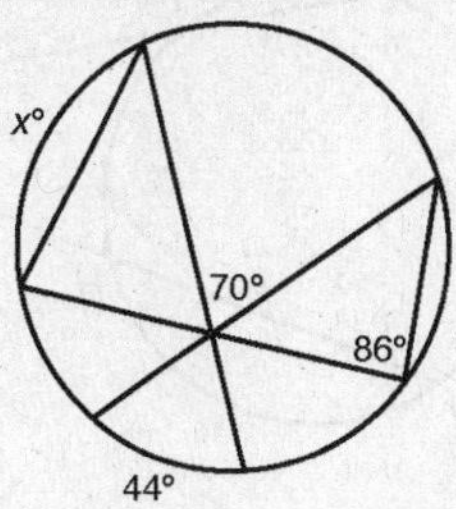

____

For Exercises 3 and 4, use the diagrams.

3. A polar orbiting satellite is about 850 kilometers above Earth. About 69.2 arc degrees of the planet are visible to a camera in the satellite. What is $m\angle P$?

____

4. A geostationary satellite is about 35,800 kilometers above Earth. How many arc degrees of the planet are visible to a camera in the satellite?

____

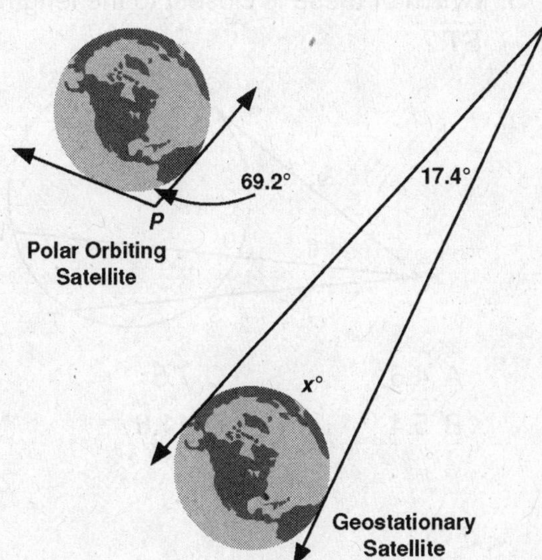

Choose the best answer.

5. What is $m\angle ADE$?

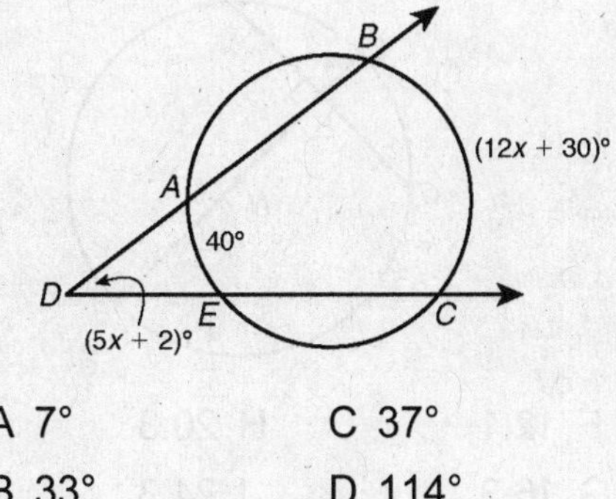

A 7° C 37°

B 33° D 114°

6. Find $m\angle VTU$.

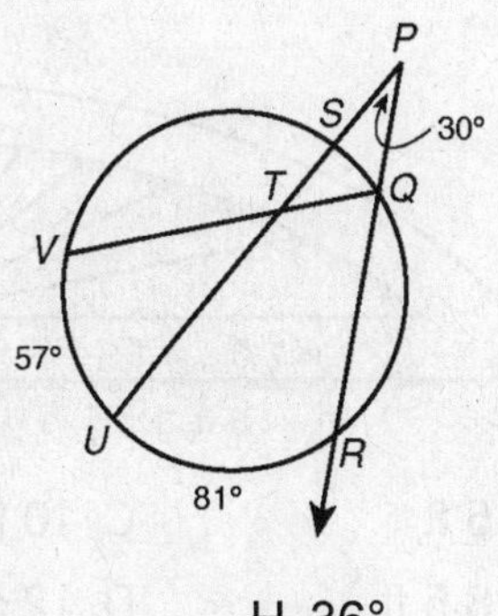

F 21° H 36°

G 29° J 39°

Name ______________________ Date ______________ Class ______________

LESSON 12-6

Problem Solving

Segment Relationships in Circles

1. Find EG to the nearest tenth.

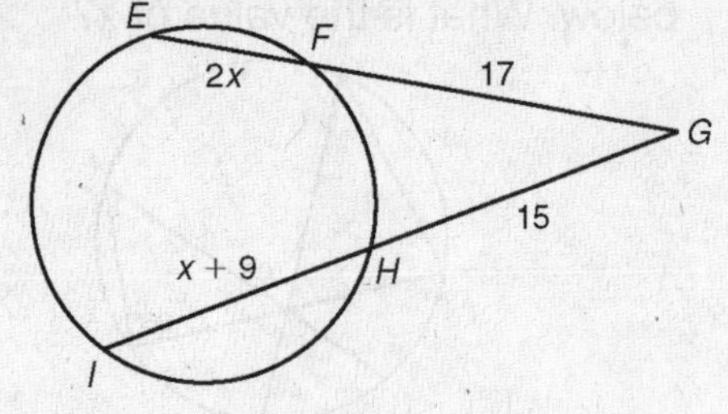

____

2. What is the length of $\overline{UW}$?

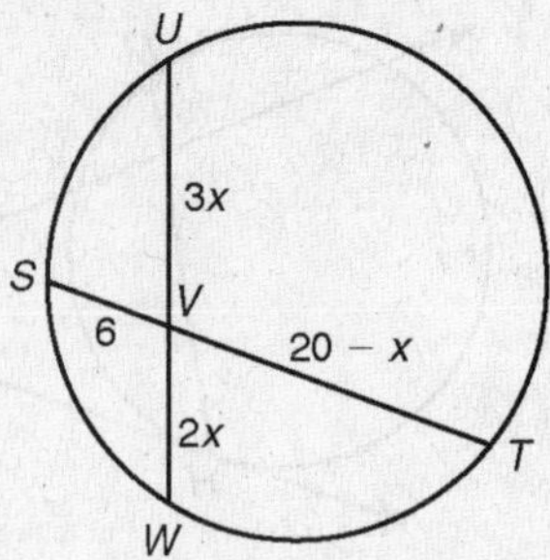

____

Choose the best answer.

3. Which of these is closest to the length of $\overline{ST}$?

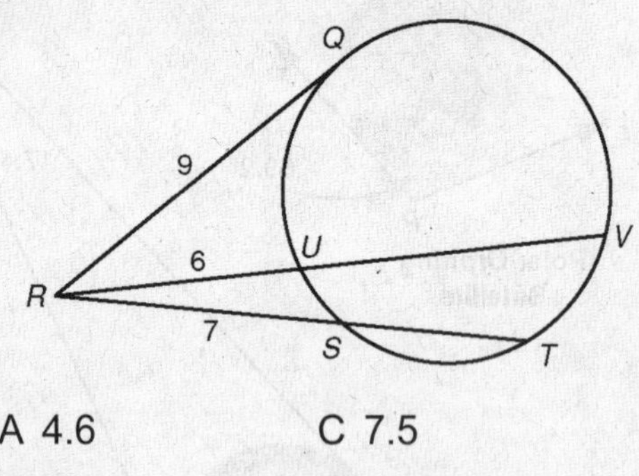

A 4.6　　C 7.5

B 5.4　　D 11.6

4. Floral archways like the one shown below are going to be used for the prom. $\overline{LN}$ is the perpendicular bisector of KM. $KM = 6$ feet and $LN = 2$ feet. What is the diameter of the circle that contains $\widehat{KM}$?

F 4.5 ft

G 5.5 ft

H 6.5 ft

J 8 ft

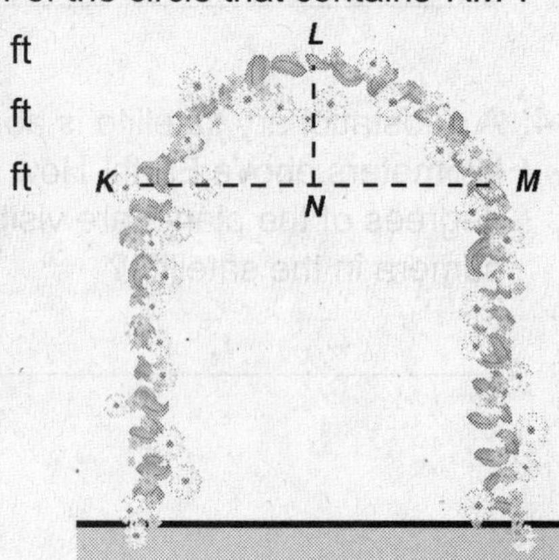

5. The figure is a "quarter" wood arch used in architecture. $\overline{WX}$ is the perpendicular bisector of the chord containing $\overline{YX}$. Find the diameter of the circle containing the arc.

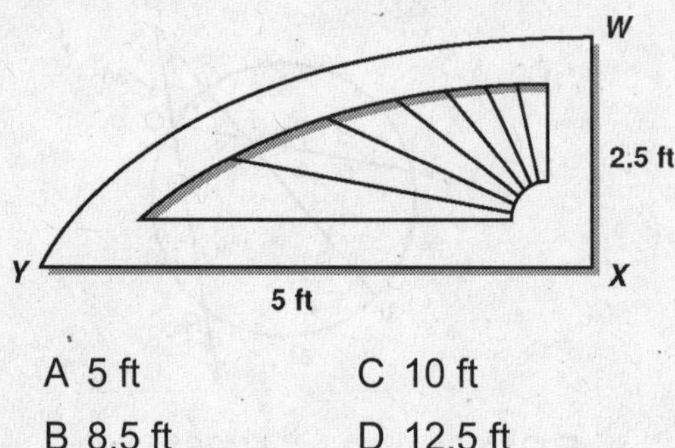

A 5 ft　　C 10 ft

B 8.5 ft　　D 12.5 ft

6. In ⊙N, $CD = 18$. Find the radius of the circle to the nearest tenth.

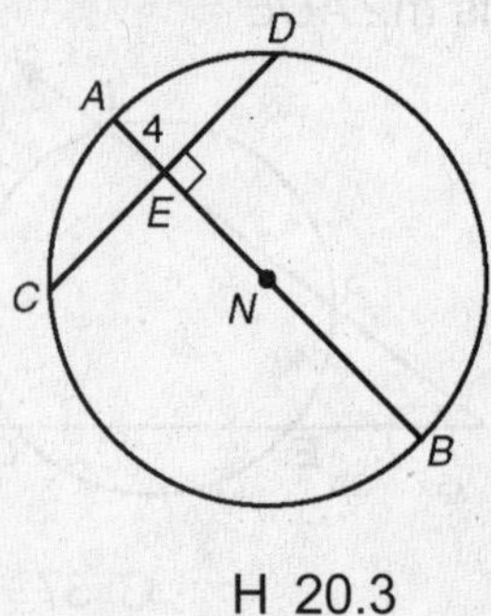

F 12.1　　H 20.3

G 16.3　　J 24.3

Name ______________________ Date ______________ Class ______________

LESSON 12-7

Problem Solving

Circles in the Coordinate Plane

1. Write the equation of the circle that contains the points graphed below.

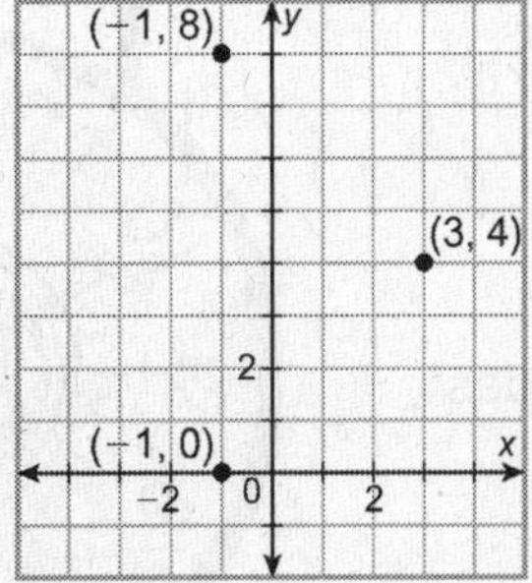

____

2. Find the area of a circle that has center *J* and passes through *K*. Express your answer in terms of π.

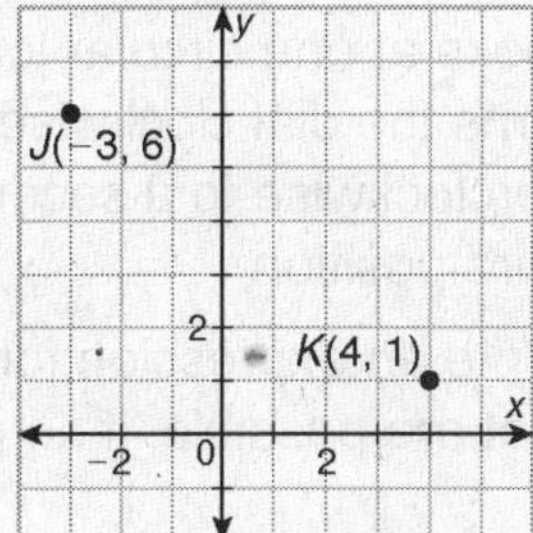

____

Choose the best answer.

3. An English knot garden has hedges planted to form geometric shapes. A blueprint of a knot garden contains three circular hedges as described in the table. Flowers are to be planted in the space that is within all three circles. Which is a point that could be planted with flowers?

A (7, 1) C (0, 5)

B (5, 1) D (0, 0)

Circular Hedge	Center	Radius
A	(3, 2)	3 ft
B	(7, 2)	4 ft
C	(5, –1)	3 ft

4. Which of these circles intersects the circle that has center (0, 6) and radius 1?

F $(x-5)^2 + (y+3)^2 = 4$

G $(x-4)^2 + (y-3)^2 = 9$

H $(x+5)^2 + (y+1)^2 = 16$

J $(x+1)^2 + (y-4)^2 = 4$

5. The center of ⊙*B* is (9, 2), and the radius of the circle is 5 units. Which is a point on the circle?

A (4, 2) C (9, 4)

B (14, 0) D (9, –5)

6. Which is an equation for a circle that has the same center as ⊙*P* but has a circumference that is four times as great?

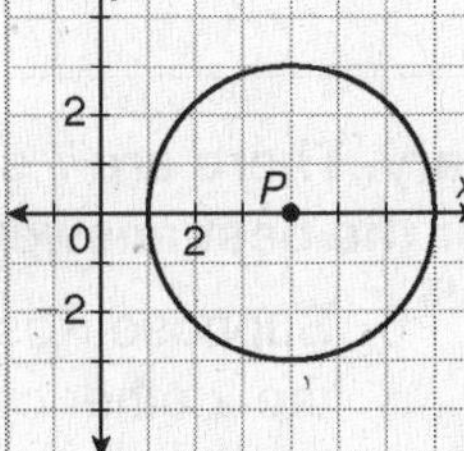

F $(x-4)^2 + y^2 = 36$

G $(x-4)^2 + y^2 = 144$

H $x^2 + (y-4)^2 = 36$

J $x^2 + (y-4)^2 = 144$

7. The Maxair amusement park ride consists of a circular ring that holds 50 riders. Suppose that the center of the ride is at the origin and that one of the riders on the circular ring is at (16, 15.1). If one unit on the coordinate plane equals 1 foot, which is a close approximation of the circumference of the ride?

A 22 ft C 138 ft

B 44 ft D 1521 ft

Name _______________________ Date _____________ Class _____________

LESSON 13-1

Problem Solving

Permutations and Combinations

Rosalie is looking at locks. The label *combination lock* confuses her. She wonders about the number of possible permutations or combinations a lock can have.

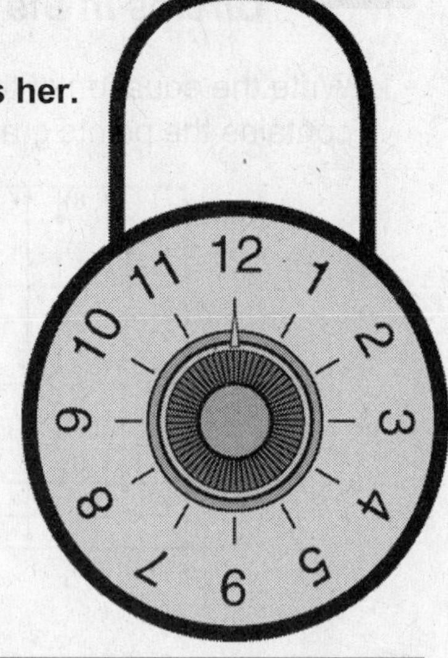

1. She looks at one circular lock with 12 positions. To open it she turns the dial clockwise to a first position, then counterclockwise to a second position, then clockwise to a third position

   a. Write an expression for the number of 3-position codes that are possible, if no position is repeated.

   ____

   b. Explain how this represents a combination or a permutation.

   ____

2. Rosalie looks at cable locks. Each position can be set from 0 to 9. How many different codes are possible for each lock if no digits are repeated in each code?

   a. a 3-digit cable lock

   ____

   b. a 4-digit cable lock

   ____

   c. a 6-digit cable lock

   ____

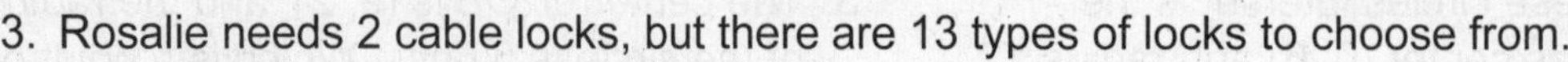

3. Rosalie needs 2 cable locks, but there are 13 types of locks to choose from.

   a. In how many ways can she choose 2 different locks? ____________

   b. Explain how this represents a permutation or a combination.

   ____

4. Explain why you think Rosalie might be confused by the label *combination lock.*

   ____

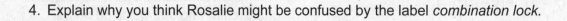

Rosalie wants to lock her bicycle near the library. There are 7 slots still open in the bike rack. Choose the letter for the best answer.

5. Rosalie arrives at the same time as 2 other cyclists. In how many ways can they arrange their bikes in the open slots?

   A 7
   B 35
   C 210
   D 343

6. Suppose Rosalie arrived just ahead of the 2 other cyclists and selected a slot. In how many ways can the others arrange their bikes in the open slots?

   F 2
   G 15
   H 24
   J 30

Name ______________________ Date ____________ Class ____________

LESSON 13-2

Problem Solving

Theoretical and Experimental Probability

As part of a grant to improve bus routes to and from school, Hogan and Jane gather traffic flow statistics for one intersection. They make a table to show their findings for between 7:45 A.M. and 8:00 A.M. on a Monday morning.

Traffic Direction	Number of Vehicles
Straight through	282
Turn north	94
Turn south	188

1. Analyze the statistics.
   a. Write and evaluate an expression for $P(N)$, the probability that a vehicle will turn north.

   ____

   b. Write and evaluate an expression for the probability that a vehicle will turn north or go straight through the intersection.

   ____

   c. Write and evaluate an expression for the probability that a vehicle will not turn north.

   ____

2. The police department gathers statistics on Tuesday. Officers count a total of 608 vehicles, of which 380 go straight through the intersection, 76 turn north, and the rest turn south.
   a. What is the probability that a vehicle will turn north? ____________
   b. What is the probability that a vehicle will turn north or go straight through the intersection? ____________
   c. What is the probability that a vehicle will not turn north? ____________
3. Does this represent theoretical or experimental probability? Explain.

____

Math Assessment Survey				
Activity	**Group Projects**	**Keep a Journal**	**Multiple Choice**	**Word Problems**
Student Response	57	18	35	10

A teacher surveys students on how they would prefer to have work assessed in math class. Choose the letter for the best answer.

4. What is the probability that a randomly chosen student prefers assessment through a group project?

   A $\frac{1}{12}$ C $\frac{19}{40}$

   B $\frac{53}{120}$ D $\frac{21}{40}$

5. Which expression gives the probability that a randomly chosen student will not want multiple-choice questions?

   F $\frac{7}{24}$ H $1-\frac{7}{24}$

   G $1+\frac{7}{24}$ J $35-\frac{7}{24}$

Name ______________________ Date ______________ Class ________

Problem Solving

LESSON 13-3

Independent and Dependent Events

The table shows student participation in different sports at a high school. Suppose a student is selected at random.

Sports Participation by Grade

	Track	Volleyball	Basketball	Tennis	No Sport
Grade 9	12	18	15	9	66
Grade 10	6	20	12	2	95
Grade 11	15	11	8	5	61
Grade 12	7	6	10	12	50

1. What is the probability that a student is in grade 10 and runs track?
   a. Find the probability that a student is in grade 10, $P(10)$. ____________
   b. Find the probability that a student runs track, given that the student is in grade 10, $P(Tr \mid 10)$, ____________
   c. Find P (10 and Tr) = $P(10) \cdot P(Tr \mid 10)$. ____________
2. What is the probability that a student is in grade 12 and runs track or plays tennis?
   a. Find the probability that a student is in grade 12, $P(12)$. ____________
   b. Find the probability that a student runs track or plays tennis, given that the student is in grade 12, $P(Tr \text{ or } Te \mid 12)$. ____________
   c. Find $P(12 \text{ or } (Tr \text{ or } Te))$. ____________
3. During a fire drill, the students are waiting in the parking lot. What is the probability that one student is in grade 12 and runs track or plays tennis, and the student standing next to her is in grade 10 and runs track?
   a. Find the probability for the first student. ____________
   b. Find the probability for the second student. ____________
   c. Find the probability for the event occurring. ____________
   d. Are these events independent or dependent? Explain.

   ____

Samantha is 1 of 17 students in a class of 85 who have decided to pursue a business degree. Each week, a student in the class is randomly selected to tutor younger students. Choose the letter for the best answer.

4. What is the probability of drawing a business student one week, replacing the name, and drawing the same name the next week?

   A 3.4 C 0.04

   B 0.2 D 0.002

5. What is the probability of drawing Samantha's name one week, not replacing her name, and drawing the name of another business student the next week?

   F $\frac{1}{85} \cdot \frac{16}{84}$ H $\frac{17}{85} \cdot \frac{16}{84}$

   G $\frac{1}{85} \cdot \frac{17}{84}$ J $\frac{17}{85} \cdot \frac{17}{84}$

Name ______________________ Date ______________ Class ______________

LESSON 13-4

Problem Solving

Two-Way Tables

1. The table shows the number of students who would drive to school if the school provided parking spaces. Make a table of joint relative frequencies and marginal relative frequencies.

	Grades 9-10	Grades 11-12
Always	32	122
Sometimes	58	44
Never	24	120

	Grades 9-10	Grades 11-12	Total
Always	32/400 = 0.080	32/400 = 0.305	0.080 + 0.305 = 0.385
Sometimes	58/400 = 0.145	32/400 = 0.110	0.145 + 0.110 = 0.255
Never	32/400 = 0.060	32/400 = 0.300	0.060 + 0.300 = 0.360
Total	0.080 + 0.145 + 0.060 = 0.285	0.305 + 0.110 + 0.300 = 0.715	1

2. Gerry collected data and made a table of marginal relative frequencies on the number of students who participate in chorus and the number who participate in band.

		Chorus		
		Yes	**No**	**Total**
Band	**Yes**	0.38	0.29	0.67
	No	0.09	0.24	0.33
	Total	0.47	0.53	1.0

a. If you are given that a student is in chorus, what is the probability that the student also is in band? Round your answer to the nearest hundredth.

____

b. If you are given that a student is not in band, what is the probability that the student is in chorus? Round your answer to the nearest hundredth.

____

Select the best answer.

3. What is the probability if a student is not in chorus, then that student is in band?

A 0.29 C 055

B 038

4. What is the probability that if a student is not in band, then that student is not in chorus?

F 0.09 H 0.73

G 0.33

Name ________________________ Date ____________ Class ____________

LESSON 13-5

Problem Solving

Compound Events

Of 100 students surveyed, 44 are male and 54 are in favor of a change to a 9-period, 4-day school week. Of those in favor, 20 are female. One student is picked at random from those surveyed.

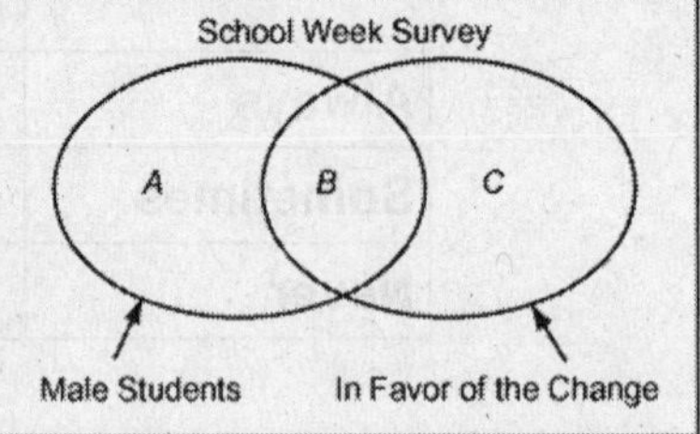

1. What is the probability that the student is male or favors the change? Use the Venn diagram.

   a. What is represented by the total of $A + B$?

   ____

   b. What is represented by the total of $B + C$?

   ____

   c. How many of those in favor of the change are male? ____________

   d. Find the values for A, B, and C and label the diagram.

   e. Write and evaluate an expression for the probability that the student is male or favors the change. ____________

2. What is the probability that the student is female or opposes the change?

   a. How many students are female? ____________

   b. How many students oppose the change? ____________

   c. If you draw a Venn diagram to show females and those opposed to the change, what is the meaning and value of the overlapping area?

   ____

   d. Write and evaluate an expression for the probability that the student is female or opposes the change. ____________

3. Of the students surveyed, 27 plan to start their own businesses. Of those, 18 are in favor of the change to the school week. Write and evaluate an expression for the probability that a student selected at random plans to start his or her own business or favors the change.

____

Sean asks each student to cast a vote for the type of class he or she would prefer. Of the students, 55% voted for online classes, 30% voted for projects, and 15% voted for following the textbook. Choose the letter for the best answer.

4. Which description best describes Sean's experiment?

   A Simple events

   B Compound events

   C Mutually exclusive events

   D Inclusive events

5. What is the probability that a randomly selected student voted for online classes or projects?

   F $\frac{33}{200}$

   G $\frac{7}{10}$

   H $\frac{1}{4}$

   J $\frac{17}{20}$